'*Cybercrimes* is a timely, comprehensive and authoritat
the subject and provides vital clarity on this dynamic
the interdisciplinary nature of the field, it is written in
ble manner for all students, making it indispensable for any cybercrime
programme.'

— *Lisa Sugiura, University of Portsmouth, UK*

'The multidisciplinary and international approach employed by Anita Lavorgna
makes this an ideal text for instructors with a diverse student population of different backgrounds and with varying interests. Expanding beyond traditional
introductory cybercrime texts, *Cybercrimes* provides a more comprehensive and
in-depth understanding of today's most relevant types of cybercrimes, and rigorously deals with the emerging challenges posed by cyberspace. The book
addresses the technical aspects of cybercrimes without getting bogged down in
unnecessary details and highlights the qualitative and quantitative similarities
and differences with traditional crimes.'

— *Bryce G. Westlake, San Jose State University, USA*

'One thing I have learned from researching cybercrime over the past 25 years is
that it is a complex issue and also a moving feast of social, technical and even
political issues. Anita Lavorgna's book does a very good job at isolating and capturing these elusive characteristics and presents the subject (which it has now
become) to the reader in a very digestible form.'

— *David Wall, University of Leeds, UK*

'*Cybercrimes* is an excellent guide to the intricacies of criminal and deviant
behaviours in cyberspace. Due to the blurring of online and offline in our
daily lives, it makes less and less sense to think of "cyber" as a unicum which
can be kept apart from our ("real") routines. Professor Lavorgna explains it
from a multi- and transdisciplinary perspective without focusing on a specific
jurisdiction.'

— *José R. Agustina, UIC Barcelona, Spain*

'*Cybercrimes* is one of the most comprehensive books on the topic I've come
across to date. Not only does it investigate all the "usual suspects", it goes a step
further by providing articulated discussions of criminological theory and can
thus be used more widely across our criminology-related courses.'

— *Brian Frederick, University of Gloucestershire, UK*

'*Cybercrimes* by Anita Lavorgna offers a timely and much-needed insight into
evolving cybercrime areas. The book provides a critical analysis of cybercrime
means, methods and responses, and the arguments are expertly illustrated by
numerous examples throughout. The topics considered cover everything from

legislative and theoretical issues to computer technologies and devices, as well as policing and governance challenges. This book is an important resource for people working with cybercrime worldwide, including students, academics and cybersecurity practitioners.'

– Tine Munk, Middlesex University, UK

CYBERCRIMES

CRITICAL ISSUES
IN A GLOBAL CONTEXT

ANITA LAVORGNA

First published 2020 by
RED GLOBE PRESS

Red Globe Press in the UK is an imprint of Macmillan Education Limited, registered in England, company number 01755588, of 4 Crinan Street, London, N1 9XW.

Red Globe Press® is a registered trademark in the United States, the United Kingdom, Europe and other countries.

ISBN 978-1-352-00911-8 hardback

ISBN 978-1-352-00904-0 paperback

This book is printed on paper suitable for recycling and made from fully managed and sustained forest sources. Logging, pulping and manufacturing processes are expected to conform to the environmental regulations of the country of origin.

A catalogue record for this book is available from the British Library.

A catalog record for this book is available from the Library of Congress.

CONTENTS

List of figures and tables   vii

List of boxes   viii

Acknowledgements   ix

1 Introduction   **1**
   The context and purpose of this book   1
   Approaching crime in cyberspace   4
   The content of this book   6

2 Outlining cybercrimes   **9**
   Introduction   9
   A brief historical context   9
   Defining cybercrimes   13
   Measuring cybercrimes   18
   Concluding remarks   27

3 Theorising cybercrimes   **29**
   Introduction   29
   Classicism and offender's decision-making   30
   Social structure approaches   35
   Socialisation approaches   40
   Critical criminology   45
   Postmodern and late-modern criminology   47
   Towards a theory for crime in cyberspace   49
   Concluding remarks   50

4 Crimes against devices   **53**
   Introduction   53
   Hackers and identity construction   54
   Attacks and vulnerabilities   61
   Internet of things   66
   Monitoring and collection of online data in state
   and corporate surveillance   70
   Concluding remarks   77

CONTENTS

5 **Crimes against persons**   **81**
   Introduction   81
   Hate speech   82
   Harassment   90
   Sex crimes   97
   Concluding remarks   111

6 **Crimes of deception and coercion**   **115**
   Introduction   115
   Frauds   115
   Extortion   131
   Concluding remarks   137

7 **Market-based crimes and crimes against property**   **141**
   Introduction   141
   Illegal markets online   142
   Intellectual propery infringiment   160
   Concluding remarks   166

8 **Political offences**   **169**
   Introduction   169
   Cyberwarfare   169
   Cyberterrorism   177
   Controlling cyberspace as political deviancy   182
   Concluding remarks   185

9 **Disrupting cybercrimes and the need
   for crime prevention**   **187**
   Introduction   187
   Policing cybercrimes   188
   Approaches to cybercrime prevention   200
   Concluding remarks   208

10 **Cybercrime research and the future of cybercrimes**   **213**
   Introduction   213
   Researching cybercrimes   213
   The future of cybercrimes   217

References   221
Index   255

LIST OF FIGURES AND TABLES

FIGURES

2.1 Information and communication technology milestones versus
cybercrime evolution: a timeline   10
2.2 Approaches to quantify the extent of cybercrimes   19
4.1 The anatomy of a DDoS attack   62
4.2 Schematising cybersurveillance   71
7.1 Byzantine generals and proof-of-work   147
9.1 The three major forces shaping today's approaches
to dealing with cybercrimes   209

TABLES

2.1 Cybercrimes typology   18
3.1 Classification of criminological theories   31
3.2 Mainstream theoretical explanations of cybercrimes   32
5.1 Types of (cyber)crimes against persons   83
6.1 Types of (cyber)frauds   116

LIST OF BOXES

2.1	Who are the victims of cybercrime?	23
2.2	How much does cybercrime cost?	26
4.1	Moral panic and the social construction of cybercrime	57
4.2	Hacktivism: civil disobedience or something else?	59
4.3	Malware	62
4.4	The privacy paradox	69
4.5	Providing anonymity and protecting data confidentiality in cyberspace	75
5.1	Problematic subcultures in cyberspace: hate sites and self-harm sites	88
5.2	Human trafficking	106
6.1	Social engineering	117
6.2	Spam	122
6.3	Doxing	135
7.1	Cryptocurrencies	143
7.2	Blockchain	145
7.3	Unauthorised access of information	148
7.4	Online criminal networks	158
8.1	Cyber-jihad and terrorist strategies in cyberspace	179
9.1	Law enforcement and data analytics	195
9.2	Implementing secure data storage	203

ACKNOWLEDGEMENTS

Writing this book has been an exciting and fulfilling project – one that would not have been possible without the support of many along the way to whom it is hard to express enough thanks.

First, I wish to express my profound gratitude for the much-appreciated encouragement received by my network of academic mentors, advisors and colleagues over the years – you know who you are. Your genuine kindness has always been inspiring and your enthusiasm for research and teaching contagious.

A big thank you also to all those who through stimulating conversations contributed to the unpacking, development and refinement of the topics, themes and ideas presented in this book. Most appreciation is due to my colleagues and the students of my criminology classes at Southampton, not only for the insightful discussions but also for embracing and valuing my disciplinary heterodoxy.

To the anonymous referees, thank you for helping to improve this work with your precise comments. For any errors or inadequacies that may remain in this work, of course the responsibility is entirely my own.

Special thanks to the Red Globe Press team and particularly my editor Lloyd Langman, who believed in my book project ever since our first chat, and project editor Peter Atkinson, who made the process smooth and pleasant.

Finally, some more personal acknowledgements. To Leonardo: the lack of good sleep and coffee during the writing of this book has been more than repaid by your presence, which has made the whole thing much more meaningful and fascinating. To Gianluca, for being supportive when my computer and my notes became the third wheel in all our trips and travels. Thank you also for your critical reflections on parts of my work and for the help with tables and figures – as always. Last but not least, a heartfelt acknowledgment goes to Eddie (Vedder), Ani (Di Franco) and Niccolò (Fabi) among others – who might never know about this book but whose music accompanied and empowered me through some challenging aspects of academic life.

Anita Lavorgna
London, November 2019

1 INTRODUCTION

The context and purpose of this book

This book presents an introduction to cybercrimes and is addressed specifically at students with different backgrounds and interests, aiming to provide them with a common language and guide them throughout the intricacies of criminal and deviant behaviours in cyberspace. Academic curricula are acknowledging the momentous change caused by the pervasiveness of cyberspace and are expanding their courses on cybercrimes. On the one hand, criminology programmes are proposing modules targeting students with (mostly) socio-legal and psychology backgrounds and supplying them with sufficient understanding of the cyber dimension of crime and deviance. On the other hand, computer science and engineering programmes are developing courses and degrees targeting students with more 'technical' backgrounds and interests. While these courses are comparable in their aim of preparing future workers for entry to the emerging cybersecurity professions, they differ in their approaches and employability prospects. Criminology courses prepare experts for work in the private sector, public administration or policing and frequently operate as a link between sector-based and technological experts, while technical courses train professionals in business or consultancy companies to design, build and control secure systems. In addition, in recognition of the intrinsic complexity of the field, new interdisciplinary and multidisciplinary degrees have been developed in an attempt to bring together the skills and expertise needed to form a new generation of highly prepared and employable students.

A big educational challenge needs to be addressed: if, on the one hand, criminology students need to understand with sufficient precision 'how' things (might) occur in cyberspace, then, on the other hand, computer science students must develop a sound appreciation of some of the 'big themes' in the social and legal sciences (think, for instance, of the debates on the shifting balance between privacy and security in cyberspace) in order to have the instruments to deal with the complexities and challenges they are likely to encounter in their future jobs. This educational challenge has broad social implications that go beyond problems of employability: in order to appreciate and preserve both our individual rights and public goods in the digital age, technical knowledge alone is not enough. Professionals working from different angles to promote and preserve security in cyberspace need to be able to critically assess the delicate trade-offs and complexities they are called to intervene in; if not, there is a risk that the remedy will be worse than the disease.

In understanding cybercrimes, there is an inherent interrelation between distinct disciplines; only a multi- and transdisciplinary approach can allow us to understand more fully the multidimensional nature of cyberspace and to underline several of the existing and emerging challenges of crime and deviancy in our times. As a consequence, even if this book is grounded in criminology, it also aims to deal rigorously with more technical aspects (without lingering on technicalities) and to give account of the broader socio-legal contexts that can be beneficial for a more comprehensive and in-depth understanding of some current and emerging problems in cyberspace. After all, students of crime and crime control are taught to look beyond the confines of their subject matter (Garland & Sparks 2000; Stratton et al. 2017). Criminology has, by its very nature, traditionally drawn upon scholarship from a wide range of disciplines, ranging from law, sociology and philosophy to economics, history and psychology. Nowadays, disciplines such as computer and data science should also be considered, to avoid irrelevancy in addressing questions of contemporary crime and deviance.

This book does not focus on a specific jurisdiction. Rather, examples from several countries are included, in an attempt to show how crime and deviance in cyberspace are global problems, with different countries experiencing comparable sets of challenges. At the same time, however, we will see how these challenges manifest themselves differently, depending on the socio-legal culture of reference; hence, effective solutions cannot ignore local specificities. Indeed, the maxim 'think globally act locally' is particularly pertinent in the field of cybercrimes (Grabosky & Smith 1998; Broadhurst 2006). After all, as Wall (2007) pointed out, even a virtual act has to resurface in the local, physical space at some point – via the offender (because a crime has to be committed somewhere), via the victim (who is victimised somewhere) or via the investigation (which has to take place somewhere).

This multidisciplinary and international approach is reflected in my academic background and developed in my research and teaching experiences: I have a background in law and international studies but have been working as criminologist since my PhD, leaning increasingly towards computational criminology; I am used to teaching a wide variety of students from different backgrounds and with different interests. In addition, I am an Italian scholar with international experience working in British academia, an (old) 'millennial' born between digital immigrants and digital natives, and I am a woman – which makes me part of a minority in relation to 'cybercrime experts'. I hope that these features will help me to bring a new perspective into the cybercrime narrative and to offer an interesting account to those approaching this fascinating area of inquiry.

Please note that we are using the plural form: cybercrime*s* and not cyber-crime. In general parlance, people still use the term 'cybercrime' for the hodge-podge of illegal behaviours that can be easily clustered together and separated from other illegal behaviours by occurring online, this being their discerning factor. As will emerge from this book, this interpretation is incorrect or at least hardly useful in comprehending sufficiently crime and deviance in cyberspace. With the blurring of online and offline in our daily lives, it makes less and less sense to think of 'cyber' as a *unicum* which can be kept apart from our ('real') routines. Digital technologies and social media in particular are so embedded in our everyday lives that we are increasingly part of a 'digital society' (Lupton 2014; Stratton et al. 2017). In the physical world, we would never equate a murder, a verbal offence after an altercation and a bicycle theft; similarly, in cyberspace, we need to be careful when distinguishing between very different sets of crimes. Over the years of criminological debate, several typologies of cybercrimes have been proposed. Trying to further the ongoing debates on how to best synthesise and comprehend cybercrimes and to define and refine what exactly we mean by the notion of cybercrime, this book proposes an updated typology (that is, a set of categories used for classification), which will be presented and explained in Chapter 2.

It is worth noting in this introduction that, while the focus of this book is on cyber-*crimes* – which by definition occur when a law is broken – we will also encounter behaviours that are *deviant* rather than illegal – that is, behaviours that break an accepted code of behaviour, even if they might not neces-sarily infringe a specific law. Think, for instance, of antisocial behaviours (including those of a violent nature) carried out in online virtual worlds or multiplayer online role-playing games such as Minecraft or Fortnite; or con-sider the creation of false new stories being propagated online. Some of these behaviours might be considered 'microdeviations' and, as such, be ignored by authorities because of the normality of deviance (Popham 2018). This approach is very common in criminology, which looks beyond strict legal definitions to examine social context and investigate why certain activities are labelled as 'crimes' while others are not. Furthermore, this is a convenient choice in a socio-legal context – that of cyberspace – which is evolving extremely fast, with legal frameworks and social perceptions on cyber-threats and risks yet to be settled. Such ongoing evolution depends not only on the emergence of technological innovations but also on the changes taking place in the political and economic arenas of our 'information age', changes that have important legal and ethical implications (Boyle 1996). Deviance and the relationship between deviance and crime have always been insightful concepts to understand the power relationships in society, as they can be used not only to label harmful behaviours but also to stigmatise and disem-power certain social groups (Adler & Adler 2006). Furthermore, observing how these concepts change through time and space affords us an excellent viewpoint of broader societal changes. These perspectives also hold true in cyberspace.

Approaching crime in cyberspace

In our hyper-connected world, it is becoming difficult to imagine a crime that does not involve an 'online' component, if only because the network infrastructure provided by the internet is an increasing part of our everyday routines. Information technology is fundamental for people to fully participate in modern society, with the internet becoming a ubiquitous and integral part in the everyday lives of many. In cyberspace, the virtual and figurative space created within the internet, offenders are finding a new environment in which to operate – one that is virtually unlimited, enabling instantaneous communication for the propagation and sale of ideas, goods and services, with huge possibilities for deception. Cyberspace is not criminogenic per se; it is simply a new social space connecting people and facilitating commerce. However, by taking some of the features that characterise late modernity to the extreme, cyberspace is particularly prone to exploitation, to the carrying out of countless illicit and malicious behaviours in very effective ways. Nowadays, in the context of ubiquitous computing – that is, the emerging trend of embedding computational capability into everyday objects, making them constantly connected – the potential for exploitation is growing even more.

A core question that will accompany us throughout the book is whether and to what extent cybercrimes are extensions of traditional crimes or whether they pose qualitatively and quantitatively new types of challenges. We will see that it can be very difficult to separate the offline from the online in our mundane experiences, as the internet's pervasiveness is what gives it its significance (Miller 2009). Hence, it is often more useful to interpret crime in cyberspace as an expansion of crime possibilities occurring in 'normal' space. This is what McGuire (2007) called 'hyperspatialisation', a term capturing the complexity of contemporary social spaces, where there is a continuity between the online and the offline realms: what happens in one space often spills over into the other, with the internet influencing our culture and our changing culture influencing cyberspace in return. Even if we accept the fact that cybercrimes are mostly adaptations or expansions of traditional crimes, this does not imply that the different system of risks and opportunities framed by new technologies does not change criminals' characteristics and modus operandi. This is why it is still heuristically useful to distinguish (crime in) the physical world from (crime in) cyberspace – after all, this is a book on cybercrimes, not on crimes in general.

Cyberspace is the setting of the activities and behaviours we will encounter in the following chapters, so it is worth expending a few lines on it before venturing on with this book. The term 'cyberspace' has an interesting genesis: it was first popularised by the American-Canadian writer William Gibson in his 1984 science fiction novel *Neuromancer*, which narrates the story of a talented hacker uncovering a conspiracy advanced by artificial intelligence in a cyberpunk dystopia. In the novel, cyberspace is a futuristic non-place which is accessed by physically connecting the brain to a computer to become part of a consensual hallucination. In its current representations, cyberspace is something different, even if, unlike most of the notions and concepts addressed in this book, it does not have an agreed definition. We generally refer to cyberspace as the social space in which or through which cybercrimes occur, a social space, generally depicted as potentially inclusive of all social groups, being global and borderless. In reality, however, this is not (yet) always the case, which is something we always need to bear in mind to properly understand cybercrimes today. Hence, before we start to discuss crime and deviancy, it is important to linger a little on the extent to which we can consider cyberspace truly inclusive, global and borderless.

It is true that cyberspace is accessible to an increasing number of people. According to the latest Internet World Stats (2019), the internet penetration rate (defined as the number of individuals who have access to the internet at home, via computer or mobile device) is almost 57 percent on a global scale, peaking to 89 percent in North America and 87 percent in Europe. Approximately 43 percent of the global population have access to social media, ranging from 6 percent in Middle Africa to 70 percent in North America (Statista 2019). With the increased use of devices such as smartphones, now owned by over a third of the world's population (Statista 2019), a growing number of people can access cyberspace from anywhere. However, one should not lose sight of the fact that about 45 percent of the world population still does not have an easy or reliable way to get online. The so-called digital divide – that is, the gap between those who do and those who do not have access to the internet – is a serious social (and technological) problem, deepening existing inequalities. Nowadays, being offline means being excluded from key opportunities to access important services or participate in political debate (Berners-Lee 2018). That is why the United Nations declared internet access to be a human right (like food and clean water) in 2016.

Even if the physical access gap is closing in most parts of the world, other gaps are still deep and wide in high-tech societies, where only people with a certain position in society (such as the young and employed, from higher-income families or those in receipt of a higher level of education) expect basic access to the internet and its services (van Dijk 2005). In certain countries, women and people living in rural areas are likely to remain offline (Berners-Lee 2018). Age is also an important discriminating factor regarding usage of the internet, with digital immigrants (those who invented technologies and systems pre-internet but became familiar with cyberspace as adults) and digital natives (those growing up in the digital age) representing different worldviews and thinking and processing information in different ways. Furthermore, while cyberspace is potentially borderless in nature, it is growing less and less so: new geopolitical boundaries are becoming embedded in its structure. Think, for instance, of the 'Great Firewall of China' – that is, a combination of technological and regulatory measures prescribed by the People's Republic of China to block access to a number of foreign internet services and to slow down cross-border internet traffic.

Finally, if we consider cyberspace as a global context of communication, it is worth underlining how it allows language socialisation and the consequent creation of a sense of collective identity to take place in new ways; physical and social cues are reduced and language choices facilitate interactions among transnational and diaspora networks around the world. After all, geographical boundaries do not coincide with linguistic ones. Besides English (which, due to its broad circulation around the world, is often perceived as a neutral language to use in multilingual contexts), online communities cluster around many other languages, sometimes giving rise to new hybrid and simplified codes (as in the case of Arabic online) (Danet & Herring 2007; Lam 2008). In a global English-centred research context, where most published research on cybercrimes focuses on English-speaking online communities, the linguistic diversity and multilingualism of the internet are things we should always keep in mind and we must be cautious in generalising research results.

The content of this book

This book comprises 10 chapters which can be logically divided into three main parts. The first part has laid the foundations of the topic with this introduction (Chapter 1), then offers a digression on the historical, legal and criminological aspects of cybercrimes (Chapter 2) and an introduction to key theoretical elements needed to better understand and interpret cybercrimes (Chapter 3). In more detail, Chapter 2 shows that, even if there is consensus on the fact that cybercrimes are serious crimes, and generally on the rise, they still lack any agreed definition: the main legal framework we have at an international level is outdated, with criminologists, lawyers and computer scientists alike proposing and debating various ways to define and categorise crime in cyberspace. The fact is that the concept of 'cybercrime', as we will see, has been socially constructed and refined through time and is still evolving. Moreover, Chapter 2 will discuss how consensus is also absent on the size of the cybercrime industry: measuring crime is not easy, and measuring crime in cyberspace can be particularly challenging. Chapter 3, on the other hand, will briefly outline the main ways in which crime has been traditionally explained by criminologists over time. In reading this chapter, you will realise how many crime theories developed years (if not decades) ago, can still help us to unpack, comprehend and analyse various forms of cybercrimes – and even to prefigure future crime manifestations.

The second, 'core' part of the book is dedicated to the most relevant types of cybercrimes. Here, you will learn about the boundaries of their definitions, key characteristics, more recent trends and the current challenges in curbing them. You will encounter real-life examples of cybercrimes and have the chance to reflect on the aptness and effectiveness of the way in which we approach them, from both an academic and a practical point of view.

We will start with crimes against devices (Chapter 4), a category encompassing various types of attacks against computers, mobile devices, smart goods, operating and security systems and networks – all sharing the fact that an act of unauthorised or otherwise unlawful access to a device took place. In this chapter, we will also discuss (more or less) lawful forms of access to data stored or transmitted through a device (so-called 'dataveillance') and reflect on the complex relationship between privacy, security and data confidentiality in cyberspace. Crimes against persons (Chapter 5) follow. Here, you will learn about numerous criminal and deviant acts (namely so-called antagonistic online behaviours, such as hate speech and harassment and sex crimes) sharing the fact that they all target other people, affecting their physical, psychological and emotional health. Our journey will continue with crimes of deception and coercion (Chapter 6), a hybrid category where we find crimes targeting an individual in a fraudulent or coercive way but where the endgame is generally financial profit. In this chapter, you will also read about some of the themes cutting across the whole book, as they are an important element of most cybercrimes, such as social engineering and the glocalism of cybercrimes. With market-based crimes and crimes against property (Chapter 7), you will encounter a broad array of illegal markets online, ranging from carding forums to darknet drug markets, as well as intellectual property infringements and specifically copyright infringements (which are the most common in cyberspace). You will have the opportunity to reflect on the human dimension of cybercrimes and on the blurring divide between their cyber and physical components. Finally, under the label of political offences (Chapter 8), we will discuss diverse behaviours (ranging from cyberwarfare to state censorship) pivoting around a political act, policy or idea. Most of these behaviours are not criminal, but they can still cause significant harm and, as such, deserve a place in this book.

The third part of the book concludes our journey by focusing on diverse mechanisms to address cybercrimes, either to prevent or disrupt them (Chapter 9) or to better comprehend and analyse them (Chapter 10). You will learn how the governance and policing of criminal or deviant online behaviour are characterised by a combination of formal and informal countermeasures. Beyond traditional state regulatory and law enforcement intervention, a central role is played by the presence of partnerships with non-governmental organisations, offering commercial and technology-led solutions, as well as self-regulatory and self-protection approaches. Trusting partnerships and cooperation are also key in researching cybercrimes, and by the end of the book, it will be clear that a new model of collaboration between the social and computer sciences is needed to effectively study crime and deviancy in cyberspace. Drawing from diverse expertise can allow us to think pre-emptively not only about cybercrimes but also about the trade-offs that, as a society, we are willing to accept when it comes to balancing privacy, security and convenience.

2 OUTLINING CYBERCRIMES

Introduction

Research on cybercrimes is a relatively new area of enquiry. Lawyers, criminologists and computer scientists in particular have paid increasing attention to crime and deviance in cyberspace and have been searching for new forms of understanding in this area. Despite broad consensus on the threats to economic and security interests posted by the cybercrime industry, an uncontested definition is still lacking and there is little consensus about the industry's size and structure. This chapter introduces the notion of cybercrimes, presenting key legal, criminological and historical elements. Here, we will briefly trace the development of how cybercrime has been socially constructed, which will help us to understand why certain behaviours are defined or perceived as criminal while others are not.

In this chapter, we also encounter and explain the rationale for the categorisation of cybercrimes used in this book. We continue by discussing how cybercrimes are measured and look at issues associated with the production of data on crime rates, which hinders a proper evidence-based understanding of the phenomenon and hence identification of the preventative actions that should be taken in response. We will see that, even if it is not possible to obtain a precise picture of cybercrimes, it is nonetheless important to be critically aware of the type of information currently available on their importance and their weaknesses.

A brief historical context

In order to understand the evolution of cyberspace – and of cybercrimes permeating it – it is useful to briefly retrace the technological, social and economic factors that have made it possible. This brief exercise should also remind us how cyberspace and cybercrimes are relatively new concepts and consequently why the study of cybercrimes is still, if not in its infancy, in its adolescence (Figure 2.1).

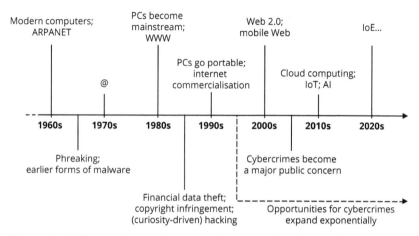

Figure 2.1 Information and communication technology milestones versus cybercrime evolution: a timeline

From a technological point of view, our story begins in the late 1930s with the development of extremely heavy (a few tons) single-task computers (the refinement of earlier attempts from the late nineteenth century) created to solve and automate specific number-crunching crises in business, academia and the armed forces. In particular, the exigencies of World War II gave great impetus to computer research. The Electronic Numerical Integrator and Computer, for instance, was a 27-tonne machine ('the giant brain') completed in 1945 to perform calculations for the hydrogen bomb design for the United States Army; the British Colossus, the first large-scale electronic computer, went into operation in 1944 (just in time for the D-Day landings in Normandy), its five tonnes being used mainly to help decipher secret German messages.

It was only during the following three decades that the creation of transistors and memory technology allowed, little by little, computers to become smaller (even if still huge by today's standards!) and fast enough to be increasingly employed not only by the military but also for commercial use. After the war, research efforts focused on the development of general-purpose computer devices, and when these started to come down in size and price, big companies, corporations and universities were able to make good use of them to increase productivity and efficiency in business accounting and scientific calculations. Mainframe computers ('big irons') made their entrance at this time.

Computers as we think of them today, however, started being invented only in the mid-1960s, when the creation of integrated circuits made them faster, smaller and cheaper (even though they were still too expensive for most households), while the introduction of time-sharing computers allowed multiprogramming (the possibility to run several tasks simultaneously), hence accommodating more users at the same time. During these years, the creation of computer monitors and the development of operating systems and graphical user interfaces made computers more accessible to the general public in terms of usability. The late 1960s witnessed the birth of the ARPANET, the world's first advanced computer network, and precursor of the internet, created by the United States in an attempt to establish military and technological superiority over the Soviet Union during the Cold War. With it, the idea of almost instantaneous communication between machines became a reality: in the early 1970s, with the development of protocols governing dialogues between machines, emails and messaging made their appearance, and the @ symbol with them.

Another big leap occurred in the late 1970s and early 1980s, when Apple, the now defunct Commodore International and IBM introduced personal computers for home and office use. These became extremely popular at the time of their release (the Commodore 64, which was introduced in 1982 became the highest-selling single computer model of all time, selling a total of 3.5 million units by mid-1986). This is when personal computers (PCs) became mainstream and the democratisation of computing really began. This context created fertile soil for cybercrimes, which before had been limited mostly to physical damage to computer systems or meddling with telecommunication networks (phreaking). However, given that most computers were still used in public and corporate organisations, at this point most cybercrimes were white-collar crimes, such as financial data theft, copyright infringements (Zavrsnik 2008; Stratton et al. 2017) or computer tampering driven by intellectual curiosity (as we will see in more detail in Chapter 4).

A momentous development occurred in 1989, when Tim Berners-Lee and his colleagues at CERN, in Switzerland, invented the World Wide Web (the information space accessible via the internet), which was initially developed to facilitate information-sharing between scientists around the world. The underlying code was made available on a royalty-free basis, which sparked collaborations and innovation around the world. The mid-1990s marked the commercialisation of the internet, which was accessible to the masses in the richest countries. This was a period of excitement led by major growth of the Web, which gave birth to many important e-companies (such as eBay and Amazon) as well as to excessive speculation: overconfidence in the market inflated the dot-com economic bubble, which by the end of 2001 caused losses equivalent to trillions of pounds of investment capital. These were also the years when new opportunities for computer crime grew tremendously: cyber-offenders could greatly expand their reach (for instance, by transmitting malware from a distance through the new and vulnerable browsers). Furthermore, offences started to be directed not only against other machines but also against the human beings behind them (Castells 2001; Stratton et al. 2017).

By the beginning of the new millennium, not only had cybercrime expanded exponentially, but it also became a major public concern. It is not a coincidence that these are also the years when cybercrimes started to receive significant coverage in news media, with a particular focus on hacking (as we will see in detail in Chapter 4), identity theft and child pornography. Traditionally, media representations have a significant influence in shaping people's perceptions not only of crime and deviance but also of the risks and possibilities offered by technological advances. So, apropos cybercrimes, media has had a pivotal role in creating expectations about what cybercrimes look like and how they might evolve. Indeed, the media crystallised the usage of the word 'cybercrime' among the general public, at a point in time when it had no specific reference point in law (Wall 2007). In fact, as we will see in the next section, it was only with the 2001 Budapest Convention that the term entered legal jargon.

To put things into context, it might be useful to remember that we need to wait until 1998 to have Google; until the late 1990s to have the first large-scale social media, instant messaging and blogging platforms (such as SixDegrees and MSM Messenger); and to the early 2000s for some of the most popular platforms such as Myspace (in 2003) and Facebook (in 2004); then 2001 for Wikipedia, 2003 for Skype, 2006 for Twitter and 2010 for Instagram. Interestingly, the increasing commercialisation of the internet soon changed the original nature of the Web: profit-driven intellectual property rights took over the idea that open sharing of information was an essential aspect of the internet in order to pursue scientific advance; surveillance technology started to be used by commercial companies first and by government agencies later (Curran 2009). At the same time, little by little, in the early 2000s, the Web 2.0 (or the 'participative Web') emerged: here, users (thanks to rich-Web and client-side technologies such as Adobe Flash and JavaScript frameworks) do not merely 'read' content but also help to generate it. On the one side, Web 2.0 further opened the possibility for meaningful interaction and collaboration; on the other side, unfortunately, it has been the basis of many of the cybercrimes we will encounter in this book.

The latest leap is related to the increasing pervasiveness and ubiquity of the internet, which has been driven by transformative technologies such as smartphones, cyber-physical systems and cloud computing. Even though the first smartphone was created by IBM in 1992, it was not until the late 2000s that smartphones achieved mass adoption in many countries, causing a real mobile revolution. As computers adopted the form of smartphones, they could be taken everywhere, allowing huge flexibility to seek or share information, communicate and even to shop. Similarly, even if precursors of cloud computing and the 'internet of things' (IoT, see Chapter 4) can be dated back respectively to the 1970s and 1980s, their use started to accelerate only after the mid-2010s, reaching the mass market a few years later and opening the way to a new dawn for cybercrimes. Another leap is probably happening right now, with new computer devices based on artificial intelligence and responding to natural language processing and with current investments in quantum computing. It might take a few years for these developments to reach their full potential and unfold the possibilities they could open up for new forms of cybercrimes.

As explained by Curran (2009), the technological evolution briefly summarised here would not have been possible without the presence of five main 'cultures of invention'. First, the military, which influenced the objectives of major technological innovations – think of the creation of the ARPANET. Second, academic computer scientists, as they were the ones actually implementing the design of the internet, trying to make it a better research tool. Third, American countercultures of the 1980s, which sought individual self-realisation through freedom from repressive convention and promoted open disclosure and social interaction. In this context, technology seemed to offer a means to escape extensive social control, emancipating the individual (Zavrsnik 2008). Fourth, the European tradition of public service, embodied by Tim Berners-Lee and inspired by the idea of opening up access to a public good and of bringing people into communion. Finally, the values of the market played a major role, countering the elitist academic approach and democratising the Web, making it more accessible to a larger number of people.

The equilibria among user-generated content, extreme commercialisation and widespread surveillance are particularly fascinating, as they show how cyberspace – at least for now – remains a contested zone, exposed to contrasting influences (Curran 2009). It will be interesting to see how the internet's architecture evolves in the future, depending on the shifting balances among those forces.

Defining cybercrimes

The legal framework

Cyberspace is not lawless: a multilevel structure of governance is already operating to regulate it, maintaining some order (Lessig 1999; Wall 2001). Nonetheless, when it comes to applicable legal principles, the internet entails several problems (both substantial and procedural) because of its peculiar features, such as the instantaneity and potential universality of traffic. Not surprisingly, with the emergence of cyber-threats, new legislation has been passed to enhance crime prevention and disruption while maintaining an equilibrium between openness and security in cyberspace.

When it comes to regulating cyberspace, there are three options (Walker et al. 2000):

- use of traditional legal approaches;
- adaptation of existing laws to cyberspace;
- creation of ad hoc cyber-law.

The third hypothesis has often been criticised by scholars: extensive new legislation does not seem necessary, the risk being that of overregulation or premature regulatory interventions (Brenner 2001; Grabosky & Smith 2001). Indeed, existing written and customary law generally provide a principled regulatory reference even if they need to be applied to new and evolving circumstances (Perry & Roda 2016). However, for the time being, the prevalent choice is to intervene with new legislation for specific types of online crimes (Lavorgna 2018a). So far, many countries have criminalised offences such as illegal access to a computer system; production, distribution or possession of computer misuse tools; computer-related fraud or forgery; computer-related identity offences; computer-related copyright and trademark offences; computer-related acts involving racism or xenophobia; computer-related production, distribution or possession of child pornography and so on (UNODC 2013).

As summarised by Clough (2010), the evolution of legislation for cybercrimes has followed successive waves, reflecting worries surrounding the misuse of computers. Initially, fears were related mostly to unauthorised access to private information and economic crimes. As the internet became more and more popular, initial concerns were joined by fears regarding remote attacks on computers, infringement of copyright and the distribution of child pornography. A new wave of crime was identified, with the increased role of the internet as a major crime facilitator for traditional crimes and especially for trafficking activities (Lavorgna 2015a, b, c).

Even if not always necessary, the introduction of new legislation may nonetheless have two major positive effects: first, by clarifying the formal state position on certain criminal activities, it sends out a clear message to (potential) offenders and impacts social values pertaining to new types of activities; second, new legislation provides the authority for legal tactics and actions to investigate new activities that previously fell short of formal prosecution (Wall 2007). Unfortunately, unnecessary regulatory intervention can also lead to unintended consequences. Grabosky and Smith (1998), for instance, envisaged the dangers of the 'forbidden fruit effect'. Some internet users might work to create alternative points of access to the material or services forbidden by law in an ideological attempt to respond to what is perceived by them as a form of censorship.

Another specific issue affecting the criminalisation of certain cyber-activities depends on the fact that these crimes generally occur in various different places, which may be under the jurisdictions of different countries (Calderoni 2010). Therefore, there is a strong need for the harmonisation of laws to avoid the anomalous situation of the same conduct giving rise to criminal liability in one jurisdiction but not in another (Grabosky & Smith 1998). For example, even if some cybercrimes (such as hacking) are already covered by substantive law in many countries, others (such as many forms of cyber-harassment) are not consistently criminalised in many jurisdictions. Hence, it is necessary to develop and expand international treaties to deal with cybercrimes and other internet-facilitated crimes, to expand extradition capacities and to set clear norms to define the priorities and competencies of each country involved (Grabosky & Smith 1998; Calderoni 2010).

This is why, besides national legislation, several legislative responses have been adopted at international and regional levels: it is not only a matter of a country protecting itself and its citizens, it is (or it should be) a matter of the world community facing similar challenges. In this regard, the most important legislative intervention was the Budapest Convention on Cybercrime. Adopted under the aegis of the Council of Europe in November 2001 and coming into force in July 2004, it is the first international convention addressing criminal behaviours online. A perfect example of the 'second wave' of cybercrime legislation (Clough 2010), in its section concerning substantive criminal law, the Convention urges Member States to criminalise four main types of criminal activities:

- offences against the confidentiality, integrity and availability of computer data and systems (illegal access, illegal interception, data interference, system interference and misuse of services);
- computer-related offences (forgery and fraud);
- content-related offences (child pornography);
- offences related to infringements of copyright and related rights.

The 'Additional Protocol to the Convention' urges states to criminalise acts of a racist and xenophobic nature committed through computer systems. Therefore, this piece of legislation has the merit to cover a broad range of online criminal behaviour, but it is not comprehensive. For instance, internet-facilitated trafficking activities (think of a large-scale drug trafficking ring in the deep Web) are not covered by the Budapest Convention, and therefore they should not be deemed cybercrimes in the strict sense, even if nowadays they are generally considered such. The Budapest Convention also promotes the adoption of appropriate legislation at a national level, the improvement of mutual assistance and investigative techniques and the fostering of international cooperation.

Overall, the Convention represents the best international response currently available to cybercrimes, as its scope goes beyond membership of the Council of Europe. Four non-Member States – namely Canada, Japan, South Africa and the United States – participated in its drafting, and some non-member countries also signed the Convention. Apart from the Budapest Convention, several other regional legal instruments on cybercrimes exist, such as the 2001 Commonwealth of Independent States Agreement on Cooperation in Combating Offences related to Computer Information, the 2005 European Union Framework Decision on attacks against information systems, the 2010 League of Arab States Convention on Combating Information Technology Offences and the 2014 African Union Cybersecurity Convention. Unfortunately, there remain substantial differences in the implementation of international and regional legal instruments, and there are gaps between different jurisdictions, with consequent problems relating to the prosecution of transnational cybercrimes (Koops & Brenner 2006; Banks 2010; Lavorgna 2018a), as we will see in more detail in Chapter 9.

Criminological perspectives

In academia, 'cybercrime' is neither well defined nor a unitary concept. After all, this term comes from science fiction and initially entered common parlance to express concerns about forms of computer misuse such as hacking, before being crystallised in law by the Budapest Convention (Wall 2012). In criminological discourse, cybercrimes are broadly interpreted as crimes generally relating to information and communication technologies (ICTs) which involve their use in the commission of offences or target ICTs themselves or in which ICTs are used incidentally in the commission of other offences (Grabosky & Smith 1998; Smith et al. 2004; Broadhurst & Choo 2011). Besides 'cybercrime', a variety of different terms have also been used, such as netcrime, hi-tech crime, computer crime, virtual crime, ecrime, I-way crime and so on. However, since the late 1990s, the term 'cybercrime' took on a life of its own, becoming part of popular parlance, and is now the word most commonly used by academics of different disciplines.

Many criminologists and criminal justice scholars have tried to unpack and categorise cybercrimes. In order to do this, the first conundrum to be solved is whether and to what extent cyberspace poses threats that are new. There is agreement that, at least potentially, the internet provides channels of communication and commerce qualitatively different from pre-existing mass media. Criminal activities not only can be carried out more quickly and more extensively but also can more easily transcend national boundaries, providing criminals with access to a potentially global arena. Scholars are more divided on whether cyberspace has allowed the existence of new types of crimes (think of spamming or malicious software), exposing its users to an array of new risks (Wall 2004), or whether some traditional criminal activities (ranging from fraud to child pornography) have merely been facilitated by the internet, which has created a new environment in which traditional crimes can prosper (Clarke 2004). In this regard, cybercrimes represent nothing more than the commission of traditional crimes by non-traditional means. As summarised by Brenner (2004, p. 5), the differences lie not so much in the elements of the offence but rather in the circumstances of its commission. Wall (2007) proposed a 'transformation test' to locate cybercrimes along a spectrum by thinking about what would happen to certain types of criminal behaviour if the online element were to be removed: at one end of the spectrum, we can find the first generation of cybercrimes (that is, traditional crimes in which a computer was used to assist traditional offending, as in the case of online drug trafficking); towards the middle of the continuum, there is the second generation of 'hybrid' cybercrimes (conventional crimes for which the internet made possible new opportunities, as in the case of global fraud); finally, only at the far end of the spectrum lie the 'true' cybercrimes of the third generation, which can exist only within cyberspace (such as spamming).

Other scholarly efforts in criminology have tried to offer typologies of cybercrimes depending on the types of crime considered. The most successful classification is undoubtedly the one proposed by Wall (2007). He distinguishes three basic groups of criminal activities, each one requiring a different legal and criminological understanding:

- computer integrity crimes
- computer-assisted crimes
- computer content crimes.

In computer integrity crimes (such as hacking, cracking and denial of service), the access system of networked computers is the object of criminal attention. Computer-assisted crimes (such as virtual robberies, scam, identity theft and espionage) encompass several deceptive and acquisitive harms upon individual or corporate victims for informational or pecuniary advantage, performed via networked computers. Computer-content crimes (such as extreme pornography, violence, harassment and hate crimes) are all those criminal activities where the content of websites and other electronic communications is obscene or offensive for a variety of reasons. Of course, the extent to which these communications are illegal varies greatly between countries. This categorisation, however, is not comprehensive. For instance, it does not include internet-facilitated criminal activities in which the Web is used as a primary crime facilitator but is not necessarily an inherent part of the criminal activity per se (Lavorgna 2015a) (for instance, internet-mediated drug trafficking). Indeed, these activities were not initially considered cybercrime in a strict sense and were excluded by the cybercrime umbrella. Nonetheless, Wall's typology has proven helpful in guiding criminological understanding for many years. Interestingly, it reflects the categorisation offered by the Budapest Convention, being a clear example of how the Convention has influenced other legal and conceptual frameworks on cybercrime (Calderoni 2010).

Our working typology

In this volume, when we explore the main types of cybercrime (Chapters 4, 5, 6, 7 and 8), we move slightly away from the classifications used in other cybercrime textbooks, as they generally assume that 'cyber' crimes are something ontologically different from 'normal' crimes and, as such, need an ad hoc typology. Even if cybercrimes have unique features that justify their study as a distinct form of crime (that is, they have a 'cyber' component that entails a unique set of challenges to be addressed), we adapt a more

Table 2.1 Cybercrimes typology

Crimes against devices	Crimes against persons	Crimes of deception and coercion	Market-based crimes and crimes against property	Political offences
Hacking	Hate speech	Fraud	Illegal markets online	(Certain forms of) Hacktivism (see box in Chapter 4)
	Harassment	Extortion	Intellectual property infringement	Cyberwarfare
	Sex crimes			Cyberterrorism
				Controlling cyberspace as political deviancy

traditional typology for the study of (traditional, offline) crimes vis-à-vis the specificities of cybercrimes.

The typology used is broadly inspired by the United Nations Office on Drugs and Crime (UNODC) international classification of crimes for statistical purposes (ICCS) (UNODC 2014) in the sense that we keep a clear distinction between acts against property, persons, the state, public order and market-based crimes such as drug trafficking and crimes of fraud and deception. To construct categories, we considered the general policy areas affected (protection of property rights, public security), the target of the act (a person, an object, the state) and the modus operandi (for example, deception or threat). Of course, we had to adapt the UNODC typology to the specificities of cyberspace and the aims of the book. Nevertheless, the ICCS provided a useful framework for guidance, the categorisation of acts being based on behaviours (similar in terms of conceptual, analytical and policy areas) rather than on legal provisions, which is particularly useful in considering phenomena evolving across diverse jurisdictions (Table 2.1).

Measuring cybercrimes

In this section, we will see whether, how and to what extent we can answer questions such as 'How many cybercrimes are out there?' and 'What is the impact of [a certain] cybercrime on society?' The answers to such questions are not trivial. A knowledge of crime levels and trends provides us with

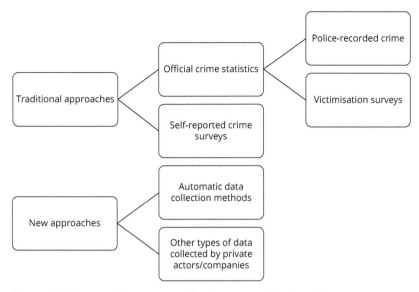

Figure 2.2 Approaches to quantify the extent of cybercrimes

a better understanding of the situation; it also determines policies and allows us to assess crime prevention and control approaches (Figure 2.2).

We will first address the two main sources of official crime statistics providing crime rates – police-recorded crime and victimisation surveys (in which people are asked about their experiences of crime over a period). A third traditional method that attempts to estimate crime is self-reported crime surveys. Here, researchers ask people to reveal information about their lifestyle and (minor) offences they have committed. Regarding cybercrimes, some academics have developed self-reporting survey data from small samples of the population (in most cases, from college and juvenile population samples) and for specific types of cybercrimes. However, this type of data, although valuable, cannot be easily generalised (Baggili & Rogers 2009; Holt & Bossler 2015).

In the offline world, police figures provide generally good estimates for rare and serious crimes (such as homicides); however, they reflect policing priorities more than actual crime rates, as they tend not to include underreported or undiscovered crimes – the so-called 'dark figure' of crimes. In cyberspace, the dark number of crimes tends to be particularly high, and the same goes for serious crimes. Police-reported crime statistics are relatively scarce and, generally speaking, do not yet provide sufficiently accurate and reliable information on the scale and scope of most cybercrimes. These limitations hinder a proper evidence-based understanding of the phenomenon and hence identification of the preventative actions that should be taken in response. There are a number of factors impeding such understanding.

First, as emphasised by Grabosky (2016), the very nature of cybercrimes makes the production of crime statistics problematic, as in most cases cybercrimes are nothing more than traditional crimes (fraud, stalking, drug trafficking and so on) committed using new methods. They are generally charged (and their statistics are therefore recorded) under statutes that reflect the substantive nature of the crime and not the tool used to commit it. Besides the lack of reporting and recording mechanisms that accurately distinguish between online and offline crimes, another problem is that more complex forms of cybercrimes cannot be easily placed into a single crime category, which severely hinders the statistical recording of such activities (McGuire & Dowling 2013). Think, for instance, of cases of phishing or ransomware, which cover more criminal offences at the same time (fraud, trespass, extortion and so forth). In most countries around the world, state agencies and institutions have not yet developed specific methods for recording cybercrimes. Even when they have done so, cyber-incidents are often not differentiated from other categories of crimes in a satisfactory way, which suggests that the extent of cybercrime remains extremely unclear. The Italian National Institute of Statistics (the main producer of official statistics in Italy), for example, provides statistics on police-recorded cybercrimes since 2010, but it recognises only online fraud and crimes against devices as distinct categories. In the United Kingdom, the Crime Survey for England and Wales (CSEW) started to include questions on cybercrimes in 2015, focusing on a limited number of computer misuse crimes such as malware, hacking and certain types of fraud. Inconsistencies in the definition and recording of cybercrimes make all types of comparative research particularly difficult and this is of the utmost importance considering the global nature of many cybercrimes. The development of cross-national common definitions (such as via the Budapest Convention and Directive 2013/40/EU in the European Union) is slowly helping to overcome this limitation (at least, for the specific types of crimes they cover), but there are still no agreed protocols and guidelines for data collection and statistical counting rules that should be applied to allow data comparison (Caneppele & Aebi 2019).

A second problem is linked to the underreporting of cybercrimes by public companies and businesses, often due to lack of awareness that some incidents are actually crimes (McGuire & Dowling 2013). Some victims, in fact, might simply be unaware that an offence has been committed (for instance, not realising they have been victims of fraud) or might have a different understanding of what counts as an offence (for example, it is sometimes difficult to draw boundaries around cases of cyber-harassment) because of lack of knowledge of the laws (which are often changing) regulating cybercrimes (Yar 2019; van de Weijer et al. 2018). Furthermore, especially regarding businesses and companies, their victimisation may not be reported to the police, as firms fear this will incur adverse publicity for their businesses; rather, many companies prefer to investigate incidents themselves

(Wall 2015). The underreporting of many forms of cybercrime is also linked to the general perception of futility in reporting incidents in cyberspace, where law enforcement agencies may be incapable or even reluctant to investigate crimes. The seriousness of cybercrimes often lies in their aggregate impact, while the impact for individual victims might be relatively low (Wall 2007). Consequently, many victims believe that law enforcement officers will not use their scarce resources to investigate 'minor' attacks. Prosecutions for cybercrimes are still relatively low around the world, leaving a huge gap between their paucity and the enormity of incidents estimated through other methods, such as victimisation surveys.

Third, even when cyber-incidents are reported, unlike for traditional crimes, this information does not flow through a single major portal – that is, the police (TechUK 2015; Wall 2015). Therefore, information gets lost. Some countries have developed a central hub for certain types of serious cybercrime. One example is provided by the US Internet Crime Complaint Centre (IC3), which, since 2000, has received and referred complaints on a wide spectrum of cybercrime matters (ranging from internet fraud to hacking) from either actual victims or a third party. Consider that over only the last four years of available data, between 2014 and 2018, the IC3 received a total of 1,509,679 complaints, with a total loss of about GBP 6 billion. In Italy, the Postal and Communication Police (one of the units of the State Police) is the only actor dealing with online child pornography. Since 2015, in the United Kingdom, the Home Office has been asking police forces to flag crimes with a cyber component, Action Fraud becoming the national fraud and cybercrime reporting centre. All these efforts are helping to build a clearer picture of cybercrime rates, but for most crimes and in most countries, the reporting of cyber-incidents remains patchy and is far from comprehensive.

Last but not least, because of how victims are perceived, certain cybercrimes suffer from specific difficulties in allowing events to become known and therefore addressed. As explained by Martellozzo and Jane (2017), victims of cybercrimes are often not recognised as victims (think, for instance, of certain victims of revenge porn), or victims might not recognise that what they have experienced is abuse (this is the case, for example, of many victims of sex crimes during the grooming phase, as we will see in Chapter 5). Moreover, there is an aura of victim blame around certain types of crime which may prevent a victim from reporting them: consider victims of online fraud, who might be seen as gullible and 'responsible' for what happened to them (Cross 2015). On top of that, in many legal traditions, victims of cybercrimes are sometimes overlooked by criminal law for doctrinal and conceptual reasons. Generally speaking, the law has high standards of proof for securing criminal convictions (which is an essential feature of the rule of law) – think, for instance, of the need to have both a clear *actus reus* (a criminal act, explicitly recognised by the law) and the *mens rea* (the offender's awareness that his/her conduct is criminal or at least of his/her culpability) for a criminal act to occur and the reliance on jurisdictional boundaries to allow its prosecution (Vincent 2017). These legal requirements, however, are not always easy to satisfy in cyberspace, which can leave the victim defenceless.

In order to assess the dark figure of crime, victimisation surveys (assessing individual or business victimisation) are used and are generally considered the best way to capture reliable statistics on crime trends. Many victimisation surveys are gradually incorporating questions on online victimisation, which should allow us to gather a more accurate, cumulative picture of the extent of certain cybercrimes (Wall 2007; Smith 2009). Unfortunately, for the time being, the situation is still unsatisfactory. In the United Kingdom, for instance, the British CSEW has incorporated questions on cyber-victimisation (fraud and computer misuse) only since 2015. The latest CSEW figures, based on interviews conducted with adults aged 16 years and over between January 2018 and December 2018, measuring people's experiences of crime in the 12 months before interview, indicate that over half of fraud incidents for the latest survey year were cyber-related, but the data available do not offer much insight for many other forms of cybercrimes. In the United States, the National Crime Victimization Survey (NCVS) collects information on criminal victimisation but focuses on non-fatal personal crimes, such as sexual assault or robbery, and household property crimes (even if an identity theft supplement was published in 2015). A more specific online victimisation survey (the National Computer Security Survey) was launched in 2006 to produce reliable industry-level estimates of the prevalence of computer security incidents against businesses in the United States, but this experience has not been repeated in more recent years.

From a comparative perspective, an additional problem is that the presence of victimisation surveys is still extremely sketchy on a global level. Many countries do not carry them out; and when victimisation surveys are carried out, this does not occur consistently in different countries (for instance, there is significant variation in methods and questioning). As a result, estimates swing widely and might be underrepresentative of the total number of victims. A review of victim surveys of selected types of cybercrimes in European countries, for example, indicates that annual crime prevalence rates range from 1 to 3 percent for online shopping fraud, that 1 to 6 percent of the population is a victim of hacking and 2 to 15 percent have been subject to malware (Reep-van den Bergh & Junger 2018).

Box 2.1 Who are the victims of cybercrime?

Victimology is that branch of criminology that focuses on victims. Over the years, an increasing number of researchers have investigated forms of cyber-victimisation and their impact on victims.

As for traditional crimes, victims of cybercrimes can be individuals, companies and society as a whole. Besides the primary victim (who experiences the criminal act), we often find secondary victims (who suffer financially or emotionally from the crime, even if they are not directly affected by it) and tertiary victims (those who experience the harm produced by the crime only vicariously, for instance when victimisation extends to the societal level). Victimisation can be objective, when victims experience material loss, or subjective, when they suffer psychological or emotional impact (Berg 2009). Just as with traditional offline crimes, cybercrime victimisation experiences produce a sense of fear in the victim, especially for individuals with low confidence in using the internet or with low social status (Virtanen 2017).

Let us imagine an online sale fraud, affecting Ms Green (individual victim) and Blue & Red Inc. (company). Both Ms Green and Blue & Red Inc. are primary victims, who directly suffer from the crime. They have both lost money (objective victimisation) and also confidence in buying items online; they might even have suffered reputational damage, as they are now considered gullible among their peers (subjective victimisation). Ms Green's family and Blue & Red Inc.'s employees are also suffering from the situation, as they have to give up a long-awaited holiday because of the loss of money or have to deal with a nervous boss; they are all secondary victims. The fraud case becomes common knowledge beyond the primary victims' inner social circles because it is reported in the press or via hearsay, provoking incremental fears in society regarding the safety of e-commerce. The people reached at this stage are tertiary victims, who might experience anxiety because of the original crime. Regarding cybercrime, therefore, we should never forget that crimes affect not only the original victim but all layers of society (Berg 2009).

According to some authors, there is an ontological difference between victims of traditional crime and cybercrimes: the latter, in fact, enter a potentially criminal social space at their own risk, led by a false sense of security due to their technological familiarity (Cox et al. 2009). This view has been surpassed nowadays, where physical and online spaces are increasingly intermingled, and being 'connected' is a normal part of everyday life, not a choice. It is true, however, that many internet users enter cyberspace with blind spots regarding good cyber-security practices, such as choosing a weak password, reusing the same password for many accounts or clicking on dodgy emails (Mitnick & Simon 2001; Hadnagy 2011). As we will see more in detail in Chapter 9, a major consequence is that individuals, rather than the state, are held increasingly responsible for security failures; in line with the 'responsibilisation thesis' captured by O'Malley (1996) and later developed by Garland (2001), victim self-help is essential in most cybercrime strategies. The problem is that there can be a thin line between making individuals responsible for security choices and victim-blaming – denying victims their status as legitimate victims.

Research on cybercrime victims indicates that, similar to what happens in offline crimes, risky routine activities and low self-control are primary risk factors explaining cybercrime victimisation: the former as they increase criminal opportunities and exposure to motivated offenders (Ngo & Paternoster 2011; Jaishankar 2011; van Wisem 2013a; Leukfeldt & Yar 2016; Junger et al. 2017; Pratt & Turanovic 2017; Bergmann et al. 2018; Kranenbarg et al. 2019), the latter as cyberspace generates the so-called 'online disinhibition effect' (Suler 2004), which causes people to behave in cyberspace with less restraint than in the physical world (Agustina 2015). Risky routine activities and low self-control approaches derive from specific theoretical criminological approaches, namely routine activity theory (Cohen & Felson 1979) and self-control theory (Gottfredson & Hirschi 1990), which will be explained to the reader in Chapter 3. Most research so far has focused primarily on youth victimisation (Kerstens & Jansen 2016), even if with some notable exceptions (see, for instance, Cross 2016 on senior victimisation), and on specific types of crimes, such as malware infections, financial cybercrime and many person-based forms of cybercrime such as harassment and identity theft (Bossler & Holt 2009; Kerstens & Jansen 2016; Reyns 2010, 2013, 2015; Reep-van den Bergh & Junger 2018). Hence, these results cannot be easily generalised.

We have seen how conventional methodologies for collecting data are not very effective for cybercrimes, with the consequence that it is difficult to find reliable 'measures' of crimes in cyberspace through official statistics. Non-traditional, automatic data collection methods are increasingly being used. For instance, in the United Kingdom, the Child Exploitation and Online Protection Centre (CEOP) has developed considerable expertise in acting as a reporting centre for the public. Thanks to the 'ClickCEOP' report mechanism (an online portal developed to offer children, parents and other concerned parties a simple and non-intimidating mechanism for gaining access to trusted safety advice, help and support), CEOP is purportedly able to use the information gathered to identify and safeguard the children involved, as well as to arrest the perpetrators (Home Office 2010). However, particularly for other types of cybercrimes and internet-facilitated crimes, there is still much work to do to develop proper avenues for reporting cyber-incidents in a way that is both easy and accurate (Lavorgna 2018a). Mechanisms such as intrusion detection systems (software applications monitoring a system or a network for malicious activity) and honeypots (a computer security tool used to 'bait' a suspect by appearing as data valuable to the attacker) are particularly promising as ways to capture information on attempts at unauthorised use of information systems or resources.

It is important to note that the private sector holds strategical information that can be used to measure cybercrimes. For example, data provided from the banking sector on losses due to credit card fraud (often committed online) offer an alternative way of measuring crime trends (Caneppele & Aebi 2019). Cybercrime data are often collected by the cybercrime control industry, which has access to important metadata and carries out its own victimisation surveys to study the market. The problem is that such an industry has a turnover of billions of pounds per year and a vested interest in emphasising the dangers of the online realm: if technological infrastructures are depicted as fragile, consumers will spend more to protect themselves and support public spending for cybersecurity (Steinmetz 2016). Moreover, there are fewer checks for quality standards on data collection and analysis, which might result in misinformation or misinterpretation (Wall 2008). Of course, this is not to minimise the security risks in cyberspace; rather, this is to remind the reader that there might be some conflicts of interest when data are collected by the cybercrime control industry, rather than by independent research bodies, and that the public should always be critical in assessing statistics and reports produced from these data (which are widely used and cited by media and policy-makers).

Before we conclude it is important to note that we do not know for sure the impact that cybercrimes are having on crime rates in total on a global level. What we do know is that, since the early 1990s, traditional property crimes and violent crimes started decreasing in the United States. Soon, a similar trend was observed in Western European countries and, according to some, even beyond – this is the 'crime drop' (Blumstein & Walman 2000; Aebi 2004). Scholars tend to agree on the existence of such a crime drop but have long debated its extension (with some scholars limiting it to Western, highly industrialised societies) (Caneppele & Aebi 2019). Debates on the crime drop are relevant in this context as they are undoubtedly connected to the evolution of cybercrime. In fact, according to some authors, the drop in certain offline crimes is directly related to the rise of cybercrimes. This is a consequence of the commercialisation of the internet, the changes it has brought to the lifestyle and routine activities of the population and the increased challenges to be met by law enforcement. According to this view, the growth of cybercrimes has quantitatively outweighed the drop in offline crimes (Caneppele & Aebi 2019). Other authors, however, disagree with this interpretation: for instance, according to Ouimet (2009), internet usage has lowered crime rates overall by changing people's routines. Not only has it confined internet users to the relative security of their houses or offices, but it has also offered information rich in crime prevention potential. Furthermore, as argued by Farrell and Birks (2018), decreasing crime rates and rising cybercrime should be interpreted as independent trends caused by broad changes to crime opportunity structures – which are security improvements against physical crimes and increased internet spread. At this time, because of the lack of reliable measures of cybercrime, it is virtually impossible to set this debate in a conclusive manner.

Box 2.2 How much does cybercrime cost?

Another way to 'measure' crime is to try to understand its cost – that is, its impact in financial terms (even though it is not always possible to reduce the consequences of most crimes to purely monetary terms). Cost estimates are very important, as they often guide society and inform interventions to prevent and reduce crime. However, they are not easy to assess. Besides the direct costs associated with an unlawful activity, a thorough examination of the cost of crime covers indirect costs, such as the cost of private deterrence, the opportunity cost of victims' time, recovery costs, costs related to emotional and physical impacts and costs to the criminal justice systems (Brand & Price 2000; Anderson 2014; Levi 2017). Even if over the last 30 years there has been tremendous progress regarding the development and refinement of methodologies to empirically estimate the cost of crime (Chalfin 2016), these estimates still have to be perfected, especially regarding crimes such as white-collar crimes and 'victimless' crimes.

Reliable estimates are considered particularly hard to achieve for most cybercrimes: on the one hand, many cybercrimes go under-reported and thus crime costs tend to be underestimated, while on the other hand, there might be vested interests among security companies and other stakeholders to exaggerate the impact of cybercrimes. In a nutshell, we know that cybercrimes represent a significant cost to society: according to a widely publicised report, for instance, the global cost of cybercrime has now reached as much as GPB 470 billion – about 0.8 percent of global GDP (gross domestic product) – even if with important regional variations (CSIS & McAfee 2018). Existing estimates can give us an idea of the order of magnitude of the problem, but we need to be aware that they originate from incomplete data and therefore lack precision.

Anderson et al. (2013) tried to figure out a framework for analysing the costs of different types of cybercrimes. According to them, the total cost to society is given by the sum of direct losses (the monetary equivalent of losses, damage or other suffering undergone by victims, ranging from money withdrawn from victims' accounts to time and effort needed to reset account credentials), indirect losses (the monetary equivalent of losses and opportunity costs imposed on society, for instance the loss of trust in online business opportunities) and defence costs (the monetary equivalent of prevention efforts, ranging from the purchase of a new antivirus to staff training). For example, a ransomware attack entails not only costs associated with the data loss (which can have a huge, immediate impact on a business) but also reputational costs, downtime costs (if a certain system needs to be shut down to deal with the infection), other financial costs associated with security-related solutions in response to an attack and potentially even emotional or physical costs, depending on the specificities of the attack (think, for instance, of an attack on critical infrastructure). What is generally easy to quantify is the criminal revenue, which is only a subset of the direct losses suffered by the victim; indirect costs can be extremely difficult to quantify.

Concluding remarks

After you read this chapter, it should be clear why defining cybercrime and categorising the diverse sets of activities brought together under its umbrella represent key analytical problems. In addition, the numerous benefits to be gained from measuring cybercrimes should be evident: the collection and analysis of crime statistics are of great value, as policy approaches and policing practices are shaped by evidence of changing trends and patterns of crime. Moreover, due to lack of reliable numbers, we cannot say anything meaningful about cybercrimes' trends and costs and even the effectiveness and efficiency of countermeasures. If traditional methods of reporting and recording crime are showing weaknesses when it comes to crime in cyberspace, new approaches have to be further explored. Cyberspace itself is a prolific source of information on cybercrime, with private actors and intermediaries such as internet service providers, social media companies, online markets and cryptocurrency exchanges being the new gatekeepers of relevant data. Consequently, alongside the challenge to improve cybercrime official statistics, there lies the challenge of finding feasible and ethical ways to access and collect these data. The fundamental role of private actors in the governance of cyberspace and the complexities of their new status as primary gatekeepers of information will be recurring themes in this book.

Another theme that will be encountered in other chapters, and that has been introduced here, is that of the social construction of cybercrimes. Particularly, we have anticipated how media have a significant influence in shaping people's perceptions of the expansion of criminal possibilities in cyberspace, as well as of the fears and expectations of harm due to technological advance. Science fiction media (beginning with the 'new wave' and 'cyberpunk' literature in the 1970s) in particular constructed much of the cultural and conceptual baggage that we can still find around the concept of cybercrime (Wall 2008). They presented a (dystopian) world where society has to deal with the constant upheaval of new technology. Since then, science fiction media have continued to contribute to the public imagination of the outcome of technological innovation in general and the increased presence of cyberspace in our daily lives. Certain media representations need to be debunked, as they create models of reality that are not in line with the facts and risk badly influencing the general public and policy-makers alike. Nonetheless, media representations have had (and can still have) an important educational role, especially insofar as they provide their public with accurate information and begin a conversation on a topic – that of cyber-crimes – that still causes confusion to many.

? CRITICAL QUESTIONS

- The 2018 report of the Office of National Statistics (ONS) in the United Kingdom revealed that 'computer misuse' (defined as any unauthorised access to computer material) has fallen by 30 per-cent over the past year, apparently driven by a reduction in com-puter viruses (Office of National Statistics 2018). The ONS itself cautioned interpretations of this finding because it looked only at changes in crime estimates over two years (questions on com-puter misuse crime were introduced in the Crime Survey for England and Wales only in late 2015, the same year that Action Fraud became the cybercrime reporting centre). The report, how-ever, was welcomed with headlines such as 'Computer crime drops 31% in England and Wales. The figures suggest that anti-virus activities are having an effect, and successful hacking attempts are also down' (*Sky News*, 19 July 2018). After reading this chapter, you ought to know that we should take this headline with a pinch of salt. What are the elements of this headline you should be careful of? Why can we not state for sure that a drop in 'computer crime' has occurred? Please discuss.

- Have you ever been a victim of cybercrime? Have you reported the crime, or not? What motivations were behind your choice?

- We have mentioned how a key issue of cybercrime underreport-ing is that businesses/companies are trying to solve the problem internally, as they are afraid of reputational damage if the com-puter breach becomes known. What could be done to break the silence associated with businesses' cybercrime victimisation?

3 THEORISING CYBERCRIMES

Introduction

This chapter provides a brief overview of a selection of criminological theories – in other words, a brief excursus on how scholars have looked at crime through history – that are key for the study and the understanding of cybercrimes. Of course, this book does not intend to be a book on theories; this chapter does not aim to engage in in-depth or exhaustive discussions about theoretical developments, their value and their critiques. Indeed, there are a number of excellent handbooks and primers that could assist you in this (see, among many, Williams & McShane 2010; Chamberlain 2015). Rather, this chapters wants to offer a brief recap of major criminological approaches to students in criminology who might have already encountered them in other modules and a crash course introducing some core criminological ideas to those readers who come from different backgrounds. Most of these approaches have been applied to cybercrimes, and you might encounter them later on in this book. In any case, you are encouraged to keep these theoretical approaches in mind when thinking about a cybercrime event: you can consider these theories as lenses thought which to think about the world, and depending on the lenses you put on, you could see different facets of the social reality and think about a cybercrime problem from different angles. A sound theoretical framework can, in fact, guide analyses and provoke critical thinking on complex topics. Theories matter not only to analyse the way others have looked at crime through different social and intellectual contexts but also to guide us in developing and testing solutions to present-day crime problems. Theories of crime are not merely part of academic debates, they are embedded in our daily lives. Every time we discuss news of a crime, hear a politician comment on crime policies or see a police officer patrolling a specific geographic area, there is a particular assumption about crime behind these events.

A selection of fundamental 'traditional' criminological approaches will be presented by gathering them according to their different focus (for instance, approaches that emphasise the role of free will vs. approaches that emphasise the influence of social or psychological aspects on criminal behaviour). A section on 'new' theories developed specifically for crime in cyberspace will follow. While there are a variety of approaches to the study of crime and its causes (criminality can be a core interest of legal scholars, phycologists, economists and even architects), over the last century and more criminology has been oriented towards sociology in studying crime and its causes. Furthermore, it has to be admitted that for many years the study of criminological theories (or, to be more precise, its international recognition) has been tremendously Anglo-centric. Consequently, we will focus mostly on sociological approaches that have been developed in the United States and the United Kingdom – a clear limitation of this chapter that is nonetheless necessary so as not to exceed the scope of this book.

We will briefly note the historical and social context in which a theory originates, something important to keep in mind as theorists do not live in isolation and their ideas are often the direct result of the broader environment. It is worth emphasising that the theories covered here are all scientific theories, meaning that they are supported by empirical evidence, systematic observations and logical soundness, and they aim for objectivity. You will see that, in explaining the causes of crime, theories can have a different level of abstraction (Williams & McShane 2010): for instance, they can have a broad scope and look at the social structure or its effect ('macro', or structural, theories), or they can look at the individual level or at how someone becomes a criminal ('micro', or process, theories). Moreover, some theories assume the presence of consensus (of values and beliefs) in society, while others hypothesise the existence of a conflictual society. Table 3.1 will assist you in understanding and comparing the theoretical approaches presented in this chapter.

Table 3.2, on the other hand, recapitulates the mainstream ways in which these theoretical approaches have been used so far to provide explanations for the main types of cybercrimes. This summary does not mean that other explanations are not possible or have never been attempted; rather, this table aims to emphasise the more used and more successful approaches that you will find briefly presented in this chapter and then applied to specific cybercrimes in the sections of this book dedicated to them.

Classicism and offender's decision-making

Classical School

Born at a time when 'criminology' did not yet exist as a discipline, the so-called Classical School of criminology brings together the ideas of several theorists (the Italian philosopher Cesare Beccaria and the English thinker Jeremy Bentham being two key figures) mostly active in the eighteenth and the early nineteenth centuries. Collectively, these theorists gave rise to ideas

Table 3.1 Classification of criminological theories

	Micro/macro	Process/structure	Determinism/free will	Consensus/conflict
Classical School	✓	✓	✓	✓
Opportunity theories	✓	✓	✓	✓
Strain theories	✓	✓	✓	✓
Subculture theories	✓	✓	✓	✓
Labelling	✓	✓		✓
Differential association	✓	✓	✓	
Social learning	✓	✓	✓	✓
General theory of crime (self-control)	✓	✓	✓	✓
Neutralisation theory	✓	✓	✓	✓
Critical criminology	✓	✓	✓	✓
Postmodern criminology	✓	✓		✓
Late-modern criminology	✓	✓		✓

Table 3.2 Mainstream theoretical explanations of cybercrimes

	Crimes against devices	Crimes against persons	Crimes of deception and coercion	Market-based and property crimes	Political offences
Classical School				✓	
Opportunity theories	✓	✓	✓	✓	
Strain theories		✓	✓	✓	
Subculture theories	✓	✓			
Labelling	✓			✓	
Differential association	✓			✓	
Social learning	✓	✓		✓	
General theory of crime (self-control)		✓	✓	✓	
Neutralisation theory	✓			✓	
Critical criminology	✓	✓	✓	✓	✓
Postmodern & late-modern criminology	✓			✓	✓
Space transition theory	✓	✓			

that are fundamental for the functioning of contemporary criminal justice systems and to the first recognised theory of criminal behaviour.

The emergence of the Classical School was deeply influenced by the work of the English philosopher Thomas Hobbes. In his 1651 book *Leviathan*, Hobbes argued that human nature would bring humanity into a permanent war of everyone against everyone (*homo homini lupus*, 'man is a wolf to a man'); the state is needed to restrain this conduct and is allowed to use as little force as possible to ensure compliance with the social contract. Furthermore, the Classical School was influenced by the rise of modern science, technology and liberal-democratic politics from the eighteenth century onwards – the so-called Age of Enlightenment or Age of Reason in Europe. These changes marked the gradual shift away from religious interpretations of human nature (that is, human beings were born into a state of original sin) towards the idea that human beings enjoy free will: they are rational and hedonistic beings, who constantly aim to maximise their own pleasure and minimise their own costs or pain (Chamberlain 2015). Both Beccaria and Bentham, for instance, argued that because the government should ideally promote happiness for the community, criminal law itself should provide the greatest good for the greatest number of people (so-called utilitarianism). Crime is committed when people think that the pleasure (the perceived benefit originating from the crime) outweighs the pain (the perceived costs). Hence, the best way to avoid crime is to focus on deterrence: according to classical deterrence theory, in order to increase the costs' perception, an individual needs to believe that his or her criminal behaviour will be certainly detected and harshly punished and that detection and punishment will occur quickly.

Classical criminology still influences thinking on crime, but contemporary approaches have suggested a number of modifications to the original ideas: 'neoclassical' approaches, for example, still recognise the importance of free will, but they also recognise that free will is generally constrained by physical and environmental conditions (such as poverty). Hence, contemporary deterrence theories have added other measures that represent inhibitions and motivations for crime, such as shame, social disapproval or the belief that a behaviour is ethical or not (Higgins et al. 2005; Chamberlain 2015). These later approaches have seldom been applied to cybercrimes – or at least infrequently in an explicit way, as deterrence ideas are often so internalised in many modern societies that they are, if nothing else, at the core of many regulatory approaches. As we will see in Chapter 7, neoclassical approaches have been used explicitly, for instance, with online intellectual property infringements (Higgins et al. 2005). Further research on deterrence for cybercrimes would be certainly welcomed to envisage effective research-led criminal justice approaches to reduce instances of criminal and deviant behaviours online.

Opportunity theories

A fundamental legacy of Classical criminology lies in its emphasis on the rationality of criminal decision-making processes. This idea is still at the core of a number of theories of crime that are very popular nowadays and that can be summarised under the label of 'environmental criminology' (as it looks at the 'environment' of specific crimes) or 'opportunity theories'. Under these umbrella terms, we can find three main complementary theories developed on predatory crimes that, while operating at different levels of explanation, share the idea that opportunity is a root cause of crime (Felson & Clarke 1998). Hence, reducing crime opportunities is seen as the best way to reduce crime: this can be implemented by identifying how offenders and victims interact in their everyday lives and consequently by manipulating the immediate environment to prevent crime commission. *Rational choice theory* (Cornish & Clarke 1986) is a micro-level theory dealing with the decision-making process that reasoning offenders undertake when they decide to commit a crime. *Crime pattern theory* (Brantingham & Brantingham 1993) is a meso-theory focused on the geographical distribution of crime that explains criminal behaviours by looking at the interactions between targets and offenders in their daily routines. Finally, *routine activity* (Cohen & Felson 1979) is a macro-theory dealing with broader societal changes affecting crime opportunities: it relates criminal activities to the everyday patterns of social interaction, starting from the idea that for a criminal act to happen there has to be convergence in space and time of a likely or motivated offender, a suitable target and the absence of a capable guardian.

Contrary to most criminological theories, which focus on the criminal predisposition of a particular social group (*why* an individual or a group commit crime), opportunity theories focus on the offender's decision-making process (the *how*) and on the immediate environmental context of offending. This approach stresses the rational elements in criminal behaviour and is crime-specific (Clarke & Cornish 1985). As efficaciously summarised by Clarke (2009), all these theories are grounded on three main assumptions: first of all, crime is intended as a real act and not as a mere propensity towards criminal behaviour and thus it is seen as the actual result of an interaction between a certain motivation and a specific situation. In other words, unlike criminological theories that try to explain why some people become criminals by looking at biological, psychological or social dispositions, environmental criminology focuses on the system of opportunities that allow a specific type of crime to happen. Second, offenders choose to commit crime because they believe this will bring them a certain type of benefit. Finally, all these theories argue that situational factors can stimulate crime: if behaviour is seen in a dynamic relationship with the environment, the propensity to commit crime depends upon immediate circumstances, which have an active role in 'readying' the (potential) criminal to act (Wortley 1997).

Opportunity theories have proven successful over the years when applied to types of criminal behaviour other than predatory crimes in the physical world, and they have shown great potential in explaining many forms of cybercrimes. Routine activity theory in particular has often been used to explain cybercrime victimisation in crimes against devices, against persons, and crimes of deception and coercion; opportunity theory-inspired approaches have been extensively used for online criminal markets. After all, cyberspace can be easily interpreted as a new *locus* characterised by being virtual, dynamic, interactive, global, commercialised and networkable.

Nonetheless, more work is needed in order to further and better test opportunity theories' resilience to technological advancements. As explained by Reyns (2017), some of the fundamental concepts of these theories (such as offender's proximity and guardianship) will have to be more carefully defined and adapted in future research, as their traditional conceptualisation does not properly cover the specificities of cyberspace.

Social structure approaches

The origins

Social structure theories all share the interpretation of crime as the result of the lack or breakdown of society's norms (so-called anomie). Hence, the origin of crime problems lies in the structures of the society itself, which need to be addressed in order to reduce crime. Different theorists have focused on different aspects and forces operating in the society to find explanations for crime and deviancy, ranging from economic inequalities and class divisions to urban geographies and cultural norms (Chamberlain 2015). Here, we will focus only on some major approaches, which have been successfully applied to cybercrimes.

Many social structure theories have been inspired by the work of David Émile Durkheim (1858–1917), a French sociologist and a founding father of modern social science. In his work, Durkheim emphasised that human behaviour (including crime and deviancy) should be interpreted and understood in sociological terms rather than mainly in biological or psychological ones, as it is often caused by social factors. In his view, crime is inevitable in society: individuals have social needs and desires (such as status, power and money) and in order to satisfy them some will violate social norms. Crime, however, is not completely negative: it serves a positive function in society, as it reinforces its moral boundaries (Chamberlain 2015). Durkheim's work heavily influenced the first department of sociology in the United States, established in 1892 at the University of Chicago, which soon became one of the dominant forces in American sociological (and, consequently, criminological) thought.

During the early twentieth century, scholars especially in the United States could not help but notice that urbanisation, heavy immigration and the limits of industrialisation (with the consequent displacement of workers) were at the basis of many of the social problems they could observe. Many scholars started to look at the city as a sort of human laboratory and studied the city and its communities, starting with the assumption that the social and the physical environments have a fundamental role in developing and changing human behaviour (Williams & McShane 2010). The diverse groups of academics associated with the sociology department at the University of Chicago are generally referred to as 'the Chicago School'. For the scope of this book, we will not linger on the approaches advanced by the

School but rather focus on three perspectives that were developed from some of the ideas central to it: (1) the rejection of individualistic explanations of criminal behaviour (which, as said above, depends instead on social structures); (2) the idea that conflict is a fundamental social process and that rules governing human behaviour vary from one culture to the other; and (3) the social-psychological theory of symbolic interactionism, which originates from the idea that human behaviour is the product of social symbols communicated between individuals and depends on the social environment (Williams & McShane 2010). Hence, there are no absolute, universal rules governing human behaviours; rather, we pick up our self-concept from our perception of what others think about us. These three central ideas are reflected in the theoretical approaches covered in this section, namely strain theories, subcultural theories and labelling.

Anomie and strain

Durkheim popularised the term 'anomie' to describe a condition of normlessness in society, in which individuals received little or no moral guidance because of the breakdown of social bonds between the individual and the community. In the aftermath of the Great Depression of the 1930s, American sociologist Robert K. Merton borrowed and adapted Durkheim's concept to explain deviance in the United States in a period characterised by socio-economic turmoil and the deregulation of social traditions. Merton (1938) redefined anomie as the disjuncture between societal goals and the acceptable means for achieving those goals; this is a result of how society is structured. According to Merton, society emphasises certain goals (such as financial success and the social status associated with it) and legitimises certain means to reach those goals (for instance, a prestigious, well-paid job). However, not everyone in society has equal access to these means: those in the lower social classes or minorities, for example, might try to work hard but never be able to achieve financial success because of the social inequalities embedded in society. In fact, despite the democratic ideology of egalitarianism and the 'American dream' (which embodies the idea that if you are honest and hard-working you will be successful), some groups in society will not be able to access the institutionalised means to success (Chamberlain 2015). The social structure is anomic and consequently certain groups in society might search for illegitimate ways of succeeding (Williams & McShane 2010).

Anomie produces strain in those who experience it. According to Merton (strain theory), people may respond to this strain with different modes of adaptation:

- conformists will accept societal goals and rely on institutionalised means even when those are restricted;
- ritualists will also play by the rules, but in this case the means will become the aspiration of the individual, as in the case of a bureaucrat with no real power who focuses only on having the paperwork filled out correctly;

- innovators accept societal goals but, when they cannot access the institutionalised means, they will rely on illegitimate means to reach their goal;
- retreatists (for instance, drug addicts, alcoholics and homeless people) are those who essentially drop out of society, as they reject both the goals and the means;
- finally, rebels are those who reject the institutionalised goals and means but also seek to replace them with new ones. Innovation, retreatism and rebellion are considered deviant modes of adaptation, with innovators being the most common deviant type.

While Merton's strain theory focused on the macro level of the social structure, subsequent adaptations of his theory looked also at the micro level of individual social interactions. In the early 1990s, Robert Agnew (1992) expanded Merton's classic strain theory to focus on the coping strategies people develop to deal with frustrations that they directly experience as a result of negative relationships with others (experienced strain), see happening to others who are close to them (vicarious strain) or may happen to them or others close to them (anticipated strain). If these strains are not properly addressed, they could lead to crime (general strain theory).

Strain theories have been successfully applied to cybercrime and especially to crimes against persons – where individuals can easily vent their frustration at others, hidden behind a screen (Holt & Bossler 2015) – as well as to intellectual property infringements, online fraud and carding (Chism & Steinmetz 2017). For instance, as we will see in the dedicated section in Chapter 8, online copyright infringement (known to many as 'internet piracy') has been explained also as the disjuncture in place between accepted goals (that is, the hyper-consumption of digital content characterising our society) and the means to access it or acquire it (Steinmetz & Tunnell 2012). Overall, however, there is still a relative paucity of cybercrime studies that have explored the potential contribution of anomie and strain approaches. Further in-depth qualitative research is needed not only to better reflect on actors' motivations but also to redefine the nature of key concepts such as strain and coping strategies in an online environment (Chism & Steinmetz 2017).

Subculture theories

In the 1950s and early 1960s – in many Western countries, a time of rise in consumerism and middle-class pride – many theorists started to focus on juvenile delinquency and specifically on its most visible form: gangs. At the same time, the different cultures studied in the Chicago School started to be referred to as 'subcultures' and to receive increasingly sociological interest (Williams & McShane 2010). Deeply influenced by Merton's work, Albert Cohen (1955) and Richard Cloward and Lloyd Ohlin (1960) among others tried to explain the group nature of urban, lower-class (male) delinquency, bridging strain theory with the heritage of the Chicago School by incorporating a cultural element in their explanations.

Cohen (1955) agreed with Merton's view that some individuals (especially working-class youths) suffer from status frustration: they are socialised to internalise societal norms (and will be evaluated by society with a middle-class measuring rod) but then are penalised by the disjuncture between societal goals and the acceptable means for achieving them because of social structures. This frustration is then expressed with aggressive behaviours and negativistic malicious acts such as vandalism. Hence, gang membership is a response to the strains experienced by young people: they cannot reach the goals of the dominant middle class and cannot acquire status by conforming to middle-class values. As a consequence, working-class youths collectively reject those values and create their own (a delinquent subculture), against which they can be judged by their peers. Within their own subculture, these youths can acquire a status and prove their masculinity by showing toughness (Chamberlain 2015) while striking back at the 'other' culture that considers them failures. By showing the link between the strain due to status frustration and delinquency as a collective solution to the problem of status, Cohen's subculture of delinquency theory places the process of becoming a criminal within a certain subculture.

This same approach is shared by Cloward and Ohlin (1960). They agree that crime and deviance originate in the unequal social structures but expand Cohen's theorisation by identifying different types of deviant subcultures, depending on different opportunity structures and the degree of integration present in a certain community (differential opportunity theory). By explicitly relying on Merton's idea of strain and recognising that social advancement is not based on meritocracy alone, Cloward and Ohlin emphasise that, for many, success in contemporary America was blocked by limited legitimate opportunities. In their view, however, strain theory was incomplete because it failed to explain why people choose one mode of adaptation over another. To solve this puzzle, they suggest looking at alternative illegitimate opportunity structures, which regulate access to crime and deviance for different types of groups. These structures depend on the delinquent subcultures present in a certain community: criminal subcultures emerge when working-class youths have access in an integrated community to pre-existing profit-making gangs and organised crime groups, from which they can learn criminal behaviour; conflict subcultures emerge when youths have access to pre-existing gangs in non-integrated communities, where the primary focus is on gaining respect and defending a certain territory with violent acts; finally, retreatist subcultures emerge when working-class youths have no access to criminal or conflict subcultures. In a way, these latter youths will find the illegitimate opportunity structures also blocked to them; gang-related activities will then be used to gain money for alcohol and drug abuse. Hence, Cloward and Ohlin suggest that subcultural patterns determine the form of delinquent and criminal behaviour and introduce a focus on learning mechanisms to explain the ongoing forms of delinquent subcultures (Williams & McShane 2010).

As already stressed by Holt et al. (2015) among others, the development and emergence of cyberspace have had a huge impact in the creation of and participation in deviant or criminal subcultures. A number of studies have looked at the features of specific types of subcultures operating online, ranging from hackers and psychonauts to hate group participants and 'pirates'. These groups, in fact, share norms, values and beliefs that are often developed as a reaction to (or are otherwise not in line with) those of the dominant culture but that are approved, justified and even normalised within their subculture.

Labelling approach

'Labelling' is the name given to various ideas and approaches that have suggested looking at crime in a different way (as a 'relative' concept), outmoding more conservative ideas. Labelling became very influential in the 1960s, significantly impacting the academic community. According to labelling theorists, we have to understand the subjective meaning of deviance for the person involved in it and shift the focus from the deviant to those doing the labelling.

As anticipated above, a key influence from the Chicago School has been symbolic interactionism, which looks at the ways in which meaning arises in social interactions through communication using language and symbols. Contrary to other social structure approaches, according to interactionist theorists, some individuals do not become criminals because of blocked opportunity structures or their socialisation; crime is rather the product of the interactions certain individuals have with others, who label a certain behaviour as 'crime'. Crime, then, is socially constructed. By starting from these premises, labelling theorists describe a general process whereby it is the external intervention (from law enforcement or significant others) to create crime. As explained by Edwin Lemert (1951), many individuals (especially children) engage in sporadic deviant acts (primary deviance): these acts generally go unnoticed and have little impact on those individuals' lives. Some deviant acts, however, will be noticed and their authors will be labelled as delinquent; they will start to internalise this new tag, which will define them negatively, affecting their self-image (secondary deviance). The labelled individuals may come to accept their self-concept as 'delinquent' and start to engage in criminal behaviour accordingly.

Working within the framework structured by Lemert, Howard Becker (the main theorist within labelling theory) illustrated how crime is the product of social interactions. In his seminal book *Outsiders*, Becker (1963, p. 9) explained how certain social groups 'create deviance by making the rules whose infraction constitutes deviance, and by applying those rules to particular people and labelling them as outsiders'. Particularly, so-called moral entrepreneurs aim to propagate their viewpoint, creating or enforcing norms in line with their understanding of what is best.

An important implication of labelling approaches is that social stigma is key not only to understand crime but also to prevent and mitigate it. Furthermore, the labelling perspective has a clear focus on how power and conflict shape society, emphasising the influence of powerful groups in society to both define and react to deviant behaviour, generally to the detriment of the less powerful. Regarding cybercrimes, this perspective is at the basis of the debates of the (de)criminalisation of certain activities, and it is necessary to understand how cybercrime has been socially constructed – a theme that will be recurrent in the book and that we will encounter in more detail, for instance, when discussing hacking and certain forms of intellectual property infringement.

Socialisation approaches

Psychosocial learning approaches

In the nineteenth and early twentieth centuries, the common belief was that crime was caused by psychological or biological impediments and that those were present in people from the lower class or otherwise considered 'inferior'. Psychosocial learning theories revolutionised our understanding of crime by arguing that people become criminals much as they become anything else – that is, through learning. Psychosocial learning theories argue that deviant and criminal behaviour depends on both our psychological features and learned behaviour. Hence, they locate the causes of crime inside the individual or in the interplay between the individual and the society. Psychosocial learning approaches are generally process theories, meaning that they focus on the process of becoming a criminal. For the scope of this book, we will cover three learning theories, namely Sutherland's differential association theory and Akers's and Bandura's social learning theories.

Edwin Sutherland, probably the most influential criminologist of the twentieth century, introduced his differential association theory in the late 1930s and further developed it in the course of his life. Sutherland's ideas originated in his observations of life in the United States during the 1920s, in the age of the Great Depression and Prohibitionism: he noted that many people who had previously not been criminal committed criminal acts as a result of their impoverished situations or because a certain behaviour (such as the production, importation, transportation and sale of alcoholic beverages) suddenly became criminal as a result of a change in the law. Hence, Sutherland rejected many commonly held beliefs about criminal behaviour as a feature of the lower class: crime was not passed down from one person to the other via genetics nor it was necessarily linked to poverty; rather, it was learned.

Sutherland's theory is based on nine fundamental principles:

- criminal behaviour is learnt;
- criminal behaviour is learnt in interaction with other persons in a process of communication;
- the principal part of the learning of criminal behaviours occurs within intimate personal groups;
- when criminal behaviour is learnt, the learning includes both the techniques of committing the crime and the specific direction of motives, drives, rationalisations and attitudes;
- the specific direction of motives and drives is learned from definitions (i.e., how one defines a situation or behaviour) of the legal codes as favourable or unfavourable;
- a person becomes delinquent because of an excess of definitions favourable to violations of law over definitions favourable to the law;
- differential association may vary in frequency, duration, priority and intensity;
- the process of learning criminal behaviour by association with criminal and anticriminal patterns involves all of the mechanisms that are involved in any other learning;
- although criminal behaviour is an expression of general needs and values, it is not explained by those general needs and values, because non-criminal behaviour is an expression of the same needs and values (Sutherland & Cressey 1978).

In the case of cybercrimes, this means that interactions with differential associates engaging in deviant or criminal activities in cyberspace will increase the actors' knowledge about (deviant or criminal) modus operandi but also about the motives needed to take part in a certain cybercrime (Boman & Freng 2017).

To sum up, according to Sutherland, people do not commit crime as personal experience but only through contact with others. The theory is deterministic: crimes do not depend on free will, but they are the result of specific social interactions. Anyone can learn criminal behaviour and become a criminal because of contacts with criminal patterns and isolation from anticriminal patterns. Interestingly, Sutherland's theory also reminds us that definitions of crime may vary across time and space: what is crime depends on legal definitions, which depend on social and political labels placed on certain behaviours in a specific country; what is deemed criminal in one society or culture may well not be a crime in another (Chamberlain 2015).

In order to better understand criminal behaviour, in the 1960s Robert Burgess and Ronald Akers proposed to integrate Sutherland's work with contributions from the field of social psychology, according to which people must be socialised and taught how to behave through various forms of direct (conditioning) and indirect (modelling) learning; in other words, behaviour is influenced by reinforcements and punishment as well as by the role models we encounter in our lives (differential reinforcement theory). Later on, Akers (1977) added the concept of imitation (a further possibility for indirect learning) and changed the title of the theory to social learning theory. Akers's theory, which over the years has accumulated a great deal of empirical support for both physical and online crimes, is therefore based on four key concepts:

- differential associations, in line with Sutherland;
- definitions, here interpreted as one's own attitudes or meaning attached to given behaviour, that define an act as right or wrong, justified or unjustified;
- differential reinforcement: that is, the trade-off between potential rewards (such as status, praise or money) or punishments that are consequences of a certain behaviour;
- imitation: that is, looking at the characteristics of role models and at whether their behaviour is rewarded or punished.

Learning is therefore seen as a dynamic process that can be encouraged, strengthened or weakened through reinforcement; whether the learnt deviance is maintained depends not only on the reinforcements available but also on their quality (namely the amount, frequency and probability of the reinforcement). Learning can happen both before the criminal act (reward opportunities and possible punishment) and after the act took place (actual reward or punishment). The social environment becomes the most important source of reinforcement, and peer association is the key factor increasing the likelihood for criminal behaviour.

Another famous version of social learning theory is offered by Albert Bandura (1977, 1986). He agrees with the main ideas of behaviourist learning theorists, but in his view, conditioning is not necessary for a behaviour to be learnt. According to Bandura, attitudes and behaviours can be learnt simply by observing and mimicking the behaviour of others (observational learning). Children, for instance, learn how to behave from the environment, mostly by observing the adults around them (models) and encoding their behaviour. Bandura's findings have important implications as regards the influence that models proposed by society (for instance, via peers, television, video games and so on) can have.

Overall, social learning theories – by focusing on how and why individuals learn criminal behaviour and the impact of significant others in this process – have been applied successfully to explain a wide variety of cybercrimes, ranging from hacking and financial theft to intellectual property infringement and several forms of cyber-hate and harassment. In order to be able to apply these theoretical frameworks in full to cybercrimes, however, there are still issues that have to be solved – in primis, to what extent online or 'hybrid' (that is, partially offline and partially online) interactions differ from face-to-face interactions. Indeed, if modalities of associations (such as the 'intensity' of association) differ greatly between the offline and the online contexts, this has important implications for the applicability of traditional forms of psychological learning approaches (Boman & Freng 2017), which might then need further adaptation to cybercrimes.

Control theories

We have seen so far how most theories of crime try to explain why individuals engage in deviant or criminal activities by identifying factors (such as strain or association with delinquent peers) pushing people into crime. By doing so, these theories assume that human nature is fundamentally good or a 'blank slate' and that crime is somehow the exception. With control theories, this central assumption shifts: according to control theorists, we live in a crime-promoting environment, where crime is a relatively easy way to fulfil a need or a desire. In a way, social control theories assume that crime is natural in a society, and it is appealing to many. Hence, according to social control theorists, the question we should ask is not 'Why do people engage in crime?' but rather 'Why do some people not engage in crime?'

Control theories were initially developed as an alternative or reaction to strain theories and, more generally, with the desire to return to the examination of the criminal behaviour (Williams & McShane 2010). Comparable to learning approaches, control theories also discuss aspects of learning and socialisation. The central idea of social control theories is that crime is the product of inadequate socialisation. Socialisation, in fact, produces controls over individuals in the form of social attachments and investments in conventional society; these controls are what prevent people from engaging in criminal behaviour. According to Walter Reckless (1967), one of the fathers of control theories, the social environment (such as a lack of opportunities for employment or delinquent peers) or individual factors (such as a risk-taking personality) can push people into crime. He identified inner and outer containments (that is, factors that insulate youth from crime, such as the presence of a consistent moral front or a person's sense of self) to explain why many individuals who were exposed to criminal influences did not turn to crime (containment theory).

In the following years, more sophisticated versions of the theory were developed. In his 1969 book *Causes of Delinquency*, Travis Hirschi argued that individuals refrain from crime because they have developed a social bond (social bond theory), and he identified four specific elements of the social bond tying an individual to the society:

- attachment (to the extent that if someone cares for the opinions of the others, they are less likely to engage in crime);
- commitment (a person who has an investment in society will follow the norms of that society);
- involvement (involvement in conventional activity is a time-consuming process, so if one is involved in conventional activities, he or she will have less time to engage in deviant behaviour);
- belief (in the way society operates).

This first version of Hirschi's theory focuses almost entirely on indirect social control. An element of internal control – that is, self-control – was added by Hirschi later on in his life. In their 1990 book *A General Theory of Crime*, Gottfredson and Hirschi suggested that internal control, and specifically low self-control, is the key element in explaining why some people refrain from committing crime or behaviours that are analogous to crime (acts that are not illegal but share the same general 'nature' as crime). Low self-control is the inability of an individual to resist a temptation towards a deviant or criminal behaviour; individuals with low self-control are more prone to engage in impulsive and risky behaviours, as they look for immediately gratifying behaviours. According to Gottfredson and Hirschi, humans are born without self-control, but they gain it through parenting (a form of direct control). In short, they argue that if parents supervise their children and recognise deviance, children will be punished and therefore will develop self-control since their early childhood. It is worth noting that more recent developments in control theory emphasise that adult social bonds (such as a quality marriage and/or a quality job) can also be relevant to explain why some people who were crime-prone youth desist from criminal behaviour during adulthood. Gottfredson and Hirschi's low self-control theory has been very popular in criminology and its testing demonstrated how low self-control is one of the best correlates of crime.

As we will see, Gottfredson and Hirschi's theory has also been applied to many forms of cybercrime, often in combination with learning theories. However, as remarked by Holt and Bossler (2015), low self-control holds as a good explanation for simple, opportunistic forms of cybercrime, but it is not a solid explication of more complex crimes where specific technical skills might be needed.

Neutralisation theory

So-called neutralisation theory is based on the idea that, even if individuals and especially juveniles are bound to the dominant value system of society by normative societal constraints (in line with the core ideas of control theories), they can still shrug off social controls so that deviant behaviour can be committed. In order to neutralise the usual commitment to societal values and avoid feelings of guilt, deviants and criminals can, in fact, rely on a number of different techniques – 'techniques of neutralisation' (Sykes & Matza 1957): (1) denial of responsibility (the offender argues that the act was caused by factors outside of his or her control, such as poverty or the influence of peers); (2) denial of injury (the offender claims that no one was really hurt by the criminal act given that, for instance, the victim can easily overcome the impact of the crime, as in the case of a wealthy person whose property was stolen); (3) denial of victim (the offender sees no real victim here, placing a social distance between him/herself and the victim); (4) condemnation of the condemners (the offenders consider themselves undeserving of punishment, as the authorities in place are considered hypocrites or crooked); and (5) appeal to higher loyalties (such as a gang or a religious belief). Hence, through these techniques, deviant or criminal behaviour is justified or rationalised, trying to make it appear to conform to the rules of society; thus, criminals avoid hurting their consciences and self-images, being able to violate conventions while avoiding negatively labelling themselves as criminals.

The applicability of neutralisation theory is particularly promising when it comes to cybercrimes, as social control mechanisms tend to be less effective in cyberspace, and, as we will see (for instance, in the cases of hacking and copyright infringements), there are many situational justifications that can be invoked.

Critical criminology

Critical criminology is an umbrella term encompassing several theoretical approaches (such as Marxist criminology, left realism, gender-based theories and cultural criminology) sharing the intent to challenge traditional forms of criminological understanding and particularly their neglect of power issues. Critical criminology approaches aim to shed light on the relationships between crime, criminal justice and the inequality and power relations existing in our society by looking at the role of class, gender and race in shaping crime definitions and criminal justice responses. For critical criminologists, the study of crime is not (and should not be) value-free. It should be evident that interactionist theories such as labelling provided the roots for the development of critical criminology. But if the labelling approach emphasises the relationship between one part of the society and its 'outsiders', critical criminology interprets society itself as being shaped by conflicts among people who have competing interests. Furthermore, in line with social structure theories, critical criminology acknowledges that social inequalities and a person's structural location in society are primary factors to explain crime and, specifically, participation in crime, how crime is defined, and the making and enforcement of laws (Chamberlain 2015).

Among the many approaches covered by the critical criminology umbrella, those focusing on social exclusion/poverty seem to be particularly relevant for discussions on cybercrimes. Left realism, for example, is a theoretical approach developed by British criminologists (such as Jock Young, John Lea and Rodger Matthews) since the early 1980s in response to populist punitive discourses advocating a zero-tolerance approach towards deviant and criminal behaviour. Left realists have focused their attention on those who are economically exploited in capitalistic societies and therefore resort to illegal behaviour to fulfil their needs and desires. They focus on concepts such as marginalisation (from the political process within a capitalist economy) and relative deprivation – that is, the idea that people engage in crime when they feel deprived in comparison with others (Lea & Young 1984; Young & Matthews 1992). In the context of cybercrimes, this view can support our understanding of many profit-driven crimes (such as frauds, extortions or market-based crimes), especially when they are carried out by unprivileged parts of the population. Similarly, approaches rooted in Marxism that critically examine the criminogenic role of the state and capitalist societies (so-called radical criminology) are of great utility to critically examine the social construction (if not the top-down intentional manufacture) of many cybercrimes and the public anxieties connected to them and to analyse the impact of cyberspace on political participation and democracy (Banks 2017).

Gender-based theories (gender is a term that refers to the socially constructed characteristics of femininity and masculinity) are also relevant when it comes to cybercrimes: crime and deviance in cyberspace, being part of the human experience, are of course influenced by gender. More specifically, certain forms of cybercrimes (and especially, as we will see, certain crimes against persons) disproportionately target women and sexual minorities (for an excellent overview on this topic, see Marganski 2017). Moreover, research has recognised the existence of a gendered digital divide when it comes to cybercrime offending: cybercrime is still a male-dominated offence category, even if variations do exist depending on the type of cybercrime (Hutchings & Ting Chua 2017). So-called feminist criminology emerged from the 1960s onwards and developed along different 'waves' and strands (ranging from Marxist feminism and radical feminism to postmodern feminism and multiracial feminism), which share a focus on gendered socio-cultural paradigms in society that inherently discriminate against women (considered as perpetrators, victims and members of the criminal justice system) both in criminological thinking and in criminal justice practice (Heidensohn 1968; Smart 1992; Daly & Maher 1998; Chesney-Lind & Morash 2013). This marginalisation of women in 'malestream' criminology is considered symptomatic of diffuse gender-based inequalities that are still present within many contemporary societies (Chamberlain 2015), which are often (more or less subtly) still patriarchal. Initially, feminist scholars focused primarily on issues of equality between men and women and differences in their offending rates and responses by the criminal justice system. Over time, however, scholarship evolved and favoured intersectional approaches (for instance, by considering relationships between gender, sexuality, race, class and ethnicity), which acknowledge gender privileges existing (and varying) across different groups of women and men.

Under the general heading of cultural criminology, we can find a number of different approaches emerging in the 1990s and pivoting around the study of the interactions between cultural dynamics (such as style or popular culture), crime and crime control. Cultural criminologists aim to describe and understand criminality as the essence of behaviour, meaning and emotions associated with a certain deviant or criminal act (Katz 1988; Ferrell 1999). In other words, we cannot understand human behaviour (the *why*) if we do not try to understand at the same time the meaning that actors attribute to the world around them (the *what*) (Yar 2017). They place the criminal act in the context of its containment by the crime control industry and its representation by the media industry. Media have a key role in cultural criminology, as media use crime and crime control as commodities to sell to consumers and have a vested interest in how a certain crime story is presented (Williams & McShane 2010). Both crime and the institutions of crime control are interpreted as cultural products; as creative constructs, they matter more as constructed phenomena than as real ones.

Cultural criminology has been deeply influenced by the work of Stanley Cohen. In his seminal 1972 book *Folk Devils and Moral Panics*, Cohen was concerned with the mods and rockers, two conflicting British youth subcultures (with a clear style identity in terms of outfits used, music listened to and so on) who were receiving impressive media coverage after a big fight between the two groups labelled them as violent and troublemakers. For the scope of this chapter, what needs to be remembered is that Cohen introduced the notion of 'moral panic' to describe the role of media in representing a certain social group as a social problem, which promotes a culture of fear through which social order and control can be maintained by those in power. As we will see, the notion of moral panic and, more generally, the role of media in the social construction of crime and deviancy is of the utmost importance when it comes to cybercrimes, whose mythology originated in media and fiction, and media and fiction still drive much of the societal reaction to cybercrimes. In the context of cybercrimes, however, traditional paradigms of cultural criminology might have to be slightly adapted. Being a horizontal network of communication, cyberspace (and especially the Web 2.0) has redefined the relationship between 'speakers' and 'audiences', making it 'blurred and broken' (Yar 2017, p. 123). Furthermore, the appeal of cyberspace as a place for cultural self-expression, where particular groups (maybe discriminated against or even criminalised in the physical world) and emerging online subcultures can transgress mainstream social norms, matters to cultural criminologists – especially when it comes to online narrations and self-representations of actors in these communities (Yar 2017).

Postmodern and late-modern criminology

In the late twentieth century, a broad philosophical movement that goes under the name of postmodernism started to distance itself from the modernist thought that had dominated the previous decades and that was characterised by the positivistic idea that human beings, aided by scientific knowledge and technology, can improve and reshape their environment. Postmodernism, on the contrary, questions assumptions on human rationality, the presence of objective reality and social progress and is rather defined by the idea that human knowledge is based on contingent and socially conditioned factors; subjectivism, scepticism and moral relativism are characteristic of postmodern epistemology. This change of disposition is reflected in criminological thinking. Postmodern criminologists attempt to debunk absolute truths by trying to deconstruct what we know about crime and also how we construct our knowledge about crime (Arrigo & Bersot 2014). In their view, racism, sexism and other forms of injustice and exploitation are the result of modernist false 'progress' and consequently they reject the grounding of knowledge about human behaviour in scientific terms (Williams & McShane 2010). For postmodern criminology, we cannot understand crime and criminal justice if we do not understand power relations in society and acknowledge that there are no universal truths (Foucault 1975); criminality is mostly a social and linguistic construct, as certain behaviours are constructed as crime by the controlling institutions. Postmodernism has had an important impact on the latest expressions of criminology approaches exemplified above, especially insomuch as postmodern theorists suggest that power is exercised not only though coercion but also by shaping reality through language; crime and deviancy themselves are socially constructed by language, and because language can also be used to resist crime construction and social restrictions, there is room for criticising definitions of crime and for political struggle.

Other theorists active since the mid-twentieth century, on the other hand, claim that modernity is not over but rather it continues and its main ideas are still pivotal in our contemporary era – which can be more properly defined as late modernity, a sort of hyper-technological version of modernity (Giddens 1990). Regarding crime and crime control, the core idea is that the rapid social and technological changes that occurred in the last 50 years have led to a new socio-political context in which the identification and management of risk have become key concerns when it comes to governing populations. In other words, in an increasingly complex and technologically advanced context, governing elites have sought to make crime more manageable and controllable – for instance, through the extensive use of surveillance (Chamberlain 2015; Jewkes 2008; Sellers & Arrigo 2017) – both offline and online.

In a time of pervasive insecurity, 'governing through crime' has thus become a quintessential characteristic of our contemporary culture of control, which spreads through most aspects of social life (Simon 2009). In addition, advancing technology can generate new insecurities; people feel insecure because of the increased perception of risk but cannot see the 'invisible' – even if omnipresent – digital threat (Beck 1992). Anxiety is a powerful social force, and because of the risk involved with cybercrimes, people can become more easily compelled to support governing elites' agendas, including solutions that tend to shift the discussion away from basic principles such as privacy and the meaningful exercise of the freedom of expression (Steinmetz 2016; Banks 2017; Wright 2017; Lavorgna 2019a).

Towards a theory for crime in cyberspace

With the growing interest in cybercrimes, an increasing number of scholars have applied traditional criminological theories (and especially the ones presented above), sometimes with minor adaptations, to crime and deviancy in cyberspace. Indeed, as lamented by Steinmetz and Nobles (2017), in cybercrime research it is quite common to find superficial applications of criminological theories, with little attention to changes in the context and processes. Other authors, however, have drawn on existing theoretical approaches and modified them significantly to capture some of the effects that cyberspace has on human behaviour. An interesting example in this direction is offered by Goldsmith and Brewer (2015), who – inspired by socialisation theorists and particularly Matza – proposed the concept of 'digital drift' to provide a better understanding of how online users might engage in or disengage from criminal networks in cyberspace and in the physical world. In at least three ways, Goldsmith and Brewer claim that cyberspace has reconfigured the social arrangements needed to carry out a criminal activity (both online and offline): (1) by weakening the bonding power of groups; (2) by expanding the range of interactions possible for a given individual; and (3) by giving individuals more power in how, when and whether they affiliate with others and take action. Hence, in their view, new technologies are allowing individuals not only to acquire criminal capability but also to limit their involvement in particular criminal networks: criminal learning does not depend anymore on face-to-face interactions over time, and individuals can drift into and out of criminal pathways more easily than before.

In addition to the adaptation of existing theories, a new explanation for criminal activities in cyberspace has been proposed by Jaishankar (2007, 2009). In his space transition theory, he considers the movement of persons from the physical world to cyberspace and the other way around, starting from the assumption that people tend to behave differently offline and online. According to Jaishankar, who aims at explaining only cybercrimes and not physical crimes too, the movement from one space to another has criminogenic features. For instance, he hypothesises that persons who repress criminal behaviour in the physical world have a propensity to commit crimes in cyberspace and that criminal acts can be exported from the physical realm to cyberspace and vice versa. We will encounter deviant and criminal behaviours – such as in cases of harassment – when the internet has been used as a shield allowing individuals to lower their inhibitions and to exhibit antisocial behaviour, with serious repercussions also in the physical world (Patchin & Hinduja 2016). This approach seems promising in explaining forms of crime that can take place entirely in cyberspace, but it does not consider criminal activities that, even if facilitated by the internet, are finalised or developed for a significant part in the physical world, such as many market-based activities. Space transition theory started to be empirically tested only recently, and preliminary results seem to show that Jaishankar's postulates are applicable to a limited number of cybercrimes (Danquah & Longe 2011).

Concluding remarks

The necessity to have a proper theory to describe and explain why and how certain individuals engage in deviant and criminal acts in cyberspace is evident in order to assist crime policy and practice to deal with offenders in the real world and to think about crime prevention. Research on cybercrimes remains largely descriptive, meaning that its primary goal is still to identify and present general trends (Boman & Freng 2017). Classical theories and especially opportunity approaches, which are based on the idea of rational choice (crime depends on a trade-off of costs and benefits) and the possibility of deterrence (if the potential costs outweigh the potential benefits), have been particularly popular when applied to crime online. Many scholars have also turned to learning, control and subcultural theories, while alternative explanations of criminal behaviour such as theories defining crime as a product of disadvantaged delinquents have been less utilised. As we will see, the combination of low self-control and learning theories proved to be particularly successful, as these approaches seem to enrich one another (for instance, low self-control is likely to be exacerbated by deviant peer association). Overall, in the effort to find a suitable theoretical framework for cybercrimes, most studies have been based on theories originally created for crimes in the physical world, and only recently has there been new attention to elaborate innovative approaches that take into consideration the peculiarities of cyberspace. Digital drift and space transition theories can be considered initial promising attempts to explain crime in cyberspace, and we can expect further endeavours to theorise the specificities of cybercrimes in the coming years.

It would be desirable for new theoretical efforts to make the most of the teachings of critical and postmodern approaches, which have had the undeniable merit of sensitising scholars to alternative meanings of crime and deviance, emphasising the idea that it is important to adopt a critical stance over discourses on crime and criminalisation. Completely value-free research is probably impossible in the social sciences (Becker 1967). Nonetheless, once we acknowledge this 'limitation', the fact that our values and beliefs shape our understanding of the social world is not necessarily a negative thing. Especially in an era characterised by rapid social and technological changes and unequal societies and often by populist discourses on crime, being critical and aware of power relations in society is likely to be the way forward to confront the challenges of crime, justice and security in a free society.

? CRITICAL QUESTIONS

- Read five recent journal articles on cybercrime events. Can you spot some of the theories/approaches mentioned in this chapter as underlying the crime narrative as presented in the news?

- How would you describe your typical routine in terms of cyberspace presence? Can you identify specific opportunities for potential criminal behaviour and for online victimisation?

- Do you think that you are living in an anomic society? Why or why not? To what extent do you think this affects cybercrimes?

- We have seen that for gender-based theories, gender is recognised as a core organising component of social structures and scholars have recognised the existence of a gendered digital divide when it comes to cybercrime offending and victimisation. A similar divide has been noted in cybersecurity, an industry suffering from a gender pay and talent gap (Poster 2018). According to some, this lack of diversity is very problematic, as it leads to blind spots in cybersecurity because of the lack of people able to see crime problems from different perspectives. Is there a gender problem in cybersecurity in your country? To what extent do you think this is a problem for crime understanding, prevention and control?

4 CRIMES AGAINST DEVICES

Introduction

With this chapter, where the 'core' part of the book begins, you will learn about the most relevant types of cybercrimes. Specifically, this chapter is dedicated to the unauthorised access to other people's devices – what is generally referred to as 'hacking'. The first part of the chapter will focus on hacking and its social construction, followed by an overview of the main types of attacks directed against devices, including smart goods, mobile devices, operating and security systems and networks. As you will see, attacks on devices encompass a broad range of activities, such as system sabotage or destruction, theft of computer resources or of confidential information, leeching (the draining of resources, bandwidth or data from a website or a network), spoofing (maliciously impersonating another device or user on a network to launch an attack) or denial of service. Some of these activities are at the basis of crimes that we will encounter later on in this book – for instance, the identity theft (a crime against persons) carried out by 'stealing' confidential information stored in a personal computer. However, the activities described in this chapter – regardless of whether they are crimes or deviant behaviours in themselves or if they are merely steps needed for more complex crimes – are all characterised by the fact that the focus is on the unlawful access to a device.

The final part of the chapter will focus instead on lawful forms of access to data stored or transmitted through a device and specifically to what is generally referred to as 'dataveillance' – that is, the practice of monitoring digital data relating to personal details or online activities, generally carried out by states and corporations. Although the monitoring and collection of online data in state and corporate surveillance are certainly not crimes if carried out according to legal restrictions, some of the techniques used to access online data (and, from a reverse perspective, to hide and protect the same data from intrusion) are the same in both licit and illicit efforts. In addition, discussing surveillance and data protection will give us the chance to start dealing with the relationships between privacy, data confidentiality and security in cyberspace, which are at the very base of many criminal opportunities that are exploited to hack our precious data.

Hackers and identity construction

Hackers are often identified as a primary threat to computer systems, organisations and individual users. Hacking can be defined as any unauthorised access to other people's computer systems (which could range from 'digital trespass' to 'taking ownership' of a computer system). Originally, however, a 'hack' was simply an innovative use of technology, bringing positive results and benefits (Yar 2019). As we will see, the notion of hacking has been constructed over time as a form of cybercriminal activity by policy-makers, law enforcement, the media and the cybersecurity industry.

Let's start with hacking's truest meaning. Scholars have identified different 'generations' of hackers, mainly reflecting hackers' changing attitudes and interests:

- During the late 1950s and the 1960s, an era when most people had never seen a computer, 'true hackers' (Levy 1984) were the pioneers of computing who experimented with and innovated the rare large mainframe computers available in facilities such as the Massachusetts Institute of Technology.
- Starting from the 1970s, 'hardware hackers' began to play a pivotal role in the computer revolution by combining and repurposing electrical and mechanical components to improve computer hardware.
- From the 1980s onwards, 'game hackers' focused on the development of software applications.
- In the 1990s, 'microserfs' (Taylor 2005) were commercially co-opted by the software industry, while 'hacktivists' marked the merging of hacking activities with the pursuit of radical political activities.

In this complex context, of course there have always been a few using their skills in a negative way. In the computer underground, 'proper' hackers started to use the term 'crackers' to identify the malicious ones, accused of having lost touch with the moral or professional motivations of the hacking movement. Often the term 'black hat' was also used to identify hackers active in identifying systems' weaknesses and carrying out attacks, while 'white hats' are those hackers active in the computer security industry (Holt 2007; Söderberg 2010). Motivations for illegal or deviant hacking differ, ranging from vandalism and destructive behaviour to intellectual curiosity, from the illegal search for profit to a political or ideological quest.

An ethical foundation for hacking can be found in the so-called *Hacker Manifesto* or *The Conscience of a Hacker* (The Mentor 1986), a seminal critical essay written by a hacker who went under the pseudonym of The Mentor. This *Manifesto* is considered a cornerstone of the prevailing hacker philosophy. Consider the following extract:

> This is our world now... The world of the electron and the switch, the beauty of the baud. [...] We explore... And you call us criminals. We exist without skin color, without nationality, without religious bias... And you call us criminals. You build atomic bombs,
>
> you wage wars, you murder, you cheat, and lie to us and try to make us believe it's for our own good, yet we're the criminals.
>
> Yes, I am a criminal. My crime is that of curiosity. My crime is that of judging people by what they say and think, not what they look like. My crime is that of outsmarting you, something that you will never forgive me for.
>
> I am a hacker, and this is my manifesto. You may stop this individual, but you can't stop us all.

Unfortunately, besides those who genuinely believe in such an ethics, the *Manifesto* has served over the years as an excuse for some individuals looking for a moral justification for their action: we should keep in mind that intruding into a computer system is in most cases a criminal act, no matter if the hacker claims he/she is moved by ethical motivations or as penetration tester (Furnell 2009). From this perspective, part of the hackers' ethos and motivations could be interpreted as part of what criminologists would call 'neutralisation techniques' (Sykes & Matza 1957) – that is, rationalisations offenders use to convince themselves that it is admissible to transgress dominant norms of conduct, thereby allowing them to deviate and justify that deviation and to help them to mitigate any feelings of remorse, guilt and shame that would otherwise be experienced in the aftermath of deviant behaviour.

Even before the hacktivism age, many hackers identified themselves as 'cyberpunks' (a cultural movement emerging in the 1970s) or 'crypto-anarchist', therefore adding a clear political dimension to their identities. In the words of internet pioneer John Perry Barlow (1996), in his 'Declaration of Independence' of cyberspace:

> Governments of the Industrial World, you weary giants of flesh and steel, I come from Cyberspace, the new home of Mind. On behalf of the future, I ask you of the past to leave us alone. You are not welcome among us. You have no sovereignty where we gather [...]

We are forming our own Social Contract. This governance will arise according to the conditions of our world, not yours. Our world is different [...]

We are creating a world where anyone, anywhere may express his or her beliefs, no matter how singular, without fear of being coerced into silence or conformity [...]

We will create a civilization of the Mind in Cyberspace. May it be more humane and fair than the world your governments have made before.

Nowadays, the countercultural potential of hacking and its positive depiction of computer enthusiasts has not completely disappeared. For instance, elements of hacking culture have often been associated with the idea that information should be free and accessible, which is at the basis of the open-source movement (see Chapter 7) (Taylor 2005, 2009).

When did hacking then become a synonym of cybercrime? The trouble began after popular media and cultural representations – such as the Hollywood films *Wargames* (1983) and *Hackers* (1995) – identified hacking as a form of criminal and deviant behaviour associated with miscreant or misunderstood (male) 'youngsters' (Yar 2005; Sela-Shayovitz 2012); the arrests of some tech-savvy teenagers self-referring as hackers and trespassing forbidden computer systems cemented this idea in the general public (Thomas 2005). In later films – such as *The Net* (1995) and *Die Hard 4* (2007) – hackers were generally depicted as amoral antiheroes or simply criminals, crystallising the social construction of hacking as a dangerous, often criminal, endeavour (Wall 2007). Even contemporary tech-inspired films and series – such as the dystopic *Black Mirror* (2011–present) – tend to present a very gloomy vision of the future, with technology enthusiasts too often unaware of the dangers we would be mindlessly clicking towards. The latter series has become a central cultural reference, showing how a slight futurological shift linked to technological abuse might produce catastrophic social and political consequences, the moral price we might have to pay and the dangerous shifts in the balance between privacy and security we will have to deal with if we acritically accept the course of action (Puech 2017). As anticipated in Chapter 2, we should not underestimate the importance of the cultural roots of cybercrimes, which frame not only how the general public see them but also how policy-makers respond (Wall 2008, 2012). The notion of moral panic can help us to better understand these dynamics.

Box 4.1 Moral panic and the social construction of cybercrime

The notion of moral panic was introduced by Stanley Cohen (1972) and soon became part of the jargon of sociologists and criminologists to describe strategies and rhetoric in the media coverage of crime and deviancy. Every moral panic has its own 'folk devil' – that is, a group of people or an episode onto whom or which public anxieties are projected: hackers, in this case. Social anxieties can be projected 'bottom-up' into moral panics, but moral panics can also be elite-engineered by 'moral entrepreneurs' (Becker 1963) for personal, commercial or political gain (Hall et al. 1978; Garland 2008; Hier 2008). In order to do so, moral entrepreneurs define a social problem as 'serious enough' to warrant attention and a desired social policy. This capacity to use media in advancing campaigns towards particular scopes has become so powerful that in recent years it has been claimed that moral panic has become institutionalised, thus becoming an integral part of the infrastructure of contemporary society (Simon & Feeley 2013).

In the context of this book, moral panic matters because of the characteristics of media reporting of cybercrime, which is often over-sensationalised (Wall 2015). This can lead to an inflation of fears and expectations of harm: there is the feeling that everyone is potentially dangerous and that threats may come from anywhere, at any moment (Beck 1992; McGuire 2007; Popham 2018). Moral panics can have very practical implications; by attracting public attention to a specific issue, they can force it onto the political agenda, allowing infrastructures of regulation and control that can have lasting effects (Garland 2008; Lavorgna 2019a). In the case of cybercrimes, this can translate into stricter laws and stringent technological countermeasures, as the discussion is framed around the need to restore law and order online (Söderberg 2010). An old-but-gold example is from the film *Wargames* (1983), which tells of a young tech-savvy boy who finds a back door into a military central computer without realising it; he thinks he is playing a war game but rather he is about to start World War III. The film had a lot of resonance in the United States, kicking off an anti-hacker panic and igniting discussions on national cybersecurity: anti-hacking bills were introduced in the course of the following year, with heavy penalties.

As explained by Wall (2008), the mythology about cyberspace and cybercrime originating in fiction rather than in facts is what blurs the line between what is real, what is not and what might exist only in the realm of technical scientific possibilities, shaping expectations about online risk. The semantic change that happened with the word hacker, which made it gain an overall negative reputation in common parlance, can be attributed in good part to moral panic.

However, it is worth remembering that the relationship between cyberspace and moral panics is twofold: if on the one hand there are moral panics *in* cyberspace (as in the case of hackers), we should not forget that moral panic can occur *through* cyberspace. Cyberspace, in fact, has a huge potential regarding the speed and the ease with which moral panics can be constructed, transmitted and amplificated, especially in the case of short-lived outbursts of concern which are facilitated by real-time rather than retrospective research (Ungar 2001; Cohen 2011; Flores-Yeffal et al. 2011).

As summarised by Steinmetz (2016), in hackers' technological subculture the worldview is still characterised by political liberalism, technological ontology (that is, interpreting the world as if it were a computer, with the consequence that human institutions are expected to work best when conditions for optimal computational performance, such as openness and efficiency, are met) and a sense of technological utopianism – the idea of 'better living through technology' (Steinmetz 2016, p. 28). State authority, on the other hand, is generally perceived (even if in a way often unreflexive and uncritical) in negative terms as controlling, inept and even leading to collateral damages. Hackers tend to share and be influenced by subcultural values and norms, such as technology (which facilitates the ability to hack), secrecy (to avoid unwanted attention from governmental institutions and crime control agencies) and technological mastery (which is proudly displayed to other hackers or outside their communities) (Holt 2007). Hacking, in a way, becomes a lifestyle for many and a specific mindset: hackers are supposed to be curious, enthused by puzzles, problem-solvers, prone to systematic, technical and unconventional thinking (Steinmetz 2016). In a way, they are those trying to engineer problems out. Boundaries among the hacking subculture are created not only as regards ethics and motivations about hacking (as in the case of 'black' versus 'white' hats) but also in the sense of technical abilities and the interest in committing themselves in developing their skills (their 'craftwork', in the words of Steinmetz 2016); poorly skilled hackers ('kiddies'), for instance, are given no respect in the community (Holt 2007).

Identity formation and social learning take place in online communities such as internet relay chats (IRLs), instant messages services, bulletin boards and social media (Mann & Sutton 1998; Zhuge et al. 2009; Lu et al. 2015) as well as offline, through a number of local meetings with hacker groups or national and international conventions (*Defcon* being the most famous one). The role of cyberspace in allowing the development of a community is of particular interest, as it allows otherwise dispersed members to find a common place that leads to a communal spirit and social bonding and learning (Castells 2001; Perry & Olsson 2009). However, we should not underestimate the role of offline experiences and upbringing. For instance, at least among hackers in the West, hacking is often a middle-class phenomenon (Steinmetz 2016): most hackers have similar educational experiences and background, as they are first exposed to technology at home, at an early age, often because their parents have technically oriented jobs.

Apart from the techniques of neutralisation (Sykes & Matza 1957) discussed above, as summarised by Yar (2005), from a theoretical point of view hacking has often been explained by criminologists through routine activity theory (Cohen & Felson 1979). Holt et al. (2015), for example, have recognised the main elements of the theory – (virtual) exposure to motivated offenders, absence of capable guardians (ranging from antivirus to personal computer skills) and presence of suitable targets (defined in terms of demographic characteristics; for instance, devices of individuals in full-time employment are more likely to be infected) – to explain cyber-victimisation. Alternatively, criminologists have focused on hacking as an act of juvenile delinquency (Yar 2005), through subcultural (Cloward & Ohlin 1960), social learning (Bandura 1977) and differential association (Sutherland 1939; Sutherland et al. 1995) theories. Sociological studies have also underlined the role of cultural influences, and in particular masculinity, in the development of hackers' identities, as traditionally hacking has been overwhelmingly a male-dominated activity (Yar 2005; Zavrsnik 2008). The gender barrier is decreasing, but problems of sexism and misogyny persist (think of the complaints *Defcon* has received over the years for displaying sexist content and for allowing a 'locker-room' attitude). A final strand of explanations offered by psychologists focuses instead on why specific individuals are disposed towards hacking: according to this perspective, 'internet addiction disorder' would explain the compulsive use of computers, also in law-breaking ways (Young 1998). This latest approach links hacking with the lack of individual self-control in a way similar to the discourse about drug addicts; interestingly, this interpretation has been adopted by some court rulings, for instance in the United States, where hackers have been banned from using computers and sent to rehabilitation centres (Söderberg 2010).

Box 4.2 Hacktivism: civil disobedience or something else?

As we have seen above, motivations behind hacking can be extremely diverse. A category of hackers deserving specific attention is that of hacktivists. For them, hacking is not about the search for profit; the pride of a hack is not in its aesthetical beauty but rather in its capacity to make a political statement. In these cases, even if hacking techniques are used, the attack does not create a high degree of concern among the general public (Holt et al. 2015), which rather welcomes (some of) its manifestations. According to a multi-country survey carried out by

CIGI-Ipsos (2016), most internet users seem to have a relatively favourable view of hacktivist groups, which are even considered an asset to hold criminal networks, large corporations and even governments accountable.

Jordan and Taylor (2004) distinguished two main types of hacktivism:

- *Mass action hacktivism* reinvents for the virtual realm traditional forms of protests, such as boycotts and street demonstrations. Think of Anonymous, which has probably been the most notorious hacktivist group since 2008. Initially, it was considered an anti-establishment collective, linked with the Occupy movement's pro-tests in 2011 and attacking mainly websites of financial institutions and opponents of free online distribution of copyrighted material. Over time, however, its scope changed: for instance, Anonymous took actions against Daesh supporters (Guiora 2017). Nowadays, Anonymous is continuing its operations mainly in the form of regional 'branches' of hacktivist groups. For example, in support of Catalan independence, in 2017 the Catalonian branch of Anonymous targeted websites run by the Spanish government: some sites were subject to so-called 'distributed denial of service' (DDoS) attacks, others defaced to display 'Free Catalonia'.

- *Digitally correct hacktivism* aims to ensure that information in cyber-space remains freely and securely available, radicalising hackers' ethos for the open Web where information flows freely and gate-keepers are not able to restrict it. WikiLeaks, the whistleblowing organisation founded in 2006 by Julian Assange, offers a good example: especially in its initial stages, it was presented as a mech-anism to fight societal corruption by increasing transparency and challenging power.

Many forms of hacktivism are often interpreted as new forms of civil disobedience – a technique of resistance and protest whose aim is to promote or achieve social or political change by peacefully breaking unjust laws. Hence, hacktivism has the potential to be a constructive agent of positive political and social change if the attack against an individual, corporation or country deemed responsible for oppressing the rights of others is carried out under a strong ethical conviction, in a non-violent way, without damaging the property of others, not for personal profit and with a willingness to accept personal responsibility for the outcome of the attack (Fioriglio 2010; Manion & Goodrum 2000; Milone 2003; Banks 2017). This view, however, is not unchallenged, with the parallelism between hacktivism and civil disobedience being often criticised. The main argument is that hacktivism, when compared with more traditional forms of activism, operates under a high degree of impunity because of the anonymity of most members and the consequent lack of accountability (Sorell 2015). Particularly Wikileaks has suffered harsh criticism for exposing information without editorial discretion, therefore harming national security, compromising international diplomacy and, even more importantly, exposing personal information of potentially vulnerable people (such as civilians working with international forces in Afghanistan in 2010 or female voters during political turmoil in Turkey in 2016).

Attacks and vulnerabilities

As anticipated above, hacking can be any unauthorised access to other people's computer systems. Hacking can occur through a variety of activities and it can exploit different types of vulnerabilities. Generally speaking, attacks can occur manually or via automatic methods such as through botnets (a combination of the words robot and network, it refers to internet-connected computers communicating between each other to complete repetitive tasks) and 'zombie machines' (internet-connected devices that have been compromised and are used to perform malicious tasks, generally without their owner being aware of it). The main consequence of automation is that it increases the speed and breadth of possible attacks and, if the attacks do not originate from the offender's device, he or she can be very difficult to trace. The Avalanche network, for instance, was used from 2009 to 2016 to distribute malware from around 20 different malware families as a communication infrastructure for other botnets and even for money mule schemes. It could involve as many as 500,000 devices worldwide per day. Investigations started in 2012 in Germany after the Windows Encryption Trojan (an encryption ransomware) blocked users' access to their computers.

DDos attacks are probably the most common use of botnets. In this case, an army of thousands of zombie computers infected by malicious code are asked to try to access the targeted system (for instance, a Web server) all at once, exceeding the capacity for the system to respond. The attacker activates 'master' zombies; these, in turn, trigger and send attack commands to 'slave' zombies, which mount a DDoS attack against the victim. As a consequence, the overwhelmed system is likely to crash for a period of time, being unable to accept new connections. The error webpage saying 'the page is unavailable' that you might have encountered while surfing online is often the result of such an attack. In early 2018, for instance, 1.35 terabits/second of traffic hit GitHub (a leading software developer platform) all at once, causing the most powerful DDoS attack recorded up to that moment. Rather than relying on a malware-driven botnet, the attackers used an amplification DDoS attack: they simply had to spoof the IP address of victims and send queries to 'memcached' systems (memcached is an open-source application designed to speed up Web applications). These systems returned to the victims 50 times the data of the queries, hindering their capacity to handle internet traffic (Figure 4.1).

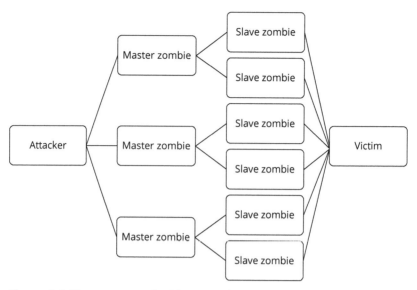

Figure 4.1 The anatomy of a DDoS attack

Box 4.3 Malware

Malware is an umbrella term including various types of malicious software:

- viruses – need a host to reproduce and transmit themselves;

- worms – capable of self-replication and self-transmission;

- trojan horses – appear to perform a useful function but have hidden destructive capabilities.

Alongside hacking, malware is one of the most recognised cyber-threats and has a long history. The Morris Worm (1988) was reportedly the first programme capable to reproduce itself and infect other computers. The worm was the result of an intellectual exercise carried out by a student in computer science at Cornell University; because of a mistake in the spreading mechanism, the worm went out of control and resulted in a denial of service (DoS) attack, causing affected computers to crash.

Malware can have different functions. We will look in detail at ransomware in Chapter 6 and focus now on examples where malware is used to unjustly monitor other people's devices. *Keyloggers* (or keystroke loggers), for instance, are a surveillance software that can be used to record the keys struck on a computer keyboard or on a smartphone, typically without the user knowing. Similarly, *spyware* permits the monitoring of someone else's device. It often (but not always) comes in the form of a trojan horse. A famous example of spyware is the software package Loverspy, which was concealed within electronic greeting cards. The software costed about GBP 55 and was explicitly marketed to monitor online activities of romantic partners; about 1,000 people bought it. The creator of the software (together with some of its users) was indicted in 2005 but has evaded capture ever since, making it onto the FBI's most wanted list in 2013.

Malware can also be used for espionage; an interesting example is provided by the 2016 'Eyepyramid' case. Here, the malware was developed and spread via spear phishing by an Italian brother and sister who worked together at a small investment firm. The malware was set to target specific high-profile victims such as members of the Italian government and law and consultancy firms around the globe, in order to gather information for better investments. The couple used hacked email accounts of persons trusted by the final, high-profile victims to infect the targeted devices with malware files, which were able to harvest information and to spread themselves to other victims via email. Malware can also be used to illegally access devices for other types of personal gain. For instance, in early 2018, a man was indicted in Ohio with the accusation of having hacked into thousands of computers through malware that enabled him to access and turn on the cameras and microphones of computers, take screenshots and record keystrokes for over 13 years. The malware was specifically programmed to alert the offender if a victim was watching pornography.

Malware either can be 'physically' integrated into the machine (for instance, via a USB key) or can be downloaded by the user (for example, if it is sent as an attachment to an email). Spam is a common way to propagate malware, such as through *ratware* (that is, mass email software that automates spam email sending), *clickjacking* (or user interface (UI)-redressing, when attackers trick users to click on a different webpage) or *malvertising* (malicious advertising). Fake antivirus programs are also used to propagate malware or defraud victims, generally via drive-by-download attacks, botnets and social engineering (for instance, a webpage displays a window in the browser pretending that the device has been infected with malware and requesting the victim to purchase a new antivirus licence) (Stone-Gross et al. 2013).

Most modern malware is relatively difficult to identify, as it defends itself against detection or removal though various stealth techniques (Furnell 2009). Cryptography is increasingly used to design malware:

cryptoworms, in particular, which are generally spread via unpatched server vulnerabilities, are set to become pivotal in ransomware, with WannaCry being one of the most notorious examples in recent years. Since 2017, cryptocurrency-mining malware has become increasingly popular: infected laptops or mobile devices are used to mine cryptocurrencies; the victim often does not even suspect that his/her device has been infected, as performance is often not impacted, or Javascript obfuscation techniques are used so that scanners cannot find miners.

Malware has been traditionally designed to target computer systems, but it is increasingly attacking mobile devices as well. Especially since 2016, several malwares targeting Android systems emerged, such as the Russian-language trojan Simploker, the rooting malware HummingBad (able to install fraudulent apps and display malicious advertisements) or the ransomware Android.Lockdroind.E (posing as a porn app, it takes control of the devices it is installed on, snapping a picture of the victim using the device's camera and including the image as part of the ransom note).

Attackers can rely on a variety of tools, ranging from port or network scanners (that is, applications designed to probe a server or host for open ports or network vulnerabilities), packet sniffers (protocol analysers that can be used to spy on network user traffic and to collect passwords) or password crackers (which allow the recovery of passwords from data that have been stored in or transmitted by a device) (Furnell 2009). Brute-forcing passwords is always a possibility: this attack is a 'trial-and-error until you succeed' method, in which the attacker tries systematically every possible combination of letters, numbers and symbols until the correct combination is discovered. This is why long and complex passwords are generally considered safer.

New techniques, however, are always emerging. One interesting example regards the new possibilities for hacking offered by the use of near field communication (NFC), a technology whose use is growing rapidly in the smartphone, contactless payment and smart camera markets, to name just a few. NFC allows the transfer of data (including payment data) among devices via an extremely short-range wireless band through bumping, tapping or swiping. The problem is that NFC was created with users' convenience, and not security, in mind. Hackers have already proven that it is possible to use an antenna to install malware on an NFC-enabled smartphone, allowing it to connect to a remote computer controlled by the hacker or to hide NFC tags in unsuspicious places that NFC-enabled devices are likely to bump up against, with people not even realising they might have been victimised.

Cloud computing, especially Software as a Service (SaaS), which allows users to connect to and use cloud-based apps over the internet to store their data, is another target that has been increasingly attacked. The problem is that many users think that by storing important information in the cloud they are mitigating the risk of being badly impacted by malicious hacking. Unfortunately, this is not the case. For instance, if files stored locally are infected with ransomware, then the backup copies held, for example, on the G-Drive will also be overwritten with the same ransomware as soon as the computer syncs. The nature of the cloud itself makes it particularly vulnerable, especially for its multi-tenancy and resource-sharing characteristics, so that the development of better security policy implementations and technological solutions to prevent, detect and react to potential attacks is the only way forward to ensure the long-term success of cloud computing services (Haghighat et al. 2015; Bonguet & Bellaiche 2017; Vidal & Choo 2018).

Indeed, we should not forget that attacks very often occur because of design faults in the targeted devices or unaddressed software vulnerabilities. Among the many examples is the hack carried out in 2015 by two members of the hacker group Linker Squad. They gained access to the Spanish mobile network operator Orange through a company website vulnerable to a simple SQL injection (that is, a code injection technique wherein an attacker can execute a malicious payload in an application's software, allowing them to steal and alter data in a website's database), which resulted in the theft of 10 million contact details from customers and employees. In late 2017, researchers discovered a severe flaw in the WPA2 protocol (a wireless security protocol), which could leave virtually all modern Wi-Fi-enabled devices vulnerable to the interception of sensitive data (including passwords and emails) and in some cases inject malware. The following year it was revealed that a flaw on a recently released Mac operating system allowed root access to the machine without the need for a password: the first time the access was denied, but the hacker just had to try a second time to be granted access.

It is not unusual for attacks to exploit previously known security vulnerabilities if they are not promptly patched. Often, vulnerabilities are discovered by multiple independent parties, which might not have an incentive to disclose what they have found to others (Herr et al. 2017). Conversely, so-called zero-day attacks take advantage of a vulnerability the same day it becomes known, exploiting it before patches are identified and then applied. Attacks can be targeted – when time and resources are dedicated towards a specific target – or they can be launched without targeting a particular person or group. Examples of targeted attacks are 'business process compromise' attacks, which affect the specific processes or machines of a specific company, business or institution with a particular aim. In 2013, for instance, drug traffickers recruited hackers to infiltrate the ICT systems controlling the movement and location of containers on the Belgian port of Antwerp, making it easier and less risky to receive drugs from the port facility. 'Bug poaching' attacks are also generally targeted: in this case, the offender compromises corporate servers and steals data in order to request a fee for information on how the attack was carried out and/or for the release of the data.

It is worth remembering that there are off-the-shelf software kits (so-called 'exploit kits') designed to identify vulnerabilities, allowing attackers who are not experts in coding to conduct their illegal activities. The exploit kits Angler (2013–2016) and Neutrino (2015–2017), for instance, were widely used for malvertising, to spread ransomware and in hacktivism campaigns.

As we will see in more detail in Chapter 9, in order to prevent and tackle attacks, there is consensus that a multilayered approach is needed. First of all, protection needs to be properly used and maintained. Think of the distribution of a new anti-malware software by cybersecurity companies, which are generally good at keeping pace with the release of new malware; the anti-malware will be effective as long as it is installed and updated by the users. This is why educating users on the best cybersecurity practices remains of the upmost importance for cybercrime prevention. Over the years, the private sector has become a fundamental stakeholder in the development of network and information systems security policies. If at the beginning the private sector was seen mainly as a victim in need of protection, it was soon perceived as an actor bearing responsibility for ensuring network resilience and also as an active policy-shaper providing technical expertise (Farrand & Carrapico 2018). It should, however, be recognised that prevention can be hard if individuals and organisations are faced with custom code that has been written specifically to target their systems (Furnell 2009).

Internet of things

The internet of things (IoT) is a concept reflecting a multi-domain environment where virtually all types of everyday objects and devices can 'talk' to each other, exchange data and be connected to the internet; moreover, the IoT facilitates new ways of communications between the people and the objects themselves. The IoT is profoundly innovating in many aspects of our daily lives, being increasingly used for a wide range of applications ranging from smart cities and emergency services to retail and healthcare. In a context where people look for easier, more convenient ways to manage their lives, increased automatisation and computerisation are generally welcomed, even when this entails moving monitoring and decision-making from humans to machines. Billions of devices are already connected to the IoT.

In healthcare, for instance, IoT-based technologies are used for medication management, glucose level sensing and electrocardiogram monitoring among other things (Ismal et al. 2015; Martellini et al. 2017). 'Connected healthcare' is promising in its possibilities to improve treatment and responsiveness by doctors, caregivers and patients themselves, but security risk cannot be neglected. First, sensitive health data could be accessed through hacking. Information might also be intercepted, modified or fabricated, service availability might be interrupted or a user's device might be compromised by interfering with the hardware components or by hacking the software, with potentially deadly consequences. In 2016, for example, the medical device manufacturer Animas from Johnson & Johnson warned that one of its insulin pumps (the production of which is now discontinued) proved to be easily hackable, which could have led to wrong levels of insulin being administered to patients.

Very popular IoT applications occur in smart homes, which can be defined as homes equipped with lighting, heating and electronic devices that can be controlled remotely by computer or smartphone. Smart homes should increase not only comfort and quality of life but also security and energy efficiency. Think, for instance, about systems that automatically adjust the room temperature depending on the user's presence or that automatically switch the lights on or off. Also in this case, however, there are security issues that need to be taken into consideration, especially keeping in mind that smart devices (which, unfortunately, are often not created with security as a top priority and do not support sophisticated security approaches) are generally considered easy to hack, with users often keeping default passwords. Poorly protected smart devices can facilitate other cyberattacks (by acting as entry points for attacks to be launched against other systems). For instance, in July 2017, hackers stole and sent to Finland 10 GB of data from an American casino by using a fish tank that was connected to the internet to regulate features such as food, temperature and cleanliness of the water. Unauthorised remote access to a smart system can also cause physical damage: doors that can be unlocked may allow a burglar to enter the premises, or heating or water systems could be hacked to cause fires or flooding. In addition, sensitive data could be accessed. In fact, smart devices collect enormous amounts of information on users by using sensors, cameras and microphones; music preferences, bills, purchases, photos and videos and even conversations could be remotely accessed (not only by offenders but also by private companies or repressive governments).

Smart wearables such as glasses for augmented reality and smartwatches are marking the overspill of the IoT, allowing us to surf the internet and get information (including information about ourselves, such as on how 'fit' we are) at all times. This is the road towards the internet of everything (IoE) – that is, the integration of people, business processes, data and things into networked connections. The IoE, in a way, extends the IoT to describe a more complex system where also people and processes, beyond devices, will be connected. The IoE could increase even further the potential security and privacy risks (Roesner et al. 2014; Martellini et al. 2017) as well as facilitate different types of criminal and deviant behaviours. As a proof of concept, Migicovsky et al. (2014) examined how smartwatches can lead to cheating in an academic environment by demonstrating a prototype cloud-backed application that would enable fraudulent students to covertly collaborate on exams. In the hope not to provide students with a new creative way to cheat during such situations, this is just an example to remember that every technological innovation comes with criminogenic opportunities that should be understood and assessed from the very beginning in order to mitigate their potential negative effects.

IoT can be described as a 'disruptive technology' (Bower & Christensen 1995), involving broad potential social and economic impacts. If IoT technology will increasingly disrupt the status quo, its impact on the social and economic welfare of citizens demands more rigorous evaluation (Ebersold & Glass 2015). In a way, the IoT is opening new legal and technical challenges that should be understood and dealt with before the massive commercialisation of smart devices.

Although attacks on smart devices are not unprecedented, their scale is changing. Furthermore, with the passing of time, attacks are becoming more complex, signalling an increase of potential threats. Approaches based on security-by-design through technologies (such as support for system auto-configuration and the automatic update of system software and firmware) are potential solutions to be further explored to assist system auto-management to enhance the security of smart devices (Lin & Bergmann 2016; Martellini et al. 2017). Consumer education, however, remains a pivotal factor to minimise the risk of attacks and their impact. For instance, the botnet Mirai, at its peak in 2016, took down high-profile websites via massive distributed DDoS using hundreds of thousands of compromised IoT devices such as home routers, netcams and air quality monitors; these devices were hacked by simply exploiting weak or default passwords. Also regarding smart and connected goods, attacks often occur because of design faults in computer systems. In 2017, for example, the lack of basic security mechanisms in the charging cards used to charge electronic vehicles in Germany was exposed: during payment, card numbers, for months, were transmitted without encryption directly to the provider in such a way that little effort was required to intercept sensitive data in order to forge charging cards or simulate charging events.

Another major problem relates to the fact that the global governance of IoT is still fuzzy. There is a lack of international regulations and shared security standards on IoT, too often resulting in self-regulation by developer companies, which are driven by profit and not by security (IERC 2015; Ahlmeyer & Chircu 2016). These gaps give advantage to countries lacking strict standards, which increases risks for consumers. Furthermore, as IoT is the basis of a global internet-based information architecture, new legal approaches for the protection of privacy need to be developed. Similarly, technical actions (such as encrypting and anonymising location data that can be attributed to an individual person) are needed to bridge the gap between IoT surveillance and the rights of individuals (Weber 2015). Sadly, the privacy implications of IoT data are still largely unaddressed. Smart home devices, for instance, are opening the way to whole new sets of privacy challenges. In summer 2017, it was disclosed that high-end models of Roomba, a famous artificially intelligent vacuum cleaner, collect data as they clean, creating house maps. Although identifying walls and furniture is necessary to make the robo-vac more effective, the data gathered could be (mis)used if shared with third parties, such as marketers trying to better target consumers. Moreover, the camera on the vacuum cleaner could be hacked, giving a real-time view of the inside of a certain house. Smart speakers such as Amazon's Echo and Google's Home have their microphones constantly listening to catch their 'wake-up word'. Of course, users are (should be?) making a trade-off between utility and privacy the moment they buy a smart device; but the fact is that users seem to be quite unaware of the potential privacy risk to which they are exposed, especially regarding the use of the data collected and its access. It is difficult to believe that so many people are consciously giving up expectations of privacy in their own homes.

Box 4.4 The privacy paradox

Privacy is a complex concept comprising the three distinct elements of secrecy, anonymity and solitude. To borrow Gavison's words, 'in perfect privacy, no one has any information about X, no one pays any attention to X, and no one has physical access o X'; consequently, a loss of privacy occurs 'as others obtain information about an individual, pay attention to him, or gain access to him' (Gavison 1980, p. 428). Privacy is essential both for individual freedom and for democracy, as it fosters the moral autonomy of citizens (Gavison 1980). Unfortunately, privacy can be very fragile and easy to erode, often without people even realising it.

Cyberspace has been changing both the magnitude and the nature of threats to privacy, making it virtually impossible for our legal systems to secure the same level of privacy we have been used to in the past. Nonetheless, the legal recognition of privacy is of the upmost importance, at least to raise awareness of the central value it should have in our lives, especially now that we live in an era where the traditional public versus private distinction has been severely challenged. We first share personal information without recognising its value, then lose control over our data once they circulate online. Publicly accessible social media pages are filled with user-generated content that often covers private and even sensitive information, discussions or images.

We should not forget that privacy manifests itself in various ways. By analysing academic literature and constitutional protection of nine jurisdictions, Koops et al. (2016) distinguished eight basic types of privacy (bodily, intellectual, spatial, decisional, communicational, associational, proprietary and behavioural), with an overlay of a ninth type (informational privacy) that overlaps, but does not coincide, with the eight basic types. Informational privacy is of the upmost importance in cyberspace, as it refers to your interest in preventing information about yourself being collected and in controlling what happens to that information even when others have legitimate access to it.

Research on online behaviour has shown that there are discrepancies between user attitudes and their actual behaviour. In other words, users are concerned about their privacy but do little to protect their data (Barth & de Jong 2017). This phenomenon is known as the 'privacy paradox' and is linked to the fact that users must agree to sacrifice some degree of privacy to enrich user experience. The privacy paradox is very common online. Think, for instance, of cookies. These are pieces of information generated by a Web server and stored in a device (or in a Web browser, in the case of 'cache cookies'). Cookies were introduced to recognise individual users and allow them to maintain their current browsing sessions, but they can also compromise users' privacy and reveal private information. For instance, tracking cookies can attribute Web traffic to an individual user (Khu-smith & Mitchell 2002; Juels et al. 2006; Englehardt et al. 2015). With the augmented pervasiveness of the internet, the privacy paradox has become quintessential in explaining people's behaviour in cyberspace. Users' decision-making seems to be increasingly moved by the search for immediate gratification and it generally takes place on an irrational level, especially when the decision-making process happens on-the-go (for instance, with mobile computing) (Barth & de Jong 2017). In order to solve the paradox or at least to limit its worst effects, there are efforts to improve users' capacity to make well-informed decisions when they are, for instance, installing a new app. These improvements, however, are unlikely to tackle the problem in its entirety, as for users it is not always feasible to decide not to use a certain app or software without being penalised in their social or working spheres.

Monitoring and collection of online data in state and corporate surveillance

Surveillance has long been recognised as a distinguishing feature of late modernity (Foucault 1975; Mathiesen 1997; Ball & Webster 2003; Lyon 2007). On one hand, surveillance constrains us by limiting our privacy; however, we increasingly rely on surveillance to maintain security and to participate in many aspects of society, both offline and online (Lyon 1994; Ball & Webster 2003; Shalhoub-Kevorkian 2012; Cortijo 2017) – consider, for instance, all the times you agree to give a company access to your data to be able to use its services, such as via an app.

Especially in activities addressed at preventing, tacking or mitigating the effects of (cyber)crimes, traditionally there is a constant tension between the need to protect users' privacy and confidentiality and the necessity to monitor suspicious or otherwise potentially criminal activities. Identifying the proper balance among these two ostensibly contradictory needs is of the utmost importance: to borrow Yar's words, this is what can define 'the future of online freedom itself' (Yar 2019). Defining what is acceptable in the interests of security is not an easy task, and there is not a fixed answer: indeed, defining what is acceptable shifts depending on cultural, political and social factors. Consider, for instance, how September 11 allowed in the United States the acceptance of the intrusive measures detailed in the 2001 Patriot Act, whose Title II (entitled 'Enhanced surveillance procedures') covers all aspects of the surveillance of suspected terrorists, those suspected of computer fraud or abuse and agents of a foreign power who are engaged in terrorist activities. Not only does the title allow the gathering of foreign intelligence information, it also permits – among other things – 'sneak and peek' warrants (that allow delayed notification of the execution of a search warrant) and roving wiretaps (that is, wiretap orders that do not need to specify all common carriers and third parties in a surveillance court order).

In more recent times, surveillance seems to have changed again: driven by security and user utility demands and pushed by technology companies, it has become 'liquid', spilling over and spreading in unimaginable (until a few years ago) ways (Lyon 2010; Bauman & Lyon 2013). It is increasingly difficult for individuals to escape the surveillance of social institutions (Haggerty & Ericson 2000; Goold & Neyland 2009; Doyle 2011; Puddephatt 2017), as the only way to stay anonymous would be to avoid engaging in mechanisms that have become standard routine in our lives (for instance, using a credit card) or to avoid any form of cyberspace whatsoever, which would be extremely limiting. Surveillance, to some degree, has become an intrinsic feature of our lives; the puzzle is about where to put its boundaries, so as to maintain a decent equilibrium with our right to privacy (Figure 4.2).

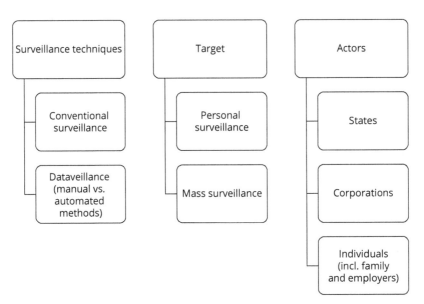

Figure 4.2 Schematising cybersurveillance

Conventional surveillance techniques have been supplanted and/or juxtaposed by personal and mass data surveillance monitoring our digital footprints ('dataveillance'). Pervasive online surveillance can take place manually (for example, monitoring social media activities by reading posts) or via automated methods (such as cookies, spyware, voice over internet protocol (VoIP) data or browser records). Automated methods change as new technologies emerge: for instance, cookies (generally small encrypted text files located in browser directories which track users across different sites, gathering information about surfing habits) used to be at the core of online monitoring but emerging technologies such as fingerprinting (which allows a website to look at the individual characteristics of any computer, such as software and plugins installed, the time zone and so on) are destined to become prevalent.

Beyond surveillance *of* the internet, there is also surveillance that *uses* the internet to monitor specific individuals – an employee, a lover, a suspect in a law enforcement investigation (McGuire 2009). Surveillance in the workplace can be particularly problematic: monitoring of emails, monitoring of internet or intranet use, and video recording of worker activities during working hours may be allowed under certain circumstances (for instance, to identify misconduct), but there is a fine line before these activities become too intrusive and illegitimate. The situation is even trickier when surveillance that uses the internet is carried out to assess workers' behaviour in their own spare time. More and more people have been fired or otherwise disciplined due to certain information on them being available online, opening a discussion on how far employers can (or should) go in supervising the private lives of their employees.

Because of its unique features, online surveillance follows a different set of rules and needs different approaches for effective safeguards (Clarke 1988). On the one side, electronic databases can make surveillance from the state and the criminal justice system more effective in determining whether our society, economy or political order is at risk; from the other side, however, ever-increasing amounts of powerful data can be used to classify, manipulate and even exclude certain people from public life (Jones 2000; Jewkes 2008; Yar 2008b, 2019). In other words, we can agree that (some) members of society need to be controlled, but who controls the controllers? Without proper mechanisms of safeguard in place, dystopic futures might be closer than expected. In 2013, Edward Snowden, an American former contractor of the US government, leaked classified information from the US National Security Agency (NSA) disclosing, among other things, the existence of global government surveillance programmes run by the NSA and the 'Five Eyes' (an intelligence alliance comprising Australia, Canada, New Zealand, the United Kingdom and the United States) with the cooperation of European countries and telecommunication companies. One year later, Vodafone (the world's second-largest mobile phone operator) admitted that several governments had placed wires within its telecoms infrastructure to listen to phone calls made over its network.

Mass surveillance systems have been used by governmental agencies in the past (just to name some of the most famous instances, the ECHELON programme that was implemented in the late 1960s by the United States and their allies and the CARNIVORE or DCS1000 that was created by the United States to monitor online communications in the late 1900s), but the scale of pervasiveness of contemporary mass surveillance is something different. After the flurry of revelations in the aftermath of the 2013 leaks, we entered a 'post-Snowden' era; how we talk about the internet has drastically changed. Now, notions of cybersecurity and IT security are no longer always aligned but they are rather often opposed. For state actors, cybersecurity is an extension of national security, which is traditionally perused also with offensive practices; but for many citizens today, advanced persistent threats include governmental agencies (such as those of the Five Eyes) compromising fundamental privacy rights (Zajiko 2018).

Beyond surveillance from the state, a form of surveillance that is revealing itself as extremely problematic is corporate surveillance. Our online activities produce an immense amount of data. Think of Google, the most popular search engine, which stores identifying information for every Web search (IP address and search phrases) for up to 18 months. If you consider that Gmail's servers – the free email service run by Google – used (until late 2017) to automatically scan emails, you can easily see the problems this might entail in terms of privacy expectations. At the core of this issue lies the fact that data created by our online activities have a monetary value: they can be used for marketing purposes, sold to other corporations as business intelligence to enable them to better tailor their products and services, and even be shared with government agencies. At the same time, there is no democratic oversight of what happens to these data. As a result, some corporations have been forming a new control elite which hoards and exploits immense amounts of data, often eluding legal constraints (McGuire 2009).

The 2018 Facebook and Cambridge Analytica data breach provides a blatant example. It was revealed that up to 87 million Facebook users may have had personally identifiable information illegitimately accessed since 2014 by Cambridge Analytica, a British political consulting firm specialising in data mining, brokerage and analysis in electoral strategic communication. Various political organisations used data from the breach to influence voter opinion, including during the Trump campaign and the Brexit vote. Beyond such an extreme example, we should note that improper uses of online data are a daily occurrence, with the transfer of sensitive information from one company to another being particularly problematic. In 2017, for instance, Grindr (a major gay dating app) gave its users the possibility to share their HIV status and last test date on their profiles, a move that was welcomed as a way to destigmatise the condition. One year later, it emerged that users' HIV status, together with information such as phone ID and GPS coordinates, were shared with third-party app-optimisation services, thus making very sensitive information far more vulnerable and at risk of being hacked.

Because surveillance is so invasive and pervasive, protection of personal and sensitive data is pivotal. The following box will briefly discuss some core technologies used to protect anonymity and privacy online. Technological approaches, however, are not the only way to improve the situation. Many legislators, often pushed by pressing requests from the civil society, are (little by little) intervening to mitigate some of the most adverse effects of dataveillance. At the global level, the situation is still extremely spotty, but things are moving on a regional level. In the European Union, for instance, in May 2018 the EU General Data Protection Regulation (GDPR) came into force, replacing the 1995 Data Protection Directive. Designed to harmonise data privacy laws across Europe and to protect European citizens from privacy and data breaches, it changed the previous regulatory landscape in many ways: among other things, the new regulation extends its territorial scope (it will apply to the processing of personal data by controllers and processors in the European Union, regardless of whether the processing takes place there or not), increases penalties for organisations in breach of the GDPR (which can be fined up to 4 percent of their annual global turnover or EUR 20 million (about GBP 18 million), whichever is greater) and clarifies that requests for consent for data processing must be given in an intelligible and easily accessible form. Furthermore, breach notifications will become mandatory where they are likely to result in a risk to the rights and freedoms of individuals, and individuals are empowered to obtain (free of charge) a copy of their personal data in an electronic format.

Last but not least, 'the right to be forgotten' has finally been recognised. Given the huge amount of data collected from and stored in different places, at all times, deletion rights are a fundamental aspect of privacy in cyberspace (Weber 2015). Under Article 17 of the GDPR, individuals have the right to have personal data erased, among other reasons, if these personal data are no longer necessary for the purpose they were originally collected, if data are used for direct marketing purposes and the individual objects to that or if the individual withdraws his or her consent for holding the data. The right to be forgotten, however, is not absolute; for instance, it does not apply in named circumstances such as if data processing is necessary to exercise the right of freedom of expression and information or to carry out a task in the public interest or in the exercise of official authority or for scientific purposes in the public interest.

Box 4.5 Providing anonymity and protecting data confidentiality in cyberspace

In order to guarantee a higher level of anonymity in cyberspace, there are several technologies that attempt to hide online interactions or disguise the identity of those engaging in them. An example is the use of proxy servers, such as in the case of anonymous remailers (servers receiving and forwarding messages without revealing where they originally came from), closed networks for file sharing or mobile virtual private networking (VPN). Anonymity is useful not only for privacy purposes but also for security, to access geo-blocked content or to circumvent censorship in certain countries. Unfortunately, most of these instruments are subject to poor security guarantees. For instance, Ikram et al. (2016) discovered that many common VPN apps expose users to privacy and security vulnerabilities, such as traffic leakages and the use of insecure tunnelling protocols. Nonetheless, these apps are still widely used.

Another fundamental way to provide anonymity in cyberspace is based on cryptographic technologies such as encryption. Encryption can be defined as 'the process of scrambling data using a mathematical algorithm so that content of the data is obscured' (Reitinger 2000, p. 113). We can distinguish among two main types of encryption, which can also be used in combination: *symmetric encryption* (which has the advantage of being faster) uses the same key for both encrypting and decrypting the files; *asymmetric encryption* uses instead a public key to encrypt the files and a private key to decrypt them. From a technical point of view, we can divide encryption methods into centralised solutions (when their architecture includes one or more central nodes concealing actual users' details, such as proxies, VPNs and SSH (secure shell) tunnels), decentralised solutions (where any system node can transmit data directly as in I2P networks) and hybrid solutions (when there is both an anonymisation mechanism and a server to coordinate the whole system) (Savchenko & Gastenko 2015). The TOR network (from the acronym of 'The Onion Router', the original software project name) is an example of a hybrid solution: probably the most notorious anonymity network, TOR is based on a free software and a volunteer overlay network of servers (nested like the layers of an onion) which facilitate the concealment of a user's location and usage from traffic analysis or network surveillance. TOR encrypts the data (including IP addresses) several times and bounces them through several randomly selected relays until the data reaches its final destination.

Anonymity tools can have a pivotal importance in building secure and trusted global information infrastructure (Denning & Baugh 2000;

Bancroft 2016). TOR, for instance, has been praised as a mechanism to support freedom of expression in countries where political activists would otherwise be censored or threatened. Of course, the same tools can be exploited by offenders to conceal their criminal activities and to make real-time communications inaccessible to law enforcement, thus frustrating communications interceptions and making it very difficult and costly for law enforcement to obtain intelligence and evidence during investigations and trials. The Janus-faced nature of anonymity tools explains why there are ongoing debates and tensions over the extent to which their use should be regulated. Encryption in particular provides a very interesting case, as nowadays it is a standard mechanism to be found in popular communication applications, such as Telegram and WhatsApp. Furthermore, many third-party email services (such as Thunderbird, Apple Mail and Outlook) allow encryption of contents of email messages and attachments from a desktop client via Pretty Good Privacy (PGP) products (which are managed by a central policy server and are therefore considered more vulnerable) or via end-to-end secure channels.

Many law enforcement agencies and security services insist on regulating the use of 'strong encryption' – which is highly resistant to cryptoanalysis – for the general public or on installing a backdoor into commercially available encryption in order to allow law enforcement the possibility to access encrypted devices if needed. These solutions, however, are harshly criticised by experts in cryptography and commercial companies alike, as banning commercial strong encryption will not make it out of reach of criminals, and the use of backdoors might simply make products more vulnerable to attacks. Digital rights organisations have also adopted a strong stance against any restriction in the use of encryption, as it is an important tool to defend the right to privacy. A key case in this regard is the FBI–Apple encryption dispute in the wake of the 2015 San Bernardino shooting, where 14 people were killed and another 22 seriously injured. The FBI recovered the iPhone of one of the shooters, which was locked with a password. The FBI announced that it was unable to access the device because of its advanced security features, including encryption, and asked Apple to create software to enable the unlocking of the phone. The company refused because such software would undermine the security features of its products. The FBI then obtained a court order to mandate Apple to provide the requested software, an unprecedented action likely to ignite a major constitutional fight between the right to privacy and security needs. In the end, though, the FBI found a third party able to assist it in unlocking the iPhone and withdrew the request.

In the United Kingdom, the government (because of the 2016 Investigatory Powers Act) technically already has the power to compel telecom providers to support law enforcement agencies in this sense, but the existing legislation has not yet been used – in order to avoid entering a difficult battle over the trade-off between privacy and security. Other countries such as Australia have been proposing similar legislation. It will be interesting to see how this situation evolves on a global level in the coming years, as opening the way to backdoors has the potential to significantly shape the future of the Web.

Concluding remarks

In this chapter, we have encountered various forms of unauthorised access to other people's devices as well as having addressed some key issues regarding the practice of monitoring digital data relating to personal information or online activities. Regardless of the actor committing the intrusion (be it a 'good' hacker, a criminal network, the state or a corporation), we should keep in mind that any action directed at the unauthorised access to, collection or distribution of, personal information may violate an individual's right to privacy, regardless of whether these actions are carried out in the name of public interest or safety (Perry & Roda 2016). Any possibility of accessing other people's devices and data is (or at least should be) carefully limited and circumscribed in law. We have also seen how hacking is a contested and often misunderstood topic: the media portrayal has boosted a negative sensationalisation of hackers' dominant subculture, which is in reality more nuanced and complex. Hacking, after all, is a skill that can be used with good or bad intentions.

Another key aspect that you should remember from this chapter is that even cybercrimes against devices, in most cases, are not confined to cyberspace but rather spill over into physical space, often serving other criminal goals. The most obvious examples probably come from the IoT and, especially, smart homes. Consider how hacked smart home devices are reportedly increasingly being used to target victims of domestic abuse, with thermostats, cameras, locks and lights being employed as tools to monitor or harass victims. As anticipated in the introduction to this book, a core question that will accompany us throughout the volume is whether and to what extent cybercrimes are 'separate' from traditional crimes or whether they provide an expansion of criminal possibilities. We are starting to see how, despite the peculiarities of crimes in cyberspace, it is often very difficult to separate the online and offline realms of our lives and consequently online and offline forms of victimisation.

- We have seen how hacking can arise from very diverse motivations. Sometimes, hackers use their abilities to stop or otherwise hinder heinous activities on the Web (such as child pornography or terrorist propaganda). Some commentators are very critical towards hackers' interventionism from both a moral and security perspective. According to Furnell (2009), for instance, 'there are other, law-abiding ways of handling sites that are found to be hosting illegal content, such as reporting them to internet service providers and the police. Even if hacking the sites was the only way they could be tackled, the task of taking them down ought to be left to someone with the legal authority to do it, rather than someone simply wanting to take a moral stand. After all, while cyber-vigilantism could have the desired result against one site, it is easy to imagine such uncoordinated and uncontrolled action disrupting a genuine investigation and preventing law enforcement from scoring a bigger hit against the wider problem.' To what extent do you agree with Furnell's view? Are there better ways you can think of in which hackers could support the policing of cyberspace?

- Sometimes, hackers might be targeting ventures that are not illegal but are not in line with their ethos. A notorious example is the 2015 Ashley Madison (a Canadian online dating service marketed to enable extramarital affairs) hack, reportedly motivated by the stupidity and greed of the company promoting it. In the hack, information about the site's users was stolen and partially released. The effects were painful: some online vigilantes looked for famous individuals in order to publicly humiliate them; extortionists started to target the victims of the hack, with one company even setting up a search engine to look for people via their email address. Significant distress was caused not only to the website's users but also to their families. In addition, as none of the accounts on the website needed email verification for a dating profile to be created, some profiles could have been there as pranks or mistyped emails (without the possibility of being deleted if not through paying a fee). Do you think it was ethically correct for hackers to expose (allegedly) deceitful partners in this way? Discuss.

- Workplace surveillance is becoming increasingly common, with some employers using a range of technologies to digitally monitor their staff, looking, for instance, at their Web-browsing patterns and emails but also social media posts. In recent years, many cases where employees were fired for posting 'controversial' material on their social media pages have reached the national and international news, with case law still under development and quite inconsistent, even within the same country. For the sake of example, let us focus on the cases of an adjunct professor in Idaho who was fired in 2018 from a religious university after posting a commemoration of the LGBTQ Pride Month on her personal Facebook page and of a British troll that in the same year was fired after joking about the death of a small baby on a 'dark humour' Facebook group; his boss was shown the posts by fellow members of the group, horrified by such cruel jokes. Many of us might be sympathetic towards the first employee, less so towards the second. Regardless of our moral stand, do you think these firings were justified? Is there a difference between the two cases because of the content of the posts? Would your answer be different depending on the fact that the private Facebook page and the Facebook group were private or 'open' to outsiders? Answer these questions as a starting point to reflecting on what expectations of privacy you have in cyberspace.

5 CRIMES AGAINST PERSONS

Introduction

This chapter focuses on a broad array of criminal and deviant acts specifically targeting other people. They are all characterised by the way in which they are noxious for an individual or a group in the sense that they (primarily) affect their psychological, emotional or even physical health. The first part of the chapter will focus on antagonistic online behaviours, namely hate speech and different types of online harassment. As denounced by Jane (2014, p. 542), 'hyperbolic vitriol [...] has become a *lingua franca* in many sectors of cyberspace'. When antagonistic online behaviour (or e-bile, to borrow Jane's words) inflicts suffering to others, it becomes problematic: psychological harm can affect the targeted individual, who might even end up withdrawing from cyberspace to escape from the persecutors. Furthermore, by normalising a hostile mode of discourse, hate speech and online harassment threaten the inclusivity and civility of both cyberspace and offline interactions. As we will see, the problem is more cultural than technological in this case, and technological solutions alone are unlikely to solve or even mitigate the problem. The final part of the chapter will move on to focus on a miscellaneous group of crimes that pivot around criminal sexual behaviours or sexually explicit material. Throughout this chapter, you should notice how there is a constant interplay between the offline and the online dimensions and between local specificities and transnational elements in the cases presented. This is the glocal aspect of cybercrimes, a pivotal feature that is too often neglected.

As academic research (and especially comparative research) on cybercrimes against persons is still in its infancy, the proposed categorisation presented in this chapter is necessarily tentative and does not aim to pigeonhole behaviours into a certain category while precluding them from fitting elsewhere. A certain degree of overlap exists between the different types of antagonistic online behaviours and the sex crimes identified: the hate and harassment-related behaviours presented in the following sections can all have a sexually based motivation or can occur in combination with the sex crimes that we will explore later on in this chapter. Think of gender or sexuality-based hate speech (targeting, for instance, a member of the LGBTQ community); of a victim trolled or bullied online by being addressed with misogynist and pejorative sexual language; of someone receiving unwanted sexual attention online, such as sexually explicit material; of rape threats or forms of simulated sexual violence ('virtual rape') used to intimidate a specific victim (Henry & Powell 2018; Choi et al. 2017). Therefore, depending on the analytical or practical needs, more fine-grained or coarse-grained classifications are certainly possible. However, the proposed categorisation is in line with most legal frameworks and allows us to have a common definitional outline, which is necessary to enhance consistency and improve analytical capacities (Table 5.1).

Hate speech

Hate is a powerful force in cyberspace. It allows both lone individuals and groups to exert power and social control in an abusive, threatening, systematic and targeted manner and to promote ideologies encouraging racial hatred, religious intolerance and other negative social views (Whine 2003; Awan 2014). This section is dedicated to hate speech, a phenomenon that pre-dates cyberspace but that – as we will see – has become extremely dangerous and harmful with the rise of the digital. Hidden behind a curtain of apparent anonymity and impunity, racists, misogynists and other fundamentalists use cyberspace to spread messages filled with intolerance and to normalise hateful rhetoric, claiming that their statements are simply opinions they have the right to express or are just cutting-edge jokes.

From a criminological perspective, exposure to cyber-hate has been successfully explained by integrating recent adaptations of routine activity (Cohen & Felson 1979) and social learning (Akers 1977) theories. Routine activity helps us to illustrate how an individual can enter into contact with dangerous people and situations: especially in the revised cyberlifestyle-routine activities perspective (Reyns et al. 2011), this approach explains how proximity to the virtual places where haters have been is the primary determinant of exposure (Costello et al. 2016; Räsänen et al. 2016). Social learning, on the other hand, clarifies why people tend to interact with those with similar ideas (flocking) and to mutually influence and reinforce each other's beliefs (feathering) (Costello et al. 2016). In cyberspace, this exposure can slip out of our control: in the words of Pariser (2011), the excessive personalisation of the algorithms managing our online searches (think of Facebook prioritising the updates of friends we interact the most with or Google refining its search results depending on our previous queries) creates 'filter bubbles', which channel us to increasingly narrow and polarised views.

Hate speech and hate crime are often confused in common parlance, but they are conceptually different (even if sometimes the distinction is very thin):

Table 5.1 Types of (cyber)crimes against persons

Antagonistic online behaviours	*Hate speech.* It is motivated by a bias or prejudice against a group and express hatred towards a collective. If a specific victim is targeted, he/she is targeted as a representative of a group. It can be a hate incident or a hate crime depending on the characteristics of the event.	
	Harassment. Behaviours that threaten, disturb or otherwise annoy one or more persons in a repetitive way.	*Stalking.* Targets an individual through a pattern of obsessive and unwanted behaviour. It can be fuelled by sexual obsession, revenge, retaliation, control or anger. *Bullying.* Targets an individual through a pattern of repeated, intentional and hostile behaviour. The bully aims to acquire prominence and respect towards the peers, reaffirming his/her social position in a social group. *Trolling.* The troll engages in conversations with the aim of upsetting people and/or to incite insulting or disruptive discussions online.
Sex crimes	*Grooming.* The preparatory stage to abuse, where confidence of the victim is gained through manipulation. *Child pornography.* The production, possession or distribution of paedopornographic material. *Forced prostitution.* Exploitative behaviours in the prostitution or pornographic business. *Image-based sexual abuse.* A wide spectrum of behaviours pivoting around the non-consensual release of pornographic material.	

hate speech does not always involve a hate crime, and hate crime does not always involve hate speech (for instance, it might rather involve a physical attack). Hate speech, however, is always a *hate incident*: it might not always rise to the level of a crime (for instance, it might not fully meet the legal requirements to be considered as such), but the hostile and harassing climate created might still severely harm a victim.

A crime becomes a *hate crime* when it is motivated by bias or prejudice against a person or a group. Even when an individual is targeted, that individual is targeted as a representative of a specific group, with certain defining characteristics (such as religion, sexual orientation, ethnicity and so on). In hate crimes, victims are targeted for what they represent. Consequently, the harm of hate crimes always goes beyond primary victimisation, as they damage the feeling of well-being and security not only of the victim but also of his/her wider community (Garland 2011).

Sometimes hate crimes are treated as a separate substantive offence, sometimes as a penalty enhancer (Gerstenfeld 2004). There is no internationally agreed definition of hate crime, with different definitions more or less narrow in focus. The 2008 European Framework Decision (2008/913/JHA), for instance, defines hate crime as 'all conducts publicly inciting to violence or hatred directed against a group of persons or a member of such a group defined by reference to race, colour, religion, descent or national or ethnic origin'. In the United Kingdom, there is no statutory definition of hate crime, but the police and Crown Prosecution Service have agreed on a common definition of hate incidents as acts motivated by hostility or prejudice based on disability, race, religion, transgender identity or sexual orientation. Some police forces, however, have adopted broader working definitions and might record as hate-motivated incidents based, for example, on age or on the belonging to a specific subculture, such as Goths. Different regulations vary to a great extent as to what kind of underlying conducts are covered as 'hate' crimes. The hate crime umbrella has been accused of covering only certain victims – such as, depending on the legal framework, those targeted because of race, religion, disability or sexuality. It has been suggested that the existence of hate crimes should rather be assessed at the micro-level, focusing on personal issues such as individual vulnerability rather than on belonging to a certain group (Garland 2011). Criticisms aside, as hate crimes are considered somehow worse than ordinary crimes, special legislation for them is generally welcomed: it can help to deter them and has the symbolic effect of stating that certain behaviours are unacceptable (Gerstenfeld 2004).

Hate speech is the most common form of hate incident (or hate crime, when it meets the criminal law threshold) in cyberspace. Hate speech is any form of communication that intends to intimidate, degrade or incite prejudicial action against an individual or a group of people on the basis of their specific attributes. Hate speech violates the rights (and even the security) of other people. It can cause loneliness, depression, anger and fear. It can also entail some long-term consequences such as the erosion of social trust and the transmission of extremist ideologies and can be a source of radicalisation (Costello et al. 2017). In other words, hate speech impugns its victims' standing as equal members of society (Waldron 2010).

In many Western countries, anti-Muslim hate provides a sadly topical example, fuelled by preconceptions on perceived terrorist and political threats. Beyond manifesting itself in the form of physical attacks, anti-Muslim hate occurs also in cyberspace. Consider, for instance, the analysis carried out by Hanzelka & Schmidt (2017) of Facebook pages of anti-Muslim movements in Germany and Czech Republic, which revealed the presence of verbal insults together with posts explicitly mentioning violent acts (killing, raping, etc.) or Miller's (2017) analysis of social media content from Australia's most prolific anti-Islam online groups. As explained in Awan and Zempi (2017), this type of hate has substantive consequences for the victims, who suffer from emotional stress, anxiety, depression and fear of online threats materialising in the physical world.

As for hate crimes, defining and regulating hate speech are tricky, as they can lead to clashes between fundamental (even if at times, at least apparently, antithetic) principles: the dignity of the victim and free speech. In liberal democracies, any kind of restriction on free speech has to remain an exception: strange though it may sound, there is generally a right of individuals to offend or disturb others, with a line usually drawn – depending on different jurisdictions – where such a right promotes hate based on certain characteristics of the victim. Consider, for instance, the 2003 Additional Protocol to the Convention on Cybercrime, concerning the criminalisation of acts of a racist and xenophobic nature committed through computer systems, which stresses 'the need to ensure a proper balance between freedom of expression and an effective fight against acts of a racist and xenophobic nature', being 'convinced that acts of a racist and xenophobic nature constitute a violation of human rights and a threat to the rule of law and democratic stability' (CoE 2003).

Nonetheless, balancing freedom of expression with the need to prohibit hate speech becomes fundamental in cyberspace, where hate speech can be particularly harmful as it easily becomes permanent, divorced from context and available to anyone (Leiter 2010). Furthermore, inflammatory, provocative or otherwise damaging material published online has the capacity to catalyse vitriol and hostility exponentially, reaching like-minded people all over the world and worsening opinion polarisation inside online echo chambers. Online platforms operators are reluctant to arbitrate and police the boundaries of acceptable content online, and in any case such delicate decisions – at the very heart of the political and democratic process – should not be left at the mercy of private, profit-driven companies.

Several countries have tried to regulate hate speech, using more or less restrictive definitions. Unfortunately, this lack of harmonisation is problematic, as gaps and loopholes in legal frameworks can easily be exploited by offenders, especially in a context – the borderless cyberspace – where unilateral efforts can be quite ineffective because of their limited jurisdictional reach. The fact is that each country's hate speech laws are rooted in the historical and constitutional tradition of that country, especially in relation to freedom of expression (Harris et al. 2009; Amnesty International 2018). In India, for instance, the need to prevent discord among various ethnic and religious communities led to the defence of freedom of speech and expression in the Constitution of the country and in several criminal and procedural laws, but restrictions can be imposed in the interest of the state, public order, decency or morality, defamation or incitement to an offence, among other things. When hate speech in the online world gave rise to violence in the physical realm, Indian states, in a few cases, limited citizens' access to the internet to resolve public order problems and to curb violence but they did so for what was arguably an unnecessarily long period of time (Arun & Nayak 2016). In Japan, where relationships with ethnic Korean residents are often tense, a Hate Speech Act was passed only in 2016 and, among its many criticisms, the act, which condemns unjustly discriminatory language as 'unforgivable', does not criminalise hate speech and sets no penalty.

With many international service providers based in the United States, the American approach is of great interest. It is deeply influenced by the First Amendment of the federal Constitution, which, it turns out, affords considerable protection to those professing online hate (Banks 2010). There is an underlying philosophical difference which reflects the extent of free speech protection among the United States and Europe: the American approach, which values very highly the individual right to self-expression, is much more permissive, with hate speech limited only when inciting imminent violence. For most European countries, democratic inclusiveness is considered a valid reason to limit hate speech, which is not protected as a valuable public discourse, to the point that hate speech 'censorship' has been extended to religious radicalism in recent years (Perry & Roda 2016). This contrasting view is at the base of many past and ongoing debates on where to draw the line on hate speech. Consider, for example, the landmark case from the early 2000s, *La Ligue Contre La Racisme et L'Antisemitisme (LICRA) and Union Des Etudiants Juifs De France (UEJF) v. Yahoo! Inc. and Yahoo! France*. In this case, two French student organisations sought to prosecute Yahoo! because it displayed Nazi memorabilia on its auction website, which is contrary to French law. The French court ruled that Yahoo! was liable and should try to eliminate French citizens' access to the sale of Nazi merchandise. However, French courts could not expand their reach into another jurisdiction: an American court ruled that Yahoo! is a Delaware corporation with its principal place of business in California and therefore American law applies. In the United States, selling Nazi memorabilia online, because of the commitment to free speech, is odious but nonetheless still protected by the First Amendment (Banks 2010).

Some contemporary American scholars, however, believe that – with sufficient safeguards – forbidding hate speech may not necessarily result in a loss of democratic legitimacy or censorship, at least as long as prohibitions on hate speech extend only to issues that are (or should be!) settled (such as race) rather than issues that are currently controversial, in order to prevent hate speech regulation from foreclosing democratic debate (Waldron 2010): considering how noxious harm from speech in cyberspace can be, the United States might have to rethink the legal protection that cyber-speech has when it seriously damages the dignity of a victim (Leiter 2010). The debate remains open.

Given the difficulties in framing and harmonising the legal frameworks, alternative mechanisms for countering cyber-hate are crucial. First, some commentators suggest private remedies, such as changing the existing legislation to make intermediaries (for instance, service providers) somehow responsible (Leiter 2010) or at least demanding that internet service providers have a more active role in regulating online content with ad hoc policies (Pavan 2017). Many social media providers already have specific mechanisms in place to counter hate speech. For instance, Twitter has a policy prohibiting 'the promotion of hate content, sensitive topics, and violence globally', which includes, among other things, 'hate speech or advocacy against an individual, organisation or protected group based on race, ethnicity, national origin, colour, religion, disability, age, sex, sexual orientation, gender identity, veteran status or other protected status' (Twitter 2017). Facebook considers hate speech any 'content that attacks people based on their actual or perceived race, ethnicity, national origin, religion, sex, gender or gender identity, sexual orientation, disability or disease' and, as such, 'is not allowed'. Facebook does, however, 'allow clear attempts at humour or satire that might otherwise be considered a possible threat or attack. This includes content that many people may find to be in bad taste (example: jokes, stand-up comedy, popular song lyrics, etc.)' (Facebook 2017). In May 2016, the European Commission together with Facebook, Twitter, YouTube and Microsoft unveiled a code of conduct that includes a series of commitments to combat the spread of illegal hate speech online in Europe, spurred by concerns that hate speech might fuel terrorism and by the rise of intolerant speech against refugees in Europe. The IT companies committed to further their efforts to tackle hate speech on their platforms by, for instance, continuing the development of internal procedures and staff training to guarantee that the majority of valid notifications for removal of illegal hate speech are reviewed in less than 24 hours. However, these companies are still harshly criticised for not doing enough to halt hate speech and extremism: especially in the wake of terrorist attacks, tech companies have been accused of missing their chances to regulate terror-related content online and to improve their take-down practices. The European Commission presented a new set of guidelines in September 2017, and the possibility of new measures to complement the existing regulatory framework on the liability of online intermediaries has also been anticipated. It will be of foremost importance to see how the delicate equilibria between free speech and the necessity to counter online content and in the allocation of responsibilities between public and private entities develop, as this will have critical consequences for the future of cyberspace.

Second, technological innovations can be used to better tackle hate speech and restrict its harms. The internet itself can, in fact, be proactively used to assist victims in reporting incidents to the police and in proving them with a community of support. Among the many examples worldwide, in India social media labs have been launched to monitor hate speech online and a WhatsApp helpline has been developed by local police forces to enable victims to report hate messages (Arun & Nayak 2016). The use of filtering software (such as firewalls) to regulate children's exposure to hate content is not new. More recently, there has been increasing attention to the potential of automatisation in detecting hate speech. The major problem to be solved is that traditional filtering (based, for instance, on keywords) does not work well with hate speech, as what can be considered as such is influenced by the cultural and discourse contexts. For years, human right groups have been warning Facebook that its platform was being used in Myanmar to promote hate against the Rohingya minority. The software for the automatic recognition of hate expression was failing as it could not understand the nuances of certain content; Burmese reviewers were needed and Facebook reporting tools had to be translated into Burmese. Only in 2018 did the company translate the reporting tools and pledge to hire more local reviewers. Natural language processing (that is, a field at the intersection of computer science, computational linguistics and artificial intelligence, dealing with the ability of a computer program to understand human speech as it is spoken) provides a promising approach to tackling this problem (Schmidt & Wiegand 2017), but the human factor is likely to remain irreplaceable.

Finally, individual responses might be insufficient to stem online hate but can still have an important role in promoting a culture of intolerance towards online incivilities and in alerting relevant authorities when they witness hate crimes or incidents (Banks 2010). Online information raising awareness and promoting 'good' content is of pivotal importance to address the cultural dimension of the problem.

Box 5.1 Problematic subcultures in cyberspace: hate sites and self-harm sites

Cyberspace has provided a fertile place for a number of problematic subcultures to flourish, as it has facilitated the creation of collective identities and cohesive movements, both locally and globally. The internet allows hate movements (and other deviant subcultures) to create an alternative channel to spread their word to the world in a community of the like-minded, reinforce the false beliefs of some and reach impressionable individuals (Perry & Olsson 2009; Yar 2019).

Hate sites are a particularly nasty manifestation of this trend. Certain hate groups prospered offline – think of the Ku Klux Klan or the skinheads – and cyberspace gave them new lifeblood. If, offline, hate groups had to recruit members by word of mouth or through flyers, online they can promote ideologies encouraging racial hatred, religious intolerance and other negative views almost unchallenged. Hate speech and cyber-harassment often occur in dispersed and uncoordinated ways, but they can also be channelled and organised into specific cyber-hotspots for haters – that is, websites or social media that are devoted in whole or in part to demeaning, harassing and humiliating individuals, groups or causes opposed by the offenders. Key cyberspace features and behavioural patterns such as anonymity, group polarisation and information cascade (a situation where each person makes a choice based on the observations or choices of others) are prime factors in the success of these sites, which end up functioning as echo chambers and ideological bubbles for distorted views of reality (Citron 2014).

Furthermore, the internet allows haters to extend internationally and hence, through hate sites, it facilitates global racist/misogynist/anti-something subcultures. For instance, one of the anti-Muslim online groups analysed by Hanzelka and Schmidt (2017), the German Pegida (*Patriotische Europäer gegen die Islamisierung des Abendlandes*), emerged in Dresden, gathered around a Facebook group and soon spread to other German cities and now there are Pegida offshoots in many other countries. The incel (involuntarily celibate) movement (whose members blame women for their sexual frustration) that inspired the deadly Toronto attack in 2018 is nothing other than a specific subculture of people gathering in various internet forums (subreddits, 4chan and dedicated websites). Unfortunately, hate sites are in large part beyond the reach of regulation in many countries, so that it is currently extremely difficult to tackle hate sites through judicial means.

Self-harm sites are a completely different phenomenon – as they are dedicated to intentionally injuring or hurting oneself – but should still receive attention in this context as a diverse manifestation of how cyberspace has allowed peculiar subcultures to emerge and flourish: while in the physical world people involved in solitary forms of troubling behaviour (generally signs of major emotional distress, such as self-injuring or suicidal tendencies) were isolated, now they have the opportunity to access global-scale virtual communities populated by like-others, where they can find advice and company (Adler & Adler 2006; Wykes 2009; Hayes et al. 2016). Websites, blogs and other social media dedicated to issues such as 'cutting', 'pro-ana' (pro-anorexia) or 'pro-suicide' are dangerously appealing for people who are depressed or in pain and especially for young people. Some of these sites can provide support and even discourage problematic behaviours but others can reinforce dangerous tendencies, with significant consequences for participants (Adler & Adler 2006; Smithson et al. 2011).

The harms are evident even if a crime might not always be present. Sometimes, however, there is one: for instance, the administrator of a pro-suicide social media group with 32 under-age members was arrested in Moscow in June 2017. And even when a crime is not present, if we look at self-harm sites through criminological lenses we should reflect on issues of responsibility, both moral and legal: when/to what extent should a website administrator or a social media platform be held responsible? How far could external control on self-harm sites go not to interfere with issues of personal liberties? And what could be done, from both social and technical points of view, to prevent and mitigate self-harm sites and their impact? After a British teenager with a self-harm Tumblr blog committed suicide in 2012, the microblogging platform changed its policy: if a user now searches for specific terms such as 'suicide', Tumblr brings up a public service announcement page directing the user towards counselling and prevention resources (Tumblr 2017). In 2017, QQ (a major Chinese instant messaging and microblogging platform) closed down a dozen self-harm networks groups in its portal and blocked search results for suspicious keyword searches. Do you think these solutions are a good compromise between harm prevention and freedom of expression?

Harassment

Harassment is an umbrella term covering a wide range of criminal and deviant behaviours that threaten, disturb, offend or otherwise annoy one or more persons in a repetitive way. Harassment is in the eye of the beholder: in order for an act to be considered harassing, a reasonable person, in possession of the same information, would think it causes emotional distress to another reasonable person (Bocij & McFarlane 2003). Of course, there can be overlap with hate speech, as offensive speech can cause emotional distress. However, hate speech might occur without the need for it to be addressed to a specific victim: think, for instance, of anti-Semitic statements on a hate site. They encourage religious intolerance and hatred, but they might be written to 'recruit' like-minded people rather than to offend a Jewish person. This section will focus on three major types of online harassment: (cyber) stalking, (cyber)bullying and trolling. While online hate speech expresses hatred towards a collective, cyberstalking or cyberbullying targets an individual in isolation. Trolling, on the other hand, might point at a collective but – as you will see – with a very different aim.

What psychologists call 'online disinhibition effect' (Suler 2004) – that is, the lack of restraint one feels in online communications – has a powerful explicatory power to make sense of antagonistic online behaviours and especially harassment. According to Suler, even if personality variables influence the extent of this disinhibition, there are six common factors that create this effect in cyberspace: dissociative anonymity (when people have the opportunity to separate their online and offline identities, they feel less vulnerable in their online actions); invisibility (which gives people the courage to do things that they otherwise would not do); asynchronicity (as people do not have to interact in real time in cyberspace, they do not have to cope with someone's immediate reaction); solipsistic introjection (the people we communicate with online are characters partly shaped by our own system of expectations and needs); dissociative imagination (some people see the online characters they interact with as existing in a different space, separate from the demands and responsibilities of the real world); and minimisation of status and authority (appearances of authority are minimised online, and people are more willing to misbehave).

From a criminological perspective, integration of self-control (Gottfredson & Hirschi 1990) and social learning (Akers 1977) theories are proving quite effective in explaining the likelihood of forms of online harassment. By focusing in particular on cases of juvenile (cyber)stalking and online sexual harassment, researchers suggest that there is a relationship between low levels of self-control and the probability of engaging in forms of online harassment. Furthermore, individuals who associate with other deviant peers are more likely to commit online deviant behaviours themselves, as they learn to perceive those behaviours as non-severe (Marcum et al. 2014; Choi et al. 2017; Marcum et al. 2017).

Stalking

In the absence of an internationally agreed definition, stalking can be broadly defined as a pattern of obsessive (and generally unwanted) behaviour by one or more persons, resulting in the target experiencing a sense of threat. Stalking can cause severe effects to the victim, impacting the individual's affective and cognitive health (such as anxiety, depression, fear and attributions of self-blame), social health (such as increased alienation and isolation, decreased trust, additional security measures and absenteeism from work) and even physical health (physical and sexual violence) (Spitzberg & Cupach 2007). Cyberstalking is an interpersonal crime that challenges the idea that physical proximity is a prerequisite for harm to occur (Roberts 2008): cyberspace allows offenders to stalk their victims from a distance, but the presence of fear is real.

Spence-Diehl (2003) distinguished among cyberstalking restricted to cyberspace; cyberstalking that begins in cyberspace but becomes offline stalking; and cyberstalking as one method of (offline) stalking. However, as cyberspace becomes ubiquitous in our lives, the distinction between offline and online stalking becomes increasingly blurred, with stalkers using elements of both. Think of a stalker following you on social media to learn your daily patterns and routines; if you post a picture taken from your smartphone without having disabled the automatic geotagging feature in the metadata, your stalker might be able to backtrack where you are even if you have not tagged or shared your location voluntarily. Or, considering the symbiotic relationship most of us have with our smartphones, think of someone installing a cell phone spying app on your mobile, operating it in a stealth mode and sending information, among other things, on the smartphone location. Worryingly, it is very easy to find these products sold and reviewed online with a simple Google search; advertised as products to check on deceitful partners and secretive teens and even to monitor employees, these apps clearly have severe implications for privacy rights, and their legitimacy is, to say the least, questionable in most jurisdictions. Yet, these major issues are not making such products less popular or less easy to download.

As explained by Pittaro (2007), the lack of an agreed definition of stalking creates ambiguities around this phenomenon, so that cyberstalking behaviours are often confused with other types of online predatory behaviours, such as online grooming (see later in this chapter) or erotomania – that is, the delusional belief that a certain person is in love with the affected individual, despite all evidence pointing in another direction. However, not all stalking is motivated by sexual obsession, as it might rather be fuelled by revenge, retaliation, power, control or even anger, which might have been precipitated by a victim's action or inaction (Pittaro 2007; Robert 2008). Cyberstalking behaviour may include, but is not limited to, the transmission of threats and false accusations, hacking, identity theft, data breaches, computer monitoring and spamming (Ogilvie 2000; Bocij & McFarlane 2003; Pittaro 2007; Reyns 2010). Cyberstalking is sometimes described as 'cyber dating abuse' when the focus is on technological invasive behaviours in romantic relationships (Marcum et al. 2017). Anyone can become a victim of cyberstalking but certain demographics (such as women and juveniles) are particularly vulnerable (Pittaro 2007).

Bocij & McFarlane (2003) categorised cyberstalkers into four different types, summarised here:

- vindictive stalkers, who are particularly malicious and use spiteful tactics;

- composed stalkers, who cause constant distress to the victim by using a variety of threatening techniques but in a calm and poised manner;

- intimate stalkers, who establish a relationship with the target, moved by obsession;

- collective stalkers, when two or more individuals target the same victim.

It can be very difficult to identify and prosecute stalkers and even more so when they operate online. First of all, stalking can have different degrees of 'intrusiveness' and it can quickly adapt to new forms of intrusion made possible by technological innovation. For legislation to be effective, it should include all experiences and degrees of victimisation and take into consideration how different individuals might differently experience disquieting intrusions and threats depending, for instance, on the gender, age, the previous relationship with the stalker and any country-specific cultural factors (Pereira & Matos 2015; Roberts et al. 2016); of course, this is impossible. Second, many countries do not criminalise stalking. Even when they do so, the 'threat' element can be difficult to prove and the lack of harmonisation between legal frameworks makes it difficult to intervene if, for instance, the stalker and the victim live in different countries (Roberts 2008). The *Council of Europe Convention on preventing and combating violence against women and domestic violence* ('Istanbul Convention'), which entered into force in 2014, criminalises stalking but only within the scope of the Convention. Many countries criminalise stalking under different names (criminal harassment, criminal menace, etc.) or rather punish perpetrators of 'proxy' offences characterised by threatening or persecuting behaviours such as domestic violence, threat and coercion (Pereira & Matos 2015; Ferreira et al. 2018).

Bullying

Cyberbullying can be defined as a form of online harassment where the offender perpetrates repeated, intentional and hostile behaviour against the victim(s) (Pereira & Matos 2015; Olweus & Limber 2018; Smith et al. 2018). It is generally considered the ICT extension of bullying: similar to many of the criminal and deviant behaviours encountered in this chapter, cyberbullying is not completely different from its online counterpart. Both bullying and cyberbullying are generally associated with young age, but they can be experienced at any age. The bully and the victim often belong to the same social context; for instance, they are in the same school or they hang around the same (physical or virtual) social communities. There is generally an imbalance of social power between the bully and the victim: through threat and coercion, the bully aims to acquire prominence and respect from their peers, reaffirming his/her social position in the group (Pereira & Matos 2015; Olweus & Limber 2018). However, this is not always the case: think of cases of celebrities – such as Ed Sheeran in 2017 and Millie Bobby Brown in 2018 – who left Twitter after receiving piles of negative and abusive comments.

Given how much life in cyberspace and offline are intertwined, the distinction between bullying and cyberbullying is becoming increasingly blurred. However, cyberbullying has some specific characteristics. What makes it distinct is that cyberbullying can be more intense and therefore more harmful, as cyberspace characteristics amplify victims' vulnerabilities and offenders' reach. As detailed by Patchin & Hinduja (2016), when operating online the bully can remain virtually anonymous, which might embolden bullies to effectuate their antagonistic agenda as it might be 'easier' to write nasty comments than to express them vocally. Apps such as Sarahah (which means 'frankness' in Arabic) have been developed with the specific aim of delivering 'constructive criticism': everyone gets a webpage on which others can write anonymous messages to them. The constructive part, however, is lost on most people and any sort of soul-crushing abusive messages can be directed at users (Sarahah was removed from most app stores in early 2018 after a viral petition on Change.org set up by the mum of an Australian teenager, appalled by the messages that her daughter was receiving). Furthermore, adult supervision is more difficult online, as certain messages might be visible only to the sender and the recipient (think of a picture or a message sent via Snapchat, which is available only for a short period of time before becoming inaccessible), and the constant presence of smartphones makes a target perpetually victimisable, without a safe place.

The harm suffered by the victim can be emotional, psychological and even physical, as the bullying behaviour might continue offline or the victim might be led to depression, self-harm and even suicide.

Social wounds (think of humiliation and embarrassment in a public setting) might also occur (García-Maldonado et al. 2011; Di Lorenzo 2012; Patchin & Hinduja 2016). It might be argued that cyberbullying can be escaped simply by ignoring or deleting the offensive messages, but this view overlooks the ubiquitous nature of ICTs and the increasing role of the virtual self to a youth's identity and self-esteem (Patchin & Hinduja 2016). In addition, cyberbullying is at times dismissed as a 'rite of passage' during one's formative years, one that at least (when limited to cyberspace) does not physically harm anyone. Dismissing the importance of cyberbullying, however, is problematic, as it can severely harm the victim and even signal a path of deviancy online (Patchin & Hinduja 2016).

Unfortunately, in the absence of harmonised legislation and even academic consensus, much of the research on cyberbullying adopts more or less strict working definitions and presents mixed findings. In addition, most research so far, even with notable exceptions (Smith et al. 2018 among others), has been carried out in Western countries, which does not allow the appreciation of cultural differences in what is a truly worldwide phenomenon. These limitations make it complicated to provide sufficient clarity to prevent and tackle cyberbullying (Tokunaga 2010; Olweus & Limber 2018). Computer science, also in the case of cyberbullying, has tried to build systems (for both computers and smartphones) to automatically detect cyberbullying within the large volume of streaming text (Nahar et al. 2014; Bigelow et al. 2016; Vishwamitra et al. 2017). However, for the system to be effective, it should stop the bullying message before it reaches the target – but as you can imagine, this creates several problems in terms of false positives and, let us not forget, of technology ethics.

Before we conclude, it is worth noting that, besides 'traditional' cases of (cyber)bullying, there are other forms of cyber-facilitated hostile behaviour (that might be seen as specific subcategories of bullying, as they often target a specific individual) that clearly exemplify the blurring divide between online and offline arenas. Consider, for instance, cases of swatting – that is, fake reports to the police hotlines to implicate innocent people (often, rival online players) in serious crimes (Philpot 2017). Swatting has led armed police forces to cause severe physical harm, as in the case of a man who in 2017 called a terrorism hotline in Maryland, causing special forces to raid the home of an innocent 20-year-old gamer and to shoot him with rubber bullets, breaking bones in his face and bruising his lungs.

Trolling

In the antagonistic online behaviours examined so far, the epicentre is the victim, who is specifically targeted and harassed for individual characteristics. In cyberbullying, for example, the offensive message is a way to hurt the feelings of a specific victim. On the other hand, with trolling, the epicentre is the harasser him/herself, who shifts the attention in an online setting onto him/herself and finds amusement in seeing the reactions of other people.

Trolling is a sort of umbrella term encompassing several types of behaviours, generally occurring within an online community, having in common the will to upset people online, making comments or engaging in activities to purposely annoy, disrupt or enrage others (Mantilla 2015). It is 'recreational nastiness' (Jane 2014). So much for netiquette, trolling can range from idiotic pranks (maybe innocent in the troll's view but probably not in the eye of the beholder) to posting vile messages on Facebook memorial pages ('RIP trolling'); from offensive and intolerant posts designed to derail a political discussion into a fruitless argument, to vitriolic statements with the sole intent to rile up total strangers. Flaming, for instance, is a particularly hostile form of trolling, where trolls incite insulting and emotional discussions online, often using profanity and *ad hominem* insults. Trolling, therefore, is a term that can have multiple (and often inconsistent) meanings, depending on the context in which the word is used, the aim of the troll and how internet users themselves constantly mobilise the meaning of the term (Coles & West 2016). Even if to a different extent, trolling can be harmful too: not only can it cause severe emotional and psychological distress (think, again, of cases of RIP trolling), but it can also deteriorate inclusiveness in cyberspace, drawing out from online conversations the voices of those who feel more vulnerable, such as minorities. At times, the term 'trolling' is used to describe certain provocative online satire but given that this connotation does not denote crime or deviancy, it will not be covered in this section.

It is unclear whether the etymology of 'trolling' derives from the fishing technique in which a baited line is dragged to catch fish or from the creature from Scandinavian folklore (Mantilla 2015). Either way, trolling developed as a sort of online subculture (the 'trollosphere'), with trolls even meeting in dedicated forums to brag about their trolling successes or gathering to harass victims for their amusement, targeting victims after others have done so (Citron 2014; Mantilla 2015). The common advice to counter trolling is 'don't feed the troll'. Although at first glance this logic seems reasonable, it should be challenged. As Phillips (2013) explains, first, trolls are not always great white sharks reacting to chum (that is, the more you throw, the more the sharks are excited and the more likely it is that other sharks will arrive. But if you stop throwing chum, the shark will lose interest). Second, the 'don't feed the troll' type of advice places all possible blame on the target (in a sort of victim-blaming rhetoric, 'don't *get* trolled!') and frames the narrative about aggressive online behaviour as if it were the aggressor's game with the aggressor's rules. Furthermore, there is good evidence that it does not always work (Phillips 2013, 2015; Jane 2017b) and in any case it does not prevent the victim(s) from reading the outrageous or abusive messages in the first place. Depending on the specific situation (the one-size-fits-all policy proves unsuccessful with online harassment), other target-empowering mechanisms might be more effective, such as unceremoniously deleting the troll's comments, naming-and-shaming the troll or other rhetorical moves to take active steps against them (Phillips 2013).

Some authors suggest distinguishing gendertrolling as a specific subcategory of online harassment: as explained in Mantilla (2015), in fact, online harassment targeting women follows a different pattern of abusive and threatening behaviours. Not only are women disproportionately targeted (70 percent of reported online harassment targets women), but when harassment is gender-based the insults have specific characteristics: they tend to branch out and often involve multiple online sites and social media, often include rape and death threats (and might involve 'in real life' interactions, adding credibility to the threat), can involve more attackers insulting in a concerted way, occur at high levels of intensity and frequency and can go on for months or even years. Insults are generally sexualised and meant to demean women as sexual objects (Nussbaum 2010; Mantilla 2015). Female activists, bloggers, politicians, journalists and academics among other categories have often been victimised online, which impacts their professional activities. Among the countless examples, some notorious ones you might remember: Bangladeshi activist and blogger Shammi Haque received death and rape threats from an Islamic extremist group for her secular views and had to move to Germany where she was granted asylum; Indian television veteran Barkha Dutt, Turkish journalist Amberin Zaman, Australian documentarist Tracey Spicer and feminist campaigner Caroline Criado-Perez (who campaigned to make Jane Austen the new face of the GBP-10 note) received rape and death threats from Twitter users in response to their views. Historian Mary Beard faced a landslide of aggressive insults on social media after defending as historically accurate a BBC video that featured a high-ranking black Roman soldier. Other famous cases of women attacked with misogynistic insults and death threats are connected to the gaming world: for instance, the harassment of video game developers Brianna Wu and Zoe Quinn and of Anita Sarkeesian, a feminist critic of the video game industry. More than 'trolling', these gender-based attacks seem to share characteristics of both bullying (attacking of a specific victim) and hate speech (as the specific victim is targeted *as a woman*, even if gender is generally not a category protected in hate crimes). Regardless of how we want to label these types of abuse behaviours – 'gendered cyberhate', as Jane (2017a) calls it, might be more accurate – it is important to recognise the peculiarities of online violence against women and girls, as the abuse-gender-cyber nexus spans several types of crimes against the person (hate crimes, harassment and sex crimes).

Sex crimes

New technology can be used to facilitate sex-related crimes both in cyberspace and face-to-face in the physical world. In this section, we will focus on some of the more serious forms of sex crimes that are directly facilitated by cyberspace: grooming, child pornography, forced prostitution and non-consensual release of pornographic material and image-based sexual abuse. We have already encountered problems of pigeonholing behaviours into boxes and definitions for analytical purposes. If possible, this challenge becomes particularly visible when we discuss sex crimes: sexual behaviours (both online and offline) can be arrayed along a spectrum from legal and accepted, to legal but deviant, to illegal and accepted or deviant (Holt et al. 2015). The position on the spectrum depends on the specific nature of the behaviour and the law and social mores of a specific group or a specific country, as there is not a fixed threshold to consider something obscene or immoral.

As a consequence, considering something criminal or deviant in cyberspace is heavily context-dependent. For instance, pornography per se (and therefore online pornography) is illegal and restricted in certain countries (such as Kuwait, Botswana and Afghanistan). In other countries (such as Mauritania, Sudan and Saudi Arabia), some forms of sexual behaviours that can be found in online pornography (for instance, same-sex intercourse) and that are completely accepted in other parts of the world can be criminalised or believed to be deviant. Considering the intricacies of legal and moral differences among countries on the topic, this chapter will focus only on those cybercrimes that are considered as such in liberal legal frameworks and that do not harm some abstract concept of 'morale' but rather harm the psychological, emotional and even physical safety of a specific victim. Similarly, we will not focus on the much-debated issues of the availability of sexually explicit material online, how this is problematic for the young users and whether, how and to what extent it should be somehow restricted (Wall 2007). Lastly, we will not enter into details of the trend of teenagers using ICTs, such as their smartphones and webcams, to carry out their own online pornography business or to enter the (underage) prostitution world. Still, it is worth keeping in mind that these phenomena are complicating the cultural narratives about teens as (always) victims of predatory adults, opening up a new set of complex socio-legal relationships enabled by new technologies and their ubiquity (Soderlund 2008).

Grooming

Both in the physical world and in cyberspace, grooming is defined as a pre-paratory stage to abuse (generally, sexual abuse), where the confidence of the victim is gained through his or her manipulation (Branca et al. 2016). The accessibility of victims is a key factor for grooming (Whittle et al. 2013): offline, it is common for offenders to abuse family members or those other-wise close to them via personal acquaintances; in cyberspace, it is very easy for sexual offenders to approach a wider pool of potential victims and to do so with relative anonymity.

You will encounter this term in relation to child pornography and online forced prostitution later in this chapter. Grooming is, in fact, a fundamental component in these crimes. However, because of the specificities of online grooming, it deserves a dedicated section. First, besides being precursory to serious harms (including physical harms), online grooming – already on its own – can cause severe emotional and psychological damage. Second, some countries – such as Australia, the Netherlands, the United States, the United Kingdom and Malaysia – have specifically criminalised online grooming (even if to a different extent and sometimes among criticism) and other countries might soon follow. In the United Kingdom, for instance, a new offence of sexual communication with a child, which anticipates the crimi-nal law protection in order to give officers the possibility to intervene before physical abuse can take place, was introduced in 2017: now, it is a crime to arrange a meeting with a child under the age of 16 with the intent of sexually abusing that child, meaning that a crime occurs even if the meeting does not take place. In Malaysia, a bill in Summer 2017 criminalised child grooming and boosted extraterritorial jurisdiction to Malaysian children from local and foreign predators and to Malaysians liable to prosecution for commit-ting similar offenses abroad; however, the proposal to also criminalise child marriage was outvoted, leaving child protection without an important weapon.

Throughout the grooming process, the victim's inhibitions are increas-ingly lowered. O'Connell (2003) identifies several stages of (child) groom-ing. Even if it should be kept in mind that they are not all necessary for grooming to take place, they offer a valid conceptual framework:

- friendship-forming stage, when the offender gets to know the victim;

- relationship-forming stage, when the offender engages with the victim on a more personal level by, for instance, discussing school and home life and creating the illusion of being his or her best friend;

- exclusivity stage, when the interaction moves to a new level, with the offender introducing ideas of trust and mutuality in the relationship with the victim, a relationship from which others are excluded;

- sexual stage, when the conversation moves towards sexualised elements.

The intensity and intimacy of the questions, of course, can vary depending on the specific circumstances of the grooming. It is generally in this final stage that the abuse begins, and this stage of the conversation can be characterised by the exchange or distribution of erotic and pornographic material or by requests that the victim send pornographic photos or videos or perform sexual acts in real-time streaming. However, it is worth remembering that not all grooming has a sexual stage as part of it. A sad but emblematic case is the one of Breck Bednar, a 14-year-old online gamer, who was groomed online and murdered in England in 2014 by the controlling ring-master of a gaming group. The fact that the victim (a boy, who was discussing gaming and tech with the offenders rather than sex) was not the 'typical' victim probably led him to ignore alarm bells about the severity of the situation before it degenerated. In Chapter 8 of this book, we will also encounter cases where grooming is used as a preparatory stage to very different criminal activities, such as terrorism recruitment.

Grooming generally involves one or more of the following: bribery, gifts, money, flattery, sexualised games and threats (Whittle et al. 2013; Black et al. 2015; de Dantisteban & Gámez-Guadix 2017). Extortion can also play an important role: victims can be blackmailed ('sextortion') to send money, or to send further pornographic material, in order to prevent sexually explicit images or videos from being made public (Kopecký 2016). Grooming (including the sexual stage) could be limited to cyberspace or it might also involve telephonic or offline meetings. Regarding offline meeting, Shannon (2008), in his analysis of Swedish cases, identifies three approaches often used by the perpetrators to persuade young victims to meet offline: the victim had been promised work (for instance, as a model), had been offered payment for sexual services, or is convinced that there is a friendship or romantic relationship with the perpetrator.

As with sexual abuse in general, there is a severe problem of underreporting with grooming: not only do a very few victims report sexual abuse (both online and offline), but victims of online grooming might not even understand that they are being abused (Martellozzo 2017). Grooming is difficult to prevent and most existing prevention messages ('do not talk to strangers') are criticised because, by demonising conversations with strangers online, they fail to acknowledge that most young people – or, generally, many people – in these years meet, converse and find friendships and romance online, even if they have not met face-to-face. Most of these cyber-formed relationships are genuine and can be beneficial (Wolak et al. 2004; Phippen 2017).

Grooming is also difficult to address because it is a multifaceted phenomenon: as both victims and offenders are not from homogeneous groups, grooming practices vary considerably in style, duration and intensity. Offenders, for instance, can be driven by the willingness to meet their victim in person or be satisfied with the fantasy provided by the grooming itself. Grooming can last minutes, days, weeks or even months, and it is not always possible to draw a precise line as to when it starts and when it ends.

A groomer might be targeting and abusing over time one or a limited number of victims or rather many victims at the same time, each involving a single instance of sexual exploitation (O'Connell 2003; Whittle et al. 2013; Winters 2017).

In both academic research and media reporting, attention is generally dedicated to young victims (often girls) lured into sexual abuse and exploitation, but victims might also be males or be older. Some young people, however, have characteristics that make them particularly likely to form online relationships, which makes them more vulnerable to victimisation: this is the case, for instance, when individuals have had high levels of conflict or low levels of communication with parents (Wolak et al. 2004). When victims are groomed online, their social media are powerful tools for offenders to easily get information on them and to identify the potential victims by looking not only at their pictures for their physical aspect but also for their psychological vulnerabilities as they emerge from their online profiles. Especially in cases of sex trafficking and forced prostitution, loverboys – young men luring girls into sexual abuse – and double-role girls – former victims that have climbed up the hierarchy in the criminal network, often as a survival strategy – often play a pivotal role in the grooming of young victims: as research carried out in the Netherlands shows, they look for girls with specific online profiles, in disadvantaged situations, around 17 years old, and isolate them from family and friends. The sexual abuse often starts when they are 18 years and one day old, so that it is more difficult to prove the element of exploitation given that the victims are no longer underage (Lavorgna 2014b).

Child pornography

Child pornography is a sensitive and appalling topic, which originated well before the internet era. Cyberspace, however, entailed major changes to this phenomenon: not only does it facilitate the encounter between a potential victim and offenders as well as distribution of paedopornographic material, but it also plays an important psychological role in the development and propagation of child pornography. For instance, the internet makes it easier for individuals who otherwise may never have actively sought offline child pornography to become casual users (Quayle & Taylor 2003; Wortley & Smallbone 2012).

Before discussing child pornography online, we need to make a terminological distinction. In popular use, the word paedophilia is often used to describe child sexual abuse. However, this could lead to inaccuracies and confusion. Paedophilia has been generally acknowledged as a psychiatric disorder (specifically a paraphilia, even if there is open debate among psychiatrists whether it should rather be considered a sexual orientation) in which an adult or an older adolescent has sexual attraction (exclusive or primary) for prepubescent children (while we have ephebophilia in the case of attraction towards pubescent or post-pubescent children). Not all paedophiles are sex offenders, as some limit their attraction to their fantasies; on the other hand, a child predator might not be a paedophile if he or she does not have an exclusive or primary sexual interest in children. Some paedophiles are active in what they call love-child movements: a famous case is the one of Frits Bernard, a Dutch clinical psychologist, sexologist and paedophile activist who was pivotal in the formation of the movement in the Netherlands. Of course, there is often an overlap between paedophiles and child predators' subcultures (Holt et al. 2010, 2015). Cyberspace has given both subcultures the chance to thrive and 'organise' better and to interact more easily. Jenkins' analysis (2001) shows clearly the diversity of individuals satelliting around relevant cyber-hotspots, who can be very diverse in terms of both the seriousness and the extent of their acts: some recognise their behaviour as deviant and others normalise it; some debate what far is too far and others just try to improve their access to paedopornographic material; some try to fulfil virtual fantasies and others admit actual abuse. Some of these individuals might pose an immediate risk to a potential victim in the offline world as well; some of them are final users of material created elsewhere, whereas others are directly involved in rapes (Jenkins 2001; Krone 2004). Although most of the offenders are men, this is not always the case: women or even other children in their early teens can be the abusers or end users (Quayle & Taylor 2003; Martellozzo 2012).

As concerns the specificities of child pornography in cyberspace, the offences might relate to the production, possession or distribution of paedopornographic material. Directly, cyberspace can allow the production of paedopornographic material (for instance, via webcams). In the 2014 Operation Endeavour, for instance, a criminal network that facilitated the live streaming of on-demand child sexual abuse in the Philippines was dismantled after a joint investigation by the United Kingdom, the United States and Australia, which resulted in 29 international arrests. Indirectly, the internet can facilitate such production through child grooming: it allows networking among child abuse perpetrators, normalising deviant behaviours within a dangerous subculture; it can be used to promote child sexual tourism (for instance, helping individuals to locate child sex tourism operators or making direct contact with child prostitutes); and it allows people to 'order' victims remotely in cases of child trafficking (Wortley & Smallbone 2012).

Interestingly, cyberspace opens new ethical questions connected to the production of paedopornographic material: what if the production of sexual material uses childish-looking avatars (for instance, in virtual words such as Second Life) or if textual descriptions are produced by adults role-playing the part of a child? (Adams 2010). Sexual ageplay in real life might be considered a fetish, but it is not illegal if it takes place between consenting adults. In cyberspace, however, the issue is more problematic as sexual ageplay tends to be considered as having indirect harms, especially as it might normalise sexual interest in children within online communities (Reeves 2013, 2018). Child pornography law seems to be moving in the direction of capturing fictitious characters and scenarios, including in erotic e-publications and sexualised fan-fiction stories (McLelland 2019), but the question is not settled yet. In order to justify criminalisation, in fact, further understanding of the extent to which avatars are to be considered extensions or reflections of real-life selves is needed (Reeves 2018).

In the context of cyberspace, possession refers to the storage of illicit material on both hardware supports and cloud platforms. Distribution of paedopornographic material can occur in cyberspace in a variety of ways, such as though webpages and websites (often, but not always, in the deep Web), emails, live broadcasting, e-groups, peer-to-peer networks, social media and mobile apps. The success of messaging apps (such as WhatsApp) and image-sharing apps (like Snapchat) has opened major possibilities for distribution. The material can be distributed among close circles to limit risks of detection, or it can be disguised and camouflaged online (for instance, among legal adult pornography).

Child pornography is a context-dependent phenomenon, so that – depending on where we position ourselves in time and space – what actually constitutes child pornography may vary. What is thought to be a 'child', for instance, varies across cultures, legal traditions and time. As summarised by Quayle & Taylor (2003), consistent with the United Nations Convention of the Rights of the Child, in Western countries we tend to end childhood with the 18th birthday and to seek legal protection from sexual and labour exploitation below that age. However, the age of consent for sexual activity varies among jurisdictions; for instance, in European countries it varies between 14 and 18 years, in the United States between 16 and 18, in African countries from 12 to 18, in Asia from 12 to 21 and so on. In practice, furthermore, it might be difficult to determine the age of an adolescent person (and therefore to assess whether pornographic material is paedopornographic material or not) from a picture, in the absence of additional information. In addition, although it is easy to identify paedopornographic material when there is a graphic depiction of sexually explicit scenes (or, at its worst, abuse), it might more difficult to do so when the material could be depicted, in the case of adults, as 'erotica' – that is, it involves sexual themes (e.g., a sexualised body) but is based on artistic grounds – and therefore it might be defended from accusations of obscenity and indecency in countries that link pornography to these notions (Quayle & Taylor 2003). It is generally recognised that child pornography varies in severity, from naked pictures and erotica to gross assault and bestiality (Jenkins 2001; Taylor et al. 2001; Wortley & Smallbone 2012).

Efforts to mitigate the problem of child pornography online are not new: if it might be impossible to completely eliminate the problem, it is possible to reduce the volume of the material online, to make it more difficult or riskier to access and to identify and arrest the more serious offenders (Wortley & Smallbone 2012). Many countries have developed new legislation against online abuse and to protect children in general and to counter human trafficking and sexual exploitation in particular (Shamim 2017). Legislative regulations are also used to compel the computer industry to play a greater role in controlling online child pornography by, for instance, making internet providers responsible for site content, requiring user verification and the preservation of users' browsing history records and requesting the use of key-escrowed encryption (which would require anyone selling encryption software to supply a trusted third party with a key to the code) (Wortley & Smallbone 2012). These approaches, however, are generally opposed by the tech industry and even civil liberties advocates and often for a good cause: key-escrowed encryption might undermine the security of a system, and holding website owners liable for illegal content posted by others would undermine free speech rights and have a devastating impact on legitimate online services, potentially implicating every online service that deals with user-generated content.

In addition, policing child pornography can be challenging. Besides traditional investigations prompted by a specific case, proactive investigations – where undercover officers are trained to pose as a child online to incite conversations with abusers seeking to groom a child – are often used in cases of child pornography (Martellozzo 2012; Winters et al. 2017). The use of undercover agents is promising but not always feasible because of the vastness of cyberspace, which would require impracticable numbers of agents. In addition, technological changes can at times hinder law enforcement efforts. For instance, since the beginning of the 2000s, VoIP technology has prompted significant changes in online communications and privacy expectations. With VoIP, audio and video communications are encapsulated via a codec (a device or software that compresses and decompresses large amounts of data) into small data packets, transmitted online and un-encapsulated at the receiving end of the communication. This is the technology at the base of services that most of us use, such as Skype, Vonage or Ooma. Unfortunately, VoIP technology is also attractive to offenders. VoIP-based services can, in fact, be used to transmit illegal material in a more secure way or even to video-stream abuse images. Lawful interceptions are made harder by VoIP technology: on the one hand, the current legal framework is often inadequate because of jurisdictional issues (in most cases, in fact, victims, offenders and the country where a VoIP service operates might be in different jurisdictions); on the other hand, there are technical problems (mostly related to the presence of security features such as encryption and the peer-to-peer structure of the network) that make it impossible to apply a one-size-fits-all interception regime (Açar 2017).

Computer industry self-regulation (such as the promptness in removing illegal sites and the establishment of complaint hotlines) and technological strategies (such as filtering techniques in search engines) are considered pivotal in tackling both grooming and child pornography online. Social media services try to exclude convicted sex offenders from their platforms (for example, Facebook's Statement of Rights and Responsibilities on registration and account security, point 6, states: 'You will not use Facebook if you are a convicted sex offender') but these rules are not easily enforceable. Apps such as Friend Verifier and dating platforms such as Gatsby let you scan for free your contact list against registered sex offenders, which can be problematic: first, they can be highly invasive of personal privacy, especially considering that, in order to be included in a list of sex offenders, the level of gravity of the crime committed can vary considerably (in some countries, the registry might include men who have urinated in public or young adults who fell in love with an underage peer, maybe just a couple of years younger); second, these lists could provide false negatives as they can match lists to media and law enforcement contacts only, and not all countries have registries for sex offenders.

Other technology-led approaches, however, are more promising. The International Communication Union (ITU, the United Nations specialised agency for ICTs) developed several guidelines for child online protection, addressed to children themselves, parents, guardians and educators, the industry and policy-makers (ITU 2016). Those addressed to industry stakeholders and developed together with the United Nations Children's Fund (UNICEF) are of particular interest. Among the several case studies and best practices presented (see ITU 2016 for further details) are a worldwide online child sexual abuse reporting portal (OCSARP) provided by the Internet Watch Foundation (IWF), which enables citizens to report online child sexual abuse content for assessment by IWF experts, and an app (HelpAPP) developed by UNICEF National Committee for Hungary, which provides instant help to children in abusive situations, as the child can call for help with one button press or send his or her GPS coordinates easily.

Of much interest is the approach developed by the Dutch branch of the leading Swiss child relief agency, Terre des Hommes, which in 2013 created a 3D model of a ten-year-old Filipino girl (named 'Sweetie'). During a sting operation based in public chatrooms and dating sites over a period of about 10 weeks, more than 20,000 individuals sought to get in touch with Sweetie, and about 1,000 potential abusers from 71 different countries offered her money for sexual acts. In this initial experiment, there were only four operators handling the chats and the large number of contacts they received made it close to impossible to deal with them all. Once again, technical solutions can come to the rescue: the use of artificial intelligence and automated chatbots can minimise human interventions in sting operations such as the Sweetie one. In February 2017, Terre des Hommes Netherlands released its Sweetie 2.0 project in Manila, which makes use of automated chatbots and more advanced tools to record and analyse interactions with potential offenders (Açar 2017). Not only can a project like Sweetie help law enforcement in their operations, but it can also function as a honey-trap, creating uncertainty in the minds of offenders and reduce the sense of freedom and anonymity they feel (Wortley & Smallbone 2012).

In addition, the analysis of big data and specifically of metadata – that is, 'data about data', information that describes other data and that has the advantage of revealing only some attributes of communications such as the date and the IP address, so as to minimise privacy intrusions – is very promising, as this approach can help to reveal suspicious patterns, therefore guiding law enforcement investigations to where they might be more effective. Consider the example offered by Açar (2017): assuming that the victim does not use anonymisation techniques to shield his/her IP address, if data analysis shows that a Filipino girl from an isolated district has online contacts with three different and relatively wealthier countries in one week, this might raise a red flag for further investigation.

Finally, the creation of more awareness in civil society is of fundamental importance: this is what leads parents to use filtering software or to be more conscious in monitoring young children's online behaviours (Wortley & Smallbone 2012; Shamim 2017). Sexual education in schools and families is also of great importance (Martellozzo 2017). Proper civil society education can also help eradicate the problem of amateurish groups of online vigilantes – maybe armed with good intentions but often causing a hindrance. In the United Kingdom, for instance, one of these groups (Letzgo Hunting, formed by a small number of mums and dads) was very active in exposing the problem of child predators online through sting operations where members of the group would pose as underage girls. However, the group was harshly criticised because it ended up intimidating and harassing innocent people too and acted in a way (posting online videos of them accusing alleged offenders) that could have interfered with official investigations, potentially allowing offenders to dart away before an arrest could be made.

Forced prostitution

Cyberspace is also revolutionising sex markets that are legal in many countries or generally considered less harmful (when the sex workers engage in sexual activities voluntarily and are not underage): offer and demand for sexual services can now meet online without time and – depending on the service – spatial restrictions, and increased privacy and anonymity make looking for commercial sex easier. In cyberspace, furthermore, the sex business is becoming more professionalised, as new ICTs provide opportunities for sex workers to organise their business as independent men/women, to discuss safety issues and minimise risks and to diversify both direct and indirect sexual services (for instance, watching live pornographic shows or participating in live sex chats) (Sanders 2009). Unfortunately, cyberspace is not immune to problems of sexual exploitation. In this section, we will focus on *forced* prostitution. We are not entering here into debates on whether prostitution is/can/should be a normal occupation or whether it is, by definition, a modern form of slavery (for a good overview, see, for instance, Siegel 2017). Moreover, we are not placing a negative value judgement on prostitution or other forms of sex work. Rather, we are firm in the assumption that, when the prostitute has not freely chosen to work in the sex industry or to work under certain exploitative conditions, then that is a form of crime that deserves attention.

Online forums, social media, dedicated webpages and even e-commerce websites have increased the visibility and exposure of victims of forced prostitution while, conversely, increasing the privacy of those abusing and exploiting them (Hughes 2002, 2004; Makin & Bye 2018; Hickle 2017). The analysis of sexuality-related commercial websites carried out by Pajnik et al. (2015) in France, Greece and Slovenia suggests that online prostitution seems more oriented to the needs of clients than to those of sex workers. Victims, once they are relegated online, are further dehumanised, while exploitative behaviours are often rationalised, normalised and eroticised, and the presence of a 24/7 community of like-minded people can positively reinforce and empower the perpetrators (Hughes 2002, 2004; D'Ovidio et al. 2009). The impact of cyberspace on online forced prostitution, however, is far more wide-reaching, as cyberspace has provided a number of market-changing opportunities to offenders.

We have discussed online grooming above and how social media can be used to target vulnerable victims. Apart from grooming, online opportunities are used in other ways to initiate contact with a victim and to facilitate her (or his) sexual exploitation. From a historical perspective, in the last century narratives on (forced) prostitution have often connected this phenomenon with human trafficking for sexual exploitation, even though these concepts only partially overlap (Weitzer 2005; Oude Breuil et al. 2011). In this section, we will focus on forced prostitution, and – at least for this book – limit the part on human trafficking to the box below.

Box 5.2 Human trafficking

Trafficking in human beings is defined as 'the recruitment, transportation, transfer, harbouring or receipt of persons, by means of the threat or use of force or other forms of coercion, of abduction, of fraud, of deception, of the abuse of power or of a position of vulnerability or of the giving or receiving of payments or benefits to achieve the consent of a person having control over another person, for the purpose of *exploitation*' (United Nations Protocol to Prevent, Suppress and Punish Trafficking in Persons, Especially Women and Children, art. 3, emphasis added).

The phenomenon of trafficking needs to be framed within the broader issue of increased human mobility. Trafficking victims are not always migrants but many of them are; and migrants and refugees are particularly vulnerable to being trafficked (UNODC 2016). The distinctive element of trafficking, however, is exploitation - which makes some commentators equate trafficking to a form of slavery. Estimates on human trafficking are always difficult to make because of the massive dark number of victims. On a global scale, thousands and thousands of victims are trafficked each year (UNODC 2016). Although all countries of the world are affected by human trafficking, its nature and extent vary significantly among geographical regions; typically, victims are transported from poorer to richer areas (Savona et al. 2009). About 40 percent of victims are trafficked domestically (that is, within the same country) while the remaining ones are moved across borders. Most detected victims are women, but children and men make up about 50 percent of the total number of victims (UNODC 2016). Sex trafficking is the form of trafficking that, traditionally, has largely informed policy and scholarly debates (Aronowitz 2009). It is characterised by a specific purpose of exploitation, namely the 'prostitution of others or other forms of sexual exploitation' (the UN Protocol, Art. 3). This expression was left undefined in order to leave its specification to different jurisdictions: national laws on sex and human trafficking are still diverse and, to a large extent, inspired by different values and traditions of prostitution and foreign migration (Savona et al. 2009; Oude et al. 2011).

Human trafficking, in both policing and research, is traditionally connected to (transnational) organised crime. Suffice it to say that the major international legal instrument to tackle human trafficking is the Protocol to Prevent, Suppress and Punish Trafficking in Persons, Especially Women and Children, which supplements the 2000 United Nations Convention against Transnational Organised Crime. However, regarding cyber-facilitated trafficking, individuals and loose networks are becoming key actors: the criminal opportunities provided by the internet facilitate the entry into the market of smaller criminal groups that can organise all stages of sex trafficking on their own rather than rely on more complex and sophisticated criminal networks: deception and recruitment of victims are now possible from afar without any input necessary from members of a criminal network on the ground (Lavorgna 2014b, 2015a).

Overall, the commercialisation of the internet has caused important changes in how human trafficking is carried out, but it is important not to over-generalise this claim: many offenders and victims still depend on their offline social networks of contacts to manage the trade. Any over-emphasis on the cyber component of human trafficking risks diverting law enforcement attention from the more traditional aspects of the crime. However, the increasing commercialisation of the internet in victims' countries of origin and its wider usage by disadvantaged sectors of society mean that, in the coming years, the cyber component in human trafficking for sexual and labour exploitation will become increasingly significant.

It is worth remembering that the internet is also used, even if to a lesser extent, as a facilitator in cases of human trafficking for labour exploitation. In these cases, internet usage is often legitimate, as it is used merely to advertise work opportunities, while the illegal element often emerges in subcontracting: online job listings are used to lure potential victims, who are then enslaved in a system of forced labour once they arrive in the destination country (Lavorgna 2014b).

Not only are victims deceived via online grooming but also with employment opportunities through the use of fake job advertisements. In many cases, victims are unaware when replying to online job alerts that the destination will be the sex industry. In other cases, the advertisement openly promotes a job in the sex industry; however, when the victim arrives in the destination country, she might be locked up and forced into prostitution. In this case, the gap between coercion and volition (as the victims, when they agree to migrate, are unaware of the conditions of future captivity) makes this a case of sex trafficking (Lavorgna 2014b).

Cyberspace has also provided market-changing opportunities to advertise sexual services. Online advertisements generally promote the licit fronts for prostitution, such as in 'adult' sections of generalist advertising websites or in specialised ones (Makin & Bye 2018). Besides advertising sexual services directly, online messages are used to publicise brothels where victims are forced into prostitution, although such messaging does not generally specify locations: instead, they might give a mobile telephone number for further information. In this way, the subsequent phase of the offender–client relationship is moved towards a less risky, offline dimension (Lavorgna 2014b). Cyberspace has also opened the way to interactive webcamming, probably the fastest-growing sector of the pornography business, equatable to forced prostitution when victims are forced to perform. Finally, ICTs also help to exacerbate the subjugation of victims, as they can be used as a tool for blackmail or intimidation: victims who resist exploitation may have compromising images and videos distributed online, which could jeopardise their reputation and – especially for victims of certain ethnic origins – make a return to their families virtually impossible. Furthermore, offenders can control victims via online cameras and handle the profits from afar: even if most criminal networks still rely on cash and offline underground banking systems, online services have been used in some cases for transferring money from victims to traffickers and between the latter and to move profits towards the exploiters' countries of origin (Lavorgna 2014b).

On a brighter side, new technologies can also provide new tools of investigation to fight human trafficking (Gerry et al. 2016), and cyberspace can prove useful to identify victims of forced prostitution. Recent research is trying to explore ways to harness information crawled online – for instance, information posted in online adverts for sexual services – to identify patterns flagging up at-risk sex workers. In fact, there are proxy indicators signalling that the sex workers might be forced into prostitution, such as when the online advertisements offer all types of sexual activity without precautions, which is strange for voluntary prostitutes. Other indicators are the recurrence of the same phone number for several prostitutes, the presence of online profiles of sex workers having a lot of similarities and ads displaying poor linguistic proficiency (Lavorgna 2014b; Skidmore et al. 2018).

Image-based sexual abuse

There is a heterogeneous spectrum of criminal and deviant behaviours that pivot around the illegal release of sexual material or the release of illegally obtained sexual material. At times, these behaviours are limited to cyberspace; other times, they are linked to offline forms of sexual or emotional abuse. This section will provide an overview of the most serious and common forms of online image-based sexual abuse, which are generally related to the non-consensual release of sexual material.

The non-consensual release of pornographic or otherwise sexual material is often, technically, a case of doxing (the intentional release online of personal information or material or of doxware if linked to extortion, as we will see in detail in Chapter 6). Of course, the unwanted release of video or pictures is not always related to sex crimes: think, for instance, of a target of bullying whose unflattering videos are released online for public mockery. However, when the material released has sexual content, the image release has specific characteristics that make it comparable, according to an increasing number of authors, to offline forms of sexual violence and abuse (Bloom 2014; Bates 2017; McGlynn et al. 2017; Powell & Henry 2017). Diverse types of criminal and deviant behaviours can be included under the umbrella of non-consensual release or otherwise online sexual abuses. For instance, the practice of sexting – sending sexually explicit messages, photos or videos – is generally a voluntary act addressed to a romantic partner in a flirtatious way, but it can be linked to forms of coercion. First, while individuals engaging in sexting might have the expectation that the material sent will not be shared with others, in reality this is not always the case, and about 25 percent of received material is forwarded to someone else (Rice et al. 2012; Branch et al. 2017). Second, research has shown that teens also send explicit pictures because of pressure from their partner or friends (Henry & Powell 2018; Branch et al. 2017; Liong & Cheng 2017).

The phenomenon colloquially referred to as 'revenge porn' is probably the most common case of non-consensual release of sexually explicit material. In the 'typical' case, provocative images or videos created in the intimacy of a relationship, or taken illegally without the subject portrayed being aware of their existence, are used by a vengeful ex-partner to seek revenge out of a broken relationship by publicly humiliating and defaming the victim. There are even dedicated websites encouraging viewers to upload material of their partners or ex-partners and allowing others to leave derogatory comments (Salter & Crofts 2015; Bates 2017). Research reveals striking similarities between the mental health effects of sexual assault and revenge porn for survivors, such as trust issues, post-traumatic stress disorder, anxiety, depression, suicidal thoughts and several other mental health effects. Non-consensual pornography can also lead to public shame and humiliation, an inability to find new partners, job loss or problems securing new employment and also offline harassment; many victims feel forced to drop out from cyberspace and to modify their offline routines (Bloom 2014; Bates 2017). Overall, legislative responses to revenge porn have been sporadic, even if they have increased in the last few years. Unfortunately, laws criminalising revenge porn in most cases focus only on the 'typical' cases, such as extreme practices of angry ex-partners, while the challenges associated with policing and with raising education and public awareness about the dangers of revenge porn have frequently been overlooked, often leaving victims without adequate protection (Salter & Crofts 2015; Bates 2017; Goldsworthy et al. 2017; McGlynn et al. 2017; Hall & Hearn 2018).

We should not forget that there are also cases of non-consensual release of sexual material where the release is not a way to seek revenge and the images were not created to fulfil the aims of pornography (Powell & Henry 2017): consider, for instance, when rapes are recorded and shared via digital devices. Among the many cases that hit the news are the infamous 2012 case of the rape of an unconscious 16-year-old girl by two high school football players in Ohio and the gang rape of an unconscious 16-year-old girl in Rio de Janeiro in 2016 and of a Dalit (the lower caste in India) girl in 2017. The perpetrators put up on social media pictures and videos of the offence, which then were circulated by other users. Such videos are also used to blackmail the victim: if he or she reports the rape, the video will be posted online (Mantilla 2015). As pointed out by Powell and Henry (2017), these cases show the inadequacy of the term 'revenge porn' and the necessity of using more overarching terminology: image-based sexual abuse.

Although men may also be victimised, the forms of online sexual abuses dealt with in this chapter are often gendered, as they disproportionately impact women (Salter & Crofts 2015; McGlynn et al. 2017; Hall & Hearn 2018). Furthermore, these hateful behaviours are used not only for revenge or as forms of control or harassment but also as expressions of masculine entitlement (Powell & Henry 2017). Together with other disturbing trends such as the distribution of rape jokes and memes, the posting of 'upskirt' photos of unsuspecting women, threats of sexual violence and the use of social media and dating sites to facilitate sexual assaults, revenge porn and other image-based sexual abuses are revealing of the nature and extent of rape culture (that is, the normalisation or minimisation of sexual violence) in cyberspace (Powell & Henry 2017).

It will be interesting – and maybe a bit scary – to see how some of the latest technological developments influence these cultural problems in cyberspace and whether and to what extent they will have a role in changing patterns (for better or worse) in online and offline sexual abuse. The emergence of virtual reality pornography is one of these developments. It promises a new use for virtual reality, with the potential to create new immersive experience: not only 360-degree three-dimensional graphics but also the possibility to replicate sensorial experiences (Wood et al. 2017). Of course, it might also offer possibilities to create a new level of revenge porn, raising ethical questions on consent, and might even push violent imagery to the extreme. A related development will be the increasing commercialisation of sex robots (or sexbots) (Levy 2012; Lee 2017). The producers suggest that sex robots could help to mitigate the risk of sexual assaults and child abuse, providing potential offenders a non-human outlet. Still, a producer company in 2017 advertised a sex robot with a 'frigid' setting, enabling men to stimulate rape; and we might need and want, as a society, to question the legality of sex robots depicting children. Some authors are starting to analyse the ethical and legal implications of sex robots in both secular and religious legal frameworks (Amuda & Tijani 2012; Sparrow 2017) and to question whether the 'rape' of a robot would be legal or not and the morality of designing a robot that lacks the capacity to explicitly refuse consent: if a robot can refuse consent, this would facilitate rape fantasies and the likelihood of users experimenting with raping (Sparrow 2017). It is probably a bit destabilising to think that technological change progresses at such a fast pace while we are still debating the basic principles of right and wrong in our societies.

Concluding remarks

Hate, harassment and (illegal/deviant) sex are powerful forces in cyberspace, and they go largely unchallenged and unregulated. The problem of under-reporting is huge, making it difficult to have reliable statistics and data to understand these problems in their full complexity. Victims often do not receive adequate support from service providers (Cohen-Almagor 2015; al-Khateeb et al. 2017; Pavan 2017). Traditional policing is also limited: not only because of the usual problems encountered when dealing with the vastness and technicalities of cyberspace but also because of problems specific to the crimes encountered in this chapter. These problems are well known in criminological research carried out on the offline counterparts of these crimes: stigma, victim-blaming, and not being taken seriously *in primis* (Henry & Powell 2018; Bates 2017). These criticisms do not hold true for child abuse and sex trafficking, which are traditionally better recognised and acknowledged as more serious, but they suffer nonetheless from another problem: the specificities of the victims and their characteristics make the surfacing of the crime extremely difficult. Awareness-raising and educational approaches that emphasise responsible and informed use of ICTs are of pivotal importance (Rice et al. 2012; Gámez-Guadix et al. 2017).

The problem, and therefore the challenge, however, is first and foremost cultural: it is not only about crime and deviance; it is often about the culture in which certain behaviours thrive (Nussbaum 2010; Phillips 2015). Ultimately, the question we should always ask is: what kind of cyberspace do we want to 'live' in? Online antagonistic behaviours and abuses should be studied, discussed and analysed without losing sight of local cultural differences and contexts and while always having an ethical and moral dimension in mind. As Jane (2015) puts it, 'a *moral* horizon is not necessarily a *moralising* horizon. It would recognise that while technological invention invariably outpaces our ability to reflect on the ethics of the use of new devices, this neither entails nor excuses a deficit of ethical reflection at all' (2015, p. 84, emphasis in the original). It can be argued that we (should) have an ethical responsibility to refrain from acting in a way that knowingly might harm our society, even in its online components: in the words of Cohen-Almagor (2015), rather than being 'netusers', we should try to become 'netcitizens', people who use the internet as an integral part of their real life and who, as such, are responsible with and accountable for our online identity as if it were our offline one. Both policy-based regulation (which may increase the traceability of real identities and subsequently users' accountability) and the voluntary disclosure of social cues (that is, logging into a certain website by simply clicking a plug-in that automatically connects the activities on the website to an existing social media account) might help to decrease anti-normative behaviours online. These approaches, however, also come with a downside, as they pose privacy concerns and monitoring risks (Cho & Kwon 2015). Once again, it becomes clear how, as a society, we need to (re)agree on the right balances and trade-offs among security, safety, confidentiality, usability and privacy to make our lives – including their online parts – better.

Before we conclude this chapter, it is also time to reflect on the *glocalism* of cybercrimes and their responses: online, there is a permanent intertwining of the global and the local dimensions, which coexist as two sides of the same coin. As cyberspace transcends jurisdictional boundaries, most cybercrimes inherently live in a transnational dimension: in most cases, the victim, the offender and parts of the technological apparatus used to perform the crime do not need geographical proximity. At the same time, however, the local element maintains a fundamental role: if we do not understand the specificities of the local contexts where cybercrimes occur, we might not be able to intervene in effective and useful ways. The example offered by Halder and Jaishankar (2017) of online harassment of women in India is particularly handy to back up this point: because of the patriarchal structure of the country, the number of cases registered and prosecuted is particularly low, for fear of social reputational damages. Women who are victims of online harassment can be further victimised by their families as they might be accused of committing infidelity. At the same time, especially in non-metropolitan cities and semi-urban and rural areas, basic infrastructures to deal with cybercrimes are missing. Further research, and especially comparative research, is truly needed to better understand the glocal features of the crimes and deviant behaviours presented in this chapter.

Further research is also needed on the characteristics of the victims: many existing studies focus on children, teens and young adults, but few have explored sensitive topics (such as sexting coercion and revenge porn) in relation to the adult population. In addition, research seems to suggest that online victims tend to be more likely to experience forms of offline violence and abuse, such as traditional forms of partner violence (Henry & Powell 2018). It is of the upmost importance to further our knowledge of the offline – online nexus from a victimological perspective to improve harm reduction and victim support.

? CRITICAL QUESTIONS

- To what extent do hate groups (such as white supremacists) have the right to propagate their ideologies online in your country? Do you think that this trade-off between freedom of speech and civil behaviour online is adequate or not? Is this different from the trade-offs in the countries we encountered as examples in this chapter?

- In August 2017, in Charlottesville (Virginia, USA), alt-right (that is, people with far-right ideologies who reject mainstream conservatism in favour of white nationalism), white supremacists, the Ku Klux Klan and neo-Nazi groups descended on the city for a rally after the city council had voted earlier in the year to remove the statue of a Confederate general. They soon clashed with counter-protesters in the city streets. At a certain point, a 20-year-old man from Ohio rammed his car into counter-protesters, killing 32-year-old Heather Heyer and leaving at least 19 others injured. Soon, hashtags and accounts on Twitter (such as #nazihunter, #goodnightaltright and @yesyoureracist) were used to identify (from pictures available) marching white nationalists. Some commentators, however, have criticised this form of online activism as it promotes a lynch mob mentality on social media and hinders the presumption of innocence principle at the basis of most democratic legal systems. Do you think that this form of online 'naming and shaming' in cyberspace can be useful or rather is it dangerous?

- If online harassment can be (at least partially) explained by integrating self-control and social learning theories, what type of prevention measures might be suggested?

- In May 2017, nearly 900 people were arrested in a major operation (Operation Pacifier) carried out by the FBI with the support of Europol and other law enforcement agencies. The arrested individuals were part of a Tor-based network of child pornography distribution; some of the arrested are suspected of direct involvement in the sexual abuses. Some civil liberties groups, however, criticised the investigation, suggesting that law enforcement agencies used malware to identify members of the paedo-pornographic ring. These practices, according to the civil liberties advocates, might undermine individuals' privacy protection on personal computers. Balancing investigative needs, the rights of victims and the right to privacy is a challenging matter. In your opinion, do the ends always justify the means? What factors should be taken into consideration to define what are/should be the limits of law enforcement investigations in cyberspace?

6 CRIMES OF DECEPTION AND COERCION

Introduction

Our journey continues with 'crimes of deception and coercion'. The position of this chapter in the overall framework – in between 'crimes against persons' and 'crimes against property' – is not a coincidence. In most jurisdictions, fraudulent acts and acts where money or other gain is obtained as result of coercion are considered alongside crimes against property: they target an individual, but the endgame is financial benefit. However, this common categorisation seemed unsatisfactory in the taxonomy adopted in this book. In fact, it soon appeared that many of the crimes encountered in this chapter which are centred on fraud, deception and coercion may fall into both the 'crimes against persons' and 'crimes against property' categories, depending on the motivation of the offender and the principal type of harm suffered by the victim. In romance scams, for instance, the prevalent harm suffered by the victim may be emotional rather than financial. In identity fraud, the motivation of the offender might go beyond the search for profit, pertaining more, for example, to the domain of revenge or envy; and the harm suffered by the victim might be more reputational than monetary. In cases of cyber-extortion, the impending threats against the victim often touch personal and intimate spheres (think of the threat to publish online private pictures), with significant psychological harm. As a consequence, this chapter gathers together diverse types of crimes where deception and coercion play a central, fundamental role. In most cases, the intent is to get money – but not always.

Frauds

Fraudulent acts preying on people's vulnerabilities are anything but new; countless victims fall for more or less sophisticated forms of scams and hoaxes. It goes without saying that cyberspace has made available a whole new set of criminal opportunities to deliberately deceive the victim. Internet frauds can be so diverse – the only limit is the scammer's imagination – that it would be virtually impossible to cover them all. Pigeon-holing internet fraud is particularly difficult, as in practice many criminal behaviours fall in between categories, having elements of two or more. Furthermore, not only – as anticipated in the introduction to this chapter – could many of the frauds encountered in this chapter be considered crimes against property but some (such as sale and review frauds) could, arguably, be included among the market-based crimes you will find in Chapter 7. However, given that any categorisation involves a choice, all major types of internet frauds that will be gathered in this section are summarised in Table 6.1.

All these types of internet fraud share a common identifying element – that is, *social engineering*. An umbrella term encompassing a broad range of diverse activities, social engineering can be broadly defined as skilfully manipulating an individual to take action in some aspects of his or her life (Hadnagy 2011). Social engineers can 'overflow' the human mind as if it were a piece of software, making humans (the 'wetware') the weakest link in the security chain (see also Mitnick & Simon 2001; Hadnagy 2011; Shackelford 2014). They are very insidious because they prey on qualities of human nature, such as the desire to be helpful, a tendency to trust people, the fear of getting into trouble and the willingness to cut corners. We all use a bit of social engineering in our

Table 6.1 Types of (cyber)frauds

Advance-fee scams	The victim is promised a large sum of money in return for a relatively small upfront payment.
Sales and charity frauds	The fraud specifically targets an online transaction where a certain good or service is offered online. In charity frauds, the donation for a worthy cause is targeted.
Fraudulent reviews and advertisement frauds	Online reviews are manipulated to fraudulently boost or kill a specific product or service; network traffic is manipulated to inflate the number of clicks and impressions from individual visitors.
Health frauds	Misleading medical information or quack therapies are fraudulently disseminated online.
Investment frauds	These frauds are similar to advance-fee scams (a victim is asked to make upfront payments pending high returns) but they specifically target investors.
Identity frauds	Various types of fraudulent behaviours having in common the fact that the scammer assumes a fake persona. Identity theft is often, but not necessarily, involved.

daily lives, as we all rely on some degree of influence and persuasion (hopefully not maliciously!) in our social relations: think about the use of flattery or emotive language. Persuasive techniques are the basis of commercial advertisements and political rhetoric, among other things. Social engineering, however, is also used in a wide range of criminal activities and no one is immune from victimisation. To a different extent, social engineering is, in fact, an important element of most cybercrimes, being a common weapon in the arsenal of a diverse range of criminals, from sophisticated crime networks involved in large-scale financial theft to a resentful employee stealing precious data from the workplace after being fired. In internet fraud, social engineering – particularly in the form that relies on a variety of psychological tricks to get a computer user to perform a certain task and/or to provide information useful to access a computer or network – is the key. Make sure you familiarise yourself with the information in the box below before moving on with the reading.

Box 6.1 Social engineering

Social engineering practices can be human-based or technology-based (Peltier 2007).

- *Human-based social engineering.* Very often, social engineering starts with gathering some background information on the victim in a non-tech way, such as through dumpster diving (it is not unusual for both individuals and companies to throw out sensitive information without shredding it first), phone calls (by posing as someone in authority or as a system manufacturer calling to offer a system update) and shoulder surfing (looking over someone's shoulder to gain, for instance, a pin code) (Long 2008; Huber et al. 2009). Low-tech methods can also be used to induce someone to perform a certain activity. In November 2016, for instance, VINCI SA (a major French concessions and construction company) was the primary victim of social engineering applied to manipulation of the stock exchange: the social engineers spread to several journalists the fake news that VINCI had fired its chief financial officer after an internal audit revealed accounting irregularities. This prompted the stock to plunge, causing a loss of more than GBP 3 billion. The fake news was sent by a phony VINCI email account, from a domain name filed only a couple weeks before in the Netherlands. The journalists, in this case, were targeted not as primary victims but as the weakest links in the chain. Social media offer a new set of tools to social engineers, with their large user base and the huge amount of information they can provide. Furthermore, they have been used to launch reverse social engineering attacks – that is, when the victims are tricked into contacting the attacker themselves (for instance, through an interesting LinkedIn profile or via common friends on Facebook). In this way, a higher degree of trust is established between the victim and the attacker (Irani et al. 2011).

- *Technology-based social engineering.* Compared with human-based attacks, automated social engineering bots have the advantage that they are cheaper in the long run, as they can deal with increasing amounts of work without requiring additional resources (Heartfield & Loukas 2016). Other common techniques are sending a virus through an attachment, using a false pop-up window asking the user to log-in again or simply leaving a USB key around the workplace with malware in it: there will always be a curious employee who will pick it up and check its contents on the office computer. Phishing (that is, inducing a victim to disclose sensitive information by using a 'bait' – as in the homophone 'fishing') is probably the most notorious example of technical social engineering. Phishing can rely on different techniques. Think, for instance, of the use of spoofed websites (that is, a fake website pretending to be the target website by adopting a similar design and URL, or even the same URL disguising a cloaked URL), clickjacking (the user is tricked into clicking on the 'wrong' button or link and is hence routed to another page, controlled by the attacker) or email spoofing (the forgery of an email header to pretend it was sent by someone different from the original sender). These types of visual deception attacks can be very effective, as most potential victims tend to ignore security cues such as a suspicious address bar (Dhamija et al. 2006). Another interesting technique is to use out-of-band authentication methods to steal users' credentials. These occur when a security code is sent to the user through a different channel (for instance, their mobile phone) in cases when the user initiated a critical action (for instance, a bank transfer). While the whole idea behind out-of-band authentication methods is to prevent an attack, in so-called verification code forwarding attacks the offender sends the user a deceptive message and, by pretending to be the service provider, lures the victim into sharing the access credentials (Siadati et al. 2017).

Human-based and technology-based social engineering is often used in synergy. In 2017, for instance, a group of hackers called ACABGang accessed the email accounts of about 50 members of the Spanish Civil Guard (a military force charged with police duties). They first took control of the online forum of the Civil Guard, which was hosted on a platform with vulnerabilities, and then, pretending to be the forum's administrators (human-based social engineering), redirected the members to a spoofed website and asked for their login details (technology-based social engineering). Those who entered their password were giving it away to the hackers.

Advance-fee scams

Probably the most notorious and low-tech form of internet scams are the so-called advance-fee scams, where the victim is promised a large sum of money in return for a relatively small upfront payment. They are also referred to as 4-1-9 scams, after the section of the Nigerian criminal code that addresses fraud: even if advance-fee scams (once carried out mainly by letter, now via email) originate from all over the world, they are still generally associated in the popular imagination with Nigeria (hence the name) and with so-called 'Yahoo boys' – that is, young Nigerian con artists looking for quick monetary reward via online frauds (King & Thomas 2009; Tade 2016).

There are many variants of advance-fee scams, but they all share the characteristic that the victim receives a contact with a request to 'help' someone in another country via a money transfer service, generally combined with a sad story justifying the request; a monetary reward is generally offered to the victim too. For most people, the social engineering behind these frauds is easy to detect, but scammers have to be believed by only a tiny percentage of people to quickly add up the numbers. In 2016, for instance, a joint operation by Interpol and the Nigerian Economic and Financial Crime Commission led to the arrest of 'Mike', the man allegedly heading a network of 40 individuals across Nigeria, Malaysia and South Africa behind scams totalling the equivalent of more than GBP 46 million worldwide. Unfortunately, reliable statistics on the extent of these scams are missing, as they are often cross-jurisdictional, there is no centralised database and many victims do not denounce the crime since they are embarrassed or they do not realise they have been victims.

Advance-fee scams often occur as romance scams or sweetheart swindle scams (Whitty 2018). In these cases, the victim (often approached via dating sites and apps) is socially engineered to develop affection towards the scammer – who generally poses under the guise of a beautiful, careful, successful and sadly alone potential partner – until a request for financial assistance is met. Romance scams can be an emotionally devastating type of fraud, as romance scammers lower victims' defences by appealing to their most intimate and compassionate side (Rege 2009; Whitty & Buchanan 2016; Whitty 2018). Scammers often use a 'sockpuppet' (fake) online identity or they 'catfish' the victim (assuming a fake identity to trick the victim into believing that they really are that person online). Although romance scams existed prior to the internet age (for instance, via post), the anonymity feature of cyberspace has given them a real boost. Online, many more individuals are enabled to participate in romantic relationships with strangers without the fear of stigma; scammers are offered anonymity and relative security from detection and are further disassociated from accountability, lowering any remorse; scammers have easy access to victims' personal information, so are able to target the more suitable ones (Rege 2009).

Advance-fee scams can take the form of business opportunity schemes. Think of a business or working opportunity allowing individuals to earn thousands of pounds (for instance, through some form of work-at-home venture). In order to make the venture a viable business, victims are asked to pay in advance a certain sum for training or other useful material. However, once the payment is made, the scammer disappears and so does the business opportunity.

Apart from the typical examples presented above, advance-fee scams can be found everywhere. An interesting variant of advance-fee scam I bumped into a few years ago concerned the sale of a piece of furniture on eBay UK (academics can have a very nomadic life and furniture has to be sold): I was contacted by a potential buyer, very keen to provide me with a very interesting and detailed story on his work in the army (which translates to 'I have a stable job, I can pay') and why, because of all his travels, he had only a small window to buy and collect the furniture (or, in other words, 'we need to finalise this asap or I cannot buy – full price – from you'). After the exchange of a few emails, when only payment had to be made, the buyer-from-the-army concocted an equally interesting and detailed story on the fact that he could not collect the furniture in person because of last-minute travel and had to send a friend instead. The friend had to rent a van but was refusing to put up the money for the rental. The buyer was travelling and could not send the money to his friend, so my only chance of selling my beloved furniture would have been to make the payment for the van. Now, at this point, as you can probably imagine, the story ended with a not-so-polite email from my side, a notice sent to eBay and the disappearance of the fake buyer. The furniture was sold, at a less than ideal price, a couple of weeks later.

Sales and charity frauds

A number of cyber-frauds specifically target online transactions: a certain 'item' – ranging from a car to a concert ticket, from a pet to a room for rent – is offered online. After the money is sent, however, the item is never delivered or an item far less valuable turns up (or is made available) instead; moreover, prices might be fraudulently manipulated. In contrast to the 'market-based' crimes we will encounter in Chapter 7, the illegal element here is not in the goods or services sold but rather in the fraudulent act, at the expense of the buyer. Besides the direct financial (and at times psychological) harm suffered by the primary victim, these frauds have wider social implications as they undermine people's trust in online commerce.

Online marketplaces (such as Amazon, Alibaba, Zalora, Bidorbuy and many more) are vulnerable to several types of sale frauds and unethical behaviours. When the sale depends on auction-style listings (such as in eBay), in-auction frauds to manipulate prices are possible (Trevathan & Read 2006). For instance, the seller might have a third-party bidding on his/ her item with the sole intent to drive the price up (shill bidding). A buyer, on the other hand, might place a low bid; a complicit third-party might enter a high bid just to discourage other bidders and then withdraw at the last minute, giving the buyer a cheap deal (bid shielding). These practices are difficult to recognise, and researchers are always trying to find new methods to prevent and detect these frauds, generally using bid data and machine learning to look for anomalies in bidding behaviours, so as to intervene before the victim incurs any monetary loss (Majadi et al. 2016).

Sale frauds can be linked to other criminal activities. For instance, triangulation frauds are often used to launder the profits from other illegal activities and to 'cash out' stolen credit card data. In triangulation frauds, the fraudsters are selling in-demand items (that they do not own yet) below the market price to attract customers. Once the sale is over, the fraudsters will use the dirty money (illegally gained from another criminal activity) to buy the item online (at its full price) and ship it to their buyer. As the legitimate buyers and sellers might not even suspect that something illegal is going on, these types of frauds are generally very difficult to detect unless the legitimate cardholder (when the fraud is linked to stolen credit card data) disputes the charge (Gregg & Scott 2008).

Another very common fraud is, of course, the non-delivery of the merchandise. Typically, someone will post a product for sale, but the item is either non-existent or not the one described in the online marketplace. If the money is sent, or the full price is paid when a parcel (containing a good of a significantly lower value) is delivered, the buyer will lose money (Trevathan & Read 2006).

We need to keep in mind that, besides the sophisticated criminal networks running large-scale operations (that sometimes reach the national news), these types of frauds are very common and generally run by unscrupulous individuals; no specific tech expertise is needed. Just one example, out of many others, among those in the local news as I write this chapter: a young man from northern Italy advertises online, at a good price, some tickets for the Coldplay gig in Milan a few weeks later; after he receives the money (a few hundred euros), he disappears. The tickets are nowhere to be found.

In order to invoke trust in online payments, escrow systems are often used: the payment is done by the buyer to an independent and licensed third party and is released to the seller only after both parties verify that the transaction has been completed as per the terms set. Of course, any technological change can lead to 'fraudogenic' consequences (Button & Cross 2017) – there is always a loophole to be exploited and escrow services are no exception. Bogus escrow services, for example, can be self-operated by fraudsters and disappear immediately after payment is received. In *overpayment scams*, the fraudulent buyer sends a (fake but realistic enough to fool most bankers) cheque or money order for more than the required sum, then asks for a refund of the difference. After the refund is sent by the victim, the cheque will bounce.

As most online marketplaces have strict policies and are taking continual steps to limit sales fraud, scammers often try to persuade targeted victims to take part in a deal outside the known marketplace; when they disappear after payment, the victim has no protection. Phishing can also be used in combination with sale frauds: fake retail websites can be used to harvest credit card information from a naïve victim, triggered into a buying mode by exceptionally good prices. The old saying 'if it sounds too good to be true, it probably is' also holds true in cyberspace. It goes without saying that social engineering tactics are constantly used, often in combination with spam and spamdexing. For instance, a spam email advertising a certain product might reflect the name of a known and trusted business label, use common file extensions (especially .zip, as most spam filters block attachments with .exe extension) or URL-shortening services (to disguise suspicious hyperlinks into plausible ones) or might be personalised to appear more reliable to the target (Broadhurst & Alazab 2017).

Last but not least, it is worth remembering that these types of frauds do not target only consumers: comparable tactics are also used in charity frauds – these are particularly amoral types of fraud, where the fraudster preys on people's sympathy for a worthy cause (to help the victims of a natural disaster or terrorist attack, to raise money for cancer research and so on) and asks them for a donation.

Box 6.2 Spam

As it often occurs within cyber-related activities, there is no agreed definition of spam. Existing definitions focus on the unsolicited nature of a message or the fact that the message is sent in bulk. The term 'spam' has a curious origin. A brand of canned meat, Spam, was at the core of a Monty Python (a British comedy group) sketch in the 1970s, where the word 'spam' was mentioned over and over in a repetitive but humorous way. Little by little, the term entered common parlance as we know it today (Wall 2004). Besides being annoying, spam can be a vector for the fraudulent schemes encountered in this chapter: think about unsolicited emails containing invitations to meet lovers or to cure male baldness. Furthermore, spam can be used to disseminate malware (malvertising) and creates impediments to the efficiency of the affected systems and internet bandwidths.

Beyond email-propagated spam, we can find spam in blogs, fire-sharing services and so on. As ICTs evolve, so does spam. Spam over internet messaging (spim) and social media has gained a lot of importance over the last decade. Most readers have probably run into suspicious discounted Ray-Ban sunglasses adverts (or similar) in their Facebook feed: this is a common scam designed to persuade users to visit a fake e-store where their personal details might be stolen. Spam via social media can be particularly tricky, as it is sent through 'friends' we tend to trust. Spammers can harvest email addresses or social media accounts by searching for publicly available lists, by illegally accessing them or by buying them in online criminal markets; otherwise, they can try to guess existing account details by randomly generating plausible ones (Broadhurst & Alazab 2017). Spam is then distributed manually or using botnets.

A comparable problem is spamdexing, which occurs when search engines (such as Bing, Ecosia or Google) are misled by black-hat search engine optimisation (SEO). As consumers tend to trust the top entries in search engines, manipulation of their ranking is used to inspire users' confidence in rough websites (Nathenson 1998). The visibility of a website depends on a number of factors (such as the keywords used), which can be fooled. For instance, (hidden or irrelevant) keywords can be added into a webpage to artificially increase its ranking (keyword stuffing). Many search engines nowadays fight against spamindexing with some success, but the issue continues on a marginal level.

Spam is generally a high-volume, low-value activity. We need to remember that, with spam, offenders' strength is in numbers – they need only a small percentage of receivers to fall for their frauds. It is difficult to gauge reliable estimates on spam-related turnover, but it has been calculated that spammers collect worldwide revenues of about GBP 150 million per year (Rao & Reiley 2012). Not all countries criminalise or regulate spam; when they do, most regulatory efforts focus on commercial or pornographic email-spam and are not very effective (Zabyelina 2017). Technological solutions have a huge impact in mitigating the problem. There are diverse counter-spam strategies, which Heymann et al. (2007) classified into three broad types: prevention-based strategies to make spam more difficult; detection-based strategies to identify and remove spam; and demotion-based strategies to decrease the ranking of spam in an ordered list. Of course, ignoring spam is always an option.

Much email spam could be prevented with mugging – that is, altering a publicly posted email address to make it unreadable to bots (thisisnotmyaddress@domainname.com would then become thisisnot myaddressATdomainname(dot)com). Among detection and demotion-based strategies, several filtering techniques have been developed to maintain a good balance between stopping unsolicited messages and allowing possibilities for anonymity (consider avoiding treating a whistle blower's anonymous mailing as spam). Because of this delicate balance, no existing solution is completely satisfactory, with 'false negatives' and 'false positives', respectively, slipping through or being stopped by filters (Hoanca 2006; Branzieri & Bryl 2008). Filtering can occur at the level of receiving end users through blacklisting or whitelisting certain addresses, but spammers can circumvent this approach by changing address or using zombie botnets. Filtering can also discard messages with certain buzzwords by calculating through mathematical models the probability that a certain email is spam (Bayesian filtering). In addition, filtering can occur at the level of the receiving server through collaborative filtering systems aggregating information across multiple spam recipients, which is convenient as it blocks spam before it is stored locally using network and storage resources. The receipt of a message can also be delayed (teergrubing or tarpitting) to slow down the server of spammers sending out large volumes of emails (Hoanca 2006; Chakraborty et al. 2016). New anti-spam strategies are continually under development (for instance, to ensure that they also work in non-English and multilingual contexts) (Alsaleh & Alarifi 2016).

Fraudulent reviews and advertisement frauds

Online reviews have become fundamental nowadays in online and offline commerce, as they are often the baseline for consumers to identify and try a new product or service. If you are looking for a nice restaurant or a cheap room for a weekend trip or need to buy a new smartphone or a book, you are likely to look online for evaluations, comments and rankings. It goes without saying that online reviews have huge importance in many of our everyday choices and for business owners alike: bad, rather than good, reviews can have an immense impact on sales. If, on the one hand, online reviews allow individuals to make better-informed choices and help promote deserving businesses, on the other, they can also be misused in a fraudulent way to spread fake information about a certain product or service, hence contravening consumer protection legislation. So-called review frauds (or opinion spam) are becoming increasingly problematic in cyberspace, as they can be used, for instance, to overemphasise the qualities of a less-than-average product or even to malign the competition, causing massive economic and reputation harm and also jeopardising trust in sharing economy platforms (Luca & Zervas 2016; Goswami et al. 2017; Hawlitschek et al. 2016). Dishonest business owners may directly engage in fraudulent reviews or pay users to write reviews from their own accounts. Fake accounts can also be created for the specific purpose of committing review frauds, and professional fake review writing services can be a powerful weapon in the hands of fraudulent opinion managers.

Another disturbing trend is that of so-called – apologies to the reader for the churlish term – 'shitstorms' (a storm of online disapproval associated in part with insulting remarks), which can cause immense corporate reputational threats in social media (Sikkenga 2017). These waves of negative comments can also be fabricated, not only by competitors or disgruntled customers but also by mean internet users for 'fun' – in other words, they are comparable to bullying or trolling but target businesses rather than individuals. Such antagonistic behaviours are generally underreported and therefore difficult to identify. In Italy, however, a case hit the national news in 2017 after a well-known blogger and columnist discussed it publicly: a restaurant in Florence was attacked on TripAdvisor, its rating dropping from 4.9 out of 5 to 3.6, after about 50 negative and offensive comments on its Facebook page by a group of buffoons, all members of a Facebook hate group.

Understandably, social media platforms have a lot of interest in addressing opinion fraud, to the point that, in 2015, Amazon sued about 1,000 people writing and selling fake reviews. Fraudulent review detection involves finding fake reviews amongst all the legitimate ones. Reviewers' behavioural patterns and the semantic features of review content provide important data to automatically identify anomalies; these anomalies can lead to fake review filtering, identification and removal (Chakraborty et al. 2016; Goswami et al. 2017; Li et al. 2017).

Other major frauds negatively affecting trust in cyberspace are online advertisement (ad) frauds, a catch-all term encompassing several activities that might occur at different stages of online advertising. The online ad industry is massive, in the order of dozens of billions of pounds per year. With this sort of turnover, it is not surprising that it has become a cybercrime target. The most serious form of ad fraud is probably traffic fraud, where the fraudsters (manually or automatically) manipulate network traffic to inflate the number of clicks and impressions from individual visitors. As revenue models for advertisers and internet or mobile publishers often depend on the traffic generated, fraudulent manipulation can increase their own revenues or exhaust those of competitors (Iqbal et al. 2018; Zhu et al. 2017). Invalid traffic (also referred to as non-human traffic, as it is generated by botnets) can therefore cause significant problems, undermining the integrity and reputation of the digital advertising industry. Botnets, in particular, allow offenders to launch large-scale click-fraud attacks in pay-per-click ad networks, where the advertisers are charged for every click on their ads (Faou et al. 2016). Methods for detecting automated traffic frauds are constantly being developed by both commercial companies and academia (Iqbal et al. 2018; Zhu et al. 2017). Methods combining computer science and social science expertise and techniques (such as the use of social network analysis to find key players to target in ad frauds) seem to be particularly promising (Faou et al. 2016).

Health frauds

Cyberspace is also profoundly altering health services, which unsurprisingly opens the way both to fascinating developments in healthcare improvements and to dangerous criminogenic opportunities. As the internet is increasingly used to support decision-making and to market health products, health frauds propagated online are becoming particularly worrisome. The problem is twofold: on the one side, 'Dr Google' is becoming the first contact point for many individuals looking up all types of medical information; on the other side, pharmaceuticals and health marketing, which are emerging as a key industry segment, are uniquely situated compared with other forms of commercial and consumer-based advertising for the type of products and services they promote (Mackey & Liang 2017). Internet-obtained information may be used to self-diagnose a medical condition, to get information on the pros and cons of potential treatments (in a sort of peer-to-peer healthcare, as described by Mackey & Liang 2017) and even to buy medical products. When fraud, deceit or simply misjudgements occur, the social implications are extremely relevant, as health-related fraudulent behaviour may cause – besides financial, physical and social harms – public health problems and loss of confidence in the professional scientific and medical norms. In fact, severe harm can be inflicted not only on the fraud victims or other people in their circle (if the fraud victims are seeking medicines or medical information on behalf of others) but also on broader society. Suffice it to note that the online spread of anti-vax information, originating from a scientific fraud, is causing outbreaks of controllable diseases such as measles and mumps in several countries (Godlee 2011; Poland & Jacobson 2011).

In Chapter 7, we will discuss in more detail criminal behaviour specific to the pharmaceutical online markets, where the sale of substandard, spurious, falsely labelled, falsified or counterfeit medical products is a core problem. For now, I would like to draw attention to a different type of online fraud, often overlooked by criminologists, computer scientists and practitioners alike: the dissemination of (medical or pseudo-medical) information and the promotion of fraudulent therapies (quackeries) in cyberspace (Lavorgna & Di Ronco 2017). Online quackeries are a concerning development in health fraud. Desperate patients are not news, and – unfortunately – they have always been and always will be vulnerable to exploitation (Cattaneo & Corbellini 2014). In this context, online communities and social media – where debates often become polarised, dissenting voices can be easily shut down and it might be difficult for naïve users to distinguish between fake and real expertise – are providing fraudsters with an ideal platform to present themselves as health gurus while being purportedly moved by the search for profit and social prestige (Lavorgna & Di Ronco 2017; Lavorgna & Sugiura 2019).

Investment frauds

We all try to make wise financial choices. If and when we have some surplus money, we might want to invest it. Financial frauds that target investors are not news, and in this case cyberspace merely provides a new wealth of opportunities for scammers. Some of these frauds take the form of the advance-fee scams covered in the previous section: a victim is asked to make upfront payments pending high returns. Think, for instance, of the sad case of the Filipino widow losing, in 2016 and 2017, about half a million GBP to a scammer when she was persuaded to partner an oil-related business in her country. The scammer pretended to be an American in love with her, while he was (reportedly) a Malaysia-based Nigerian, part of an international ring specialising in investment fraud.

Online investment frauds, however, can also work differently. Some offenders have (partially) shifted into cyberspace very traditional types of fraud, such as cold-call investment frauds. In these cases, unexpected contact is generally made by a fraudulent investment company (traditionally via telephone, now often online) to persuade the victim to invest in high-return ventures. Once the money is obtained by the company, it can be very difficult for the victims to get it back, as the company disappears. A recent case saw the arrest of five individuals allegedly running a multimillion investment fraud syndicate that preyed on 2,000 victims across Australia. Victims were promised huge returns on share market investments via high-pressure sale tactics. The scam revolved around new software, allegedly able to tell the victims which shares to buy and sell; bogus websites and fake online magazines with fraudulent information on the company and its investment products were used to gain the victims' trust.

Ponzi and Pyramid schemes are very common types of investment fraud. There have been many notorious Ponzi schemes over the last few decades, which played a big role in the 2007 US financial crisis and global economic downturn that followed. The scheme gets its name from Carlo (Charles) Ponzi, who was born in Italy in the late 1800s and who immigrated to the United States and then Canada. While working in the postal service, Ponzi realised that money could be made by capitalising on differences in postal stamp rates among different countries. He hired foreign collaborators to buy international postal coupons (which can be exchanged for postal stamps) in countries with weak economies in order to exchange the stamps back into a favourable foreign currency and finally into American funds. Regulations governing international exchange rates and postal organisations kept him from actually realising any profit, but Ponzi was nonetheless able to brag about this investment opportunity. Soon, hundreds of people invested in his 'business', with numbers increasing as the scheme grew. Ponzi realised huge profits, early investors being paid by using the investments of later investors. However, the impressive turnover drew suspicion. After a while, a journalistic investigation noted that, in order to cover the investments made by the investors in Ponzi's scheme, there would need to be more than 160 million postal reply coupons (while only about 27,000 were actually available). The journalistic inquiry caused panic among the investors, Ponzi was obviously not able to pay them back and the scheme collapsed. Investors lost millions of dollars (Artzrouni 2009; Albrecht et al. 2017). Cyberspace is also vulnerable to Ponzi schemes. One example is the E-zubao case, which was considered the biggest Ponzi scheme in Chinese history (Albrecht et al. 2017).

E-zubao was founded in 2014 by the then 34-year-old Ding Ning as a shadow banking, peer-to-peer lending platform, matching investors with companies looking for finance. The company grew quickly and was very attractive to those unable to qualify for loans from Chinese banks. Less than two years later, E-zubao stopped trading. In early 2017, 21 people were arrested, including Mr Ning, on suspicion of embezzling 50 billion yuan (GBP 58 billion) from 900,000 investors. It seems that 95 percent of the investment projects were fake (managers created fake borrowers paying huge rates on loans to perpetuate the fraud), while the company was hoarding new capital from new investors, largely in order to pay off existing investors (Albrecht et al. 2017).

Pyramid schemes are comparable investment frauds, the main difference being that, whereas in Ponzi schemes the fraudster engages directly with all investors, in pyramid schemes, early investors are expected to recruit new investors and so on. We will encounter cryptocurrencies in the next chapter. For now, it is worth pointing out that, according to some commentators, cryptocurrencies might be vulnerable to pyramid schemes. Some investors speculate in cryptocurrencies, expecting their value to increase all the time (underestimating their potential volatility). The problem is that many investors end up in schemes where their initial investment is multiplied if they sign up new investors through referral links; this form of multilevel marketing increases exponentially the 'basis' of the pyramid; consequently, when the investment plan is fraudulent, the fraudster will eventually walk away with the victim's stolen cryptocurrencies, making the whole pyramid collapse (Vasek & Moore 2015; Bartoletti et al. 2017).

Identity frauds and identity thefts

'Identity' is a multidimensional concept with philosophical, psychological, sociological and legal implications. Discussions on 'the self' are beyond the scope of this book, but it is worth remembering that identity relates to notions of self-image, individuality and social presentation (our *persona*, how we present ourselves to the world). Legal concepts of identity aim to distinguish one person from another by using, for instance, the 'attributed identity' we acquire at birth (our name, date of birth, etc.), the 'biographical identity' we acquire during our lives (qualifications, passport, etc.) or the 'biometric identity' that depends on certain physical characteristics (fingerprints, iris patterns, etc.) (Clough 2015). As explained by Clough (2015), although the misuse of identity information also exists offline, identity-related crimes are becoming ever more connected to cyberspace as our means of identification are increasingly electronic and our identity information is stored online. Furthermore, in cyberspace, we acquire an 'online identity' (or 'internet persona'), a new social identity (or more identities) which may or may not coincide with our real name. Even our online identity, unfortunately, can be misused.

This section is dedicated to identity fraud and identity theft. Although these two terms are often used interchangeably to include a number of identity-related crimes, there are some subtle differences between the two: first, so-called identity theft is precursory to identity fraud (or, to put it differently, identity fraud is generally the result of identity theft); second, the identity used in an identity fraud might be that of a fictitious person (meaning that identity theft might not be necessary to carry out identity fraud, as identities might be completely or partially fabricated). For example, as reported by Rege (2009), romance scammers often construct their online persona by inventing ad hoc online profiles, with pictures acquired from modelling sites. To create further confusion, this fraudulent behaviour is at times called 'synthetic identity theft'. From a legal point of view, 'theft' is generally defined as the physical removal of an object (which is stolen without the consent of the owner), with the intention of depriving the owner of it permanently. Identity theft, therefore, is not a 'theft' in a technical sense but this terminology, by now, has become ingrained in the common language.

When identity theft occurs, the impostor uses the personal information he/she obtained to impersonate one or more victims across a period of time spanning hours to years. Information can be obtained in a variety of ways, from accidental data leakage or hacking to social engineering (Smith 2009). Once an identity is 'stolen', the scammer can use it to commit diverse and often multiple types of identity frauds, ranging from benefit and loan frauds to credit card and bank frauds (Finch 2007; Berg 2009) or to spread fake news. In the more extreme cases, identity thieves might assume the victim's identity in daily life (this is sometimes called 'identity cloning') or in the virtual world and especially in social media ('profile cloning') (Rizi & Khayyambashi 2013). Think, for instance, of fake social media accounts assuming the identity of politicians, such as Pakistani politician Ayesha Gulalai Wazir or of public figures such as model Laura Hunter, whose fake online identity was used to pretend she was a pro-Donald Trump activist blogger (with almost a million followers) and position her as an online chamber of resonance for bogus stories (such as Bill Clinton's involvement in an illicit sex ring) to channel conservative voters' outrage. Accounts of human rights activists and journalists in Venezuela hit the news in 2017 when they became the targets of so-called double-switch attacks on Twitter, to spread fake information. In these cases, first the hacker takes over a social media account and switches the username and then creates a new account under the original username (often displaying the same name and profile picture). In this way, the original user is unable to recover the original account, as he/she does not know the new account name of their original account and their original account name is now registered to the hacker.

In addition to direct financial, social and emotional harm (generally, most financial costs are borne by institutions providing credit or facilities), victims will waste a lot of time restoring their credit, name and reputation. Moreover, identity theft can seriously undermine a victim's sense of trust and even self (Berg 2009; Golladay & Holtfreter 2017). From the cases of identity fraud described above, you can see how it can also harm the reliability of online information and indirectly manipulate the democratic process. Fear of cyber-identity theft and fraud is generally high – to the point that these activities have been labelled as 'moral panic' (Monahan 2009) – decreasing people's trust in using the internet to conduct, for instance, financial operations (Roberts et al. 2012).

Another illustrative and emblematic case of identity theft was the 2012 hacking of Mat Honan, a tech expert and *Wired* author. Honan wrote a detailed explanation of what happened to him in the magazine (Honan 2012a), which is very useful in understanding the danger of blind spots in ID verification systems, the harm associated even with a low-tech instance of identity theft and the importance of backing up data in secure locations. To cut a long story short, a security gap (now resolved) in the connection between an Amazon account and an AppleID was used by a hacker to pose as Mat Honan and to quickly take down many of his digital accounts: Amazon, Apple iCloud, Gmail and Twitter, plus the (work-related and private) data he stored on his three Apple devices. In more detail, the hacker found online Honan's '@me.com' account, a hint that Honan had an AppleID and iCloud account. He then called Amazon, posing as Honan, and asked to add a credit card to his account (it is not hard to imagine that someone has an Amazon account, and for such an operation, the only information required was the name, a billing address (that was easily found online) and an associated email address). The hacker then called Amazon again and said he had lost access to his account. By providing Honan's name, a billing address and the new credit card associated with the account, Amazon allowed the impostor to add a new email address to Honan's account. With this information in hand, the hacker went to Amazon's website and sent a password reset to the new email address; now in full possession of Honan's Amazon account, the hacker could see the last four digits of all the credit cards associated with that account. This was enough to pass Apple's ID verification. At this point, the hacker – still posing as Honan – called Apple support and requested a password reset on Honan's @me.com account and even though the hacker could not answer any of the security questions, he got a password reset, as he could provide a billing address and the last four digits of the credit card. Apple issued a temporary password, which was all that was needed to access iCloud. At this point, the damage was done: all data on Honan's iPhone, iPad and MacBook were deleted and the hacker also started tweeting hate messages from Honan's Twitter account. With a bit of luck, a lot of patience and a certain amount of money, Honan was able to recover most of his data (Honan 2012b). His story is a harrowing reminder of the dangers we might face when we lean too much towards 'usability' in the usability versus security trade-off and that we do not fully own our accounts' security (Honan 2012b).

The extent of identity-related crimes is difficult to establish. Not only do terminological confusion and the range of agencies that may respond to victims' complaints make recording problematic, but also many jurisdictions have no systematic framework for gathering such information. Furthermore, as often happens with fraud, identity-related crimes are likely to be under-reported, as individual victims may not even realise they have been victimised and organisations may be reluctant to report a crime for fear of reputational damage (Clough 2015). To mitigate the problem, over the last two decades, besides biometric tools (think of thumbprint recognition in many smartphones), several approaches to automatically detect anomalies in online behaviours have been developed. Among the most important are keystroke dynamics during login verification; keyboard and mouse activities (behavioural biometrics); and changes in a subject's behaviour as the node of his/her online social networks (Kolaczek 2009; Moskovitch et al. 2009).

Extortion

'Coercion' is the action of compelling a victim to do some act against his/her will under the threat of intentionally performing or refusing to perform an action, committing a crime or disclosing a victim's secret. Legal definitions aside, extortion can be broadly defined as the act of obtaining a profit (such as money, property or a service) by coercion. It always involves a threat (that is, a loss will be caused to the victim unless a certain demand is met). Blackmail can be seen as a subset of extortion, where the offender threatens to reveal (true or false) information about a person to someone else. In cyberspace, two main types of extortion have made their appearance: ransomware and doxware. This section is dedicated to them.

However, it is worth remembering that, besides ransomware and doxware, a third (and probably, despite its name, less scary) threatening form of online extortion/fraud is scareware: in this case, the victim receives a message saying that something illegal was found in his/her computer and the authorities will be informed if a fine is not paid or that a certain device has been (allegedly) hacked and a bogus cybersecurity company is offering help to fix the problem. In short, fear is used to get victims pay a fee, even if there might not even be a real risk to their data (for instance, in many cases, users might overcome the threat simply by clearing their browsing history and cache). For instance, a Latvian man was indicted after extradition in Minnesota in 2017 and accused of installing malware on the computers of readers of an online newspaper. The malware unleashed a series of pop-up warnings tricking users into purchasing purported 'antivirus' software to regain control of their computers. The phony software, if purchased, stopped the pop-ups but left the malware hidden in the computers, ready for future use. For those refusing to pay for it, all data stored in the computer remained inaccessible. Another recent example is given by a vulnerability in the iPhone Web browser (now fixed), which allowed scammers (posing as law enforcement) to display an endless loop of pop-up windows, preventing victims from using the browser unless they paid a fine for (allegedly) viewing illegal pornography or downloading pirated music.

Ransomware

Ransomware is comparable to the situation of taking a hostage for ransom, where money is extorted by the threat of not releasing the hostage. The hostages, in the case of ransomware, are data, whose access is denied until a ransom is paid. Unfortunately, ransomware is becoming one of the most common cybercrime problems: cybersecurity companies are consistently reporting that since 2016 the number of ransomware attacks has steadily increased. The types of harm suffered by the victims can be significant and quite diverse, as hostage data can be anything ranging from a client portfolio built over many years to the pictures of your favourite holiday.

The two main types of ransomware are encrypting ransomware and locker ransomware. The former (which has become prevalent) prevents the victim from accessing certain data, as they are encrypted and cannot be decrypted without knowing the key; the latter prevents the user from logging into the device or from using a certain app. Some recent functions even allow the removal of backups and shadow copies on infected computers and permit offenders to communicate with the infected systems. Developers often do not participate directly in ransomware campaigns but rather sell their tools online in the form of complete ransomware or as ransomware builders (that is, *ransomware construction* kits that allow people without advanced programming skills to assemble ransomwares with specific functions). Ransomware as a service (RaaS) is very tricky from a cybersecurity perspective, as it potentially opens the way to serious cybercrimes to offenders with limited tech abilities. In particular, as many trojan ransomware are accessible as source code, anyone with some mediocre capacity of programming could release his/her own version of a trojan.

The ransomware landscape is continually changing. Over the years, several ransomware families have been coded in different programming languages, as offenders constantly try to avoid detection by security products. CryptoLocker, for instance, was an encrypting ransomware whose original version was distributed in 2013 and taken down the following year by a consortium of law enforcement agencies, cybersecurity companies and academic research centres from multiple countries during Operation Tovar. Its approach was widely copied and became so infamous that the word CryptoLocker almost become a synonym for ransomware. Locky is a locker ransomware released in 2016. Rather than being installed through a trojan or through a previous exploit as with most malware, Locky uses macros (viruses written in a programming language embedded inside a software application) installed via email attachments. It is expected that ransomwares targeting the master boot record will become increasingly common: in 2016, for instance, newly released ransomwares (such as Petya and Satana) were able to leave computers unable to boot into their operating system. The ICT industry in recent years has developed security standards – such as 'locked' and 'signed' (with an encryption key) bootloaders – to ensure that computers and smartphones boot only using trusted software; however, old devices (and those whose software and operating systems are not updated) are left vulnerable.

The WannaCry attack is an infamous example of a large-scale encrypting ransomware: within one day of its May 2017 launch, it reportedly infected 230,000 computers in over 150 countries, including the German railway company Deutsche Bahn, parts of the British National Health Service and the Colombian Instituto Nacional de Salud, the largest telecommunications service provider in Portugal, PT, and several universities around the world. Luckily enough, a few days later, a British-based computer security researcher found a 'kill switch' for the ransomware, temporarily stopping and slowing down the infection. The 'big cases' such as WannaCry are those hitting the news, but it is mainly small and medium-sized businesses that are targeted by ransomware, as they are easily technologically outgunned. These cases, however, rarely reach the news as most companies prefer to silently pay or in any case to keep everything quiet not to have reputational damages. The significant dark number remains a major problem in studying and under-standing the impact of ransomware. As one example among many: in June 2017, five people were arrested in Ile-de-France as part of the investigation of a ransom demand of the equivalent of GBP 450,000 towards an English finance company. A French-language blocking ransomware (*rançongiciel*, in French) was used.

Public administrations such as health systems, because of their organisa-tional complexity, the value of their data and the fact that they tend to lag behind other leading industries in securing vital data, are relatively easy tar-gets of cyber-attacks (Kruse et al. 2017). Think, for instance, of the case of the hospitals in North Rhine-Westphalia, the most populous state of Germany, in 2016. Through phishing via email spoofing, ransomware was installed in the system, causing severe impact to ongoing operations as doc-tors could not access patients' records. In the United Kingdom, the NHS Digital (2019) (the body that provides national information, data and IT systems for health and care services) admitted there had been an increase in ransomware attacks (apart from the WannaCry incident in May 2017), even if it denied evidence that patient data had been compromised. Only one month later, in June, the healthcare services in the Indian Sawai Man Singh Hospital were paralysed as a ransomware virus struck its online system. In 2018, Singapore suffered its worst hacking attack so far when hackers infil-trated the computers of SingHealth, its largest group of healthcare institu-tions, and stole the personal data of 1.5 million patients, 160,000 of whom had their outpatient prescriptions stolen as well.

While ransomwares are designed mostly to attack Windows systems (which account for about 90 percent of the global computer base), more recently hackers have been developing ransomware specifically targeting MacOS users. In 2016, KeRanger was the first fully functional encrypting ransomware infecting OSX and specifically the Transmission BitTorrent client installer. In 2017, it was reported that MacRansom was developed and sold as RaaS in the deep Web – easily available to anyone willing to pay a commission of 30 percent on the revenue generated in bitcoins. Although MacRansom is still less sophisticated than its equivalent on Windows, it shows that no one should assume that their devices are exempted from things like ransomware attacks. The trend is likely to continue, as MacOS users are still an underexploited target group for offenders.

Ransomware has been demonstrated to be able to attack cloud-based software as a service (SaaS) collaboration tools such as Google Drive or Dropbox, which are increasingly used by both individuals and companies to store and share data. The cloud was long advertised as a particularly safe storage option but it is not an exception to the threat. Attacks to the cloud can actually be particularly infectious, as their impact can be multiplied by infecting the files in every connected device. Cerber, for instance, has impacted millions of users since 2016 through a phishing campaign; by using a text-to-speech module, it can even read the ransom note aloud – a shrewd way to further impress victims. In addition, families of ransomware (such as Small and Fusob) have been designed specifically to target smartphones and even IoT devices. A variant of the Android lock-screen Trojan ransomware FLocker, for instance, targets smart TVs, pretending to be a message from a law enforcement agency accusing the potential victim of visiting banned adult websites and then demanding about USD 200 worth of iTunes giftcards as ransom. FLocker first tries to obtain admin privileges in the device; if this does not work, the ransomware will freeze the device's screen and deliver a payload and the 'ransom' file. Once the device has been effectively infected and locked, it collects, encrypts and sends to the offender all the device's data it can access.

Doxware

Doxware (or leakware) is the threat to release copies of private information, photos, videos, documents, emails and so on stored in your device if you do not pay a certain sum. In other words, someone blackmails you to keep some secrets quiet. Doxing, unfortunately, can be quite effective from an offender's point of view: even if a victim can limit the impact of ransomware by keeping separate backups of data, there is not an easy way to circumvent vile blackmailing such as this. The name comes from a combination of the words doxing and ransomware.

Box 6.3 Doxing

Doxing is a specific form of privacy violation which refers to the act of intentionally releasing online actual (or believed to be actual) personal information (such as emails, photos, physical addresses and so on). The word derives from the phrase 'dropping documents' and originally was a form of revenge in the 1990s hacking subculture entailing the exposure of the real identity of individuals attempting to maintain online anonymity (Douglas 2016). Doxing can be used for blackmailing (that is, doxware) but not necessarily so. Besides being used to threaten and blackmail a victim, doxing can serve the intent of humiliating, intimidating or punishing the target (Citron 2014; Douglas 2016). The information revealed might already be partially or totally available to the public but perhaps only in a dispersed form. What makes it doxing is presenting the information in such a way that promotes harassing or otherwise damages a specific individual or group of people.

Douglas (2016) distinguishes between three types of doxing:

- *Deanonymising doxing*, in which personal information establishing the identity of a formerly anonymous individual is released. The most notorious example is probably the dox of the alleged bitcoin founder Nakamoto (a pseudonym) by a journalist, which raised important debates on the ethics of doxing in journalism. Another notorious example is the doxing of another famous pseudonym, the acclaimed Italian novelist Elena Ferrante. The writer always treasured her anonymity to protect her privacy and her writing freedom, but a convincing answer to the mystery surrounding her true identity was revealed in 2016. Interestingly enough, also in this case the journalists responsible for the doxing were harshly criti-cised, as doxing was seen as a form of harassment.

- *Targeting doxing*, in which personal information revealing specific details of an individual's circumstances that are usually private (such as information that allows an individual to be physically located) is divulged. Think of the release by Anonymous of lists of supposed KKK members and sympathisers or the 'kill lists' released by Daesh, which include names, addresses and emails of soldiers but also politicians, religious leaders and so on who spoke out against the terror group.

- *Delegitimising doxing*, in which intimate personal information that damages the credibility or reputation of that individual is revealed. Revenge porn is an example. Other famous examples are the sto-len database of 32 million people who used the (hacked) cheating website Ashley Madison, which was posted in the open Web in

2015, and the publicly searchable database created by the International Consortium of Investigative Journalists containing the information of thousands of offshore companies, trusts and foundations from the Panama Papers, the Offshore Leaks and the Bahamas Leaks investigations.

As can be inferred from the above, the ethics and (il)legality of doxing are often a grey area. If in certain cases (think of the 'kill lists' or revenge porn) the wrongfulness of the act is unquestioned, in many other cases the situation is not so clear-cut. What if doxing exposes serious wrongdoing? Could the context in which information is released cause a reasonable fear for the security of a doxed individual? Could doxing be a gateway to cyberstalking or to cyber-vigilantism? Interesting food for thought is provided by the Chinese case of the so-called Human Flesh Search Engine (Gao & Stanyer 2014; Chang & Poon 2017): this strange terminology was used by the media to describe a form of doxing, here imagined as an online practice of 'human hunting', involving hundreds or thousands of online users targeting an individual to track them down in real life. On the one hand, this practice was harshly criticised for exposing people to public humiliation and online vigilantism; on the other hand, it was praised in its political dimension when it led to the revealing of misdemeanours and corrupt practices by public officials, which caused their removal from positions of power. Douglas (2016) argues that doxing may be justified where it reveals wrongdoing but only to the extent to which this is in the public interest and the information released is strictly necessary to reveal that wrongdoing; revealing extra information is unjustified. The debate remains open.

An interesting case of doxware pertains to AlphaBay, a major dark Web marketplace shut down in a coordinated action by law enforcement agencies in the United States, Canada and Thailand in July 2017. Allegedly, before being shut down, AlphaBay paid an extortionist to protect the real-life identities of a former administrator and several employees of the site. AlphaBay staff confirmed that they paid the initial ransom request but not the additional amounts demanded by the extortionist after the first payment was completed.

If you are a box set addict, you probably remember when in 2017 a hacking group (the Dark Overload) claimed to have stolen the forthcoming season of Netflix's *Orange is the New Black* and demanded a ransom payment following a threat to release several episodes online. It has been reported that ransom money was paid by a Hollywood post-production studio but some episodes were released nonetheless, allegedly because the FBI was involved. The Dark Overload released a statement claiming that they are 'in the business of earning vast amounts of internet money', that 'Hollywood is under assault' (The Hollywood Reporter 2019) and that they were going to release more stolen programming. A few months later, HBO's *Game of Thrones* was hit particularly hard with a doxware attack, probably by a different group of hackers.

Law enforcement agencies and cybersecurity experts are mostly consistent in advising victims not to pay the demanded fee in cases of cyberextortion: in fact, this paying might give offenders an incentive to ask for more money or to victimise more people. Furthermore, there is no guarantee that data will be returned, unblocked or not divulged. In recent years, several projects trying to assist victims of cyber-extortion have been created. No More Ransom is probably the most important one: launched in July 2016 by a partnership between the National High-Tech Crime Unit of the Netherlands' police, Europol's European Cybercrime Centre and two cybersecurity companies, it offers an online platform providing decryption tools to ransomware victims as well as prevention advice.

Concluding remarks

This chapter has provided an overview of cybercrimes pivoting around deceptive and coercive behaviours. As anticipated in the introduction, profit is often the key motivation for these crimes but this is not always the case. Given the diversity of the crimes encountered and the broad spectrum of the possible motivations at their core, it is likely that a broad range of criminological theories and approaches might come in useful to provide us with a framework to better understand them. Interestingly enough, however, most theoretical efforts so far have focused on how offenders target potential victims. Victimisation research suggests that offenders may cast big nets, but the behaviour of potential victims is the discriminating factor between those who are victimised and those who are not. Adaptations and integrations of opportunity approaches and especially routine activity theory (Cohen & Felson 1979) and self-control theory (Gottfredson & Hirschi 1990) are proving particularly successful in providing indicators of victims' vulnerability, showing how impulsive people are overall more involved in risk-enhancing online routines (van Wilsem 2013b). In more detail, routine activity theory explains what puts individuals at risk of victimisation in the first place, as certain online victim routines (such as online purchasing and social networking) facilitate opportunities for victimisation because of the accessibility, visibility or proximity of the victim to a motivated offender, target attractiveness (such as individuals who provide a lot of personal information online) and lack of guardianship (for instance, not using a good antivirus and ad blocker). Overall, routine activity theory is also proving its utility in explaining crimes at a distance, which suggests that situational crime prevention techniques focusing on online banking, e-commerce, communicating and downloading activities could be particularly effective in reducing victimisation (McNally & Newman 2008; Miró Llinares 2011; Reyns 2013; Choi et al. 2016). Self-control theory, on the other hand, is proving successful in demonstrating the relationship between low self-control behaviours and exposure to online victimisation, which is due, for instance, to how people with low self-control respond differently to fraudulent online communications (Holtfreter et al. 2008; Pratt et al. 2010; Reyns & Henson 2016).

This chapter has also given us the opportunity to further our reflection on the glocalism of cybercrimes, introducing some policing aspects that we will re-encounter towards the end of the book. In regard to the crimes analysed in this chapter, it can be argued that cyberspace has led to the globalisation of both fraud and extortion, with (some) offenders moving online or starting new criminal enterprises online to expand the pool of potential victims and to exploit jurisdictional boundaries to avoid detection and prosecution (Button & Cross 2017). However, this does not mean that all cyber-frauds and extortions have moved to cyberspace or that they all have an international element; some still require offline interactions between the parties involved and might well occur within geographical proximity. Recent research shows that, in many sale frauds, the victims and the perpetrators are in the same country (Levi et al. 2017). We should not forget that cyber-crimes always have an offline and local dimension (Lusthaus & Varese 2017). In addition, the impact of cybercrimes is generally suffered at the local level, and there are local specificities we need to be aware of if we want to understand cybercrimes to their full extent and develop effective counterstrategies. This challenge is not going away; rather, it becomes more and more urgent to address, as cyberspace increasingly penetrates our lives and routines, also within demographics and geographical areas that were once less implicated. Hence, in order to limit the harms suffered by a small business suffering from a ransomware attack or by individual targets of advance-fee frauds, sufficient staff with cybercrime expertise and support systems should be present at every level to reduce the impact of cybercrime-related harms. Unfortunately, because of a lack of resources, in most countries specialist services are still used only for major cases, often in metro-cities, while smaller neighbourhoods are often not properly assisted.

? CRITICAL QUESTIONS

- Financial damages related to cyber-frauds can be very significant for both individuals and companies. We live in a time when attacks are increasing in frequency. The risk of these cyber-threats, however, is also an opportunity for insurers, which are developing products and solutions in this area. Given that unlimited cover could be problematic for insurers (as it might result in massive losses for them) and that insurers tend not to cover customers who have not taken minimum security protection (such as updating their malware protection), to what extent do you think insurers should cover the costs of cyber-frauds? In articulating your answer, please consider the level of public awareness and the technical specificities of cyber-risks.

- In Chapter 4, we discussed hacker subculture and its ethics. Online extortion is an area where the idea of 'hacking for a good cause' is challenged. Also within the hacker community, certain attacks (for instance, ransomware on hospitals) have been condemned as treacherous. Do you think that these attacks are a sign that the hacker community and its ethics are changing, or rather of the heterogeneity of the hacker subculture?

- In 2016, a senior British police officer was accused of victim-blaming when he said that victims of online fraud should not be refunded by banks if they fail to protect themselves from cybercrime, as this would reward bad behaviour rather than incentivise people to adopt basic security practices (such as updating their antivirus software, improving passwords, doing backups). This view is very widespread: it is often said that many victims of online fraud and extortion might have avoided victimisation or at least mitigated the harms suffered had they taken reasonable precautions. To what extent do you think this can be considered victim-blaming? If so, what might be the negative consequences of such an attitude? If not, to what extent should victims be held responsible for their victimisation? In your answer, please consider the level of public awareness and the technical specificities of cyber-risks.

- If cyber-frauds and extortion victimisation can be (at least partially) explained by routine activity theory, what type of prevention measures might be suggested? Identify at least three situational crime prevention strategies and critically discuss their potential strengths and weaknesses.

7 MARKET-BASED CRIMES AND CRIMES AGAINST PROPERTY

Introduction

This chapter focuses on (cyber) market-based crimes and property crimes. Market-based crimes are here broadly defined as illicit and illegal trades – where *illegal* refers to the trade of a product forbidden by law because it endangers some fundamental interests of society (such as heroin or stolen credit card information) and *illicit* to the trade of a product that could be legally traded under different circumstances (such as in the case of certain pharmaceuticals). It would be unfeasible to provide an overview of all possible criminal markets online: as for legitimate markets, anytime that there is a potential overlap between the demand and the offer of (illegal or illicit) goods or services, a criminal market is created. This is why in the first part of this chapter you will encounter a selection of criminal markets active in cyberspace: some of these markets (like the carding one) are active practically only online, others (such as those in recreational drugs) have been significantly changing online but their offline component is still prevalent. Some of these markets are active almost exclusively in the 'deep Web' (that is, the part of the Web that is not indexed by search engines) and generally in that part of the deep Web that is the 'dark Web' (which requires a specific software or configuration to access, such as the Onion Router (Tor)-based forums); others rely on the surface Web (also open Web or 'clearnet', the regular unencrypted part of the Web), such as on social media accounts, to reach a wider pool of potential customers.

In this chapter, we will also discuss some important forms of property crimes for which cyberspace has changed, or is changing, the rules of the game. Those targeting banks and financial institutions will be encountered when we discuss the online trafficking of credit cards and bank account information in the section on financial theft, carding and crimeware markets. Later in this chapter, we will discuss a specific form of property – intellectual property – and to what extent, if at all, certain forms of its online infringements can be considered forms of 'theft'.

Illegal markets online

Market-based crimes are criminal activities well rooted beyond cyberspace too. Cyberspace, however, has allowed new criminal markets to emerge and created whole new sets of challenges and opportunities for both offenders and law enforcement bodies. In this first part of the chapter, we will deal with how the internet is changing the characteristics of criminal endeavours (regarding both the carrying out of the crimes and the patterns of relations in and among criminal networks) as well as the dynamics of social and institutional control. Market-based crimes are continuously evolving criminal activities, as they are pliable to innovations and transformations in technologies, in the market economy, in the law enforcement action and in the policy agenda. Looking at them is like attempting to take a snapshot of a constantly evolving phenomenon. Nonetheless, trying to identify common patterns and trends is a necessary starting point to enhance crime prevention and disruption while maintaining a balance between openness and security on the internet.

Market-based crimes are typical examples of economic crimes: the profit motive is what motivates the existence of a certain criminal enterprise. As cyberspace has introduced a completely different approach towards the creation, management and control of money, before we look into specific types of illegal markets online, it is worth a digression into transmission (and even the creation!) of money online. Since the 1990s, several digital currencies – that is, currencies stored and transferred electronically – have been created, allowing instantaneous and borderless transactions. Digital currencies can be of different types: they can be centralised (when there is a central control over the money supply, as with PayPal) or decentralised; some rely on cryptography, some do not; some allow the reversal of payments (so-called 'soft digital currencies', as in the case of credit cards), some do not. Only some interact with physical currencies: virtual currencies, for instance, are a subgenre of digital currencies that are not intended for use in 'real life' and are generally used by gamers across the Web to buy, for instance, avatar clothing, weapons and virtual furniture (Mennecke et al. 2007; Hamari & Keronen 2017). It should be noted, however, that the features of digital and virtual currencies change all the time. For instance, virtual currencies are increasingly having an actual value, with practices such as Real Money Trading (RMT, exchanging in-game currency for real cash) becoming increasingly common (Balnaves & Madden 2016; Switzer & Switzer 2016; Nazir & Siu Man Lui 2017). If we look at the broad arena of digital and virtual currencies with our criminological hat on, we can foresee a number of deviant and criminal activities that could occur: think, for instance, of hackers who might steal virtual currencies from gamers (Kim et al. 2017).

Many examples in this section will focus of soft digital currencies, which are still the most widely used forms of money that can be affected in and through cyberspace: online banking systems are becoming increasingly common and banks and financial institution constantly trade, transfer and manage money through the Web. Nonetheless, there is a specific subset of digital currencies – so-called cryptocurrencies, sets of digital assets that use cryptography to secure their creation and usage in a decentralised way rather than relying on central authorities – that have become particularly important for the political economy of cybercrimes, as they are increasingly used in market-based crimes. Cryptocurrencies were released in the late 2000s during a wave of discontent for the existing monetary systems at the beginning of the global economic and financial crisis. Motivations behind cryptocurrencies are diverse and depend on cryptocurrencies' unique features: their integrity and non-falsifiability rely on mathematical properties rather than on physical properties or faith in central banks, they do not demand the sharing of personal data and transactions are irreversible (Moore & Christin 2013; Pérez-Marco 2016). However, there are still many unknowns and 'moral ambiguities' (Dierksmeier & Seele 2018) associated with existing cryptocurrencies and their possible developments, so that reactions are very divided. In any case, cryptocurrencies are of great importance as they are changing the perception of what money is or could be (Halaburda & Sarvary 2016). According to economic theory, money serves as a medium of storing value (the ability to buy goods and services in the future), a medium of exchange (to make payments) and a unit of account (to measure the value of items). For the moment, cryptocurrencies serve as money only for relatively few people and to a limited extent: they are used mainly as stores of value rather than as media of exchange or units of account and only in parallel with traditional currencies (Ali et al. 2014). However, this situation might change, as cryptocurrencies are gaining acceptance from consumers, entrepreneurs and investors. Consider that the social media giant Facebook is said to be finalising plans to launch its own cryptocurrency. The next box is dedicated to cryptocurrencies and the following one to the technology at the basis of many of them.

Box 7.1 Cryptocurrencies

Bitcoin, the first decentralised peer-to-peer cryptocurrency, was created in 2008 by an anonymous author (or group of authors) under the name of Nakamoto (2008). The author(s) is (are) allegedly part of the cypherpunk community – a cyber-subculture that combines cyberpunk and individualism and promotes the use of strong encryption to preserve privacy (Pérez-Marco 2016). Since then, numerous cryptocurrencies have been created (such as Litecoin and Peercoin), although bitcoin remains the most important one; it is not easy to assess whether its success depends on its design or on its first-mover advantage (Bonneau et al. 2015).

Cryptocurrencies represent important technical innovations. Bitcoins, for instance, are produced through a process called mining. 'Miners' are members of the bitcoin community who provide computational power to assist with the verification of new payments and add transaction records to bitcoin's public ledger of past transactions (so-called blockchain). In this way, it is possible to distinguish legitimate bitcoin transactions from attempts to re-spend coins already spent elsewhere. As with new gold mined from the ground, new bitcoins are brought into the system from mining: miners are rewarded with a certain number of bitcoins and are paid some (low) transaction fees. In this way, new currency is issued and incentives are created for more people to join the system (Lavorgna 2015b). Bitcoins are a fixed-money supply system: *the maximum number of bitcoins to be mined is limited to 21 million (to be reached by 2040) by the Nakamoto protocol*. It should be noted, however, that a fixed supply is not an inherent feature of cryptocurrencies (Kaskaloglu 2014).

Cryptocurrencies have some enthusiastic supporters. The mathematician Pérez-Marco (2016, p. 8), for instance, welcomes the 'technology coup' that can bring back to the citizens the ownership of money, overcoming our 'outdated' and centralised financial system; cryptocurrencies are considered more secure and less erosive of individual liberties as they better protect the privacy of those involved in economic transactions (Halaburda & Sarvary 2016; Swam 2016). Cryptocurrencies might also help social inclusion, as they can make micro and cross-border payments easier and provide a solution for the 'unbanked' – those with no access to banking services (Vigna & Casey 2015; Pérez-Marco 2016). On the other hand, cryptocurrencies are considered problematic at different levels as they escape national regulations: for now, the legal status of decentralised cryptocurrencies varies significantly across countries, with some banning them (for instance, Ecuador, Bolivia and Kyrgyzstan), others (the majority) trying to regulate their use and some (such as China and Russia) looking for some sort of state cryptocurrency. On the macro-level, at least for now, cryptocurrencies do not pose a risk to financial stability. However, should they become more widespread, economists believe that they could harm economic systems: they might lead to high volatility in prices, without the presence of centralised control systems able to adjust inflationary pressure (Ali et al. 2014).

At the meso- and micro-levels, the unique features of cryptocurrencies make them exploitable for a number of criminal activities, and the whole history of cryptocurrencies has been associated with cybercrime (De Filippi 2014; Kethineni et al. 2018). In the case of bitcoin, for instance, there are mechanisms to hide the money trail, such as the mixing service: this allows users to transfer bitcoins to a mixer pool, which then transfers back in small transactions the same amount of coins to different addresses under the control of the initial user. Both the values of the transactions and the timing are randomised to avoid tracking (Lavorgna 2015b; Reynolds & Irwin 2017). Several analyses have focused on the use of cryptocurrencies as the preferred payment method in illegal online trades (Martin 2014a; Van Hardeveld et al. 2016), in ransomware cases (Liao et al. 2016) and for money-laundering (Brown 2016). Cryptocurrencies have been linked to the funding of a number of terror attacks in Europe and Indonesia, as terrorist organisations are trying to mitigate the risks associated with traditional fund transfer methods (Irwin & Milad 2016). Cryptocurrencies are also at a risk of fraud and theft (Moore & Christin 2013; Ali et al. 2014). The most famous case is probably the one of Mark Karpelès, CEO of the (then world-leading, now failed) bitcoin exchange Mt Gox. He was charged in September 2015 by Japanese prosecutors for embezzlement, being accused of having manipulated account balances and stolen bitcoins (an amount valued at millions of dollars) from customers. It has also been claimed that certain cryptocurrencies might work as a Ponzi scheme (Vasek & Moore 2015; Bartoletti et al. 2017).

Box 7.2 Blockchain

The blockchain system, as anticipated in the previous box, is the real breakthrough in terms of technological innovation at the basis of cryptocurrencies. The blockchain system, in fact, has provided a good enough solution to the 'Byzantine generals' problem' (Lamport et al. 1982), an agreement problem built around some imaginary generals who have to make a decision whether to attack or retreat and can communicate the decision among themselves only via one messenger. The generals are aware that some of them might be traitors, but they still need to agree on a common plan of action or there might be disastrous consequences. With cryptocurrencies, a common decision (consensus) between several parties (computers rather than generals) is needed for the correct functioning of the system, but we know that some parts of the agreement might send a deceitful message (through the digital communication system, aka the messenger). Thanks to the blockchain system, it is possible to include a 'proof-of-work' – that is, a piece of data that is time-consuming and resource-intensive to produce but easy for others to verify. In other words, in order to validate any message sent between parties, a piece of information is added; the mathematical characteristics of this piece of information make it very lengthy and expensive (in terms of resources) to tamper with (it is worth noting that some developers are now moving towards a 'proof of stake' mechanism, which depends on a validator's economic stake in the network). In the case of bitcoins, for instance, miners create 'hashcash' (cryptographic algorithms) proofs-of-work, which serve to validate the blockchain transaction log. Therefore, thanks to the blockchain system, cryptocurrencies such as bitcoin are considered fault-tolerant systems (meaning that they continue to function to a level of satisfaction even in the presence of faults): for the first time, it is possible for a distributed network to reach an agreement about every transaction that takes place. Furthermore, it is now possible not only to record those details but also to make these records mathematically impossible to forge (Halaburda & Sarvary 2016; Pérez-Marco 2016).

Because of the solution it provides, the blockchain system has applications that go well beyond cryptocurrencies: a sort of super-sophisticated account ledger, it has the potential to decentralise how we store data and manage information, shifting the power away from centralised authorities. In other words, it is a new tool for organising complex systems, allowing for more transparent, efficient and secure coordination – at least in theory – as it creates permanent records of all data changes in a way that cannot be altered or deleted without leaving a record.

Among the countless applications, blockchain is starting to be used for identity-management systems, land registries and healthcare records, to prevent event ticket frauds and to track the supply chain for virtually all types of products (think, for instance, of the possible impact this can have in terms of countering counterfeit goods frauds). The car industry is also starting to explore blockchain's potential, with companies like Toyota presenting in 2017 plans to use blockchain to monitor and distribute information about the safety of autonomous vehicles, to tackle frauds and to create usage-based insurance products. Another innovative application pertains to smart contracts – that is, a computer protocol designed to facilitate the negotiation and verify and/or enforce the performance of a contract. The blockchain platform Ethereum has already introduced smart contracts among its functionalities. By providing a higher level of security compared with traditional contracts (as they can be made self-executing and self-enforcing), smart contracts would reduce many of the transaction costs associated with traditional contracting. Furthermore, the idea is that the replacement of legalese with computer code would reduce potential points of contention, as computer codes do not have the nuance of human languages. However, this approach could also entail a few negatives: interpretation is fundamental in legal reasoning and a certain degree of flexibility is often necessary to ensure fairness, equality and justice.

All these blockchain applications are still highly experimental and are changing very quickly, but their potential far-flung implications are indisputable. There will be the need to regulate (and to understand how to regulate) blockchain technology in ways that have yet to be fully explored under existing legal theories (Wright & De Filippi 2015; Halaburda & Sarvary 2016; Swam 2016) (Figure 7.1).

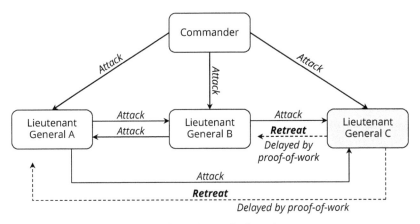

Figure 7.1 Byzantine generals and proof-of-work

Financial theft, carding and crimeware markets

Over the years, cybercrimes affecting the banking and financial sectors have come increasingly under the spotlight because of the severe financial harm they can cause – from both an individual and a societal point of view – and because they are becoming more frequent by the day. These crimes have in common the fact that, at some point, very important data – that is, financial information – is 'stolen' or otherwise compromised on individual or institutions. As already explained in the section on identity theft, (financial) data cannot be the object of 'theft', strictly speaking, even if this is the terminology that has become prevalent. Financial theft can occur in different ways, many of which we have already encountered in previous chapters:

- via low-tech fraudulent schemes such as those encountered in Chapter 6. Think, for instance, of IBAN redirection frauds, where the victim (often a company with financial interests in several countries) receives a fraudulent email from a business partner notifying that all future payments are to be sent to a different, new IBAN;

- via hacking or attacks, like those encountered in Chapter 4;

- in a mixed high-tech/low-tech way, such as in cases of 'card-non-present' transactions (Smith 2009). These transactions are very common when the physical card does not need to be involved for a payment to occur (for instance, when the transaction is finalised via phone or via an online form). If the thief has access to the card numbers, the authority of the cardholder will not be checked. Card numbers can be accessed through illegal hacking or carding or simply by taking note of them during a payment: in certain countries such as the United States, for instance, table-side wireless credit card machines are less common than in Europe, while it is common to hand the credit card to a waiter, who will use the information present on the card to complete the payment.

Of course, financial information is not the only type of valuable data that can be 'stolen'. Take a look at the following box before proceeding with the rest of the chapter.

Once financial information has been accessed (for instance, though phishing or by using credit card skimmers at ATMs), data can be used directly by the offender or it can be sold online in dedicated markets. Data are valuable and some are willing to pay a lot for it.

Box 7.3 Unauthorised access of information

The 'stealing' or unauthorised access of personal identifiable details of someone else goes generally under the label of information (or data) theft (Okeke & Shah 2016). Information, however, is typically not the object of theft but rather of unlawful copying or appropriation – hence, we will refrain from using the 'theft' label, at least in this section. Here, we are encountering forms of unauthorised access of information that are focused specifically on financial information, but unauthorised access of information can be linked to many other cybercrimes. It can occur to individuals, companies or public institutions alike and can depend on a wide array of motivations: it could, in fact, be motivated by revenge, greed, patriotism, jealousy and so forth. The victim might be aware of the data breach or not realise it until it is used for something else; the victim might retain a copy of the data or data might be compromised so that the victim 'loses' them; the data breach might be intentional or not.

The offender might be a stranger or someone well known to the victim. The insider threat problem is an ever-present problem faced by any organisation and the more difficult to deal with: an employer already has legitimate access to a system and at times it might be hard to determine whether an act is malicious or part of a legitimate activity. Trying to minimise the risk of false positives researchers are trying to combine task analysis, artificial intelligence and risk analysis to identify anomalous behaviour of employees (McGough et al. 2015). Besides the obvious case of the insider who actively 'steals' or compromises information with bad intentions (or – in the case of a whistle-blower – with intentions that might be good from his/her own perspective but still bad from the organisation's point of view), we might have a negligent employee falling victim to a social engineering attack or an employee circumventing a procedure to take a shortcut to complete the job or to take some work home (McGough et al. 2015). Common policies such as 'bring your own device' can provide a lot of benefits to both productivity and staff morale but can also facilitate data breaches.

Common techniques to unlawfully access information are podslurping and bluesnarfing: the former is used to download a large amount of data from a computer of the corporate network (manually or with the help of dedicated software to search for important hidden files), whereas the latter exploits Bluetooth connections (a high-speed but short-range wireless technology for exchanging data devices) to copy data from wireless devices without leaving any evidence of the attack (Cavalancia 2010). Attacks that remain undetected by the victim (stealth attacks) can be extremely dangerous, as data access could go unnoticed for years, producing damage without the victim being able to fix the situation.

Of course, the commercialisation and ubiquitousness of ever-new technological products – think of the IoT or wearable tech – entail a lot of new challenges and new approaches to data security. The underlying problem is that too often convenience and usability are more important than security for developers and users alike, and the security frameworks currently in place are not considered adequate to properly cover emerging technologies. IoT security, for instance, is still implemented mostly through a self-regulation process: a lack of security in current IoT implementations, a lack of detailed IoT guidelines in current security standards and a lack of IoT laws and regulation at both national and international levels are still hindering key security requirements in this sector (Ahlmeyer & Chircu 2016). Regarding wearable tech (such as activity-tracker devices that measure data such as heart rate, quality of sleep and other personal fitness-related metrics), the personal data stored in them can be extremely valuable from a financial point of view, as it can be used to assess health risks. Think of how valuable this could be for an unscrupulous health insurer.

Carding is an umbrella term generally used to describe all the practices surrounding illegal credit card markets. It can be linked to a wide range of criminal practices: for example, in the case of an account takeover, the unauthorised use of a credit or debit card account goes hand in hand with identity theft (Peretti 2009). In this section, we will focus on carding forums – that is, the online criminal markets where financial information is traded. Carding forums, however, are only part of a larger underground illegal eco-system comprising markets – so-called crimeware markets – commercialis-ing other types of data, software or services used to facilitate a cybercrime (Gordon & Ford 2006). In crimeware markets, we can find, beyond financial information, stocks of spam services or compromised email accounts, spyware, ransomware or other malware services, hacking services, DDoS software or services, botnets, exploit kits (software designed to identify and exploit vulnerabilities in a system), cashier or money-laundering services, cybercrime tutorials and much more (Motoyama et al. 2011; Kigerl 2018). In a way, crimeware markets are generally built around the phenomenon of cybercrime-as-a-service, which poses a growing concern as it allows people with no or low technical expertise to become a criminal threat, defying the myth that cybercriminals are necessarily technical geniuses (Webber & Yip 2012). Although most research so far has focused on Tor-based forums, those are not the only convergence settings for criminals. Hosting providers and content distribution services such as CloudFlare (a cybersecurity and network company that allows customers to encrypt connections to their sites for free) are often exploited for crimeware markets and other criminal forums as ways to proactively protect the forum from a potential takedown (Butler et al. 2016).

If we look specifically at carding forums, in terms of content the messages posted in the forums can be broadly categorised as advertisement and sensitive data (Franklin et al. 2007). Advertisements are used to connect the actors in the market – sellers and buyers. Among the products advertised are credit or debit card numbers and their CVV (the pin number at the back of the card), dumps (an e-copy of the magnetic stripe of a credit or debit card), plastics (a card with an unwritten magnetic strip that can be turned into a fake one) and access to accounts on places like eBay or PayPal (Holt & Lampke 2010; Holt et al. 2016). Hacking and cash-out services are advertised as well (Holte & Lampke 2010). Mules (who act as middlemen who receive compromised funds and generally send the bulk of the cash overseas to the main offenders after keeping a small percentage for themselves) are very sought after (Florencio & Herley 2010; Leukfeldt et al. 2017a), and certain services advertise suggested possibilities of collusion with legitimate providers, such as bank staff (Hutchings & Holt 2015; Leukfeldt et al. 2017b). Sensitive data publicised in the forum are rare and generally do not contain enough information to be useful (Franklin et al. 2007). Most transaction details are contained in private messages and discussed outside public forums, in places less readable by law enforcement (Franklin et al. 2007). For instance, it their analysis on Russian and English forums, Holt et al. (2016) noticed that one of the preferred methods of contact, apart from personal emails, was the ICQ protocol, which is owned by a Russia service provider and hence is less readably accessible by US law enforcement. The hidden nature of the real negotiation makes it virtually impossible for researchers to know the actual prices paid (Holt et al. 2016). We know that advertised prices are generally low (making this a potentially high-return crime) and they depend on the type of data (for instance, standard cards are less valuable than Platinum accounts), the country of origin, the level of trust in a certain seller and even the quantity of items to be purchased: in fact, sellers often offer special discounts for major or returning buyers (Herley & Florencio 2010; Holt 2012; Hutchings & Holt 2015; Holt et al. 2016).

'Trust' is a word fundamental to understanding illegal markets, to the point that carding forums have been described as 'networks of trust' (Webber & Yip 2012, p. 195). Carding forums and crimeware markets in general are classic examples of 'lemon markets' – that is, markets that exhibit asymmetric information as buyers are unable to distinguish the quality of goods and easily identify potential rippers (Akerlof 1970; Franklin et al. 2007; Herley & Florencio 2010; Dupont et al. 2017). Furthermore, vendors and buyers cannot turn to the traditional enforcement and protection system should, for instance, a payment not be received or a product be substandard: they obviously cannot rely on consumer rights or sue a vendor because an item was faulty. Hence, there are several mechanisms in place to make sure that trustworthy and reputable vendors are identified and that rippers are banned from the marketplace. We should remember that black markets are not without rules. In most cases, explicit rules of conduct are outlined within the forum and also sellers usually set their own terms (for instance, in terms of products replacement) (Hutchings & Holt 2015). Forum administrators are responsible for the overall good functioning of the market. They can verify users or their products, ban untrustworthy participants or moderate their activity and encourage buyers and sellers to undertake transactions only with verified forum members. Buyers can provide reviews and feedback, which helps to identify the more reliable vendors (Franklin et al. 2007; Holt & Lampke 2010; Odabaş et al. 2017). Other mechanisms to reinforce trust are prowess demonstrations (for instance, by posting tutorials), which are used as forms of indirect advertising and to establish an informal hierarchy among participants, and crime display, used not only to test whether someone is an undercover agent but mainly to assess the expertise of a potential partner (Lusthaus 2012). Hence, reputation is the primary tool that users have in carding forums and it is attached to their nicknames; it is so important that some nicknames are treated like brands (Yip et al. 2013).

This centrality of reputation has inspired law enforcement to look for new and more effective ways to counter illegal online markets given that standard law enforcement techniques, as we will see in more detail in Chapter 9, enjoy very limited success. Some of these new techniques attempt to 'lemonise' the market in order to create quality uncertainty: in this way, those selling good-quality products and services cannot compete with those selling poor-quality ones and with their low prices (Hutchings & Holt 2015). For instance, in so-called slander attacks, an intruder uses false defamation against sellers and buyers to undermine their verified status (Franklin et al. 2007). Another mechanism employed to create an appearance of mistrust between buyers and sellers is the use of 'sybil' or slander attacks (Franklin et al. 2007; Holt et al. 2016): numerous identities (sybils) are forged to control the reputation system of a peer-to-peer network, therefore undercutting its participant verification and review system.

Digital currencies and especially cryptocurrencies are the preferred methods of payment in illegal online markets, as they allow quick and relatively anonymous interactions among users (Holt 2012). Escrow services are often used as payment system: as in many legal online markets, escrow services are an important tool to boost confidence in e-commerce; they act as middlemen in transaction by receiving items by both the parties involved and sending them on to the intended recipients only after every party has delivered the item. Of course, there is a loophole to be exploited in every innovation: in a bogus escrow scam, a fake escrow service is set up by the scammer which assures the victim that the expected item (sent by the same scammer or by an accomplice) has already been sent. After the victim sends the item as well, the fake escrow service closes down, leaving the victim without a way to recoup the losses. Another way in which escrow services can be misused is through 'exit scams': in this case, the escrow service is run by the market operators, who at a certain point decide to make off with the money held up to that point. A famous case is that of the online drug market Evolution Marketplace, which ended in 2015 after its administrators disappeared with millions in cryptocurrencies; the site vanished soon after.

The variety of participants of crimeware markets makes it hard to identify common motivations. Existing research suggests that the desire for higher social status and the lack of legitimate ways to it (for instance, because of previous wrongdoing), disconnection from society and peer recognition are core elements to understand forum members' motivations (Webber & Yip 2012). Once again, an integration of different theoretical approaches seems to be particularly successful in explaining online criminality. According to the interpretation proposed by Webber and Yip (2012), first, social strain (Merton 1938) gives us a framework to understand the attractiveness of certain cybercrimes for those seeking to achieve a higher status in society: carding forum members, for instance, would then present the characteristics of Merton's innovator, retreatist and rebel combined, as they self-represent themselves as fighting and beating the system. Second, techniques of neutralisation (Sykes & Matza 1957) explain why many offenders seem to perceive their actions as (relatively) victimless (for example, the financial crime is not seen as against an individual but against the banks that will compensate the victim). Finally, social learning theories (Akers 1977) and specifically differential association (Sutherland 1939) help us to interpret the importance of positive reinforcement and the exchange of tutorials among forum members. Researchers on criminal markets online have also relied extensively on opportunity theories to look not so much at the motivations for crime but rather at *how* a certain crime is carried out and, potentially, to identify points of intervention – both in crimeware markets (Hutchings & Holt 2015) and in internet-facilitated (traditional) criminal markets (Lavorgna 2014a, c, 2015c), such as the ones covered in the following section.

Internet-facilitated criminal markets

Not only does cyberspace provide space for 'new' criminal markets, but it also facilitates traditional crimes perpetrated in the physical world. This section will focus on internet-facilitated trafficking activities: having no borders, the virtual word is indeed extremely attractive for criminals involved in (often transnational) illegal and illicit trades, who can take advantage of greater international mobility and more rapid and secure communications. Trafficking activities, in fact, affect all countries of the world, even if different trafficking patterns depend on the specific item traded. Thanks to the inherently transnational character of the internet, the physical location of criminal actors is less important than it was before, providing them with the opportunity to operate in countries where there are loopholes in legislation and security that can be exploited or to easily connect with distant criminal peers. As already remarked, it would be unfeasible to cover all the relevant criminal markets; this is why we will focus only on those selling controlled psychoactive substances or other drugs and counterfeits (with a specific focus to counterfeit pharmaceuticals), which have been at the centre of much research. Nonetheless, once you have understood the main criminal mechanisms at stake, you should see how this 'market approach' can help you think of any other market-based criminal activity independently; consider, for instance, internet-facilitated trafficking of weapons (Rhumorbarbe et al. 2018), cultural objects (Brodie 2015) or wildlife (Lavorgna 2014a).

Among all trafficking crimes, drug trafficking is probably the one where the role of the internet has received more scholarly attention. 'Drug' is a term of varied usage that indicates any chemical agent that alters biochemical or physiological processes. In the context of the international security agenda, controlled drugs are those listed in the schedules annexed to two international treaties: the 1961 Single Convention on Narcotic Drugs – which considers mainly plant-based products such as cannabis, coca, opium and its derivatives but also synthetic narcotics such as methadone – and the 1971 Convention on Psychotropic Substances – which extended the international drug control system to include substances such as amphetamine-type drugs, sedative-hypnotic agents and hallucinogens. Depending on the schedule they are listed in, drugs are subject to different control regimes. The last core international treaty dealing with drug trafficking is the 1988 United Nations Convention Against Illicit Traffic in Narcotic Drugs and Psychotropic Substances, which adds additional legal provisions for enforcing the 1961 and 1971 conventions in order to consolidate international cooperation between law enforcement bodies. The 1988 Convention also regulates chemicals used to manufacture controlled drugs. Besides these international legal instruments, all modern nations have regulatory frameworks that prohibit the importation, manufacturing, growth, distribution, sale and use of a variety of drugs. However, efforts to counter drug trafficking suffer from the presence of so-called new psychoactive substances (NPSs, sometimes called 'designer drugs' or 'legal highs'), an umbrella term indicating all those drugs that are not yet under regulatory control but that may pose a public health threat (Lavorgna 2014c). Harms caused by drug trafficking affect individuals, private-sector entities, governments and the social and physical environment (Paoli et al. 2013); they can be very diffuse and pervasive, ranging from the loss of material interests, privacy and reputation to the loss of life and other physical and psychological damages.

Cyber-hotspots for recreational drugs – hubs where all interactions among all actors involved in drug trafficking are facilitated (not only drug sales but also, for instance, the recruitment of drug mules) – are present in both the surface and the dark Web (Lavorgna 2014c). In the surface Web, sellers and buyers can easily 'meet' on commercial or auction websites or in social networks; these platforms can inform searchers of (online and offline) places both to buy drugs as well as offer instruction to cultivate plant-based drugs or to manufacture synthetic drugs. This is common especially for cases regarding NPSs or 'soft' drugs such as cannabis – that is, drugs that are generally considered less socially reprehensible or that run on the edge of legality and for which differences among national legislations can be easily exploited (Lavorgna 2014c). Most criminal markets for recreational drugs, however, concentrate in dark Web forums in what are often described as 'cryptomarkets' as they rely on advanced encryption to protect their users' anonymity (Martin 2014b). Anonymity, once more, is key for the success of the market: users rely on coded names to conceal their identity and use cryptocurrencies as the preferred method of payment. If anonymity is a benefit as it makes forum users less detectable by law enforcement, it is also a cost as the detachment between physical and online identities forces participants to establish trust in different ways (Lusthaus 2012). As in crimeware markets, customer reviews and feedback are very important to enable sellers to build their online reputation. Forum administrators have, once again, a crucial role in reducing or eliminating scams, and – at least in the most successful markets – they proactively help participants to manage conflicts, maintain trust and support a cohesive community (Morselli et al. 2017). In return, they keep for themselves a small percentage (generally 2 to 4 percent) of the transaction value for every sale. Overall, online drug markets are perceived as safer markets, as from the one side they provide a less violent alternative to conventional drug distribution and from the other they empower consumers to get more information regarding the quality of the products they are purchasing (Martin 2014b, 2016).

An important innovation in online drug trafficking can be attributed to the active presence of psychonauts – that is, people who take drug themselves – entering the market, often as small-scale traders promoting positive drug experiences (van Hour & Bingham 2013). Nonetheless, most trades are increasingly dealt with by professional dealers, with a small number of forum users being responsible for a large proportion of sales (Munksgaard & Demant 2016; Décary-Hétu & Giommoni 2017). Drugs are generally delivered via the postal service, without any physical interactions among buyers and suppliers (Lavorgna 2014c). Packaging is professional and designed in such a way as to avoid the unwanted attention of the postal services or customs. Van Hout and Bingham (2013), for instance, describe a case of LSD being well hidden in a Christmas card. Drugs are generally shipped in small quantities to fit regular post envelops (Martin 2014b). Some vendors advise their customers of security-related risks (for instance, a common piece of advice is to supply real names for delivery to avoid being identified as suspicious by the postal services and flagged for further investigations or to use pseudonyms and never to have items posted to the place of residence), but most sellers down-play the risks and focus on securing the trust of potential customers (Martin 2014b; Aldridge & Askew 2017).

The most notorious cryptomarket, probably because it was the first to hit international headlines, was Silk Road, initiated in 2011 and shut down by the FBI in 2013 (Barratt 2012; van Hout & Bingham 2013). Many other markets are active nowadays, some targeting an international clientele, others a more local one (such as the Finnish Valhalla or Silkkitie or the Swedish Flugsvamp); recent research suggests that national and regional forms of distribution are becoming dominant (Demant & Munksgaard 2017). When cryptomarkets are disrupted by law enforcement operations, they are generally replaced by new markets: crime displacement is high and research indicates that police operations have some deterrent effect (but limited in time to one or two months) (Décary-Hétu & Giommoni 2017). In general, traditional policing approaches are not effective to monitor online drug markets: given the expanding volume of global trade, it is easy to see how it is extremely difficult for postal services and law enforcement to intercept and investigate drugs in transit, and monitoring online forums (which might be in a foreign language or use a rapidly evolving jargon) can be extremely resource-intensive.

Innovative approaches (like the attempts to lemonise the markets that we encountered in the previous section) and technological solutions are becoming prevalent in preventing, countering and mitigating internet-facilitated criminal markets. Automatic techniques (such as machine learning and natural language processing) for extracting meaningful data to identify market trends have been increasingly investigated by cybercrime experts (Portnoff et al. 2017). An example of a combination between traditional and new policing approaches is 2017's Operation Bayonet. First, AlphaBay, a Tor-based online market selling illegal goods (mainly drugs but also stolen credit cards and weapons), was taken down by the FBI after a joint operation between several organisations worldwide, including Dutch police, Europol and Thai authorities. The young Canadian Alexandre Cazes, a multimillionaire computer expert and alleged mastermind behind AlphaBay, was arrested in Thailand in July 2017 on charges of drug trafficking and money laundering; unfortunately, he was found dead in jail (apparently, he took his own life) while waiting to meet prosecutors pushing to extradite him to the United States. It appears that

Cazes was found out because he made the mistake of leaving his personal email address visible online in old posts, and when he was discovered he was still logged into the AlphaBay website as the administrator. Seized assets included millions in fancy properties and in bank and cryptocurrency exchange accounts registered to offshore financial centres. With the end of AlphaBay, Hansa was predicted to become one of the leading markets (as it allows the use of a multi-signature wallet for every transaction in cryptocurrencies, meaning that all funds require the signatures of multiple people before they can be transferred, which makes this system even safer than the traditional escrow system). However, the Dutch National Police quietly seized the Hansa server in Lithuania in June 2017 and took over the website; this law enforcement success was not disclosed until a few weeks after AlphaBay was taken down (moreover, the FBI waited for a while before announcing they were behind the disappearance of AlphaBay, so as not to scare its users), which gave AlphaBay users enough time to migrate to Hansa and the Dutch Police and FBI enough time to log transactions and identify both buyers and sellers – allowing an alleged total of 10,000 physical addresses to be unveiled. At the time of writing, information is being shared with law enforcement agencies in other countries, depending on the addresses discovered.

The second example of an internet-facilitated criminal market is the one in counterfeit pharmaceuticals for human use. Despite the obvious benefits of being able to purchase medicines via the internet, this form of e-commerce presents a major problem: in fact, according to the World Health Organization, up to 50 percent of pharmaceuticals sold online are spurious/falsely labelled/falsified/counterfeit (SFFC) drugs (WHO 2010), which makes this criminal activity a form of intellectual property infringement too. We should keep in mind that accurate measures of the extent of this lucrative business are difficult to obtain, but there is agreement that the problem is of a massive, global scale leading not only to financial harm but also to serious physical harms and even death (Attaran et al. 2011; Clark 2015). Whereas developing countries have long suffered from the presence of counterfeit medicines because of loopholes in their traditional distribution channels, in developed countries the internet is thought to be the only significant way in which counterfeit medicines may enter the market, as the legal production and supply chains are generally safer because of control policies set by national authorities (Lavorgna 2015c).

The online trade in counterfeit medicines is generally related to the presence, since the 1990s, of spam (Zabyelina 2017) and of online pharmacies – that is, retail pharmacies that operate partially or exclusively over the internet and that ship orders to customers by mail (Orizio & Gelatti 2010). Besides legal online pharmacies, which respect the legal framework of the country where they are established, there are, in fact, fake online pharmacies (which seemingly sell only medicine but in reality operate frauds and phishing activities) and illegal online pharmacies (which are the main system for selling counterfeit medicines, at least in Western markets). The inherent transnational nature of these activities entails that it is not always easy to draw a line of the legality of the pharmacy, as different jurisdictions have very different regulations on the topic and the legal landscape has been changing in recent years. Generally speaking, there are severe variations across states on how the public can access pharmaceuticals online; whereas an increasing number of countries are allowing the sale of 'over-the-counter' products (which can be sold directly to buyers without a medical prescription), only a minority of countries (such as the United Kingdom, Germany and Sweden) allow 'prescription only' medicines also to be sold online. Consequently, an online legal pharmacy could be accessed by customers from a country where such a sale is considered illegal (Lavorgna 2015c).

All types of pharmaceuticals can be found online, ranging from 'lifestyle drugs' (pharmaceuticals that are assumed voluntarily to improve appearance or certain aspects of personal life, such as drugs for erectile dysfunction, obesity and male pattern baldness) and anti-HIV drugs to opioid analgesics and psychotropic substances that can also be misused by drug addicts. Online pharmacies have changed over the years in response to increase public and law enforcement awareness of the problem of counterfeits, which are becoming more sophisticated. Yet, they remain the major cyber-hotspots for pharmaceuticals, even though currently they are no longer the only ones: especially with apropos doping products and lifestyle drugs, social media have become increasingly important in selling and advertisement (Lavorgna 2015c; Hall & Antonopoulos 2015, 2016). Because of the primary need to reach a large number of potential clients, illegal and illicit trades in pharmaceuticals are carried out mostly in the surface Web. However, cryptomarkets are also used, with highly abused pharmaceutical medications often sold in conjunction with recreational drugs in the deep Web (Lavorgna 2015c).

Social engineering is employed to create a feeling of trust and commitment. Through a range of marketing strategies, sellers try to target specific types of consumers who might be more prone to trust them because they feel part of the same social group: think of the case of social media targeting athletes for the sale of doping products (Antonopoulos & Hall 2016) or people interested in alternative treatments for the sale of fake 'natural' products (Lavorgna 2015c). Specific efforts are also made to obtain the trust of clients online, with sellers actively trying to reassure clients with the set-up of fictitious customer services in online pharmacies or promoting endorsements of their products via social media (Hall & Antonopoulos 2015; Lavorgna 2015c). Around forums and other social media, subcultures normalising and glamorising dangerous behaviours (such as the taking of drugs without medical checks) thrive, with dangerous consequences (Hall & Antonopoulos 2015). For instance, in the United Kingdom in early 2018, there were debates over a spate of Xanax-related hospitalisations, supposedly related to a growing number of adolescents accessing the tranquilliser online as a cheap way to 'self-medicate' against mental health problems but also for recreational use and to groom victims of sexual assaults.

Box 7.4 Online criminal networks

This section on online criminal markets gives us the chance to discuss how cyberspace has not only changed criminal behaviours and activities but also intervened in patterns of relationships among deviant actors. A growing number of studies show that over the years the Web has impacted the organisational life of crime. This is particularly true for international criminal markets that traditionally have been linked, in their offline components, to organised crime. Organised crime, however, it is not a neutral and aseptic notion but one that is deeply imbued with historical and cultural elements, as it evokes the idea of a bigger interpersonal and social threat compared with non-organised crime: the idea is that what individuals can do, organisations can do better (van Duyne & van Dijk 2007; von Lampe 2008; Siegel & van de Bunt 2012).

Many academic and non-academic articles and reports have described various types of organisational structures involved in cybercrimes and especially market-based cybercrimes as organised crime, but some researchers are more critical in applying the organised crime label (for a literature review, see Lavorgna 2016; Leukfeldt et al. 2017a): according to the latter, enough consistent and solid evidence to make analogies between online criminal networks and offline organised groups is missing, especially keeping in mind the recommendations of organised crime scholars on the fact that we need something more than some forms of organisational structure (such as a certain level of continuity of the criminal activity, violence, corruption or alliances with the political and economic elites) to have organised crime (von Lampe 2008). Debates on the use of the organised crime label in cyberspace are not merely speculative and scholastic but have a real practical significance: over-estimating organised crime's involvement in a crime can attract more resources and additional legal powers, especially regarding intrusive surveillance measures (Lavorgna & Sergi 2016; Lavorgna 2019, 2019a) and can orient law enforcement's responses and the general public's reactions alike. For instance, linking drugs and organised crime's violence is a powerful symbolic device at the core of public support for drug prohibition, but what if this does not hold true in online distribution markets? (Martin 2014b).

Existing empirical evidence – which unfortunately is still quite limited and has a strong European/Anglo-Saxon focus – suggests that alongside (more or less) organised criminal groups, most criminal groups operating online are formed of loose and transient networks of relationships. Being critical on the fuzzy use of the organised crime rhetoric, of course, is not intended to deny the presence of certain organised crime groups online or the seriousness of many forms of cybercrime. This definitory attention does not deny that certain criminal networks operating online have a high degree of sophistication (Holt et al. 2016) and attempt to regulate and control production and distribution of products and services: in online forums, as we have seen, administrators and moderators can offer a certain degree of third-party enforcement over certain transactions and regulate access to criminal markets. However, contrary to the physical world, even if forum administrators and moderators try to retain customers, there is no system of enforcement, no opposition against competitors and no control over distribution (Lusthaus 2013): a ripper might try to access the forum with another name or with the nickname of someone with a good reputation on another forum. Hence, some key organised crime characteristics are missing. Notable exceptions have been found when the offline and local dimensions of the criminal network are very strong, such as in the case of the Romanian groups studied by Lusthaus and Varese (2017): in this case, for instance, high numbers of individuals professionally geared towards online frauds are concentrated in particular towns and in particular neighbourhoods; they are often also involved in offline activities that allow them a certain control of the territory, such as loan sharking and extortion, and have links with politicians and law enforcement authorities. But these cyber-organised crime groups are formed under very specific local circumstances, and we should be careful not to generalise their features to the majority of criminal actors operating in cyberspace.

Sophisticated criminal networks aside, it is interesting to note that the Web opened the way to small-time criminals and newcomers, even if with a potential global reach (Lavorgna 2015a). Jaishankar (2009) has already underlined that a peculiar problem of online crimes is that, at least potentially, they cut across a wider spectrum of society and most typical people could hypothetically join a network of offenders or start a criminal career on their own, especially if we consider that only low technical skills are required to enter many criminal markets. Many actors involved in illegal activities often do so in an occasional or semi-professional way (for example, they might be employed in the ICT sector or in a bank or in parallel legitimate trades) and there are often many connections between legal and illegal services offered online and between online and offline activities (Bijlenga & Kleemans 2018).

Intellectual propery infringiment

In cyberspace, there is a specific type of property rights that can be seriously affected and therefore need specific protection: intellectual property (IP) rights. As defined by the World Intellectual Property Organization (WIPO), IP refers to creations of the mind (such as inventions), literary and artistic works, designs and symbols, names and images used in commerce (WIPO 2017). IP law is the body of rules governing legal rights (such as ownership and accessibility) of both tangible and intangible but valuable items, both in cyberspace and in the physical world. IP law has the arduous task to find an equilibrium in the shifting balance between the need to promote innovation and creation (giving authors an incentive for their work through specific protections such as patents, trademarks and copyright) and allow access to scientific, industrial, literary and artistic knowledge and experience – therefore fostering an environment in which innovation and creativity can thrive (Landes & Posner 2003; Netanel 2003; Gosseries 2008; Lambrecht 2017). A patent is the set of exclusive rights granted by a government (therefore, it is a territorial right) for an invention capable of industrial application for a certain period of time, in exchange for detailed public disclosure of the details of the invention. A trademark is the sign (it could be a name, a logo or other) that distinguishes the goods of a given enterprise from those of its competitors, and it is used to indicate the source of a certain product. A copyright is the set of rights protecting the creator's work – ranging from music and films to software and academic articles – from others using it without the creator's permission.

In this section, we will focus mostly on copyright infringements, which are the most common type in cyberspace. In order to promote innovation and creation before the expiration of the creator's IP rights, some exceptions are in place: for instance, according to the United States' doctrine of 'fair use' (which has equivalent provisions in many other countries, such as the 'fair dealing' one in the United Kingdom's Copyright, Designs and Patents Act), a small amount of copyrighted material can be used for a limited and trans-formative purpose (for example, to comment upon or criticise the original work) without permission from the copyright owner. This is the reason you can photocopy only one complete chapter or extracts of up to 10 percent of a book from a British University library but not the entire book.

Although IP protection varies among different jurisdictions (for instance, the originality threshold for a work to be protected under copyright law is relatively low in countries such as the United Kingdom and China), some common elements are generally present, as the legal systems need to be nimble and coordinated enough for creative businesses to operate in a global environment (Terralex 2017). A number of international conventions – starting from the 1886 Berne convention for the Protection of Literary and Artistic Work – and regional agreements – such as many provisions of European law – are in place to enable copyright-protected goods and services to move among countries.

IP law, in short, protects the 'intangibles', establishing exclusive or derivative property rights over original forms of intellectual production for a certain number of years (generally beyond the creator's lifetime), after which the creative work enters the public domain (Lessing 2004; Wall & Yar 2009). As cyberspace is inherently constructed by intangibles, it should be self-evident to the reader that the commercialisation of the internet and the emergence of ever-changing technologies have had an impressive impact on the implementation and management of IP, opening the ground to a whole bundle of new challenges. Cyberspace, among other things, allows the transmission of intangibles rapidly, bypassing many distribution costs as well as border controls. The copies disseminated are virtually identical, as their quality generally does not deteriorate in the process.

Every technological change has brought with it new challenges for IP protection: from 'warez' sites since the 1990s for the illegal software distribution, to protocols for peer-to-peer file-sharing such as BitTorrent since the early 2000s, to the rise of streaming services allowing users to view or listen to copyright-protected material directly in the browser without the need to download it. In regard to the current challenges, suffice it to think how smartphone apps have become the major culprit for illegal music downloads in recent years. Or how digital media allow people to share, shape and remix copyrighted content (Ekstrand & Silver 2014). The viral distribution of memes and GIFs is creating new sets of issues in ways that were never imagined before: memes and GIFs can have both artistic and commercial value, meaning that their sharing could undermine the copyright owner's ability to control how their work is shared, its proceeds and the derivatives it could produce. Many over the internet might be sharing and modifying memes and GIFs (increasing their value), but the initial picture or sequence was at some point created by someone who is likely to hold the copyright – in fact, adding a few lines to create a catchy meme generally does not change the copyright ownership. As is often the case in cyber-matters, the jurisprudence is still not settled.

If we want to see how IP infringement is regulated, we need first to insert the usual caveat: different legal systems have different approaches and every jurisdiction has its own way of addressing this issue. Some have been traditionally more tough in addressing IP violations: in Germany, a country with a well-organised publishers' guild and strong economic interests in this field, for instance, breaking copyright law to illegally share files can carry the risk of huge fines or even gaol time (James 1996). Others are more relaxed. However, some general trends can be identified. First, IP rights have expanded significantly over the last four decades in terms of their duration, scope and reach (Lessing 2004). Second, even if IP infringement disputes have traditionally been resolved by targeting the individual infringers through direct negotiation or civil remedies, an increasing number of cases have been targeting the service providers and have been prosecuted via the criminal justice system or through 'notice and take down' processes to block users from accessing suspect websites. This depends on the fact that IP disputes have become increasingly common and complex because of advances in technology and the relative anonymity enjoyed by the individual infringers. These changes have been successfully explained as attempts of securitisation – that is, the escalation of the politicisation of a topic, which transforms it into a matter of 'security'. As explained by Farrand and Carrapico (2012), although the civil remedies had the goal of rectifying a market failure by regulating the relationship between private parties, IP infringements are now increasingly seen as a threat to consumers, economies and even governments by linking them to organised crime groups (which is very often not the case). As a consequence, strict criminal sanctions are soaring.

Often, the term 'piracy' is used to refer to the unauthorised copying of digital goods and services (such as audio files, videos, software products and so on). However, framing copyright infringement as piracy is not value-free: it implies that the crime is so serious as to be comparable to attacking ships on the high seas. The world 'theft' is also used, denying the specificities of intangible and creative goods – that is, if someone else takes and uses an idea or an intangible product, the copyright holder is not deprived from them as if a physical object was stolen – compared with other types of property, to emphasise the monetary harm suffered by the copyright holders. In 2013, a district court in the United States came to the point of banning the Motion Picture Association of America (the trade association representing the six major Hollywood studios) from using pejorative words such as 'piracy', 'theft' and 'stealing' during a trial as they could misguide the jury (*Disney Enterprises Inc. v. Hotfile Corp.*, 11-20427, S.D. Fla. 2013). Nonetheless, this sort of framing is still broadly used in common and even academic parlance.

The copyright industries – those who create, produce and distribute copyright materials, such as music, movie and software-related industries – have a clear vested interest in overstating their losses for lobbying purposes. The costs of copyright violations, however, are still open to debate: some research suggests that, for instance, those downloading movies for free might never have paid for the same content, meaning that there is no real loss for the movie industry (McKenzie 2017). The copyright industries are also those who generally push for the criminalisation of IP infringement practices and for the demonisation of copying and sharing practices (Yar 2008a, 2019). These actors tend to stress that copyright infringements are not victimless crimes, but they hit independent artists and major corporations alike. The starving artist cliché and more or less successful 'anti-piracy' campaigns have often been used to stress the seriousness of IP violations. Among the many campaigns, one of the most notorious ones – where piracy was compared to stealing a car, a handbag and a television among other things – was done under the auspices of the Motion Picture Association of America in 2004. The farcical representations and parodies of this campaign (which can be found on YouTube quite easily by the curious reader) probably became even more famous than the original video (Cvtkovski 2014).

Despite these efforts, many people still commit IP violations on a routine basis, as in most cases there is no social shame or stigma attached to it (Lysonski & Durvasula 2008; Cvtkovski 2014). Furthermore, many artists over the years (among others, Lady Gaga, Shakira, Joss Stone, Neil Young and Ed O'Brien and Thom Yorke from Radiohead) have stated that they do not think that certain types of copyright violations (in the music industry) should be criminalised. Rather, they believe that sharing their work allows the democratisation of music, the creation of communities of shared interests and the ability to reach a wider public. In other words, cultural creativity also depends on allowing the free use of cultural heritage (Condry 2004; Lessing 2004), and a merely legal and political focus on IP infringement would ignore fundamental aspects of file-sharing – failing to recognise its importance in the development, for instance, of music cultures (Condry 2004). In 2000, singer and visual artist Courtney Love wrote an iconic letter to the music industry:

> Today I want to talk about piracy and music. What is piracy? Piracy is the act of stealing an artist's work without any intention of paying for it. I'm not talking about Napster-type software. I'm talking about major label recording contracts. [...] Recording artists have essentially been giving their music away for free under the old system, so new technology that exposes our music to a larger audience can only be a good thing. Why aren't these companies working with us to create some peace? There were a billion music downloads last year, but music sales are up. Where's the evidence that downloads hurt business? Downloads are creating more demand. Why aren't record companies embracing this great opportunity? Why aren't they trying to talk to the kids passing compilations around to learn what they like? [...] Now artists have options. We don't have to work with major labels anymore, because the digital economy is creating new ways to distribute and market music. (Love 2000)

Moving beyond the music industry, we should remember that the existence of a wide range of IP rights on intangibles is not a given. The open access movement, for instance, advocates free access to research outputs rather than making them available through a subscription business model via publishing companies. The idea is that researchers should be able to access online, download, read and use academic journal articles, subject to proper attribution of authorship, but free of most copyright and licensing restriction (Suber 2012). Regarding software development and distribution, the most notable example is given by the GNU Project, as the basis of the free-software (or 'open source') movement launched by Richard Stallman in the early 1980s. As explained by Stallman himself, 'free' here 'refers to freedom, not price': in fact, 'there is no contradiction between selling copies and free software', which is built around 'the ideas of freedom, community and principle' (Stallman 1984). Hence, freedom is about the possibility to run and modify a program as you wish but also to redistribute the copies (gratis or for a fee) as part of a cooperating community. Alternative production and distribution models like the one presented here are still non-mainstream in copyright industries, but it is worth keeping an eye on them as they might become more widespread in the coming years, as ways towards better and faster innovation.

Even if IP violations are socially widespread, most research so far has focused mainly on young people and especially on university students (Gray 2012). Once again, research indicates that, among the theoretical approaches that have been used to explain IP infringements, self-control (Gottfredson & Hirschi 1990) and social learning (Akers 1977) theories can be effectively combined to explain why online forms of copyright infringement are attractive to certain individuals – namely those who have low self-control and have socially learned digital piracy (Higgins et al. 2007). In more detail, Higgins et al. (2007) demonstrated that social learning theory has an important explicatory power on the intentions to 'pirate' movies: using data from American college students, they showed that the link between low self-control and the illegal download of movies is exacerbated by association with peers engaging in the same behaviour. In addition, research suggests that the lack of punishment certainty hinders punishment severity from working as a proper deterrent (Higgins et al. 2005), in line with the teachings of the Classical School. Furthermore, general strain theory has been used effectively to explain IP infringements, which have been interpreted as the result of a social and cultural disjuncture between socially approved means and goals (Larsson et al. 2012; Steinmetz & Tunnell 2012): the idea is that our 'consumer society' pushes us towards hyper-consumption (also regarding media content); 'pirates' are simply those who replace socially approved ways to access digital content with illegal ones (Steinmetz & Tunnell 2012).

As stressed by Gray (2012), an ongoing problem is that many studies are acritical of the assumption that IP infringements are always to be considered criminal: indeed, these types of violations are often not perceived as something illegal or deviant and are barely considered amoral or unethical (Hinduja 2007). The mainstream legalistic approach, unfortunately, ends up equating crime and deviancy and fails to recognise that some forms of copyright infringement are socially accepted in many countries and there is no social shame associated with it (think, for instance, of users of services such as SoundCloud sharing and remixing copyrighted tracks). However, in order for a law to be effective, its subjects should feel morally inclined and culturally obliged to conform to legal norms, which is also in line with the teaching of Bentham and the Classical School (Hinduja 2007). As stressed by Hinduja (2007), research should then focus on identifying what individuals conceive as fair when it comes to online copyright and its infringement, as any legal intervention that does not take this complexity into account is likely to fail in its intent.

Many efforts have been put in place to counter online copyright infringements, focusing on both the demand side (punishing individuals consuming illegal material or providing them with incentives for legal consumption) and the supply side (targeting sites supplying access to illegal content) (Daneher et al. 2017). In terms of punishment, one of the most famous cases remains that of Kim Dotcom, the adopted name of the German-Finnish creator of Megaupload, a popular file-hosting and -sharing site that was taken down in 2012. Mr Dotcom was charged with criminal copyright infringement by the United States Department of Justice; as he resides in New Zealand, the extradition battle is still open. Meanwhile, however, in 2013 Mr Doctom launched a new similar service (Mega), which is encrypted client-side: in this way, Mega cannot be held responsible for the content of uploaded files as it does not have the encryption key to view the content. This, again, demonstrates the flaws of traditional law enforcement approaches in tackling online IP violations. The provision of legal alternatives to access cultural material online, such as Netflix, has generally been welcomed as contributing to changes in the distribution and exhibition model of the entertainment industry (even if the perils associated with these new phenomena have also been underlined, as generally these platforms are geared towards business interests rather than towards a commitment to art and ideas – see, for instance, McDonald & Smith-Rowsey 2016). In any case, the provision of these legal alternatives seems to have only a partial effect on digital IP violations. Elswah (2016), for instance, studied movie downloaders in Egypt (who, before Netflix expanded in the Middle East in 2016, had no alternative legal access to movie channels) and demonstrated how Netflix is not succeeding in providing a legal alternative to illegal downloading, at least in a developing economy for which subscription packages are still too expensive.

As demonstrated by Daneher and colleagues (2017), the effectiveness of supply-side interventions depends on whether they sufficiently increase consumers' search and transactions costs for finding alternative sites supplying access to illegal content. Still, the question remains as to whether these efforts should be adopted – a question whose answer should entail a better understanding of the long-run effects of copyright and its violation in terms of creative output and social welfare (Daneher et al. 2017).

Technological innovations are also used to mitigate online IP infringements. Among the bottom-up initiatives, an interesting example is that of KODAKOne, a blockchain application of the old photography company Kodak. An image rights management platform, KODAKOne allows photographers to register both new and archive work that they will then be able to license within the platform and to sell securely, as they will have cryptographic proof of the ownership of photos. In regard to the top-down initiatives, it is worth remembering that, in the context of the Digital Single Market Strategy, the new IP enforcement strategies proposed by the European Commission entail that video-sharing platforms embrace automated anti-piracy systems – that is, sophisticated technological tools capable of recognising content that right-holders have already identified as their own. This would support and promote the (so far unregulated) informal notice and take-down procedures developed by private companies (Jacques et al. 2017). The way in which technology can be used to tackle online violations is certainly a fascinating development but such a course of action should be problematised: as stressed by Jacques et al. (2017), in fact, the privatisation of decision-making vis-à-vis when online content is blocked, filtered or removed worsens the current problem of lack of accountability of digital intermediaries, which are ultimately left to decide what unauthorised use is an infringement to be enforced. In the long run, this entails the risk of negative impacts on cultural diversity, as these private intermediaries make their decision on the basis of profit maximisation, not the thriving of artistic and cultural expression.

Concluding remarks

In this chapter, we have encountered a number of criminal behaviours motivated mainly by the quest for profit; some take place almost entirely in cyberspace, others have a prevalent offline component but cyberspace is changing them in meaningful ways. In particular, the use of the internet has made it easy for newcomers as well as for local criminals dealing with offline small-scale crimes to move online to start or to expand a criminal business (Treadwell 2012; Lavorgna 2014c). After all, many of the crimes covered in this chapter are relatively low-tech.

There is a genus of property crimes that we have not covered in this chapter as they manifest themselves mainly in the physical world and have not been changed in their main features by new technologies, but it is important nonetheless to mention them here for the sake of completeness: internet-facilitated property crimes – that is, traditional types of property crimes (think, for instance, of a burglary) that are increasingly facilitated by the unique combination of spatial and temporal information available in social media and in apps' geolocation features. Here, the blurring of the divide between online and offline is extremely evident. Wearable technology and geolocation-enabled mobile applications in particular create a significant risk of disclosure of confidential information online. As demonstrated by Stottelaar et al. (2014), for example, sports tracking apps (which are used to record data about exercises such as running or cycling on a map) make available a unique combination of spatial and temporal information about personal routine activities (such as the route followed by a runner, its duration and even the home address, as this is generally the place from where the run starts and stops). The data available can enable criminals to target a potential victim both at home and en route, as knowing where a target lives or when he or she will be outside home becomes easily predictable. Also in this latter case, changes in how the internet is commonly employed by typical users are at the core of specific shifts in criminal activity.

Another common theme addressed in this chapter concerns the blurring divide between the cyber and the physical components of many of the crimes addressed. In order to understand cybercrimes, we have to acknowledge that behind cyber-attacks there are persons (and often products) that physically exist. On the one side, there is a local, human dimension that needs to be understood if we want to better understand cybercrimes' dynamics and hence improve our prevention and countering strategies (Lusthaus & Varese 2017). On the other side, if we focus only on the online aspects of cybercrimes, we risk losing sight of the offline infrastructure that enables them. Think, for instance, of the importance of the postal delivery service in facilitating most market-based crimes (as this guarantees, for example, that the drug traded online reaches its customers) (Hall & Antonopoulos 2015); this is a postal service that in our globalised and connected world deals with huge volumes of packages from all over the world and that for obvious reasons cannot screen everything. Reducing criminal opportunities in cyberspace is not enough to counter most cybercrimes if we do not take into consideration the broader societal and economic transformation that the digital revolution also entails offline.

? CRITICAL QUESTIONS

- Which type of recent/upcoming technology do you think will have the greatest impact on online criminal markets? Why? What type of impact will this have on the characteristics of criminal markets? And on their policing?

- We have seen how blockchain technology has the potential to change, among other things, how we do business, spend and transact. In your opinion, will blockchain revolutionise our daily life?

- In 2018, researchers discovered forbidden data (copyright violations, malware and illegal content including child sexual abuse images and links) that were injected and permanently hosted in the public ledger of transactions in the blockchain (Matzutt et al. 2018). The fear is that blockchain could become a safe haven for hosting and sharing illegal data. Given that no methods are currently available to wipe this type of data, to what extent do you think it is ethical to allow everyone to add unmoderated data to the public ledger? Do you think that this type of problem will hinder blockchain's potential?

- Is digital copyright infringement common in your country? What type of deterrent strategies are there in place? To what extent do you think they are effective? Do you believe that digital copyright infringements will improve or get worse (in your country/globally) as time goes on?

8 POLITICAL OFFENCES

Introduction

In this chapter, the reader will encounter diverse behaviours in cyberspace grouped by the fact that they all pivot around a political element, being the final aim of said behaviour a political act, a policy or an idea. Not all the behaviours encountered are criminal; many are deviant or are otherwise in a grey area where the construction of social norms is still keeping pace with the opportunities given by technological developments. Still, all the cyber-activities covered in this chapter can cause significant harm and, as such, have been deemed suitable for a place in this book.

The first part of the chapter will deal with cyberwarfare, which as you will see manifests itself in many different forms; some (such as information pollution) can be particularly subtle and difficult to eradicate and are becoming a distinguishing feature of political life in cyberspace. The second part of the chapter will focus on cyberterrorism, as by definition its scope is inherently political. Finally, the chapter will cover cases of 'political deviancy', where state actors tend to exploit cyberspace to limit civil and human rights of – depending on the case – their opponents or their own citizens. Cyberspace, in this way, becomes a dangerous instrument of control.

Cyberwarfare

Warfare is the set of all the hostile activities undertaken against an adversary or enemy. It is not the equivalent of war and can be undertaken by state and non-state actors alike (Szafranski 1995). The pervasiveness of cyberspace and specifically the unavoidable reliance on ICTs by both military and civilian institutions have opened new scenarios in warfare, and the security of cyberspace soon became a high strategic interest for states (Grabosky 2016; Domínguez-Bascoy & Bauzá-Abril 2017; Rowe 2017). Think, for instance, of the Russian cyberwarfare between 2014 and 2017 after the outbreak of the war in eastern Ukraine: during the siege of the Donetsk airport, Russia was able to jam GPS, radios and radar signals, crippling communications and impeding Ukrainian troops from using radios and phones for hours at a time (Grabosky 2016). The attacks in Ukraine have raised the concerns by the international community on the potential vulnerabilities of critical infrastructure across industries, a topic to which the first part of this section will be dedicated. We will focus specifically on cyberattacks carried out by state actors, which are particularly interesting as they show the limits of the existing international framework in dealing with new forms of discord among states.

The international community has long discussed the challenges cyberspace presents in case of cyberwarfare (and, potentially, cyberwar). Nongovernmental efforts such as the *Tallin Manual* (Schmitt 2013) have clarified how established principles in international law (such as the condition of self-defence, proportionality and necessity) can be applied to cyber-operations. In line with this view, scholars argue, among other things, the importance of constraining cyberwarfare on ethical grounds and on the 'just war' theory to minimise unnecessary harm towards civilians (Buchan & Tsagourias 2012; Cornish 2017; Rowe 2017; Sleat 2018). Nonetheless, it remains to be seen how these approaches and interpretations will be implemented in practice in the near future.

The remaining parts of this section will address other forms of cyberattacks that are significantly impacting relationships among states in the internet era. Specifically, we will address the issues of contemporary variants of information warfare and of cyberespionage – that is, gaining illicit access to confidential information via cyberspace.

Cyber-attacks against critical infrastructures

Attacks against critical infrastructures can target military as well as civilian facilities such as water, power and heath supplies, critical manufacturing and food production, hence directly threatening human health and well-being (Hardy 2010; Grabosky 2016). Though still relatively rare, these types of attacks, unfortunately, are already a fact. As reported by Martellini et al. (2017), for instance, an employee's laptop was used as an entry point to install a malware capable of affecting the operations in a water treatment plant in the United States in 2006; in late 2015, a DoS attack triggered a power outage in a power plant and multiple substations in Ukraine; in late 2016, a DDoS attack disrupted the heating system of several houses in Finland for more than a week.

Only a limited number of cyber-attacks have been publicly attributed to nation-states, but the number of attacks allegedly ascribed to state actors or their 'proxies' – that is, non-state actors used by state actors (Maurer 2016) – is much higher. Historically, the most famous one has probably been Stuxnet, a computer worm reportedly created in a joint United States-Israel operation and first discovered in 2010. It targets so-called supervisory control and data acquisition (SCADA) systems, an industrial control system architecture that uses computers and networked data communications for high-level process management. Stuxnet is deemed responsible for causing substantial damage to Iran's nuclear programme, wreaking physical damage (it destroyed about a thousand centrifuges in the nuclear enrichment facility of Natanz) by means of a cyber-attack. Stuxnet is considered a gamechanger in cyber-defence, as this was the first time that extensive physical damage was done through malware capable of precision targeting: in fact, the worm was designed specifically to unleash its payload only when entering a SCADA system matching the specific characteristics of the Iranian one. Furthermore, Stuxnet helped to move discussions about cyberwarfare from hypothetical scenarios to reality, forcing the world to recognise the potential damage that cyberweapons could cause (Denning 2012).

In recent years, many large-scale attacks have been attributed to North Korea, one of the most isolated countries of the world. The typical North Korean does not have access to the internet but only to the country's national intranet service, called Kwangmyong, which is walled off from the outside world. Connections to the global cyberspace are monitored and are generally available only for government departments, trading companies and a few more. Despite this isolation, North Korea has long relied on the use of cybertechnology to develop its poor economy, creating a pool of experts with good hacking abilities. Hacking activities have been denied by the North Korean regime, but reportedly they have been used for both political and economic reasons. For instance, the Lazarus Group – which is behind the 2014 attack on Sony Pictures – has links to North Korea. The hack, one of the biggest corporate breaches in recent history, gave access to personal information of thousands of employees and to unreleased films; the hack was also considered part of the successful effort to stop a movie satirising North Korean leader Kim Jong-un from being released (Guiora 2017). Although the attack on Sony Pictures is not an attack on critical infrastructure, it shows the interconnectedness and the similarity of attacks targeting other key industries such as entertainment and telecommunications. Allegedly, North Korea has been launching attacks more and more consistently towards foreign sensitive targets in a real cyberwarfare effort. More recently, the same Lazarus Group would have been involved in the WannaCry ransomware attack and in cryptocurrency theft, allegedly using the profits to reduce the pressure of financial sanctions.

Typical points of entry for attacks against critical infrastructures are Highly Critical Wireless Networks (HCWNs) – that is, commercial wireless systems used to support a critical function. Nowadays, HCWN technology is part of many industries and is increasingly used in IoT devices. HCWNs are widespread at a global level and are increasingly employed in developing countries in Africa and Asia, where 'new' wireless infrastructures are often preferred to 'old' wired ones (Martellini et al. 2017). The problem is that the same type of industrial control system software is often used by several actors;

hence, once a vulnerability is discovered, attackers can remotely affect a variety of industries from all over the world.

This is why early warnings are of extreme importance. Many countries have mechanisms and points of reference in place to quickly collect and, if needed, share relevant information. On a global level, one of the most important ones is the United States National Cybersecurity and Communications Integration Center's Industrial Control Systems, which works to reduce risks within and across all critical infrastructure sectors by partnering with law enforcement agencies and the intelligence community. It also collaborates with international and private-sector Computer Emergency Response Teams to share information on control systems-related security incidents and mitigation measures. In preventing and responding to attacks to critical infrastructures, technical solutions such as anomaly detection systems sensitive to network traffic-based disturbances (to be integrated into industrial control applications) are of the upmost importance; network probing and surveillance might, in fact, signal an imminent cyber-attack (Haller et al. 2019). Once again, however, we should not forget the importance of the human factor, especially considering that many of today's critical infrastructures are operated by people who are not computer experts. Beyond the implementation of suitable risk management strategies and security technologies, security awareness training (which should cover the various social engineering security threats) remains fundamental (Ghafir et al. 2018).

In attacks on critical infrastructures, the physical damage is generally indirect. However, recent events such as a cyber-attack in 2018 against a petrochemical plant in Saudi Arabia, which was designed not only to shut down the plant but also to trigger an explosion, suggest that there might be an escalation in international hacking. Reportedly, the only thing that prevented the explosion was a mistake in the malware code used. As advanced cyber-attacks are expected to intensify in the near future, critical infrastructure organisations need to keep improving their security, ideally being prepared to operate even if there is a threat active on their network.

Information warfare and information pollution

Particularly likely to occur in cyberspace is information warfare (Szafranski 1995) and specifically its contemporary variant, the manipulation of information to obtain a competitive advantage over an adversary (Wall 2007). From a historical perspective, information warfare is nothing new. However, the contemporary impact of fabricated content is revolutionary, at least because of the presence of innumerable platforms hosting and reproducing this content (Wardle & Derakhshan 2017).

The weapon of choice in contemporary information warfare is 'fake news', which can be defined as news that is verifiably false and that purposely tries to mislead the reader. As lamented by Wardle and Derakhshan (2017), however, this terminology seems inadequate to describe the complexities of modern information warfare and it has been used by politicians to discredit news organisations they find disagreeable, thus becoming a mechanism to undermine the free press. A better way to conceptualise fake news is to consider it a form of *information pollution* on a global scale, which can manifest itself as misinformation (when false information is shared but no harm is meant), disinformation (when false information is knowingly shared to cause harm) or malinformation (when genuine information is shared to cause harm) (Wardle & Derakhshan 2017).

The issue of information pollution has become so pivotal in recent years that in 2016 the Oxford Dictionaries named as word of the year 'post-truth', an adjective defined as 'relating to or denoting circumstances in which objective facts are less influential in shaping public opinion than appeals to emotion and personal belief'. The direct and indirect impacts of information pollution are difficult to quantify (Wardle & Derakhshan 2017) but we know it can impose heavy social costs: misinformation, disinformation and malinformation make people less knowledgeable, can undermine democratic processes, sharpen existing socio-cultural divisions, make people more sceptical towards legitimate news producers and reduce the incentives to invest in accurate reporting (Allcott & Gentzkow 2017).

Information pollution is successful because it is cheap to obtain, difficult to identify and enjoyable: it is more pleasant for a consumer to read partisan news in line with his or her system of beliefs, rather than something questioning them (Allcott & Gentzkow 2017), and many people might not have the cultural instruments to distinguish what is fake from what is not. Social media are often used for information pollution as they can act as echo chambers where all participants are ideologically aligned. Sometimes, however, entire websites are fabricated to spread mis- or disinformation: some (such as *NewsThump* in the United Kingdom, *Le Gorafi* in France, *Lercio* in Italy or *The Onion* in the United States) are openly satirical humour websites, taking a swipe at current affairs; others, however, can be extremely dangerous as the false news they publish is disguised as factual. Another way to manipulate narratives online to promote a specific agenda is so-called astroturfing, the practice of creating an impression of widespread grassroots support for a policy or individual – where little such support actually exists – by using fake pressure groups or multiple online identities (Popham 2018). Astroturfing usually takes place on social media, blogs, forums and in the comment sections of newspaper websites. It is not illegal, but it is certainly a 'deviant' practice that hinders the smooth functioning of democratic processes.

In the effort to reduce information pollution, social media companies and researchers alike are trying to improve technologies for automatically detecting, for instance, fake accounts and bots and for reducing and deprioritising updates from sources consistently posting clickbait headlines

(Kumar & Geethakumari 2014; Lazer et al. 2018). Worrisomely, information pollution is likely to become even more difficult to identify: technological sophistication (think, for instance, of artificial intelligence able to reproduce a specific voice) can make it easier to modify audio and video files, which we generally consider trustworthy as we tend to believe what we hear and see firsthand. This issue is becoming particularly problematic now that the new generation of generative adversarial networks (GANs, a class of artificial intelligence algorithms used in unsupervised machine learning) is capable of synthesising videos from large volumes of training data with minimum manual editing (Li et al. 2018). A software tool made available in 2018 (DeepFake), for example, can create videos in which human faces are replaced, leading to the falsification of persons' identities in the video. Forensics experts are trying to find ways to expose fake videos, a task that is becoming increasingly challenging as the quality and efficiency of the techniques to generate realistic-looking videos have significantly improved. Li et al. (2018), for instance, developed a method based on detection of eye blinking in the videos, a physiological signal that still is not perfect in fake videos. However, as technology improves, the task of forensics experts becomes harder and harder.

Some 'fake news enterprises' are run by young individuals or small companies for profit. Sensationalist information, in fact, can generate easy money: if some news goes viral, it creates traffic to a certain website. No matter if the content is real or not, this traffic draws advertising revenue, often through services such as Google AdSense. Information pollution, however, can also be motivated by politics or ideology. Some creators or providers of information pollution do so to favour their preferred political candidates, playing with the fears and prejudices of voters to influence their voting plans. Notorious examples are the attempts of private companies to influence elections in the United States, Brazil and Europe through social media and the behaviour of certain Leave campaign groups in the Brexit Referendum (Allcott & Gentzkow 2017; Peters 2018; Wardle & Derakhshan 2017; UK Parliament 2018). Some issues of electoral information pollution are (allegedly) state-sponsored and this problem is quickly reaching a global scale. Already in 2013, South Korea's National Intelligence Service has been accused of trying to affect public opinion ahead of the political elections via Twitter (Grabosky 2016). In 2017, Taiwan's ruling party bolstered its cyber-defences against fears that hacker groups linked to the Chinese government were trying to influence local polls scheduled for 2018 after the party's website and staff computers were allegedly tampered with. Russian state-sponsored inference in American and European elections since 2016 has been the object of numerous enquiries.

Fake social media profiles are often used. These profiles can be created or bought online: a fake social media profile with an American name costs about 50 cents, whereas with a Russian name it costs about 10 cents. As reported in a series of congressional hearings in the United States, before the

2016 presidential election Russian agents published over 130,000 messages on Twitter, over 1000 videos on YouTube and disseminated inflammatory posts that reached 126 million users on Facebook. A notorious example of a fake persona is Jenna Abrams, a well-known freewheeling American blogger pushing divisive views on sensitive political topics such as segregation and immigration. Jenna, however, was not real: she was instead the fictional creation of 'the Internet Research Agency', a Russian troll farm.

Unfortunately, our existing legal framework is no longer fit for purpose to address these new challenges for democracy, and at the moment of writing many regulatory agencies are starting to take action to mitigate the problem. New forms of resilience against misinformation and disinformation need to be built into our political systems (UK Parliament 2018), but the task is not easy. Once again, the role and responsibilities of social media companies in this context are pivotal. For instance, in the United States, during investigations probing Russian electoral interference, representatives of Facebook acknowledged that the social network sold ads during the 2016 presidential campaign to a Russian company seeking to target voters through a number of fake accounts run by trolls and automated bots. Interestingly, the majority of ads run by these accounts did not specifically reference the presidential election or Donald Trump; they were rather focusing on amplifying and polarising divisive and controversial socio-political issues, such as gun rights and immigration. Russian imposters have also been found elsewhere, such as on Twitter, Instagram, YouTube and even Pokémon Go. Social media companies have started to find solutions to their political misuse, employing both technical and non-technical solutions. Facebook tried to respond to the criticism that it had failed to detect and respond to the use of its platform to spread divisive and fake political content during the 2016 presidential election by implementing a postcard verification system. The idea is that people who want to purchase political advertising on its site will receive via ordinary mail a specific code, hence they will need an American physical address; in this way, false online personas adopted from abroad to push election-related ads should be prevented from acting. Similarly, Facebook blocked political advertising from groups based outside Ireland ahead of the country's abortion vote in May 2018 – a vote that was expected to be tight (even if, in the end, Ireland voted by landslide to legalise abortion) and that could attract the interest of foreign powers. It remains to be seen whether this approach will suffice to block or at least limit foreign inference in electoral processes. What is certain is that cyberattacks to democracies are major threats that will need constant multidisciplinary efforts to be identified, obstructed and prevented.

Cyberespionage

As information relevant to national security and economic intelligence is increasingly stored and transmitted online, cyber political (and industrial) espionage is becoming prevalent (Grabosky 2016; Buchanan 2017).

Cyberespionage is often carried out as an advanced persistent threat (APT) – that is, a set of covert and continuous sophisticated cyber-attacks over a long period of time. For instance, reportedly, Chinese spies may for years have been accessing sensitive commercial and intelligence secrets of almost 30 US companies through a small hardware chip inserted into servers, hence compromising the United States' technology supply chain. In most cases, however, APT relies on malware to exploit system vulnerabilities and on an external command and control system to monitor the target continuously. This type of attack requires capability and resources and represents one of the most challenging cybersecurity threats. Early detection and mitigation of APT activities are not easy and require a combination of different techniques based on human security intelligence and big data analytics (Marchetti et al. 2016).

Other examples of APT have been carried out by the hacker groups identified as Guccifer 2.0 and Fancy Bear. In June 2016, Guccifer 2.0 stole emails from the United States Democratic National Committee and leaked them to WikiLeaks and the media months before the elections, together with forged material. Guccifer 2.0 claimed to be a hacker from Romania, but investigations in 2018 suggest that he was instead a member of Russia's GRU intelligence agency; allegedly, the hacker failed to activate his VPN client before logging into a social media account, leaving an IP address on a server in France, which could be traced back to the GRU's headquarters in Moscow – as the saying goes, everyone makes mistakes. The cyberespionage group Fancy Bear, which is also reportedly associated with GRU, has since the mid-2000s targeted government and military organisations by using zero-days vulnerabilities, phishing and malware to compromise targets. It is deemed responsible for a number of major attacks, such as against the NATO, the United States Democratic National Committee, the Organisation for Security and Cooperation in Europe, the German Parliament and citizens of the Russian Federation who are considered political enemies of the Kremlin.

Cyberespionage efforts can be also be one-offs. In late 2018, for example, the Dutch government accused Russia's GRU of targeting the Organisation for the Prohibition of Chemical Weapons (OPCW, the world's chemical weapons watchdog) through a close-access hack operation: allegedly, after a failed remote cyber-attack, four GRU agents arrived in the Netherlands, parked a rented car as close as possible to the OPCW headquarters in The Hague and tried to access its computer systems through specialist hacking equipment. At the time, the OPWC was investigating the attempted assassination of two Russians in the United Kingdom as well as a chemical weapons attack in in Syria.

Besides using advance technologies, cyberespionage can rely on low-tech approaches and specifically on social engineering, such as by using fake personas. Consider the following examples; in both cases, (fake) attractive cosmopolitan young women were used as honeypots to attract victims. Between 2014 and 2016, Safeena Malik was claiming to be a young activist active on social media and interested in human rights. She contacted activists, journalists and trade unions offering research and asking for information, generally soliciting the recipient to open a Google Docs link. Safeena, however, was not real and her messages were phishing attempts targeting people working on human rights issues across Qatar, as cybersecurity experts at Amnesty International discovered. In 2016 and 2017, a certain Mia Ash, a photographer in her mid-twenties, was using social media to lure men working in strategically important industries to complete a survey. Mia was in fact a team of hackers believed to be working for the Iranian government, who were using the survey to send malware.

Cyberterrorism

Terrorism can be defined as an act, by an individual or a group, intended to kill, injure or otherwise harm one or more persons as a way to instil fear and anxiety in others; it has the purpose of advancing a specific political, religious or social cause, generally trying to undermine confidence in the existing political structure. The notion of cybercrimes intersects that of terrorism in two main ways, expanding the reach of terrorism towards cyberspace through a change of means or targets.

In line with most academic literature (see, for instance, Denning 2000b; Flemming & Stohl 2001; Weimann 2005; Stohl 2006), we should consider as cyberterrorism only those attacks directed via cyberspace towards a physical (such as a critical infrastructure) or an online target. Of course, cyberterrorism could translate into everything from a minor hack to a major attack on critical infrastructure (Denning 2009). All these acts, however, are characterised by a specific modus operandi: the terrorist attack would not be possible offline. Conversely, the use of the internet as a mere facilitator for terrorists' activities offline (for instance, recruiting a suicide bomber online) should not be considered cyberterrorism (Rogers 2019). We will briefly cover internet-facilitated terrorism in a box below.

It is worth spending a few words on the importance of correctly defining (cyber) terrorism and to distinguish it from other phenomena such as hacktivism (see box in Chapter 4). We have already seen that there is a thin line between hacktivism and civil disobedience. In contrast, at least in theory, the line between hacktivism and terrorism should be quite thick. In reality, however, this is not always the case. If the threshold to define an act as (cyber) terrorism is set too low, there is a risk of covering forms of hacktivism with draconian anti-terrorism legislation. As reported by Hardy (2010), for example, the broad Australian definition of terrorism would cover lesser forms of political protest, such as the series of DoS attacks against the Australian Parliament House website launched by Anonymous in 2010 in response to proposed Web censorship regulations. Once again, we should not dismiss definitory issues as merely academic but always remember that they entail very serious practical implications.

Luckily for us, so far cyberterrorism (in a narrow sense) has seldom occurred, with cyberspace being mostly used by terrorists as a means rather than as a target. Nonetheless, cyberterrorism has received attention particularly by governments, media and cybersecurity companies as something likely to occur and to threaten cybersecurity on a large scale. After all, cyberspace is a venue where harm (generally not physical harm but perhaps economic harm) can be done at little cost and risk (Denning 2009; Guiora 2017; Armenia & Tsaples 2018).

Fears about terrorist cyber-attacks have a long history, even if most of the attacks that have occurred so far are relatively small-scale. Already in 1997, for instance, an organisation calling themselves the Internet Black Tigers (a subgroup of the Liberation tigers, a Tamil militant organisation waging a secessionist nationalist insurgency in Sri Lanka) attempted a DoS attack by bombarding various Sri Lankan networks with emails. In the late 1990s, the so-called millennium bug or 'Y2K problem', probably one of the century's bigger hypes, acted as a catalyst for public fears. For those of you who are younger, it is worth remembering that the issue was around a class of computer bugs that could have made the year 2000 indistinguishable from 1900 at the change of the century because many programs represented four-digit years with only the final two digits. This issue, though potentially problematic, was oversold as a major, dramatic problem by cybersecurity experts who, among other things, advised that 'cyberterrorists' would use it to sabotage computer systems (Stohl 2006). It was only in the post-9/11 socio-political context, however, that concerns with radical Islamist terrorism tied the threat of large-scale cyberterrorism to groups such as al-Qaeda and Daesh.

There is still a general reluctance to label the sorts of attacks that have occurred so far as cyberterrorism as the effects have not been comparable to the large-scale terrorist attacks we have sadly become used to in the offline world (Denning 2009). For instance, it was only in 2016 that a 20-year-old Kosovan computer science student was charged in the United States with cyberterrorism after he hacked into a military website and sold Daesh a list containing personal information of about 1300 government employees and military members. This was the first time such a charge had been given.

Even if there have not been attacks where cyberterrorism has mirrored the type of destruction and harms generally associated with conventional forms of terrorism, the state of alert remains high: we are often reminded that we are vulnerable to cyberterrorism and that attacks might occur anytime (Anderson 2004; Stohl 2006; Klein 2018). These types of attacks are certainly possible and we need to be prepared for them. However, their likelihood is scarce. Hence, it is important to debunk what Yar (2019) has called the 'rhetorics and myths of cyberterrorism', a moral panic fuelled by private and public security agencies trying to secure greater power and resources. We should keep in mind that cyberspace is not the best target for terrorists. Given that terrorists – according to the utility principle – want to maximise their rewards while minimising their efforts, cyberspace could make many targets extremely difficult targets to access. First, state and corporate critical infrastructure is generally heavily protected and largely isolated from public networks, which makes it extremely difficult to hack; in addition, many cyber-attacks would require a very high level of sophistication and considerable knowledge and skills in order to be carried out, which makes conventional attacks comparably cost-efficient (Flemming & Stohl 2001; Stohl 2006; Yar 2019). It remains to be seen whether and to what extent the growth of cybercrime-as-a-service, by making tech expertise widely available, might change this situation, increasing the likelihood of cyberterrorism.

Box 8.1 Cyber-jihad and terrorist strategies in cyberspace

There is no doubt that cyber-technologies are influencing how terrorists behave. As many other entities do, terrorist groups use the internet to secure many of their organisational goals through more efficient means (Stohl 2006). On the one side, terrorists can enjoy the ubiquity, secrecy and globalism offered in cyberspace; on the other side, however, they are also exposed to a new set of risks, as their activities might leave an electronic trail. Suffice it to think that researchers in cybersecurity are suggesting the use of Web-crawling and analysis techniques such as online social networks, text mining, supervised learning and natural language processing methods to automatically monitor and detect online communications by violent extremist groups (Chen et al. 2013; Scanlon & Gerber 2014).

For the sake of clarity and brevity, this box focuses on online strategies of jihadist groups, as they provide the most internationally widespread terrorist threat nowadays; however, we should keep in mind that similar strategies are exploited by other international or domestic terrorists and extremist groups, regardless of the fact that they are motivated by political, religious, social or racial ideologies.

Because of the relative anonymity allowed by VoIP, encrypted messaging apps, emails and message boards, the internet is consistently used to facilitate communication both to support existing intra-organisational relationships and to reach a wider audience as well as for planning purposes. For instance, the encrypted app Telegram was allegedly used for the planning of the attacks in Paris in 2015 (Al Adwan & Lind 2017). A major consequence is that cyberspace gives terrorism the possibility to be more geographically dispersed and to rely more effectively on fluid networks rather than on hierarchies (Brown & Korff 2009; Denning 2009). Cyberspace is also exploited for the gathering of important resources and information (such as maps, footage, instructions for bombmaking and so on) as well as for fundraising and financing. Funds can be raised through donations, crowdfunding campaigns, or cybercrimes – typically frauds and financial crimes.

The most revolutionary criminogenic opportunities the internet creates for terrorists, however, are probably those allowing them to carry out propaganda online, creating a sense of belonging to a community of like-minded people, and those allowing education and even training of supporters online. Through online propaganda, terrorists can radicalise and recruit individuals – often very vulnerable young people, including a large number of young women and adolescent girls (Edwards 2017). Militant texts can be spread quickly and with virtually no limitations, given the difficulties of monitoring the dissemination of dangerous content online. Online propaganda and training have the capacity to increase public support for terrorists' causes, normalising terrorists' behaviour (Brown & Korff 2009). These activities often take place in ad hoc jihadist websites: as stressed by Brown and Korff (2009), websites are cheap to create but can easily look professional, increasing the allure of the group and the message. Dedicated apps and social media (Al Adwan & Lind 2017) as well as generalist commercial networks, mainstream social media and online video games are also widely used (Choi et al. 2018), with Twitter and Ask. fm being particularly effective for disseminating jihadist content to a large audience (Al Adwan & Lind 2017).

In cyberspace, terrorists can easily present facts in the way that best fits their ideology (Denning 2009; Holt et al. 2015) and communicate directly with supporters and even with potential recruits – so-called 'armchair jihadis', people who can contribute to the terrorist efforts via online freelance propaganda or cyber-attacks but who might also be recruited to become operational offline. For instance, since 2010, al-Qaeda in the Arabian Peninsula (AQAP) has published *Inspire*, an English-language online magazine used by all al-Qaeda branches and affiliates to disseminate radical jihadist views as well as to provide instructions and techniques for how to carry out terrorist attacks. The magazine format and the engaging writing style make this online platform particularly effective in promoting a terrorist agenda to newcomers.

Broadcasting videos online has also become very popular, being especially appealing and convincing to the young and less literate. We are all sadly aware of the beheadings and torture of hostages carried out by jihadists, broadcast on terrorists' online channels and then reported by mainstream media (Stohl 2006). As remarked by Stohl (2006), this tactic is not new: one of the first examples dates back to the Japanese embassy hostage crisis in Peru in 1996, when the Marxist-

Leninist group Túpac Amaru Revolutionary Movement (MRTA) took hostage hundreds of high-level diplomats, government and military officials and business executives attending a party at the Japanese Ambassador's residence in Lima. The MRTA not only used cyberspace to spread their political ideas but also published a videoclip of members preparing for their mission. So, videos are used not only for propaganda but also in psychological warfare (Grabosky 2016), as they feed the climate of fear at the basis of terrorists' agenda.

A discussion on cyberterrorism would not be complete without a (brief, not to exceed the scope of this book) discussion on cybersecurity. As explained by Guiora (2017), in fact, cybersecurity and cyberterrorism mirror each other: cybersecurity is the response to cyberterrorism, and cyberterrorism can be mitigated by effective cybersecurity. Cybersecurity can be defined as 'the effort to protect information, communications, and technology from harm caused either accidentally or intentionally [and] to ensure the confidentiality, integrity, and availability of data, resources, and process through the use of administrative, physical, and technical controls' (Guiora 2017, p. 11).

If from the one side the internet can be a powerful facilitator for terrorism, on the other side it can also be used in cybersecurity and specifically to gather intelligence and to tackle and mitigate terrorists' efforts. Terrorist use of new technologies gives intelligence agencies the opportunity to use active (such as through malware) or passive (such as traffic or network analysis) attacks on terrorist devices to gather important data (Xu & Chen 2008; Denning 2014). Furthermore, intelligence agencies can infiltrate forums to affect trust, jeopardise the spread of dangerous information and disrupt terrorists' operations and to challenge terrorists' legitimacy (for instance, regarding their Qu'ranic interpretations) by flooding relevant channels of communication with mis- or alternative information (Brown & Korff 2009; Denning 2009).

The collection of online information for anti-terrorist purposes is often at the core of heated legal and political debates, with significant differences among jurisdictions. The principle of proportionality is generally key, with many jurisdictions setting both substantial and procedural rules for online surveillance and data-gathering. For instance, the European Court of Human Rights and the European Court of Justice have developed standards according to which a specific legal basis is needed for any collection, storage, use, analysis and sharing of personal data for law enforcement and anti-terrorist purposes. Among other things, legislation must clearly define the procedures to be followed for the authorisation of such surveillance measures, limits on the time for which information can be retained and provisions on the grounds on which data can be accessed (Brown & Korff 2009).

Overall, anti-terrorism has given significant impetus to contemporary surveillance and, more generally, is influencing policy decisions on cyber-defence at both the national and international level (Denning 2000a; Guiora 2017). Even if many anti-terrorism provisions are initially adopted as emergency measures, with the passage of time they tend to be included in general law, thus presenting a challenge to citizens' privacy rights (Brown & Korff 2009). A major issue is the fact that many of these measures end up profiling or targeting not just (potential) terrorists; indeed, for the most part, they affect us all, with intrusive mass surveillance capturing data on our activities (Brown & Korff 2009). We are giving up freedom, but the extent to which this leads to an increase in security is not fully clear yet.

Controlling cyberspace as political deviancy

As anticipated in Chapter 4, cyberspace has often been intended as a transcendent place, a spaceless realm, almost as if it were outside of terrestrial jurisdictions (Barlow 1996). As noted by scholars such as Lessig (1999), however, the arguments proposed by digital libertarians tend to ignore how the internet has been slowly moving towards an architecture of control. Rather than interpreting cyberspace as a transcendent place, we should situate it within the world of politics and history (Bomse 2001). From this perspective, forms of political deviancy in cyberspace can be seen in governments' attempts to use communication and information technologies to limit human and civil rights of both their citizens and opponents.

State surveillance and censorship: some issues of responsibility

Technology, especially in areas of conflict, where part of the population is considered a security threat, has been extensively used to control people's acts and lives, turning cyberspace into a new place of surveillance. In Chapter 4, we have already encountered discussions on surveillance (including state surveillance) and data protection. Now, we need to develop this issue a bit further, looking at the role of tech companies in furthering governmental agendas against the free Web. Technology companies, in fact, have a major role and responsibility in internet governance, even if they often do not fully acknowledge it. In light of a lack of international mechanisms regulating surveillance technology, surveillance tools are sold by so-called digital era mercenaries (a handful of companies based in the United Kingdom, Germany, Italy, France and the United States) to countries such as China, Iran, Syria and Uzbekistan – countries that are on Reporters Without Borders' list of 'enemies of the internet' (Reports Without Borders 2014). Surveillance products are designed to enable government agencies to circumvent anonymising techniques such as data encryption and are used to spy on critical journalists and internet activists, in violation of human rights and freedom of information (Moini et al. 2017).

Furthermore, internet companies are prone to submit to the censorship demands of authoritarian regimes. Twitter has been accused of censoring journalists: in Turkey, for instance, a local content management tool has been used to block access to tweets and accounts from certain geographical areas. Facebook has reportedly developed software to stop certain content from appearing in users' news feeds in specific geographic areas, allegedly to satisfy the Chinese regime's censorship requirements (the 'Great Firewall of China', a combination of technological and legislative actions by the People's Republic of China to regulate the internet domestically, which includes blocking access to certain foreign websites) and concomitantly to be able to expand its reach further into the Chinese market. Growing criticism has been moved against Facebook regarding its moderation policies and the deletion of relevant content such as political cartoons or photos (Moini et al. 2017).

At the core of the problem lies the fact that, especially over the last few years with the decline of American hegemony over internet regulation, countries leading the so-called balkanisation of the internet (the splintering of the internet along geographic and commercial boundaries) and blocking large amounts of content have been trying to increase their role in internet governance (Mueller 2017). A major consequence is that in the meetings of the Information Society, one of the main multilateral platforms on internet governance, binding international mechanisms designed to prevent authoritarian regimes from subjecting their citizens to mass censorship and surveillance were never adopted. Similarly, no legal framework is yet in place to control 'digital era mercenaries': most national and international legislation lacks proper regulation of internet surveillance, data protection and surveillance technology exports vis-à-vis international human rights norms and standards (Moini et al. 2017).

A detailed overview of the issue of the role of private actors in the development of internet governance would be well outside the scope of this book, but I hope that this brief section has encouraged you to think about how criminologists, as well as computer scientists, cannot fully understand the role and use of technologies without connecting them to the broader socio-political context. Particularly, when thinking about tools designed to enhance 'security', we should keep in mind that 'security' – as much as 'crime' – is socially constructed. Tech companies and the cybersecurity industry do not operate in a vacuum but rather as part of complex systems that might be riven by injustice, unequal power relations and even human rights violations.

Political mobilisation shutdowns

If certain technologies have turned cyberspace into a place of surveillance, we should not forget that technology can also be used as a tool for the empowerment of civil society and specifically as an instrument of e-resistance towards oppressive power relations. 'Hacktivist' technologies have been designed over the years to support self-expression, privacy and security for both local and global civic networks (Deibert 2003). For instance, Shalhoub-Kevorkian

(2012) showed the potential of cyberspace to create deterritorialised spaces for political activism and resistance in the Palestinian context in Jerusalem, allowing for mobilisation of the population. The role of social media has been considered pivotal for a number of political uprisings and especially during the Arab Spring – a series of protests and demonstrations across the Middle East and North Africa starting in 2010 in response to oppressive regimes and low living standards. However, it is worth noting that although Western media significantly emphasised the role of social media in the Arab Spring, Middle Eastern activists tend to play down this role (Hassan 2012).

A disturbing trend is that of governments using internet shutdowns for political purposes. Between 2016 and 2018, for instance, some African countries resorted to this measure in trying to disperse political dissent, creating a series of problems for the affected population. In late 2017, the Camerounaise government shut down the internet in its English-speaking southwest and northeast regions after a series of protests. Similarly, a few weeks later, Gnassingbé's government in Togo cut off the internet for about a week while trying to limit the anti-governmental mobilisation of young people. In both cases, however, the dissent was emboldened rather than defeated by the shutdowns, with affected people mobilising offline as the shutdown was felt as a major intrusion, something that could not be accepted.

Criminogenic elements in edemocracy

eDemocracy is a form of government in which citizens should be able to participate equally in decision-making processes (for instance, being able to have their say in the proposal, development and creation of laws). It is expected that fundamental democratic practices, ranging from discussing matters of public interest to voting in electoral processes, will occur increasingly online. An instrument of political self-determination, eDemocracy is generally welcomed as a catalyst of democratic involvement, which might contribute to reducing democratic disengagement and deficits in many countries (Korthagen et al. 2018; Richardson & Emerson 2018). We have already encountered in previous sections how cyberspace has aided in the enhancement of political communication, making it possible for a large segment of the population both to consume and to produce news media and political discourse (Müller & Schulz 2019). Similarly, the internet has been used as a tool for political action and organisation.

For the purposes of this book, it is important to draw attention to the fact that the same devices and software enabling eDemocracy represent potential for different types of cybercrime and cyber-deviant behaviours. First, they could be used as a vector for hackers, which could severely hinder election results. For instance, Italy's populist party Five Star uses an online platform ('Rousseau') to survey members on policies, conduct online primary votes and receive donations; the platform has been hacked several times (until now, for demonstration purposes). Second, as already addressed above, with a move towards the multiplicity of sources and perspectives on events that can be found online, there is a danger of 'selective exposure' in which political news is selected on the basis that it matches the predispositions, ideologies and beliefs of the audience member (Müller & Schulz 2019). Last but not least, there are specific challenges related to the use of e-platforms and of remote e-voting via the internet from any location, especially in terms of the responsibility of intermediaries. Devices and software for eDemocracy are generally developed by the private sector, whose vested interests might open the way to deceptive behaviours and manipulation in the absence of proper mechanisms for transparency and accountability.

Overall, there is consensus that existing mechanisms for eDemocracy, for now, cannot replace physical systems. For instance, as reminded by Richardson and Emerson (2018), in eDemocracy, developing a hack-proof voting system is not enough to validate it. Any new system should match or improve the protections our current systems have evolved over the centuries, including auditability, data security, duress protection, identity verification and vote privacy. We are not there yet, and the successful hacking of existing discussion and voting platforms should remind us that giving new technologies a more central role in the democratic process is no guarantee that the process will be de facto improved.

Concluding remarks

As explained in the introduction, the various behaviours grouped in this chapter share the fact that they all pivot around a political element and can cause significant harm. These behaviours also share the fact that they test the cyber-resilience of our countries and specifically the endurance of the democratic values and mechanisms many of us have the luck to be used to. The cyber-risks encountered in this chapter cannot be avoided; we can try to reduce them to an acceptable level, but we also need to make sure that our political infrastructures can be protected and can resist even if they are severely hit (Dunn Cavelty 2013).

There are two key take-home messages from this chapter. First, we should never ignore the central role that tech companies have gained in the political arena nowadays. They can be important enablers of positive change, but they also have the burden of serious responsibilities when it comes to impacting citizen awareness and engagement and electoral processes. Tech companies can also enable attacks that may impact significantly on relationships among states, allowing new forms of cyberwarfare and cyberespionage. After the unprecedented level that large-scale attacks have reached in the last few years, in April 2018 more than 30 major global technology companies (joined by dozens more in the following months) signed the Cybersecurity Tech Accord, pledging not to assist any government in offensive cyber-attacks and to establish new partnerships with public and private actors to better coordinate vulnerability disclosures and improve cybersecurity globally. Athough the commitment made by the signatory companies is commendable, the fear is that the Accord's impact might be limited simply to marketing. The agreement, in fact, lacks any teeth, some major companies did not sign and it is likely that many governments will not embrace its principles. However, as we have seen in this chapter, state actors often have a pivotal role in the launch of cyber-attacks; without a clear commitment by national governments in joining the efforts, the private sector is not in a position alone to prevent the rise of political offences in cyberspace in their many forms.

Second, the reader should reflect on the importance of multi- and interdisciplinarity in understanding the type of cyber-attacks addressed. The challenges to be met go well beyond criminology and computer science and enter the domain of disciplines such as international relations, political science and ethics. The problem, once more, is that it is not always easy, or feasible, for experts from different areas to talk and work together. As stressed by Happa and Fairclough (2017), many experts in political disciplines, as well as many stakeholders such as politicians, lawyers and business owners, lack the necessary technical background to make the correct decisions in dealing with cyber-attacks. Conversely, technical aspects are better understood by cybersecurity analysts, but many do not have the societal, political, legal or financial knowledge to fully understand the repercussions and the implications of their decisions. Hence, the best way to forward an informed and effective approach to counter political cybercrimes is to promote discussions among experts from different domains in order to take into account both technical and contextual considerations.

? CRITICAL QUESTIONS

- What was the most important cyberwarfare story in the news over the last couple of months? Was the cyber-attack attributed to a specific actor? If so, was it a state or a non-state actor? Are there details on how they were able to figure out who did it? Discuss how the news media reported the story.

- What mechanisms of deterrence can be envisaged in cyberspace? Do they differ for state versus non-state actors?

- We have seen how the weapon of choice in contemporary information warfare is information pollution (so-called fake news). In your opinion, what makes a topic a good choice for information pollution and why? Please identify a recently published piece of fake news in your country. What persuasive strategies have been used? What type of details have been included to make the story appear credible? How can we identify the story as 'fake'?

9 DISRUPTING CYBERCRIMES AND THE NEED FOR CRIME PREVENTION

Introduction

The previous chapters make it clear to the reader that cybercrime is not only the flavour of the month but is a real-time, critical and complex issue to address. In a domain where technology is fast-moving, an effective response requires timely, consistent and extensive effort. Since the late 1990s and early 2000s, contemporary law enforcement and regulatory agencies have increasingly invested in resources and building expertise to counter cybercrime, with most countries having (or having under development) national laws or policies on cybercrime investigation, prosecution and prevention, often inspired by those adopted by North American and European governments (UNODC 2013; Lavorgna 2018a). Contrary to what is often believed, cyberspace is not a lawless and unpoliced 'far west' – or at least not completely. As we will see in this chapter, several mechanisms are now in place to regulate, police and manage many of the threats explored in this book.

Unfortunately, for a variety of reasons presented in the following pages, traditional methods for the formal control of cyberspace are not fully effective. The varied and complex nature of cybercrime defies a single-policy solution or best strategy but rather necessitates a combination of diverse context-specific instruments. Furthermore, law enforcement and regulatory solutions need frequent adaptation in response to the inevitable, new and rapid changes. A wide array of strategies and measures to reduce the risk of cybercrime and its potentially harmful effects have been adopted in the process of trying to address the multiple causes of crime (UNODC 2013).

In general, the governance and policing of online behaviour are characterised by a combination of formal and informal elements directed towards the disruption and prevention of cybercrimes, prevention being considered the most potentially effective way to control them. Countermeasures in cyberspace include, beyond traditional state regulatory and law enforcement intervention, the presence of multi-agencies and partnerships with non-governmental organisations, commercial and technology-based solutions, self-regulatory and surveillance initiatives run by a wide array of online managers and the element of self-protection by prospective victims of cyber-crimes (Lavorgna 2018a). These different and multifaceted approaches will be presented in this chapter.

Policing cybercrimes

Criminal justice institutions, and particularly law enforcement agencies, retain a pivotal role when it comes to fighting crime in cyberspace. Despite the undeniable effort expended in keeping pace with new challenges posed by cyberspace and the existence of a number of operational successes, several problems still hinder the effectiveness of cybercrime policing. Overall, law enforcement and regulatory agencies seem to lack the capacity to control a large number of cybercrimes, the overall impression being that law enforcement operations dealing with cybercrime are addressing only the tip of the iceberg. Not only is ICT-related knowledge often alien to law enforcement and legal cultures, but the slow evolution of legal frameworks and limited reach of national jurisdictions are putting law enforcement in cyberspace at a huge disadvantage because of the remarkable speed with which cybercrimes occur and the ephemeral and inherently cross-border nature of digital information (Broadhurst 2006; Calderoni 2010; Davis 2012). Traditionally, law enforcement agencies are reactive rather than proactive, local rather than global, and resist responding to change. Resistance to change generally emanates from the bureaucratic organisational structure of law enforcement agencies but can also come from experienced personnel reluctant to be reassigned to a different unit or to new tasks involving extensive training (Burns et al. 2004; Davis 2012). In this context, unconventional approaches to crime management are under development in an attempt to incapacitate offenders, disrupt criminal activities and reduce harm.

Criminal justice challenges

As outlined above, police units are experiencing severe difficulties in fighting cybercrime. Indeed, modern policing institutions have been designed to deal effectively with low-volume, high-impact crime and are profoundly hampered when it comes to processing cybercrimes, which are often high-volume (even if low impact) (Dupont 2017). As reported by Wall (2007), the risk is that they fall into the so-called *de minimis trap*: given that many cybercrimes lead to low-impact victimisations that cause large aggregated losses that spread globally, policing strategies will generally not prioritise them in their agendas (with the exception of some specific forms of serious offending, such as the production of child pornographic images). Many police units are already overwhelmed with traditional crime and might not be willing to use their scarce resources to investigate a criminal incident they perceive as relatively minor and potentially not prosecutable, because the offenders might be difficult to identify (Burns et al. 2004; Lavorgna 2014c, 2015a; Grabosky 2016; Leppänen & Kankaanranta 2017). An unfortunate consequence is that the (perceived and, at times, actual) lack of effective law enforcement entails a general perception of futility in reporting incidents in cyberspace, where law enforcement may be incapable or even reluctant to investigate crimes.

Inadequate resources are consistently lamented in the literature. Law enforcement officers continue to lack adequate personnel, training and equipment to investigate cybercrimes, especially regarding local law enforcement agencies with small jurisdictions or those located in poorer countries (Davis 2012; Lavorgna 2018a). Specialised/centralised units or task forces are often created to deal with serious cybercrimes, especially in larger and state-level agencies (Willits & Nowacki 2016). By contrast, local law enforcement agencies, which are the natural contact point for the general public, often lack specific cybercrime experience apropos intervention and collection of evidence (Burns et al. 2004; Holt & Bossler 2015). Even in countries considered to be at the forefront of cybercrime investigations, such as the United Kingdom, problems in local units persist. This is emphasised by Holt et al. (2018) in a study examining the perceptions of police constables and sergeants across England and Wales regarding cybercrime, where local law enforcement officers generally recognise the fact that online crimes are a frequent occurrence but spend only a relatively small portion of their time addressing them. Similarly, in the Netherlands, even high-volume crimes such as hacking and e-fraud often never enter the criminal justice system or else leave it too early because of lack of capacity throughout the police organisation (Leukfeldt et al. 2013). In less well-resourced countries, on the other hand, most local police stations do not even have access to the internet, because of lack of resources or, as lamented by Algarni (2013) regarding Saudi Arabia, lack of trust. Computers are often in short supply and training opportunities may be scarce or inadequate. On a global scale, the situation is anything but rosy.

An additional limitation regarding law enforcement is that many traditional procedural provisions do not translate well to cyberspace, and technical difficulties in gaining investigative access to virtual 'places' and conversations without in-depth technological knowledge needed to uncover relevant information impede the process of law enforcement. National approaches to cybercrime investigative powers differ greatly. When cyber-specific legislation (for instance, to ensure expedited preservation of computer data and obtain stored subscriber data) is in place, most countries still report a lack of legal power for more advanced measures of remote computer forensics – that is, the collection, examination and reporting of digital evidence (Sommer 2004; UNODC 2013). Even if most countries have begun to put in place specialised structures for the investigation of cybercrimes, in developing countries in particular, these are not well resourced and a large majority of law enforcement officers lack basic computer skills and equipment (UNODC 2013).

Online investigation requires a mix of traditional and new policing techniques. A multidisciplinary approach, covering a wide range of both technical and non-technical skills and knowledge, is therefore vital when investigating cybercrime (Sommer 2004; Hunton 2010). Cyber-skills shortage and mobility are major problems in cybersecurity, with the cybersecurity industry lamenting the shortage of well-prepared and talented professionals. For public agencies, the problem is even bigger, as state salaries generally cannot match those in private industries. Law enforcement agencies in many countries are starting to pay increasing attention to hiring personnel with strong computer skills. The latest United Kingdom National Cyber Security Strategy (Home Office 2016), for instance, has a whole section ('Develop') dedicated to the road forward on strengthening cybersecurity skills in the country and addressing the shortage of current cybersecurity specialists, the lack of young people entering the profession, insufficient exposure to cyber- and information security concepts in computing courses, the lack of qualified teachers in these topics and the absence of established career and training pathways in the profession. Indeed, the task of developing a pool of capable cybersecurity experts is not a trivial one.

Furthermore, there are problems in matching and complementing the different skills required in (cyber) law enforcement: ideally, you need people with excellent technical capabilities and a good background in criminology and policing, or people with criminology and policing expertise, who have the ability to 'talk' with colleagues coming from a more technical background. Interdisciplinary and cross-disciplinary abilities will be key in preparing the law enforcement of the future, but – once more – this will entail organisational and institutional changes, which are likely to be resisted. A change in the attitudes and dynamics of law enforcement agencies is hence urgently needed. Indeed, more than two decades ago, Goodman (1997) stressed how, unless police departments started planning for and training on combating cybercrime immediately, it would be impossible to keep up with the challenges posed by new and emerging technologies. Law enforcement officers should not only meet the expertise and skills of their criminal counterparts but, rather, exceed them. Since Goodman's appeal, many things have changed. During the last few years in particular, resources have been put in place by many countries and efforts made to create and reorganise police units to better carry out online investigations, but progress is still too slow.

The lack of available resources within law enforcement agencies is partially alleviated by the support of external consultancies trained in security management and computer forensic science (Grabosky & Smith 1998). In order to effectively police cyberspace, law enforcement agencies increasingly need to team up with other actors, particularly from the private sector. Public–private partnerships are developed through formalised cooperation between governmental authorities and important stakeholders (Boes & Leukfeldt 2017). This trend has been observed, studied and generally welcomed by many researchers in Western countries, but such partnerships are not always possible in countries with a different ideological, socio-economic and political context. In Saudi Arabia, for example, the lack of public–private partnership culture and autocratic view of the state so far has limited the possibility of devolving some aspects of online policing to commercial businesses and private-sector agencies, impeding the emergence of plural policing in cyberspace experienced in other parts of the world (Algarni 2013). However, although the public–private partnerships approach can be of much practical utility, it should be deployed with caution; indeed, the partial 'privatisation' of online security can bring problems of transparency and accountability unless extensive security checks are put in place in order to ensure that confidential technical information is properly managed.

As the challenge of prosecuting crimes in cyberspace can be viewed as a key one in the coming years (Buono 2010), appropriate training should also be provided for prosecutors and judges in order to acquaint them with the complexities that cybercrime cases might present and furnish them with sufficient expertise to deal with them. Many international organisations and individual countries have started to engage in this training process but improvements take time. For instance, in the United Kingdom, the Crown Prosecution Service (CPS, the principal prosecuting authority for England and Wales) started in-house training of high-tech crime specialist prosecutors and caseworkers across the country to increase awareness and capability within the organisation (Home Office 2010). The Council of Europe, through its Cybercrime Programme Office (C-PROC) in Romania, supports countries worldwide in the strengthening of their criminal justice capacity to investigate cybercrimes and secure electronic evidence through training, networking and specialisation according to the Budapest Convention on Cybercrime. As part of this process, C-PROC also deals with the training of judges, prosecutors and law enforcement officers. The main aims are to enable institutes to deliver cybercrime training based on international standards, to equip the largest possible number of future and practising judges and prosecutors with basic knowledge on cybercrime and electronic evidence and to provide advanced training to a critical number of judges and prosecutors and support their continued specialisation (Council of Europe 2009). The GLACY (2013–2016) and GLACY+ (2016–2020) projects, a joint effort of the European Union and the Council of Europe, are intended to support states around the world (with the GLACY+ project focusing on countries in Africa, the Asia-Pacific and Latin America and the Caribbean region) by strengthening their capacity to apply legislation on cybercrime and electronic evidence and enhancing effective international cooperation in this area (Council of Europe 2017). As one of the outcomes of these initiatives, for instance, in March 2018, the first introductory 'training of trainers' course on cybercrime and electronic evidence for the ASEAN (Association of Southeast Asian Nations) region took place in Manila.

Law enforcement investigations

Defence and intelligence agencies, rather than police services, tend to receive the bulk of public funding to counter cybercrime (Dupont 2017). Computer emergency response teams, designated with specific responsibilities for cyber-protection, have been created in many countries, such as Italy (CERT Nazionale Italia, IT-CERT), the United Arab Emirates (Arab Emirates Computer Emergency Response Team, aeCERT) and the United States (Department of Homeland Security United States Computer Emergency Readiness Team, US-CERT), among others. Regarding police services, in many countries, specialist units concentrate their expertise in cybercrime, their precise operational remits varying from force to force. These units generally share a number of strategic and tactical responsibilities, ranging from contributing to national strategies on cybercrime, delivering training programmes and cooperating at the national and international level to coordinating and conducting investigations, offering specialised support to non-specialised units and examining digital evidence. Jewkes and Yar (2008) classified these units into four main types: scientific support units carrying out forensic examination; departments gathering online information on major crimes; units with a broader remit to investigate offences with a cyber-element; and units that investigate paedophile networks. In most countries, however, in recent years, this distinction has become increasingly blurred. Examples of specialised units are the Technological Investigation Brigade in Spain, the Federal Computer Crime Unit in Belgium and the National Cyber Crime Unit in the United Kingdom. Though relatively successful, these units are building experience and developing standards as they go (Lavorgna 2014c), and there are, as yet, no solid data to properly assess their effectiveness.

Beyond traditional policing techniques, online investigations require the use of new techniques and approaches to uncover relevant information, sometimes in new, creative ways. Grabosky and Smith (1998) categorised the policing techniques typically used in cyberspace as tapping (the interception of telecommunications systems), bugging (listening and recording private conversations), tracking (locations), spying (monitoring and recording visual and sound information through video surveillance devices), hacking (obtaining unauthorised access to a computer network) and scanning (scanning electromagnetic radiation emitted from computers and converting them into visual images). Specific forms of particularly serious cybercrimes, such as the grooming of children for sexual exploitation, may require specific and aggressive investigative techniques, such as undercover investigation tactics (Grabosky 2016). Another innovative approach is the use of so-called honeypots – that is, online 'traps' set for criminals interested in specific information. Typically, a honeypot consists of a site that appears to be part of a network but is actually isolated and being closely monitored by whoever sets the trap. For example, during Operation PIN-The Virtual Global Taskforce in 2003, a website containing images of child abuse was created as bait for persons looking online for child pornography. Everyone entering the website was confronted with a law enforcement message stating that his or her details had been captured and transmitted to the relevant national authorities. In this way, details of (potential) offenders were captured and potential offenders were deterred. Honeypots are considered valid tools not only to detect potential offenders but also to collect important data on the statistical properties of cyber-attacks, which can be of great help in understanding them better or even predicting them (Zhan et al. 2013; Wall 2015; Bossler 2017).

Different countries still differ greatly on what they are/are not allowed to do when it comes to cybercrime investigations, with regulations and practices still evolving in the quest to balance investigative needs and human rights. A major problem with cybercrime is that online investigations invariably involve issues of privacy. Limits and safeguards have to be set globally to provide effective guarantees against abuse. The legal and ethical implications, however, are often unclear (for instance, regarding the admissibility of evidence) given that existing legislation in most cases does not yet consider specifically the legality of online undercover operations and monitoring activities (Lavorgna 2018a). Existing legislation was often developed when technical possibilities were different and does not adequately cover the specific features of high-tech investigations. Case law comes into play in adapting legal standards to contemporary needs but its development is patchy, uncoordinated among different jurisdictions and subject to continual changes. For example, in the so-called 'Scurato case', in July 2016, the Italian Supreme Court ruled that wherever a crime is particularly serious (i.e., if it falls within the concept of organised crime or terrorism), it is possible to carry out electronic surveillance in private dwellings, even if no criminal activity was undertaken inside them. In this case, however, the Court distinguished between 'online search' and 'online surveillance', the former including the possibility of making a copy of certain data, which is then transmitted to the investigation bodies, allowing interception of the information flow taking place between different devices and thereby enabling the remote monitoring of whatever is displayed on a certain screen, said through a microphone or keyed in via a keyboard (Vaciago & Ramalho 2016). However, in late 2016, the Italian Supreme Court (ruling on the 'Eyepyramid case', see Chapter 4) said that it was also legitimate to use trojan software for online searches or for less serious types of crimes if carried out via electronic means.

Cyberspace can also be a powerful resource for law enforcement regarding the collection of evidence. When technology is used instrumentally or incidentally in the commission of an offence, devices can store important data that can be used as digital evidence (think, for instance, of metadata present on mobile phones, browsing histories, email and so on) (Holt et al. 2015). Digital evidence has specific characteristics that make it peculiar to process: it is intangible but also volatile and potentially massive in quantity, which can make it very difficult to use in practice (Grabosky 2016). The increasing use of digital evidence is posing new sets of challenges to investigative techniques, as prosecutors need to collect evidence according to evolving best practices in order to have it accepted in court. One basic issue concerns authorship: who was using the device when the relevant data were produced? Biometric analyses focusing on keyboard stroke dynamics (looking, for instance, at the user's rhythm in typing), forensic stylistics (qualitative analyses looking at 'idiosyncrasies' in the language) and computational stylometric analyses (considering quantifiable language features such as phrase length or vocabulary frequency) are some of the methods used to try to answer this question (Chaski 2005). Other issues concern the use of best methods to collect evidence and ensure it is not tampered with, the reliability of computer programmes that might otherwise create inaccuracies in the outputs and the extent to which service providers may be required to assist law enforcement bodies in collecting evidence during their investigations (Grabosky 2016). However, because of the fast pace of development in digital technologies, it is difficult even for the forensic experts to keep updated and react in a timely way to emerging tools and techniques for handling and analysing digital evidence (Choo & Dehghantanha 2018). Cloud computing systems and the IoT, for instance, require more complex and time-consuming digital evidence acquisition (often from different jurisdictions) and analysis, with uncontroversial and internationally recognised standards and guidelines yet to be developed (Taylor et al. 2010; Nieto et al. 2018).

We should not forget that cyberspace is also a resource for law enforcement vis-à-vis improved possibilities to interact with the general public (for instance, to ask for information on investigative leads, to provide alerts on criminal incidents or to manage emergencies) (Crump 2012; Holt & Bossler 2015; Nhan et al. 2017). This is, to some extent, applying the practices of community policing to cyberspace – that is, the idea of facilitating interactions between police and citizens to promote legitimacy and best control crime at the local level by encouraging citizens to take responsibility (Manning 1991). Recent research, however, suggests that, although the potential to transform police–citizen engagement through social media would be fascinating, embedding social media into police communications remains problematic: new technologies are not sufficient to transform cultural dynamics within law enforcement agencies (many officers are, in fact, sceptical of the idea that community engagement should play a role in their work) and organisational changes are resisted (Bullock 2018). Moreover, although 'internet sleuthing' and the public taking active roles online over perceived injustice can potentially offer great help to investigations, it can also go terribly awry, pushing rushed false information (willingly, accidentally or even subconsciously – for instance, to blame the political opposition).

Box 9.1 Law enforcement and data analytics

Social media mining (the extraction of massive amounts of raw social media data to discern patterns and trends), sentiment analysis (also known as opinion mining, the process of computationally identifying the emotional tone behind a piece of text), natural language processing (the application of computational techniques to analyse interactions between computers and human natural languages), machine learning technologies (the application of artificial intelligence allowing computer systems the ability to 'learn' and improve performance in a certain task without being explicitly programmed) and biometric software applications (to identify or verify a person by analysing their unique physical characteristics) are some of the proposed tools that might help in detecting criminal incidents quickly or even preventing them before they occur (Williams et al. 2013; Middleton & Krivcovs 2016; Hardyns & Rummens 2017; Aghababaei & Makrehchi 2018; Andrejevic 2018; Wilson 2018). Think, for instance, of machine learning technology as a way of targeting malicious coding, identifying it as it appears without requiring (much) additional human intervention, the use of sentiment analysis on Twitter to monitor civil unrest (so-called 'neighbourhood informatics', see Williams et al. 2013) or facial recognition technology to scan tens of thousands of people in a crowd to identify potential suspects.

The use of automatic trawling and big data analytics for policing, however, does not come without problems. First, there are technical challenges to be addressed in *datification*: big data, especially when occurring in real time or when used to identify situations and incidents that require immediate response, are not easy to manage and important data need to be identified and prioritised among a white noise of basic rumours and potentially misleading information. Second, especially in the context of predictive policing – that is, the use of statistical analytical techniques to prevent crime by, for instance, identifying likely targets for police intervention or to solve past crimes – there are no certainties provided by the data but only projections of patterns based on computational models. Because of the complexity of human behaviour, the results obtained might be spurious and vulnerable to change (Smith et al. 2017) but the officers relying on them and the general public might overestimate the reliability of these results, as they might not fully understand the mechanisms behind them.

In this context, it is of utmost importance to understand the theories behind these models to be able to critically assess the results (Chan & Bennet Moses 2016) and to use big data for the estimation of crime patterns in conjunction with more 'trusted' forms of data (Williams et al. 2017). Even more importantly, these new possibilities for crime control create potential legal and ethical challenges, posing potential threats to civil liberties and inequality. Rather than (more or less accountable) governmental actors, private companies (such as social media companies) have more and more power over some of our basic rights, which might be threatened by unaccountable algorithms. These algorithms are not perfect and they can reinforce biases in society and in policing activities – after all, they are only as good as the data they are trained on and this data can have problems of racism or sexism. As a consequence, they risk reinforcing negative 'labelling' (Becker 1963) or perpetuating the over-policing of certain segments of the population; they might lead to ethnic profiling and neglect core principles such as the presumption of innocence (Ferguson 2012; Shapiro 2017). When the automatisation of processes of data gathering and analysis traditionally undertaken by social scientists takes place, they should be involved in the design of the algorithms, as they can bring to the table a lot of experience to address potential biases of the machine (Williams et al. 2017); furthermore, social scientists should retain the capacity to question automated decisions in light of their analytical and theoretical interpretations. The creation of increased accountability and transparency around the use of big data – and more honesty concerning its limitations – is essential if emerging technologies and analytical possibilities are to be used more extensively in policing activities.

Finally, there has also been increasing attention paid to the possibilities for law enforcement to automatically mine streams of data to inform their investigations or to better focus their efforts. The use of so-called data analytics can potentially bring a lot of efficiency to law enforcement routines, but – as we will see in the following box – it could also give rise to worrisome developments.

The need for international cooperation

The global nature of cybercrime entails additional specific issues for traditional law enforcement, with jurisdictional conflicts, disparities and problems with police and judicial cooperation being the main challenges.

Jurisdiction conflicts can be either 'positive' or 'negative'. In the case of positive conflicts, more than one state might have jurisdiction over a given offence (for instance, because the same offence might target victims located in different states). Should this case arise, states should consult with each other to determine where the prosecution should take place but international collaboration (also under the umbrella of the Budapest Convention on Cybercrime) is not injunctive on this. In the case of negative conflicts, none of the states involved can prosecute or prefer not to prosecute (for instance, because of lack of resources). This second possibility is not uncommon when it comes to cybercrimes.

Jurisdictional disparities are also problematic because they can cause forum shopping (that is, the attempt to have a legal case heard in the jurisdiction thought most likely to provide a favourable judgement). Furthermore, because of the *nullum crimen sine lege* principle (a person cannot face criminal prosecution for an act that was not criminalised before the criminal act was performed), policing and prosecution might be impeded if countries where certain cyber-events have not (yet) been criminalised are involved (Wall 2007). In deliberately targeting their activities in or through jurisdictions where regulation, legislation or investigative capacities are known to be poorer, cybercriminals can minimise the risk of their activities being discovered or punishment being suffered.

In both crime control and crime prevention perspectives, cross-border investigations and other forms of cooperation are therefore of the utmost importance to ensure time-critical responses to help negate attacks as well as to secure evidence. The systematic sharing of information across jurisdictions has become pivotal. When information-sharing is not effective, critical information can be overlooked, ignored or even lost as a result, with cybercriminals successfully committing their attack or getting away with their actions. However, information-sharing is still extraneous to most police cultures, as it is not yet considered by many police forces to be part of their normal routines (Lavorgna 2018a), and in any case international law enforcement cooperation can be slow and expensive (Paquet-Clouston et al. 2018). Inter-agency rivalry, issues of jurisdiction and authority and even personality conflicts can complicate information-sharing and investigations needing interstate cooperation. Regarding international cooperation, lack of foreign language proficiency and issues of distrust towards certain countries on how they manage police and judicial data simply worsen the situation.

A wide range of governmental institutions and agencies are needed to support crime disruption and prevention initiatives in the area of cybercrime and criminal justice responses, to the point that there is still confusion from the public as to which agency is responsible for dealing with certain cybercrimes (Sommer 2004). Apart from at the national level, where generally a specific governmental institution (national law enforcement authority or a specific ministry) is responsible for coordinating the prevention and combating of cybercrime, cross-border initiatives for law enforcement and judicial cooperation, as well as cross-sector multi-agencies, are often used to facilitate and enhance the international prevention and combating of cybercrimes (UNODC 2013; Lavorgna 2018a). Combined, these agencies and organisations offer a platform not only for crime disruption and prevention but also to set future research, policies and operational agendas (Wall & Williams 2014). Some of these infrastructures (such as Eurojust or the Financial

Action Task Force), however, are not specialists on cybercrime, so will not be dealt with here. Beyond these organisations, fully institutionalised forms of cross-border cooperation in place at both regional and international levels are now focusing on cybercrime. The European Union Agency for Network and Information Security, for instance, is a centre of expertise for cybersecurity with the aim to improve network and information security for the benefit of the citizens, consumers, enterprises and public-sector organisations of the European Union. It works as a hub for the exchange of information and best practices to help prevention, awareness-raising and cooperation between different actors in the information security field, notably by developing public/private partnerships with industries.

International and transnational law enforcement is increasingly playing a central role in preventing and countering cybercrimes. For instance, Interpol (the intergovernmental organisation that facilitates cooperation between the criminal police forces of 192 countries) has expanded its scope to deal with cybercrime by building a new centre in Singapore with the aim of becoming a global coordination body on detection and prevention, relying on three core strategies: harmonisation of efforts across different sectors in order to share expertise while avoiding duplication of activities; capacity-building; and operational and forensic support. In this perspective, it is worth underlying that a key component of this new Interpol facility is the Cyber Fusion Centre (a multi-stakeholder environment bringing together law enforcement specialists and industry experts), providing real-time monitoring and analysis of malicious internet activity and giving member countries the intelligence and expertise required to investigate cybercrimes more effectively.

At the regional level, emblematic for the increased attention directed towards the international policing of cybercrime was the creation of the European Cybercrime Centre (EC3) at Europol (the European Union agency for law enforcement cooperation), launched in January 2013 to strengthen the law enforcement response to cybercrimes in the European Union and specifically to contribute to faster reactions in the event of online crimes. EC3 aims to support member states and the European Union's institutions in building operational and analytical capacity for investigations and cooperation with international partners in the following areas of cybercrime: that committed by organised groups to generate large criminal profit, such as online fraud; that which causes serious harm to the victim, such as online child sexual exploitation; and that which affects critical infrastructure and information systems in the European Union. EC3, however, may be subject to two main criticisms: first, it might not serve as a model for the development of countermeasures in the vastly different socio-cultural and economic circumstances found in less developed countries (Khoo 2003); second, its mandate largely reflects the vision of treating cybercrimes as separate realities from other forms of serious crimes. Nonetheless, it remains a deserving example of the way forward to foster regional cooperation.

Unluckily, in other regional areas of the world, international cooperation is not always possible or fully effective. In Latin America, for example, despite examples of multilateral initiatives carried out with positive results, a comprehensive, unified and coherent regional strategy to counter cybercrime is still missing (Lavorgna 2018a). As mentioned above, one of the main factors hindering cooperation is distrust between states. Whereas some practical problems of information exchange are ultimately resolvable, issues of *trust* are more challenging to address (Aldrich 2004; Hufnagel & McCartney 2017). Specific political circumstances or differences in legal traditions can also limit mutual assistance in terms of investigative or judicial cooperation. For instance, a common legal framework on police cooperation does not exist between the four different jurisdictions of Greater China (Mainland China, Hong Kong, Macau and Taiwan) even if a number of formal agreements were established bilaterally. Here, cross-border law enforcement is still predominantly based on informal cooperation mechanisms (Hufnagel 2017). For Taiwan and China specifically, most forms of cooperation occur through third-party organisations and can work only when relations are not strained. This issue badly reflects on cybercrime investigation and prosecution, not only between these two countries but also for third parties, as malicious online activities between Taiwan and China can also affect others (Chang 2013). In recent years, however, informal mutual help in cybercrime investigation has begun to take place, at least in cases of economic crime where no government element is involved and which both countries suffer from (Chang 2013).

Apart from the institutionalised forms of cross-border cooperation encountered so far, multi-agency partnerships (that is, agencies bringing together different types of stakeholders, ranging from governmental organisations and research institutions to non-governmental organisations and private-sector providers) are being built to embark on and consolidate networked trust relationships, where information is more easily shared (Wall 2007). After all, the blurring of traditional clear-cut distinctions between public and private when it comes to crime prevention and control is a characteristic of many contemporary societies (Garland & Sparks 2000). Cybercrimes are simply encouraging this trend to go further. There are different types of multi-agencies, with different geographical and functional scope. For instance, the Society for the Policing of Cyberspace, based in Canada, aims to enhance international partnerships among public and private professionals to prevent and combat crimes in cyberspace. It includes various types of partners, ranging from law enforcement and criminal justice professionals to corporate security and academic institutions. The Anti-Phishing Working Group, founded in 2003, is an international consortium encompassing more than 2000 institutions worldwide, ranging from financial institutions and solutions providers to law enforcement and governmental agencies. It operates through a United States-based and incorporated non-profit organisation and a research foundation based in Barcelona. A final example is provided by the China Internet Network

Information Centre, the administrative agency responsible for internet affairs under the Ministry of Information Industry of the People's Republic of China. Within this framework, the Anti-Phishing Alliance of China was founded to tackle cybercrime in cooperation with all major Chinese online commerce stakeholders, including all major Chinese commercial banks and Web hosting companies. It is not easy to assess the effectiveness of these partnerships but they certainly have the merit of facilitating a climate of trust and cooperation among different actors (Lavorgna 2018a).

We have seen how, especially since the late 1980s, many forms of international cooperation have emerged to tackle problems collectively but these approaches are not always sufficiently effective. Furthermore, problems might be due to the existing 'digital divide' between different countries, with disadvantaged states subject to cyber-insecurity being more vulnerable to cyber-attacks (Gamreklidze 2014). Given the limitations of traditional crime control methods in cyberspace, much effort has been directed at crime prevention. In this case, a mix of traditional and new approaches is required.

Approaches to cybercrime prevention

Although public police are generally expected to take care of the greater share of policing and regulating behaviour because of their traditional consensual relationship with the state and its citizens, their real role in cyberspace is small overall and suffers major limitations, with other actors and different preventive strategies playing larger roles (Sommer 2004; Williams & Levi 2017; Farrand & Carrapico 2018; Porcedda 2018). In this section, we will focus on the role played by the private sector and the general public, who not only are core stakeholders when it comes to cybercrime but also are in a very important position to contribute to the mitigation of cybercrime issues.

The emerging approaches to cybercrime prevention to be discussed are in line with the 'responsabilisation thesis': the state power recognises its limits in ruling some aspects of society and consequently agrees to shift some of the responsibility for crime control to other actors, such as individuals, communities and businesses (O'Malley 1996; Garland 2001). This responsabilisation manifests itself through 'preventative partnerships' that are a common feature of contemporary society, their creation being led by the wider socio-political processes of late modernity, especially neoliberalism (Garland 2001). The importance of this partnership is becoming bigger and bigger in the cyberspace arena, where the state's role is diminished, if only for the practical challenges it cannot face on its own.

Commercial solutions

When it comes to cybercrime prevention, commercial businesses are both part of the problem and part of the potential solution. On the one hand, many companies are unwilling or unable to ensure proper levels of cybercrime pro-tection (Paquet-Clouston et al. 2018). However, they could exercise a mean-ingful role in the prevention of cybercrimes through the use of more rigorous management practices (for instance, by using improved mechanisms to verify online identities) and by relying on new technologies (as in the case of the adoption of biometric security measures, which evaluate bodily elements or biological data for identity verification). Although companies are increasing their spending on cybercrime prevention, many of them do not have clearly defined internet security policies or action plans to cope with cyber-attacks. This problem particularly affects companies based in more deprived areas or small and medium-sized enterprises, which are often left to navigate their way through the cyberworld without having sufficient resources or in-house exper-tise to increase their cyber-resilience and to keep their IT security updated and effective (Almadhoob & Valverde 2014; Jansen et al. 2016).

Unfortunately, in today's world, for many companies, a cyber-attack is not a matter of *if* but of *when*, the big challenge being not only to prevent it but also to promptly identify and respond to the breach when it occurs. Hence, increasing attention is being paid to the importance of raising busi-ness confidence and awareness of online safety and security (for instance, by providing easy-to-understand information on the threats via the use of spe-cific campaigns). In order to achieve these goals, key terms for cybersecurity need to be explained in user-friendly language and simple best practices (such as changing passwords periodically and never sharing them with any-one else, never using a word found in the dictionary, logging off or locking one's personal computer when away, copying and storing information in a secure location, not providing personal information in response to any email, keeping the firewall turned on and so on) need to be clearly emphasised. In addition, guidance and security-related information needs to be provided to users to enable them to perform effective security measures (such as choosing a strong password) (Furnell et al. 2018).

The nature and extent of the basic duty of care expected from users, how-ever, evolve with changes in the cybercrime scenario. For instance, the usual advice given to users in the past was to make sure they had good, updated antivirus software. However, it is becoming increasingly clear that, although this is necessary, it is not sufficient: cybercriminal tactics have changed but modern antivirus software often does not update fast enough to recognise many forms of attacks and is becoming less and less effective at protecting devices. Relying only on prevention-focused products, as a consequence, can give companies a false sense of security, paradoxically making them vulner-able to social engineering-driven attacks, for instance. Furthermore, although these awareness-raising approaches are certainly well meant, they risk becom-ing box-ticking exercises that avoid engagement with the actual context-specific concerns of individuals and businesses alike. As an alternative way of managing the risk of cyber-attacks, the cyber-insurance market is growing but its expansion is still limited by the fact that cybercrime costs are difficult to estimate. Damaging cyber-events are rare but may have large negative impacts (they are a 'tail risk', in insurance jargon) and it is extremely difficult to bring together insurance-related requirements with the reality of constantly evolving technologies. As a consequence, cyber-insurance is still very expensive and relatively rare (Bolot & Lelarge 2009; Meland et al. 2017; Tosh et al. 2017).

A degree of self-regulation may also be exercised by telecommunication carriers, service providers and other tech companies to ensure that safety and security are factors taken into account when designing services and that criminals are deterred from exploiting potential crime opportunities in the online environment. These for-profit businesses themselves, which have a great vested interest in security and public trust in the use of new technologies, may deliver products and services to minimise the risk of abuse and to assist individuals in defending themselves. Indeed, the private sector has become over the years a fundamental stakeholder in the development of network and information systems security policies: if at the beginning the private sector was seen mainly as a victim in need of protection, it soon became perceived as an actor bearing responsibility for ensuring network resilience and also as an active policy shaper by providing technical expertise (Farrand & Carrapico 2018). After all, computer security is a thriving and profitable industry, for both crime prevention and the provision of damage control services in the aftermath of an attack on telecommunications systems. Some of these companies are proactively trying to define themselves as key players in crime control and cybersecurity. In 2013, for instance, Microsoft opened a Cybercrime Center in Redmont, Washington, with the aim of combining in-house and cross-industry expertise to better fight crime on the internet. In 2017, the same company announced the opening of a new Cybersecurity Engagement Center in Mexico that would serve the wider Latin American region to help Microsoft's clients (citizens, private-sector companies, police forces and governments) with protection from attacks as well as offering ways to detect them and find solutions. The development of the Center has been an important step in improving cybersecurity across the whole region.

Other companies are trying to address the enforcement gap in cyberspace by using, among other things, private enforcement to monitor cyberspace and uncover illegalities in their platforms – as in the case of banking or money transfer companies (PayPal, for instance), which often employ teams of specialists who monitor transactions 24/7, dedicated software to identify anomalous transactions and who work with the authorities to shut down fraudulent websites. For instance, if you buy things online with your credit or debit card, you might receive a text message from your bank asking you to confirm the transaction, especially if it is not in line with your usual spending habits.

The engagement of private companies in the provision of security, however, is not unproblematic and it raises a number of dilemmas. Although pluralisation of security may be welcomed in the sense that it presents a number of opportunities for positive, efficient and flexible cooperation among multiple actors, we should not forget that when it is carried out by for-profit organisations, security becomes a product to be sold, and for businesses it can be more (economically) convenient at times to transfer the cost of a cyber-threat rather than minimising it for the public good (Bures 2018). Furthermore, the legal responsabilisation of commercial actors, especially in the tech business, is still very porous (Walker et al. 2000): a coherent international legal framework that accounts for social objectives has yet to be established, even if the matter is receiving increasing attention and there is growing political pressure to better regulate the untamed freedom of powerful tech companies. After the 2018 debates around the Facebook/Cambridge Analytica scandal (see Chapter 4) and the consequent loss of faith in social media voluntary codes of conduct to avoid the illegitimate usage of the data they collect, it is likely that stricter legislation and heavy sanctions will at least be discussed. After all, intervening in finding new balances between profit maximisation and social good for tech companies (powerful gatekeepers, whose decisions affect millions) is probably one of the main challenges to be met in our times (Berners-Lee 2018).

Box 9.2 Implementing secure data storage

Secure data storage refers to the manual and automated processes and technologies used to ensure the security and integrity of stored data. It applies to very different devices, ranging from hard disk and USB drives to cloud computing and data warehouses (central repositories of corporate information coming from multiple data sources within a company; as such, they can be among the most sensitive targets in an organisation). Secure data storage has to prevent unauthorised access to the data, while keeping them available to the right users when needed, and must keep a record of activities performed by users. Secure data storage may include the security software (such as data encryption or protection against malware) or the physical protection of the hardware on which the data is stored (in terms, for instance, of infrastructure security).

There are numerous examples of recent major data breaches linked to unsecure data storage. To name a few, in 2015, the Ashley Madison website (a Canadian online dating service marketed to enable extramarital affairs) was breached and information about the sites' users was stolen. Some of these data were released, with a number of users receiving extortion emails and many more (and their families) experiencing significant distress. In late 2016, a massive hack against Uber exposed data of almost 60 million users and drivers. Reportedly, the hackers were able to obtain unencrypted data stored on Uber's

Amazon Web Services account. Uber initially refrained from notifying the individuals and regulators but rather paid USD 100,000 to keep the breach quiet and delete the data. In 2017, an attack against Equifax, a major American consumer credit reporting agency, potentially compromised sensitive information of 143 million citizens, including their social security and driver's license numbers. In the same year, personal data of millions of South Africans (including contact details, ID numbers and income) were leaked, remaining publicly online for months, and a database backup file held by the Deeds Office was compromised. These types of data breaches can create the risk of harm from identity theft or fraud and also cause victims to experience anxiety and fear (even if so far there has not yet been consistent case law on these issues and many data breach lawsuits are still dismissed in courts for failure to allege sufficient harm, see Solove & Keats Citron 2018). The underlying problem is that often data not directly relevant to the business are collected, employees without a need-to-know necessity can access them and personnel is not sufficiently educated on key cybersecurity issues. Besides, in 2018, the Facebook/Cambridge Analytica case provoked discussions on the problem of private companies collecting huge amounts of data on individuals to monetise these by selling them to other organisations (which may then mishandle them).

Generally speaking, it is a company's responsibility to ensure compliance with data protection regulations and best standards in data storage. Systems used by commercial outfits, however, are not always particularly secure, as there is often a trade-off between meeting users' preferences and ensuring high levels of data protection. This issue is becoming increasingly evident with the cloud, as many data owners (individuals and businesses alike) are outsourcing their data storage and protection to third-party (cloud) companies. For instance, most cloud storage systems (such as the popular Google Drive and Dropbox) encode users' data with an encryption key and generally keep and store the key as well. This is most convenient but less secure, as the key might be misused or stolen, leaving data vulnerable, often without the data owner knowing.

An alternative is to use structured encryption (a way to ask a system to do computational work without the system knowing what kind of work it is doing) to protect a file before uploading it onto the cloud. In this way, the encryption key remains open to the user, meaning that the service provider cannot 'see' the files stored, but this also means an additional 'step' of effort for the user before being able to store the data, rather than being able to modify the file directly from the cloud. Furthermore, this can be problematic when the cloud is used for data-sharing, especially if the data owner changes some of the users' access privileges. Homomorphic encryption (a technique used to operate on encrypted data without decrypting it), proxy re-encryption schemes (that allow a third party to alter data that has been encrypted for another party by re-encrypting it under a different set of keys without de-encrypting it first) and blockchain technology have been proposed as alternative frameworks for secure data-sharing (Samanthula et al. 2015; Zyskind et al. 2015).

Technological solutions

Technology itself can be used in various ways to prevent cybercrimes. Both in the design process and in successive stages, it is possible to identify vulnerabilities and implement crime control policies that, by intervening in the codes and structures of ICT technologies, can 'design out' crime. Some solutions are extremely common, such as giving usernames and passwords to gain access to a secure network. More sophisticated solutions envisage, for instance, eliminating certain vulnerabilities in the internet Domain Name System (DNS) infrastructure (how internet domain names are located and translated into IP addresses) to reduce specific cybercrimes such as 'pharming' (a cyber-attack intended to redirect a website's traffic to another fake site) or to build a better and usable design to shield users from spoofing (Hallam-Baker 2005; Dhamija et al. 2006). Furthermore, technology can provide a wide range of solutions, supplying secure mechanisms to reduce opportunities for crime and impede (potential) offenders: a simple and well-established system we encountered in Chapters 6 and 7 is that of escrow payments as a way to ensure trust in e-commerce. Coding itself can help to prevent crime by becoming a sort of 'law' in cyberspace: if we can virtually regulate every aspect in the use of online spaces and services by means of trusted systems created by codes, codes become those influencing people behaviours and attitudes (Lessig 1999). As a system of regulation, codes can be extremely pervasive but also rapidly adaptive to emerging needs (Williams 2007) and, as such, should be effective in preventing illegalities (such as fraud) by reducing uncertainties (for instance, in the online delivery of a service). In this way, the architecture of the Web itself is what can create areas of freedom or of control, with the consequence that those controlling the codes are also those in charge of pivotal decisions not only about practicalities of policing cyberspace but also about its underlying ethics and values in general.

Technological interventions, however, do not come without problems and criticism. Incorporating security as a guiding principle in designing new products and software is often not a priority, as it can be costly and time-consuming. In the trade-off (or, at best, the false dichotomy) between usability and security, developers often lean towards the former, even when this might not be fully justified. As explained by Caputo et al. (2016), this approach is often due to gaps in training and awareness and to bias towards the idea that 'developers know best', which makes it culturally difficult for many developers to accept guidance by usability and security specialists, often perceived and dismissed as 'people who cannot code'. Furthermore, technological interventions tend to address only the effect rather than the cause of crimes and risk interfering with the free flow of information or invading individual privacy. Technological solutions tend, in fact, to shift the privacy-security balance in favour of the latter. Although in cyberspace serious offenders are a small minority of users, with most technological solutions all users are unfairly affected through being monitored (or potentially monitored) in most of their online activities. Furthermore, although technological solutions may reduce criminal opportunities (for instance, by restricting access to specific ICTs), they might also inadvertently limit opportunities for their positive and constructive use. Think of the presence of Web filtering software (such as parental control software), which might accidentally lead to preventing access to educational websites, or how the use of backdoors in encryption might help law enforcement in apprehending criminals but also diminish personal security when exchanging information in a highly secure manner for legit actors.

Self-help, education and online vigilantism

Given the complexities and the vastness of cyberspace, victims' self-help – or at least the exercise of prudent behaviour by prospective victims – is generally considered the first line of defence against cybercrime, for both individual and commercial victims. As advocated by Brenner (2003) among others, a proactive and collaborative approach is needed in cyberspace: in other words, a system of distributed security, in which citizens assume responsibility for discouraging the commission of cybercrime. After all, since its beginning, the culture of the internet has favoured self-regulation among users, rather than external intervention from state actors, in the attempt to preserve cyberspace as a space free from potential interference and/or censorship (Yar 2019).

So far, unluckily, many companies still have no clear policies on how to deal with cyber-incidents or cyber-attacks and may be resistant to acknowledging or reporting a cybercrime because of the risk of adverse publicity. Individuals might not be sufficiently informed and therefore do not even know they have been victimised or they might not know of simple precautions to avoid victimisation. Cyberspace, however, is simply an expansion of the physical social space where crime might occur. Just as no one would leave a costly smartphone unattended in a lecture hall or a wallet in full view on a busy train, internet users must get used to taking a series of precautions in the online environment. As a consequence, information and education play a major role in cybercrime prevention: many potential victims remain unaware or poorly aware of the dangers they face and it is therefore of utmost importance to provide them with greater knowledge of the risks they might encounter. Behavioural research indicates that is also necessary to educate individuals on the effectiveness of the various behaviours they can adopt to protect themselves (Crossler et al. 2019).

As mentioned above, a wide range of different programmes have been established to enhance general education in cybersecurity at different levels, often joining forces with internet service providers to develop an online culture that expunges unacceptable behaviours, such as virtual stalking and harassment (MS-ISAC 2005). Indeed, through education, social values can be shaped and users made aware of what is acceptable behaviour in cyberspace (Lavorgna 2018a). Some countries have developed and implemented education programmes and platforms. In the United Kingdom, for instance, the scheme 'Get Safe Online' (presenting itself as a leading source of unbiased, factual and easy-to-understand information on online safety) has been created as a public–private sector partnership supported by the government and leading organisations in banking, retail, internet security and other sectors. In 2017, the Department for Digital, Culture, Media and Sport launched a GBP 20 million cybersecurity training programme aimed at young people in school, to support and encourage schoolchildren to develop some of the key skills needed to work in the growing cybersecurity sector. Many countries, however, do not have comprehensive initiatives in place (Kortjan & von Solms 2013) or even make attempts in that direction. Nevertheless, in Nigeria, for instance, the Cyber Crime Prevention Programme has proved effective in enhancing students' knowledge and attitude to cybercrime prevention, irrespective of students' computer literacy level (Amosun et al. 2013). In Qatar, in addition to a Cybercrime Prevention Law, a National ICT Strategy and a website detailing safe practice guidelines for internet usage have recently been developed (Foody et al. 2017). Although most education and awareness campaigns are organised at the national level (UNODC 2013), a few examples at the regional and international levels also exist. Examples are those organised by institutions such as the European Union (for instance, the European Cyber Security Month, the European annual awareness campaign that takes place each October across Europe to promote cybersecurity among citizens) and technology companies such as Google (with tools such as the Safety Centre for families to get practical advice on how to protect children online and Internet Legends, a programme designed to give children skills to stay safe and act responsibly online).

In parallel, as cyberspace has become more and more popular and populated, several solutions of auto-regulation and monitoring have become increasingly widespread, especially regarding the mitigation of illegal or deviant content online. Structured cyberplaces where people interact (such as forums and online groups) rely on the presence of mediators to prevent discussions from becoming disruptive and to ensure that community members adhere to acceptable standards of behaviour. Similarly, unofficial norms to inhibit low-level incivilities via peer pressure (so-called netiquette) exist and are constantly evolving. After all, compared with formal policing, online communities are 'closer' to the users and in a better position to try to instil a sense of shared responsibility among their members. Examples are reputation management systems and online shaming to ostracise the wrongdoer or as a way to reintegrate him/her into the community (Wall & Williams 2007; Williams 2007).

The increasing sophistication of many cybercrimes, however, is calling into question the effectiveness of some of these mechanisms, so that more sophisticated systems have been developed, such as online vigilantes (Williams 2007). Citizens concerned about the presence of undesirable content in cyberspace have given rise to online private monitoring and informal surveillance, the underlying idea being that where formal social control is weak, due to the enormity of the environment to be controlled, collective responses of users and e-patrol groups can assume a prominent role. For instance, there are groups of anti-criminal activists – such as CyberAngels – who patrol websites to help keep the internet safer (from child pornography and cyberstalking, in the case of this group) and promote online safety education programmes (Lavorgna 2018a). Overall, internet vigilantism (or 'digilantism', Nhan et al. 2017) can allow concerned citizens to be empowered online and to achieve some form of social justice while satisfying their personal need for participation or 'having fun' (Chang & Poon 2017). Unfortunately, as we have seen in Chapter 6 when dealing with the phenomenon of cyber-crowdsourcing and 'human flesh searches', vigilantism can also take a turn for the worse: in the attempt to shame or punish illegal or immoral behaviour, it can become a witch hunt, with innocents unjustly dragged through the mud.

Concluding remarks

In this chapter, we have seen how the design, development and implementation of control and preventive measures against cybercrimes are moving in three different directions: *up* (towards the transnational or international level), *down* (towards individual responsibilisation) and *out* (towards privatisation and commercialisation) (Figure 9.1).

The development and implementation of these measures should be undertaken with care, so as not to unduly limit the potential advantages inherent in the new technologies or hinder other fundamental values – such as privacy and freedom – under the aegis of security. The openness of cyberspace is fundamental to promote the free flow of ideas and innovation, to deliver the economic benefits of globalisation and to strengthen democratic ideals. We cannot ignore that the process of 'hyperspatialisation' of our lives carried out by new ICTs, and specifically by the internet, has transformed the relationship between deviance and control (McGuire 2007). Cyberspace is now a pervasive and integral part of society, which generates crime and deviance as well as new forms of surveillance and regulation: in this way, key dimensions of social systems have

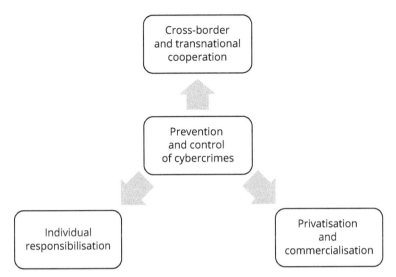

Figure 9.1 The three major forces shaping today's approaches to dealing with cybercrimes

been reshaped. For instance, traditional law enforcement is not enough to ensure safety on the internet, and site operators and internet users, often without any specific training, have an increasing role in monitoring and reporting criminal behaviour online. From the brief overview provided in this chapter, it should be clear not only that there is no single best strategy for the control or prevention of cybercrimes but also that security in cyberspace increasingly depends on a wide range of institutions as well as victim self-help, market forces and technology. After all, the pluralisation of security actors is a characteristic of many contemporary societies. This feature is simply becoming more apparent in cyberspace, with formal and informal systems of control, run by both state and non-state actors, being increasingly involved in the prevention, disruption and mitigation of cybercrimes.

If this pluralisation of actors opens up many possibilities for enhancing cybersecurity and resilience, it also brings with it certain problems. Not only can it complicate organised and coordinated responses to prevent or tackle cybercrimes but, as underlined by Powell (2001) and Paquet-Clouston et al. (2018) among others, it can also cause a so-called collective action problem. A secure system can, in fact, be considered a public good depending on many actors; although every actor would be better off cooperating with the common goal (that is, a secure system), these actors may fail to do so because joint action is discouraged by the fact that everyone is waiting and hoping for someone else to research and invest in security, so as to be able to free-ride rival consumption, maximising their individual interest. In cyberspace, as elsewhere, this can lead to severe inefficiencies, with free-riders exploiting the situation and otherwise proactive players being deprived of the right sets of incentives to invest in security.

Finally, given the glocalism of cybercrime countering and prevention, it should be clear how the global nature of cybercrime entails additional international cooperation. Before we conclude, however, two core challenges need to be further emphasised. First, cooperation is set to fail if we do not prioritise addressing the power disparities between the Global North (especially English-speaking nations) and the rest of the world when it comes not only to digital divides but also to setting standards for online policing, regulatory structures and surveillance practices (Mann & Warren 2018). These disparities can, in fact, hinder the practicalities of law enforcement and judicial assistance and, even worse, loosen and worsen privacy and transparency standards in the handling of data. Second, many mechanisms in place for international cooperation are necessary and promising but still limited in their scope and reach; in order for them to become more effective, possibilities for sharing data and resources should be augmented at least at the regional level, but the political climate in many countries does not make this easy. The discussions around Brexit – the departure of the United Kingdom from the European Union – offers a good example. Although both parties would be better off if they were to maintain or even increase collaboration in cybersecurity, because of the need to renegotiate many data- and intelligence-sharing procedures, after Brexit the United Kingdom will lose influence and access to full transnational cooperation, making it more fragile and less accountable (Hillebrand 2017). This is likely to entail serious negative effects in the prevention of cyber-attacks, their investigation and prosecution and for cyber-resilience at different levels (Lavorgna 2018b). Because of the rise of populism and nationalism in many countries, a worrisome trend might emerge, restricting or most probably slowing down the road to further cooperation.

? CRITICAL QUESTIONS

- Situational Crime Prevention (SCP), an approach to crime control grounded in the idea that opportunity is a major driver for crime (Felson & Clarke 1998), has been used as an analytical framework in the attempt to interfere with criminals' risk/benefit ratio and therefore to prevent and disrupt criminal activities rather than merely curb them through the might of the criminal justice system. SCP, in fact, seeks to alter the 'near' or immediate causes of crime by modifying the decisions that precede its commission (Clarke 2008). The reduction of crime is achieved through 25 mechanisms that can be reduced to five main opportunity-reducing techniques: (1) increase the offender's perceived effort; (2) increase the risk; (3) reduce the rewards; (4) reduce provocations; and (5) remove the excuses (Clarke 1992; Cornish & Clarke 2003). In practice, some techniques of SCP are already used to counter many forms of cybercrime, even if sometimes they are not explicitly recognised as such. Please discuss the crime prevention approaches introduced in this chapter in the light of the five main SCP opportunity-reducing techniques and use this framework to identify other possible crime prevention approaches in cyberspace.

- The advent of any new technological innovation seems to cause a 'crime harvest' (Pease 2001), followed by a retrospective effort to deal with it, in a continuous cycle of innovation-harvest-reactive interventions, often in a technological arms race. To what extent do you think this approach is effective and/or sustainable? What might be alternative ways to mitigate crime in cyberspace without hindering its openness?

- We have discussed how the development of new technological products often does not favour security enough and how this problem is at least partially caused by cultural barriers (for instance, among developers, security experts and sales and marketing professionals) (Caputo et al. 2016). Think of and discuss potential approaches to overcome these cultural barriers and facilitate communication among experts.

10 CYBERCRIME RESEARCH AND THE FUTURE OF CYBERCRIMES

Introduction

Chapter 9 made it clear to the reader that the prevention and countering of cybercrimes are complex issues, where cooperation is key: on the one hand, a trusting partnership between the academic world, the private sector and law enforcement is necessary to tackle the new challenges of cybercrimes in an effective way; on the other hand, genuine collaboration among disciplines is increasingly needed to overcome the challenges of researching crime and deviance in cyberspace. In this concluding chapter, we will reiterate how, given the multidimensional nature of cyberspace, multi- and transdisciplinary expertise is needed to address the challenges of the future. First, we will see how a new model of collaboration between the social and computer sciences is needed to effectively research crime and deviancy in cyberspace. Second, we will consider some of the likely threats, opportunities and potential future developments that are at the margins of current thinking about cybercrimes. Besides the pluralisation of security actors offering formal and informal systems of prevention and control, drawing on the expertise from a number of different social, technological, economic and political disciplines (and beyond) is probably the only way to seek out and understand the potentially insidious future scenarios. Furthermore, this gives us the possibility to think proactively about crime and deviancy and the trade-offs we are willing to accept as a society between privacy, security and convenience.

Researching cybercrimes

Digital data and methodological challenges

For the scope of this book, cyberspace has been not only a place of interest because of its criminogenic features but also a data hunting ground for researchers of different disciplines. You might exploit the wealth of data for your dissertation, in writing a report for your company or out of pure curiosity. The accessibility, variety and wealth of data available online on a broad range of criminal and deviant behaviours constitute a treasure trove of information for researchers using the Web as a space or a tool of investigation.

Digital data can be collected manually or automatically. Manual collection of online data can take different forms: for instance, the researcher might perform active or passive virtual ethnography or might look at text and images to be analysed though a variety of analytical methods. In any case, the data-gathering approach involves mostly copying and pasting online content from webpages, social media and so on. It goes without saying that this process can be quite time-consuming, even if it has proven effective in providing in-depth knowledge on the characteristics of online criminal and deviant activities and groups.

Automatic collection involves the use of software to gather digital content, giving the researcher access to larger datasets. As summarised by Décary-Hétu and Aldridge (2015), the three main methods for the automatic collection of digital data are:

- mirroring (or Web crawling, that is, the indexing and copying of webpages);

- active monitoring (the monitoring of synchronous and ephemeral online communications, such as those on certain social media, their analysis and extraction of the required information);

- leaking (a form of doxing in which information posted on discussion forums, including private messages or administrative information, is willingly made public by someone, such as an offender trying to harm the competition in online criminal markets).

Whereas manual collection methods closely resemble research methods with a long tradition in the social sciences, automatic collection methods often require innovative approaches and skills generally associated with those with a more technical background. The explosion of digital data available will certainly create new opportunities for our understanding of crime and deviance in cyberspace. However, we should not forget that possessing more data is never a substitute for having high-quality data and that high-quality data are not a given when it comes to the combination of complex human behaviours and approaches to collect relevant data which are mostly still under development and refinement. There is currently both an opportunity and a responsibility for social scientists to be cautious and critical in the usage of big data, as the risk of relying on biased or partial data to make mistaken or even ethically concerning claims to knowledge is just around the corner (Halford & Savage 2017).

Ethical and disciplinary issues

Unfortunately, the absence of consensus regarding online methodologies and ethics practices is an issue that severely complicates academic research in this area (Martin 2016). Most academic disciplines, and especially those researching human subjects, have long-standing ethical codes and guidelines to ensure that every study follows legal requirements, respects and protects the rights and welfare of the research subjects and does not have major negative spillovers (Zimmer & Kinder-Kurlanda 2017). Most research frameworks and ethical standards traditionally used by researchers and ethical boards are inadequate to respond to the new challenges and possibilities of online research, especially in a sensitive area such as cybercrimes.

Major issues concerning privacy, confidentiality and research validity need to be discussed and adapted to the ever-changing online scenario, where privacy policies and terms of use evolve rapidly, individuals rashly share sensitive information and it is often tricky to understand which national or international standards apply, given the cross-border nature of many online activities (Zimmer & Kinder-Kurlanda 2017). Is it ethical, for instance, to pretend to be someone you are not or to withhold information when engaging with online communities for research purposes? Should researchers obtain informed consent from people they are observing online and, if so, how? This would be virtually impossible when studying thousands of individuals. Moreover, when and to what extent are researchers under an obligation to inform law enforcement if they witness an illegal act? To what extent do internet users have an expectation of privacy when active in 'public' online spaces? And how can we determine whether and to what extent an online space is 'public' or 'private'? (Sugiura et al. 2012; Martin 2016; Zimmer & Kinder-Kurlanda 2017).

In other words, there is a necessity to find new balances between mitigating risks to both researchers and research subjects and allowing the exploration of uncharted research territories. Without sound ethical standards, severe harm could be inflicted on the actors involved (think, for instance, about exposing the identity of members of online communities) as well as to society in general (if the broader socio-economic and political context of the research is not taken into consideration). Overly conservative approaches and decisions from ethics boards, on the other hand, could discourage researchers from approaching a novel and interesting research area or even hinder the possibility of carrying out fundamental research for the public good. It is safe to conclude, in line with Zimmer and Kinder-Kurlanda (2017), that current discussions on online research and ethics can only be part of an ongoing conversation: there is insufficient consistency or agreement on current practice to talk about 'ethical research online' but we should all aim for 'ethically informed' research practices to guide, case by case, our decision-making.

Researching cybercrimes is also one of the domains where the need for multi- and interdisciplinary approaches is most evident. Research on illegal online markets presents an interesting example. There is already a solid (and growing) body of research on various types of criminal and semi-criminal markets in cyberspace, both on the surface and in the deep Web, showcasing a broad and diverse range of methodologies (Martin 2016). In looking at online activities, we can distinguish between traditional social sciences approaches (ranging from interviews with law enforcement or offenders to analysis of judicial documents), approaches adapted from social sciences (such as active or passive online ethnography) and new methodological approaches, often borrowed or absorbed from computer science (especially when it comes to more or less sophisticated ways to crawl data online) (Décary-Hétu & Aldridge 2015). As asserted by Martin (2016), however, the multitude of approaches can hardly be effective if the disciplines involved do not work together. Researchers with a computer science background, for instance, are in the position to use and advance highly technical methodologies to gather more or better-quality data but often lack in-depth understanding of criminological, socio-economic, political or psychological knowledge to proficiently interpret those data. The risk is for the methodology to guide the research question rather than the other way around. On the other hand, criminologists generally lack sufficient technical proficiency to be able to access relevant data, to the point that many researchers are simply reluctant to approach cybercrimes in their research endeavours.

The need for a 'symphonic' approach

As we have seen, different disciplines have an interest in digital data. Regarding digital data on crime and deviance, (generally speaking) data scientists, big data specialists and data analysts have the analytical, statistical and computing skills to make the most of them, while criminologists have the expertise to ask relevant research questions and to meaningfully interpret these data. Traditional criminology and the social sciences in general, however, are facing major methodological and technical challenges, summarised by Williams et al. (2017) as the six 'Vs':

- volume (which refers to the huge amount of relevant information constantly uploaded on computer networks);

- variety (which relates to the heterogeneous, messy and unstructured nature of these data);

- velocity (which refers to the speed at which digital data are generated and propagated);

- veracity (which relates to issues regarding the quality, authenticity and accuracy of digital data);

- virtue (which relates to the ethics of using digital data in research);
- value (which relates to the possibility of extracting meaningful information).

A reaction is the emergence of 'computational criminology' – which defines itself through the use of digital sources of data – as an expanding research field.

As stressed by Halford and Savage (2017), when it comes to big data analytics, a new model of collaboration between the social and computer sciences is needed, a model that integrates computational skills with theoretical, methodological and empirical expertise to study the social world. After all, social and computer scientists are divided by differences in perspective because of their different intellectual traditions but these differences are not unbridgeable epistemological chasms (Di Maggio 2015). The 'symphonic approach' proposed by Halford and Savage – that is, a different way to do big data by pursuing key social questions across multiple data streams including, but not limited to, new forms of digital data – should also be welcomed when it comes to questions on crime and deviance. In other words, if we acknowledge the limitations of much existing research on the digital world (which is often based on a narrow conflation of data sources, specific analytical techniques and monodisciplinary expertise) when it comes to the investigation of complex social issues, we should try to become methodologically pluralist and be able to combine old and new data sources by exploring their contradictions and complementarities (Halford & Savage 2017, p. 9).

However, nobody can be an expert at everything. Hence, the challenge is to try to provide criminologists and social scientists with a sound understanding of cybercrime issues and to equip cybersecurity students and professionals with the skills and mindset to approach the topic in a more cross-disciplinary way. The goal is not to replace or trivialise each other's expertise but rather to learn a common language to better cooperate.

The future of cybercrimes

Thinking about cybercrime prevention and mitigation is complex because these are constantly changing problems. Without going too far in imagining potential futures shaped by major technological novelties that might (or might not) occur in the following years, we can easily see how (more or less) recent innovations have the potential to significantly change how we interact with cyberspace and its criminogenic features and open the way for new (more or less) intrusive ways to secure cybersecurity and control. To mention some examples, the introduction of the IoT and cyber-physical systems into the manufacturing environment is currently launching a new industrial revolution – industry 4.0 (Martellini et al. 2017); these changes will pave the way for cyber-threats in areas where they are currently still limited. Innovations in biometric security, such as the use of digital social biometrics obtained by looking at social media patterns, could open the way to new methods in security and authentication applications (Gavrilova et al. 2017) but there is also the potential for disturbing scenarios in terms of intrusions into our private sphere. Technologies that are currently considered at the forefront of cybersecurity (and of potential cyber-threats when they are criminally exploited) might become obsolete with the next technological innovations. Blockchain, for instance, might be surpassed by new consensus protocols; encryption as we know it might be broken by quantum computing, which offers an exponential leap in processing power.

We have seen throughout this book how it is already increasingly difficult to separate the online and offline realms in our lives, with the consequence that, in many cases, cybercrimes are not confined to cyberspace but rather spill over into the physical space, expanding criminal possibilities through technology. Boundaries are likely to become even more blurred: with the next big waves in computer interfaces, we might encounter standalone augmented-reality headsets (probably replacing our smartphones), creating a world where physical and digital lives blend even more. The implantation of mini radio-frequency identification (RFID) chips in individuals as a new payment and identification option was piloted by a Wisconsin technology company in 2017. We do not know yet whether chips implanted between our thumb and index finger will become a part of our future, but it is nonetheless of great importance to carefully discuss the security implications of this type of technology before it becomes widely used. And let us not forget emerging challenges such as those linked to robotisation. The robotics industry, for example, is seeing the emergence of humanoid robot co-workers to be used in areas such as hospitality, education and healthcare. Some are remotely controlled; others are starting to rely on artificial intelligence (AI) technologies. In both cases, the machine could be hacked, paving the way for new types of crimes. Even more interestingly, should AI-enabled robots become highly or completely autonomous, there are questions to be addressed regarding allocation of responsibility and accountability in the event of a criminal or deviant act as well a redefinition of what 'deviant' might mean for a next-generation robot. Once again, better definition of the role and responsibilities of commercial companies in this context will become pivotal.

Melvin Kranzberg, an American historian writing more than three decades ago, listed 'six laws of technology' in an attempt to emphasise society's unease with the pervasiveness of technology (Kranzberg 1986):

1) Technology is neither good nor bad; nor is it neutral.

2) Invention is the mother of necessity.

3) Technology comes in packages, big and small.

4) Although technology might be a prime element in many public issues, non-technical factors take precedence in technology policy decisions.

5) All history is relevant, but the history of technology is the most relevant.

6) Technology is a very human activity – and so is the history of technology.

In our current times, Kranzberg's laws are still very relevant, as they make us consider how most technology-related problems arise when we do not think and plan ahead regarding the unforeseen consequences that might appear with the large-scale use of apparently benign technologies when they interact with our social ecologies. There is no absolute good or bad when it comes to innovation: a new technology can be good or bad, depending on its geographical and cultural context and its use, abuse or misuse by human beings. This acknowledgment, however, cannot be interpreted as a way to relinquish responsibility for those devising, creating and disseminating innovation. Critical awareness across the technology industry is slowing the process of building up, with employees of major companies such as Google, Amazon and Microsoft demanding greater insight into how the technologies that they build are deployed and students from top institutions protesting at tech companies' involvement in government work, especially in developing military technology (Conger & Metz 2018). All too often, however, tech companies seem reluctant to fully recognise the responsibilities that come with their immense power.

Regardless of what the future holds in terms of new criminogenic opportunities, there are a few important lessons that we can learn from our current knowledge of cybercrime and cybersecurity. First of all, in a context that will keep evolving into further complexity, if nothing else because of the speed of technology-driven changes, a sound theoretical understanding can prove useful in making sense of why and how certain individuals engage in deviant and criminal acts, facilitating thinking and strategies for crime prevention and control and harm mitigation. Second, in spite of the potentially global nature of the new challenges to be met, we should never forget to consider and try to comprehend the local and human dimensions of technology-enabled crimes. No matter how futuristic a technological innovation may sound, only by bringing the local and human elements into the equation can we contextualise the issues at stake, improve our understanding and devise effective approaches to limit new and emerging forms of crime and deviancy. Last but not least, we should keep in mind a major transversal theme encountered in this book – that of the social construction of cybercrimes and specifically of how people's perceptions on the criminogenic features of technological advancement are shaped and informed by the media as well by public discourse. Hence, we should keep an open mind but also be critical and attentive when reading about technological developments depicted as exciting or scary, promising or alarming, depending on the source we are using.

Once again, cross-disciplinary education and cooperation between criminologists, philosophers, historians, economists, political scientists and many more could provide us with a way forward to make the most of the creative power of human beings. This book is intended to be a contribution in this direction. Regardless of your background – be it criminology, computer science, law, politics or something else – by now you should have learned a common language, as the socio-technical basis of a crucial, often challenging, but certainly fascinating topic.

REFERENCES

Açar KV (2017) Webcam child prostitution: an exploration of current and futuristic methods of detection. *International Journal of Cyber Criminology* 11(1):98–109

Adams A (2010) Virtual sex with child avatars. In Wankel C & Malleck S (eds.) *Emerging ethical issues of life in virtual worlds*. Charlotte: Information Age Publishing

Adler Pa & Adler P (2006) The deviance society. *Deviant Behaviour* 27(2):129–114

Aebi MF (2004) Crime trends in Western Europe from 1990 to 2000. *European Journal on Criminal Policy and Research* 10(2–3):163–186

Aghababaei S & Makrehchi M (2018) Mining Twitter data for crime trend prediction. *Intelligent Data Analysis* 22(1):117–141

Agnew R (1992) Foundation for a general strain theory of crime and delinquency. *Criminology* 30: 47–66

Agustina JR (2015) Understanding cyber victimization: digital architectures and the disinhibition effect. *International Journal of Cyber Criminology* 9:35–54

Ahlmeyer M & Chircu AM (2016) Securing the Internet of things: a review. *Issues in Information Systems* 17(4):21–28

Akers RL (1977) *Deviant behaviour: a social learning approach*. Belmont: Wadsworth Pub. Co

Akerlof GA (1970) The market for 'lemons': quality uncertainty and the market mechanism. *The Quarterly Journal of Economics* 84(3):488–500

Al Adwan & DB Lind (2017) How to counter the extremists on social media. In Niglia A, Al Sabaileh A & Hammad A (eds.) *Countering terrorism, preventing radicalization and protecting cultural heritage. The role of human factors and technology*. Amsterdam: IOS Press BV

al-Khateeb HM, Eoiphaniou G, Alhaboby ZA, Barnes J & Short E (2017) Cyberstalking: investigating formal intervention and the role of corporate social responsibility. *Telematics and Informatics* 34(4):339–349

Albrecht C, Morales V, Baldwin JK & Scott SD (2017) Ezubao: a Chinese Ponzi scheme with a twist. *Journal of Financial Crime* 24(2):256–259

Aldrich RJ (2004) Transatlantic intelligence and security cooperation. *International Affairs* 80(4):732–753

Aldridge J & Askew R (2017) Delivery dilemmas: how drug cryptomarket users identify and seek to reduce their risk of detection by law enforcement. *International Journal of Drug Policy* 41:101–109

Algarni AF (2013) Policing Internet fraud in Saudi Arabia: expressive gestures or adaptive strategies? *Policing and Society* 23(4):498–515

Ali R, Barrdear J, Clews R, & Southgate J (2014) The economics of digital currencies. *Bank of England Quarterly Bulletin*, Q3

Allcott H & Gentzkow M (2017) Social media and fake news in the 2016 elections. *Journal of Economic Perspectives* 31(2):211–236

Almadhoob A & Valverde R (2014) Cybercrime prevention in the kingdom of Bahrain via IT security audit plans. *Journal of Theoretical and Applied Information Technology* 65(1):274–292

Alsaleh M & Alarifi A (2016) Analysis of web spam for non-English content: toward more effective language-based classifier. PLoS One 11(11):e0164383

Amnesty International (2018) Spain: counter-terror law used to crush satire and creative expression online. <https://www.amnesty.org/en/latest/news/2018/03/>

Amosun PA, Ige OA & Choo KKR (2013) Impact of a participatory cybercrime prevention programme on secondary school students' attainment in crime prevention concepts in civic education and social studies. *Education and Information Technologies* 20(3):505–518

Amuda YJ & Tijani IB (2012) Ethical and legal implications of sex robot: an Islamic perspective *OIDA International Journal of Sustainable Development* 3(6):19–28

Anderson R, Barton C, Böhme R, Clayton R, Eeten M, Levi M, Moore T & Savage S (2013) Measuring the cost of cybercrime. In Böhme R (ed.) *Economics of information security and privacy.* Heidelberg: Springer

Anderson DA (2014) Cost of crime. In Marciano A & Ramello GB (ed.), *Encyclopedia of law and economics.* New York: Springer

Andrejevic M (2018) Data collection without limits: automated policing and the politics of framelessness. In Završnik A (ed.) *Big data, crime and social control.* Abingdon: Routledge

Anderson A (2004) Risk, terrorism and the Internet. In Clarke D (ed.) *Technology and terrorism.* New York: Routledge

Antonopoulos GA & Hall A (2016) 'Gain with no pain': anabolic-androgenic steroids trafficking in the UK. *European Journal of Criminology* 13(6):696–713

Armenia S & Tsaples G (2018) Individual behavior as a defense in the 'war on cyberterror': a system dynamics approach. *Studies in Conflict & Terrorism* 41(2):109–132

Aronowitz AA (2009) *Human trafficking, human misery. The global trade in human beings.* Westport: Praeger

Arrigo BA & Bersot HY (2014) Postmodern criminology. In Bruinsma G & Weisburd D (eds.) *Encyclopedia of criminology and criminal justice.* New York: Springer

Artzrouni M (2009) The mathematics of Ponzi schemes. *Mathematical Social Sciences* 58(2):190–201

Arun C & Nayak N (2016) *Preliminary findings on online hate speech and the law in India.* Berkman Klein Centre Research Publication No. 2016-19

Attaran A, Bate R & Kendall M (2011) Why and how to make an international crime of medicine counterfeiting. *Journal of International Criminal Justice* 9(2):325–354

Awan I (2014) Islamophobia and Twitter: a typology of online hate against Muslims on social media. *Policy & Internet* 6(2):133–150

Awan I & Zempi I (2017) 'I will blow your face OFF' – virtual and physical world anti-Muslim hate crime. *British Journal of Criminology* 57(2):362–380

Baggili I & Rogers M (2009) Self-reported cybercrime: an analysis on the effects of anonymity and pre-employment integrity. *International Journal of Cyber Criminology* 3(2):550–565

Ball K & Webster F (2003) *The intensification of surveillance: crime, terrorism, and warfare in the information age.* London: Pluto Press

Balnaves M & Madden G (2016) Social games and game-based revenue models. In Willson M & Leaver T (eds.) *Social, casual and mobile games. The changing gaming landscape.* London: Bloomsbury

Bancroft A (2016) Challenging the techno-politics of anonymity: the case of cryptomarket users. *Information, Communication & Society* 20(4):497–512

Bandura A (1977) *Social learning theory.* Englewood Cliffs: Prentice Hall

Bandura A (1986) *Social foundations of thought and action. A social cognitive theory.* Englewood Cliffs: Prentice-Hall

Banks J (2010) Regulating hate speech online. *International Review of Law, Computers and Technology* 24(3):233–239

Banks J (2017) Radical criminology and the technocrime security-capitalist complex. In Steinmetz KF & Nobles MR (ed.) *Technocrime and criminological theory.* Boca Raton (FL): CRC Press

Barlow JP (1996) *A declaration of independence of cyberspace.* Electronic Frontier Foundation. <https://www.eff.org/cyberspace-independence>

Barth S & de Jong MDT (2017) The privacy paradox – Investigating discrepancies between expressed privacy concerns and actual online behaviour. A systematic literature review. *Telematics and Informatics* 43(7):1038–1058

Barratt MJ (2012) Silk Road. eBay for drugs. *Addiction* 107(3):683

Bartoletti M, Carta S, Cimoli T & Saia R (2017) Dissecting Ponzi schemes on Ethereum: identification, analysis, and impact. CoRR, abs/1703.03779

Bates S (2017) Revenge porn and mental health. A qualitative analysis of the mental health effects of revenge porn on female survivors. *Feminist Criminology* 12(1):22–42

Bauman Z & Lyon D (2013) *Liquid surveillance. A conversation.* Cambridge: Polity Press

Beck U (1992) *Risk society: towards a new modernity.* London: Sage

Becker HS (1963) *Outsiders: studies in the sociology of deviance.* New York: Free Press

Becker HS (1967) Whose side are we on? *Social Problems* 14(3):239–247

Berg S (2009) Identity theft causes, correlates, and factors: a content analysis. In Schmalleger F & Pittaro M (eds.) *Crimes of the Internet.* Upper Saddle River: Pearson Prentice Hall

Bergmann MC, Dreißigacker A, von Skarczinski B & Wollinger GR (2018) Cyber-dependent crime victimization: the same risk for everyone? *Cyberpsychology, Behavior, and Social Networking* 21(2):84–90

Berners-Lee T (2018) The web can be weaponised – and we can't count on big tech to stop it. *The Guardian,* 12 March

Bigelow JL, Edwards A & Edwards L (2016) Detecting cyberbullying using Latent Semantic Indexing. *Proceedings of the First International Workshop on Computational Methods for CyberSafety.* CyberSafety@CIKM

Bijlenga N & Kleemans ER (2018) Criminals seeking ICT-expertise: an exploratory study of Dutch cases. *European Journal on Criminal Policy and Research* 24(3):253–268

Black PJ, Wollis M, Woodworth M & Hancock JT (2015) A linguistic analysis of grooming strategies of online child sex offenders: implications for our understanding of predatory sexual behaviour in an increasingly computer-mediated world. *Child Abuse & Neglect* 44:140–149

Blanzieri E & Bryl A (2008) A survey of learning-based techniques of email spam filtering. *Artificial Intelligence Review* 29(1):63–92

Bloom S (2014) No vengeance for 'revenge porn' victims. Unravelling why this latest female-centric, intimate-partner offense is still legal, and why we should criminalize it. *Fordham Urban Law Journal* 42(1):233–289

Blumstein A & Wallman J (2000) *The crime drop in America.* Cambridge: Cambridge University Press

Bocij P & McFarlane L (2003) Seven fallacies about cyber stalking. *Prison Service Journal* 149(1):37–42.

Boes S & Leukfeldt ER (2017) Fighting cybercrime: a joint effort. In Clark R & Hakim S (eds.) *Cyber-physical security. Protecting critical infrastructure*, vol 3. Cham: Springer

Bolot J & Lelarge M (2009) Cyber insurance as an incentive for Internet security. In Johnson ME (eds.) *Managing information risk and the economics of security*. Boston: Springer

Boman JH & Freng A (2017) Differential association theory, social learning theory, and technocrime. In Steinmetz KF & Nobles MR (ed.) *Technocrime and criminological theory*. Boca Raton (FL): CRC Press

Bomse AL (2001) The dependence of cyberspace. *Duke Law Journal* 50:1717–1749

Bonguet A & Bellaiche M (2017) A survey of denial-of-service and distributed denial of service attacks and defences in cloud computing. *Future Internet* 9(3):43

Bonneau J & Miller A (2014) FawkesCoin: a cryptocurrency without public-key cryptography. *Security Protocols Workshop*

Bonneau B, Miller A, Clark J, Narayanan A, Kroll JA & Felten EW (2015) SoK: research perspectives and challenges for Bitcoin and cryptocurrencies. *IEEE Symposium on Security and Privacy*

Bossler AM (2017) Need for debate on the implications of honeypot data for restrictive deterrence policies in cyberspace. *Criminology & Public Policy* 16(3):681–688

Bossler AM & Holt TJ (2009) On-line activities, guardianship, and malware infection: an examination of routine activities theory. *International Journal of Cyber Criminology* 3(1):400–420

Bossler AM and Holt TJ (2010) The effect of self-control on victimization in the cyberworld. *Journal of Criminal Justice* 38(3):227–236

Bower JL & Christensen CM (1995) Disruptive technologies: catching the wave. *Harvard Business Review* January–February, pp. 43–53

Boyle J (1996) *Shamans, software, and spleens: law and the construction of the information society*. Cambridge: Harvard University Press

Branca CMC, Grangeia H & Cruz O (2016) Grooming online em Portugal: um studio exploratório. *Análise Psicológica* 34(3):249–263

Branch K, Hilinski-Rosick CM, Johnson E & Solano G (2017) Revenge port victimization of college students in the United States: an exploratory analysis. *International Journal of Cyber Criminology* 11(1):128–142

Brand S & Price R (2000) *The economic and social costs of crime*, vol 217, Home office research study. London: Home Office

Brantingham P & Brantingham P (1993) Environment, routine, and situation: toward a pattern theory of crime. In Clarke RV & Felson M (eds.) *Routine activity and rational choice, advances in criminological theory*, vol. 5. New Brunswick: Transaction Publishers

Brenner SW (2001) Is there such a thing as 'virtual crime'? *California Criminal Law Review* 4(1):1–72

Brenner SW (2003) Toward a criminal law for cyberspace: distributed security. *Berkeley Electronic Press Legal Series*, Paper 15

Brenner SW (2004) Cybercrime metrics: old wine, new bottles? *Virginia Journal of Law and Technology* 9(13):1–52

Broadhurst R (2006) Combating the cybercrime threat. In Bidgoli H (ed.) *Handbook of information security*. Hoboken: John Wiley & Sons Inc

Broadhurst R and Choo RRR (2011) Cybercrime and online safety in cyberspace. In Smith CJ, Zhang SX & Barberet R (eds.) *Routledge handbook of international criminology*. Abingdon: Routledge

Broadhurst R & Alazab M (2017) Spam and crime. In Drahos P (ed) *Regulatory theory. Foundations and applications*. Canberra: Australian National University Press

Brodie N (2015) The Internet market in antiquities. In Desmarais F (ed.) *Countering illicit traffic in cultural goods: the global challenges of protecting the World's heritage*. Paris: International Observatory on Illicit Traffic in Cultural Goods

Brown I & Korff D (2009) Terrorism and the proportionality of Internet surveillance. *European Journal of Criminology* 6(2):119–134

Brown SD (2016) Cryptocurrency and criminality. The Bitcoin opportunity. *The Police Journal: Theory, Practice and Principles* 89(4):327–339

Buchan R & Tsagourias N (2012) Cyber war and international law. *Conflict & Security Law* 17(2):183–186

Buchanan B (2017) *The cybersecurity dilemma. Hacking, trust and fear between nations*. Oxford: Oxford University Press

Bullock K (2018) The police use of social media: transformation or normalisation? *Social Policy and Society* 17(2):245–258

Buono L (2010) *Investigating and prosecuting crimes in cyberspace: European training schemes for judges and prosecutors*. ERA Forum 11(2):207–218

Bures O (2018) Contributions of private businesses to the provision of security in the EU: beyond public-private partnerships. In Bures O & Carrapico H (eds.) *Security privatization*. Cham: Springer

Burgess RL & Akers RL (1966) A differential association-reinforcement theory of criminal behaviour. *Social Problems* 14:128–147

Burns RG, Whitworth KH & Thompson CY (2004) Assessing law enforcement preparedness to address Internet fraud. *Journal of Criminal Justice* 32:477–493

Butler B, Wardman B & Pratt N (2016) REAPER: an automated, scalable solution for mass credential harvesting and OSINT. *APWG Symposium on eCrime Research*

Button MR & Cross C (2017) Technology and fraud. In McGuire MR & Holt JT, *The routledge handbook of technology, crime and justice*. New York: Routledge

Calderoni F (2010) The European legal framework on cybercrime: striving for an effective implementation. *Crime, Law, and Social Change* 54(5):339–357

Caneppele S & Aebi MF (2019) Crime drop or police recording flop? On the relationship between the decrease of offline crime and the increase of online and hybrid crimes. *Policing: A Journal of Policy and Practice* 13(1):66–79

Caputo DD, Pfleeger SL, Sasse MA, Ammann P, Offutt J, Deng L (2016) Barriers to usable security? Three organizational case studies. *IEEE Security and Privacy* 14(5):22–32

Castells M (2001) *The Internet galaxy: reflections on the Internet, business and society*. Oxford: Oxford University Press

Cattaneo E & Corbellini G (2014) Taking a stand against pseudoscience. *Nature* 510:333–335

Cavalancia N (2010) Preventing data loss by securing USB ports. *Network Security* 11:18–20

Chakraborty M, Pal S, Pramanik R & Ravindranath Chowdary C (2016) Recent developments in social spam detection and combating techniques: a survey. *Information Processing and Management* 52(6):1053–1073

Chalfin A (2016) Economic cost of crime. In Jennings WG (ed.) *The encyclopedia of crime and punishment*. Hoboken: John Wiley & Sons

Chamberlain JM (2015) *Criminological theory in context*. London: Sage

Chan J & Bennet Moses L (2016) Is big data challenging criminology? *Theoretical Criminology* 20(1):21–39

Chang LYC (2013) Formal and informal modalities for policing cybercrime across the Taiwan Strait. *Policing and Society* 23(4):540–555

Chang LYC & Poon R (2017) Internet vigilantism: attitudes and experiences of University students towards cyber crowdsourcing in Hong Kong. *International Journal of Offender Therapy and Comparative Criminology* 61(16):1912–1932

Chaski CE (2005) Who is at the keyboard? Authorship attribution in digital evidence investigations. *International Journal of Digital Evidence* 4(1):1–13

Chen Z, Liu B, Hsu M, Castellanos M, Ghosh R (2013) Identifying intention posts in discussion forums. In *Proceedings of NAACL-HLT. Association for Computational Linguistics, Atlanta*, 1041–1050

Chesney-Lind M & Morash M (2013) Transformative feminist criminology: a critical re-thinking of a discipline. *Critical Criminology* 21(3):287–304

Chism KA & Steinmetz KF (2017) Technocrime and strain theory. In Steinmetz KF & Nobles MR (ed.) *Technocrime and criminological theory*. Boca Raton (FL): CRC Press

Cho D & Kwon KH (2015) The impacts of identity verification and disclosure of social cues on flaming in online user comments. *Computers in Human Behaviour* 51(A):363–372

Choi KS, Scott TM & LeClair DP (2016) Ransomware against police: diagnosis of risk factors via application of cyber-routine activities theory. *International Journal of Forensic Science & Pathology* 4(7):253–258

Choi KS, Lee SS & Lee JR (2017) Mobile phone technology and online sexual harassment among juveniles in South Korea: effects of self-control and social learning. *International Journal of Cyber-Criminology* 11(1):110–127

Choi KS, Lee CS & Cadigan R (2018) Spreading propaganda in cyberspace: comparing cyber-resource usage of Al Qaeda and ISIS. *International Journal of Cybersecurity Intelligence & Cybercrime*: 1(1):21–39

Choo KKR & Dehghantanha A (2018) *Contemporary digital forensics investigations of cloud and mobile applications*. New York: Elsevier

CIGI-Ipsos (2016) *Global survey on internet security and trust*. Centre for International Governance Innovation & Ipsos. <https://www.cigionline.org/internet-survey-2016>

Citron DK (2014) *Hate crimes in cyberspace*. Cambridge: Harvard University Press

Clark F (2015) *Rise* in online pharmacies sees counterfeit drugs go global. *The Lancet* 386(10001):1327–1328

Clarke R (1988) Information technology and dataveillance. *Communications of the ACM* 31(5):498–512

Clarke RV & Cornish DB (1985) Modelling offenders' decisions: a framework for research and policy. *Crime and Justice* 6:147–185

Clarke RV (ed.) (1992) *Situational crime prevention. Successful case studies*. New York: Harrow & Heston

Clarke RV (2004) Technology, criminology and crime science. *European Journal on Criminal Policy and Research* 10:55–63

Clarke RV (2008) Situational crime prevention. In Wortley R and Mazerolle L (eds.) *Environmental criminology and crime analysis*. Cullompton: Willan

Clarke RV (2009) Situational crime prevention: theoretical background and current practice. In Krohn MD, Lizotte AJ & Penly Hell G (eds.) *Handbook on crime and deviance*. New York: Springer

Clough J (2010) *Principles of cybercrime*. Cambridge: Cambridge University Press

Clough J (2015) Towards a common identity? The harmonisation of identity theft laws. *Journal of Financial Crime* 22(4):492–512

Cloward RA & Ohlin LE (1960) *Delinquency and opportunity: a theory of delinquent gangs*. New York: Free Press

Coles A & West M (2016) Trolling the trolls: online forum users' constructions of the nature and properties of trolling. *Computers in Human Behaviours* 60:233–244

Cohen A (1955) *Delinquent boys: the culture of the gang*. New York: Free Press

Cohen S (1972) *Folk devils and moral panics: the creation of the Mods and the Rockers*. London: MacGibbon and Kee

Cohen S (2011) Whose side were we on? The undeclared politics of moral panic theory. *Crime, Media, Culture* 7(3):237–243

Cohen LE & Felson M (1979) Social change and crime rate trends: a routine activity approach. *American Sociological Review* 44(4):588–608

Cohen-Almagor R (2015) *Confronting the Internet's dark side. Moral and social responsibility on the free highway*. Cambridge: Cambridge University Press

Condry I (2004) Cultures of music piracy. An ethnographic comparison of the US and Japan. *International Journal of Cultural Studies* 7(3):343–363

Conger K & Metz C (2018) Tech workers now want to know: what are we building this for? *The New York Times*, 7 October

Council of Europe (CoE) (2003) Additional protocol to the convention on cybercrime, concerning the criminalisation of acts of a racist and xenophobic nature committed through computer systems. <https://www.coe.int/en/web/conventions/full-list/-/conventions/rms/090000168008160f>

Cornish DB & Clarke RV (eds.) (1986). *The reasoning criminal. Rational choice perspectives on criminal offending*. New York: Springer-Verlag

Cornish DB & Clarke RV (2003). Opportunities, precipitators and criminal decisions: a reply to Wortley's critique of situational crime prevention. In Smith MJ & Cornish DB (eds.) *Crime prevention studies no. 16*. New York: Criminal Justice Press

Cornish P (2017) Deterrence and the ethics of cyber conflict. In Taddeo M & Glorioso L (eds.) *Ethics and policies for cyber operations*. Cham: Springer

Cortijo B (2017) A conceptual and legal approach to the cyberspace: the dilemma security versus freedom. In Ramírez J & García-Segura L (eds.) *Cyberspace. Advanced sciences and technologies for security applications*. Cham: Springer

Costello M, Hawdon J, Ratliff T & Grantham T (2016) Who views online extremism? Individual attributes leading to exposure. *Computers in Human Behaviour* 63:311–320

Costello M, Hawdon J & Ratliff TN (2017) Confronting online extremism. The effect of self-help, collective efficacy, and guardianship on being a target for hate spec. *Social Science Computer Review* 35(5):587–605

Council of Europe (2009) *Cybercrime training for judges and prosecutors: a concept*. Project on Cybercrime & Lisbon Network. Department of Information Society and Action against Crime. Strasbourg: Directorate General of Human Rights and Legal Affairs

Council of Europe (2017) Global Action on Cybercrime Extended (GLACY)+. <https://www.coe.int/en/web/cybercrime/glacyplus?desktop=false>

Cox III RW, Johnson TA & Richards GE (2009) Routine activity theory and the internet crime. In Schmallager F and Pittaro M (eds.) *Crimes of the Internet*. Upper Saddle River: Prentice Hall

Cross C (2015) No laughing matter. Blaming the victim of online fraud. *International Review of Victimology* 21(2):187–204

Cross C (2016) 'They're very lonely': Understanding the fraud victimisation of seniors. *International Journal for Crime, Justice and Social Democracy* 5(4):60–75

Crossler R, Bélanger F & Ormond D (2019) The quest for complete security: an empirical analysis of users' multi-layered protection from security threats. *Information System Frontiers* 21(2):343–357

Crump J (2012) What are the police doing on Twitter? Social media, the police and the public. *Policy & Internet* 3(4):1–27

CSIS & McAfee (2018) Economic Impact of cybercrime – no slowing down. Centre for Strategic and International Studies & McAfee. <https://www.mcafee.com/>

Curran J (2009) Reinterpreting Internet history. In Jewkes Y & Yar M (eds.) *Handbook of Internet crime.* Cullompton: Willan

Cvetkovski T (2014) The farcical side to the war on media piracy: a popular case of Divine Comedy? *Media, Culture & Society* 36(2):246–257

D'Ovidio R, Mitman T, Jamillah El-Burki I & Shumar W (2009) Adult-child sex advocacy websites as social learning environments: a content analysis. *International Journal of Cyber Criminology* 3(1):421–440

Daly K & Maher L (eds.) (1998) *Criminology at the crossroads: feminist readings in crime and justice.* Oxford: Oxford University Press

Danaher B, Smith MD & Telang R (2017) Copyright enforcement in the digital age: empirical evidence and policy implications. *Communications of the ACM* 60(2):68–75

Danet B & Herring SC (eds.) (2007) *The multilingual Internet. Language, culture, and communication online.* Oxford: Oxford University Press.

Danquah P & Longe OB (2011) An empirical test of the space transition theory of cyber criminality: investigating cybercrime causation factors in Ghana. *African Journal of Computing & ICTs* 4(2):37–48

Davis JT (2012) Examining perceptions of local law enforcement in the fight against crimes with a cyber component. *Policing: An International Journal of Police Strategies & Management* 35(2):272–284

de Dantisteban P & Gámez-Guadix M (2017) Estrategias de persuasión en *grooming online* de menores: un análisis cualitativo con agresores en prisión. *Psychosocial Intervention* 26(3):139–146

De Filippi P (2014) Bitcoin: a regulatory nightmare to a libertarian dream. *Internet Policy Review* 3(2):43

Décary-Hétu D & Aldridge J (2015) Sifting through the net: monitoring of online offenders by researchers. *The European Review of Organised Crime* 2(2):122–141

Décary-Hétu D & Giommoni L (2017) Do police crackdowns disrupt drug cryptomarkets? A longitudinal analysis of the effect of Operation Onymous. *Crime, Law and Social Change* 67(1):55–75

Deibert RJ (2003) Black code: censorship, surveillance, and the militarisation of cyberspace. *Millennium: Journal of International Studies* 32(3):501–530

Demant JJ & Munksgaard R (2017) *Kryptomarkeder i en dansk og skandinavisk kontekst.* Copenhagen: Justitsministeriets Forskningspulje

Denning DE (2000a) Activism, hacktivism, and cyberterrorism: the internet as a tool for influencing foreign policy. *Computer Security Journal* 163:15–35

Denning DE (2000b) *Cyberterrorism*. Testimony before the Special Oversight Panel on Terrorism Committee on Armed Services U.S. House of Representatives, May 23, 2000. <http://www.cs.georgetown.edu/~denning/infosec/cyberterror.html>

Denning DE (2009) Terror's web: how the Internet is transforming terrorism. In Jewkes Y & Yar M (eds.) *Handbook of Internet crime*. Cullompton: Willan

Denning DE (2012) Stuxnet: what has changed? *Future Internet* 4:672–687

Denning DE (2014) Framework and principles for active cyber defence. *Computers & Security* 40:108–113

Denning DE and Baugh WB (2000) Hiding crimes in cyberspace. In Thomas D & Loader BD (eds.) *Cybercrime: law enforcement, security and surveillance in the information age*. London: Routledge

Dhamija R, Tygar JD & Hearst M (2006) Why phishing works. *Proceedings of the SIGCHI Conference on human factors in computing systems*, pp. 582–590

Di Lorenzo M (2012) Nuevas formas de violencia entre pares: del bullying al cyberbullying. *Revista Médica del Uruguay* 28(1):48–53

Di Maggio P (2015) Adapting computational text analysis to social science (and vice versa). *Big Data & Society* July–December, pp. 1–5

Dierksmeier C & Seele P (2018) Cryptocurrencies and business ethics. *Journal of Business Ethics* 152(1):1–14

Domínguez-Bascoy J & Bauzá-Abril B (2017) War-like activities in the cyberspace: applicability of the law of armed conflicts. In Ramírez J & García-Segura L (eds.) *Cyberspace. Advanced sciences and technologies for security applications*. Cham: Springer

Douglas DM (2016) Doxing: a conceptual analysis. *Ethics and Information Technology* 18(3):199–210

Doyle A (2011) Revisiting the synopticon: reconsidering Mathienen's 'the Viewer Society' in the age of Web 2.0. *Theoretical Criminology* 15(3):283–299

Dunn Cavelty M (2013) *A resilient Europe for an open, safe and secure cyberspace*. Swedish Institute of International Affairs, Occasional Papers #23

Dupont B (2017) Bots, cops, and corporations: on the limits of enforcement and the promise of polycentric regulation as a way to control large-scale cybercrime. *Crime, Law and Social Change* 67(1):9–116

Dupont B, Côté AM, Boutin JI & Fernandez J (2017) Darkode: recruitment patterns and transactional features of 'the most dangerous cybercrime forum in the world'. *American Behavioral Scientist* 61(11):1219–1243

Ebersold K & Glass R (2015) The impact of disruptive technology: the Internet of Things. *Issues in Information Systems* 16(4):194–201

Edwards SSM (2017) Cyber-grooming young women for terrorist activity: dominant and subjugated explanatory narratives. In Viano E (eds.) *Cybercrime, organized crime, and societal responses*. Cham: Springer

Elswah M (2016) Netflix vs. Illegal downloading: digital movie piracy in Egypt (August 2016). <https://doi.org/10.2139/ssrn.2882715>

Englegard S, Reisman D, Eubank C, Zimmerman P, Mayer J, Narayanan A & Felten EW (2015) Cookies that give you away: the surveillance implications of Web tracking. *Proceedings of the 24th International Conference on World Wide Web*, pp. 289–299

Facebook (2017) What does Facebook consider to be hate speech? <https://www.facebook.com/help/135402139904490?helpref=uf_permalink>

Faou M, Lemay A, Décary-Hétu D, Calvet J, Labrèche F, Jean M, Dupont B & Fernande JM (2016) Follow the traffic: stopping click fraud by disrupting the value chain. *14th Annual Conference on Privacy, Security and Trust (PST)*

Farrand B & Carrapico H (2012) Copyright law as a matter of (inter)national security? The attempt to securitise commercial infringement and its spillover onto individual liability. *Crime Law & Social Change* 57:373–401

Farrand B & Carrapico H (2018) Blurring public and private: cybersecurity in the age of regulatory capitalism. In Bures O & Carrapico H (eds.) *Security privatization. How non-security-related private businesses shape security governance.* Cham: Springer

Farrell G & Birks D (2018) Did cybercrime cause the crime drop? *Crime Science* 7:8

Felson M & Clarke RV (1998) Opportunity makes the thief: practical theory for crime prevention. *Police Research Series*, Paper 98. London: Home Office

Ferguson AG (2012) Predictive policing and reasonable suspicion. *Emory Law Journal* 62:259–325

Ferreira C, Matos M & Antunes C (2018) Pathways towards new criminalisation: the case of stalking in Portugal. *European Journal of Criminal Policy and Research* 24(3):335–344

Ferrel J (1999) Cultural criminology. *Annual Review of Sociology* 25:395–418

Finch E (2007) The problem of stolen identity and the Internet. In Jewkes Y (ed.) *Crime Online.* Cullompton: Willan

Fioriglio G (2010) *Hackers.* Rome: Edizioni Nuova Cultura

Flemming P & Stohl M (2001) Myths and realities of cyber terrorism. In Schmid AP (ed.), *Countering terrorism through international cooperation.* Wien: International Scientific and Professional Advisory Council of the United Nations Crime Prevention and Criminal Justice Program

Florencio D & Herley C (2010) Phishing and money mules. Information Forensics and Security (WIFS). <https://www.microsoft.com/en-us/research/publication/phishing-and-money-mules/>

Flores-Yeffal NY, Vidales G & Plemons A (2011) The Latino cyber-moral panic process in the United States. *Information, Communication & Society* 14(4):568–589

Foody M, Samara M, El Asam A, Morsi H & Khattab A (2017) A review of cyberbullying legislation in Qatar: considerations for policy makers and educators. *International Journal of Law and Psychiatry* 50:45–51

Foucault M (1975) *Surveiller et punir. Naissance de la prison.* Paris: Éditions Gallimard

Franklin J, Paxson V, Savage S & Perrig A (2007) An inquiry into the nature and causes of the wealth of internet miscreants. *ACM Conference on Computer and Communications Security (CCS)*

Furnell S (2009) Hackers, viruses and malicious software. In Jewkes Y & Yar M (eds.) *Handbook of Internet crime.* Cullompton: Willan

Furnell S, Khern-am-nuai W, Esmael R, Yang W & Li N (2018) Enhancing security behaviours by supporting the user. *Computer & Security* 75:1–9

Gámez-Guadix M, De Santisteban P & Resett S (2017) Sexting entre adolescentes españoles: prevalencia y asociación con variables de personalidad. *Psicothema. Revista Annual de Psicologia* 29(1):29–34

Gamreklidze E (2014) Cyber security in developing countries, a digital divide issue. *The Journal of International Communication* 20(2):200–217

Gao L & Stanyer J (2014) Hunting corrupt officials online: the human flesh search engine and the search for justice in China. *Information, Communication & Society* 17(7):814–829

García-Maldonado G, Joffre-Velázquez VM, GJ Martínez-Salazar & Llanes-Castillo (2011) Ciberbullying: forma virtual de intimidación escolar. *Revista Colombiana de Psiquiatría* 40(1):115–130

Garland D & Sparks R (2000) Criminology, social theory and the challenges of our times. *British Journal of Criminology* 40:189–204

Garland D (2008) On the concept of moral panic. *Crime, Media, Culture* 4(1):9–30

Garland D (2001) *The culture of control: crime and social order in contemporary society.* Oxford: Oxford University Press

Garland J (2011) Difficulties in defining hate crime victimisation. *International Review of Victimology* 18(1):25–37

Gavison R (1980) Privacy and the limits of law. *The Yale Law Journal* 89(3):421–471

Gavrilova ML, Ahmed F, Azam S, Paul PP, Rahman W, Sultana M & Zohra FT (2017) Emerging trends in security system design using the concept of social behavioural biometrics. In Alsmadi I, Karabatis G, Aleroud A (eds.) *Information fusion for cyber-security analytics. Studies in computational intelligence*, vol 691. Cham: Springer

Gerry FQC, Muraszkiewicz J & Vavoula N (2016) The role of technology in the fight against human trafficking: reflections on privacy and data protection concerns. *Computer Law & Security Review* 32:205–217

Gerstenfeld BP (2004) *Hate crimes: causes, controls and controversies.* London: Sage

Ghafir I, Saleem J, Hammoudeh M, Faour H, Prenosil V, Jaf S, Jabbar S & Baker T (2018) Security threats to critical infrastructure: the human factor. *Journal of Supercomputing* 74(10):4986–5002

Giddens A (1990) *The consequences of modernity.* Palo Alto: Stanford University Press

Golladay K & Holtfreter K (2017) The consequences of identity theft victimization: an examination of emotional and physical health outcomes. *Victims & Offenders* 12(5):741–760

Godlee F (2011) Wakefield's article linking MMR vaccine and autism was fraudulent. Editorial. *The British Medical Journal* 342

Goldsmith A & Brewer R (2015) Digital drift and the criminal interaction order. *Theoretical Criminology* 19(1):112–130

Goldsworthy T, Raj M & Crowley J (2017) 'Revenge porn': an analysis of legislative and policy responses. *International Journal of Technoethics* 8(2):1–16

Goodman MD (1997) Why the police don't care about computer crime. *Harvard Journal of Law and Technology* 10(3):465–494

Goold BJ & Neyland D (eds.) (2009) *New directions in surveillance and privacy.* Cullompton: Willan

Gordon S & Ford R (2006) On the definition and classification of cybercrime. *Journal in Computer Virology* 2(1):13–20

Gottfredson M & Hirschi T (1990) *A general theory of crime.* Palo Alto: Stanford University Press

Gosseries A (2008) How (un)fair is intellectual property? In Gosseries A, Marciano A & Strowel A (eds.) *Intellectual property and theories of justice.* London: Palgrave

Goswami K, Park Y & Song C (2017) Impact of reviewer social interaction on online consumer review fraud detection. *Journal of Big Data* 4(15):1–19

Grabosky PN & Smith RG (with the assistance of Wright P) (1998) *Crime in the digital age. Controlling telecommunications and cyberspace illegalities*. New Brunswick: Transaction Publishers

Grabosky PN & Smith RG (2001) Telecommunication fraud in the digital age: the convergence of technologies. In Wall DS (ed.) *Crime and the Internet*. London: Routledge

Grabosky P (2016) *Cybercrime*. Oxford: Oxford University Press

Gray K (2012) Stealing from the rich to entertain the poor? A survey of literature on the ethics of digital piracy. *The Serials Librarian* 63(3–4):288–295

Gregg DG & Scott JE (2008) A typology of complaints about eBay sellers. *Communications of the ACM* 51(4):69–74

Guiora AN (2017) *Cybersecurity. Geopolitics, law, and policy*. New York: Routledge

Hadnagy C (2011) *Social engineering: the art of human hacking*. Hoboken: Wiley & Sons

Haggerty KD & Ericson RV (2000) The surveillant assemblage. *The British Journal of Sociology* 51(4):605–622

Haghighat M, Zonouz S & Abdel-Mottaleb M (2015) CloudID: Trustworthy cloud-based and cross-enterprise biometric identification. *Expert Systems with Applications* 42(21):7905–7916

Halaburda H & Sarvary M (2016) *Beyond Bitcoin. The economics of digital currencies*. London: Palgrave

Halder D & Jaishankar K (2017) *Cyber crimes against women in India*. New Delhi: Sage

Halford S & Savage M (2017) Speaking sociologically with big data: symphonic social science and the future for big data research. *Sociology* 51(6):1132–1148

Hall A & Antonopoulos GA (2015) License to pill: illegal entrepreneurs' tactics in the online trade of medicines. In Van Duyne PC, Maljevic A, Antonopoulos GA, Harvey J & Von Lampe K (eds.) *The relativity of wrongdoing*. Nijmegen: Wolf Legal Publishers

Hall A & Antonopoulos GA (2016) *Fake meds online: the Internet and the transnational market in illicit pharmaceuticals*. London: Palgrave

Hall M & Hearn J (2018) *Revenge pornography: gender, sexuality and motivations*. Abingdon: Routledge

Hall S, Critcher C, Jefferson T, Clarke J & Roberts B (1978) *Policing the crisis: mugging, the state, and law and order*. London: Macmillan

Hallam-Baker P (2005) *Prevention strategies for the next wave of cyber crime. Network Security* 10:12–15

Haller P, Genge B & Duka AV (2019) On the practical integration of anomaly detection techniques in industrial control applications. *International Journal of critical Infrastructure Protection* 24:48–68

Hamari J & Keronen L (2017) Why do people buy virtual goods: a meta-analysis. *Computers in Human Behavior* 71:59–69

Hanzelka J & Schmidt I (2017) Dynamics of cyber hate in social media: a comparative analysis of anti-muslim movements in the Czech Republic and Germany. *International Journal of Cyber Criminology* 11(1):143–160

Happa J & Fairclough G (2017) A model to facilitate discussions about cyber attacks. In Taddeo M & Glorioso L (eds.) *Ethics and policies for cyber operations*. Cham: Springer

Hardy K (2010) Operation Tritstorm: hacktivism or cyber-terrorism? *UNSW Law Journal* 33(2):474–502

Hardyns W & Rummens A (2017) Predictive policing as a new tool for law enforcement? Recent developments and challenges. *European Journal of Criminal Policy and Research* 24(3):201–218

Harris C, Rowbotham J & Stevenson K (2009) Truth, law and hate in the virtual marketplace of ideas: perspectives on the regulation of Internet content. *Information and Communications Technology and Law* 18(2):155–184

Hassan K (2012) Making sense of the Arab Sprig: listening to the voices of Middle Eastern activists. *Development* 55(2):232–238

Hawlitschek F, Teubner T, Adam MTP, Borchers NS, Moehlmann M & Weinhardt C (2016) Trust in sharing economy: an experimental framework. *International Conference on Information Systems (ICIS)* 37

Hayes JF, Maughan DL & Grant-Peterkin H (2016) Interconnected or disconnected? Promotion of mental health and prevention of mental disorder in the digital age. *The British Journal of Psychiatry* 208(3):205–207

Heartfield R & Loukas G (2016) A taxonomy of attacks and a survey of defence mechanisms or semantic social engineering attacks. *ACM Computing Surveys (CSUR)* 48(3):art.37

Heidensohn F (1968) The deviance of women: a critique and an enquiry. *British Journal of Sociology* 19(2):160–175

Henry N & Powell A (2018) Technology-facilitated sexual violence: a literature review of empirical research. *Trauma, Violence, & Abuse* 19(2):195–208

Herley C & Florencio D (2010) *Nobody sells gold for the price of silver: dishonesty, uncertainty and the underground economy.* Microsoft technical report MSR-TR-2009-32

Herr T, Schneier B & Morris C (2017) *Taking stock. Estimating vulnerabilities rediscovery.* The Cyber Security Project, Harvard Kennedy School – Belfer Center for Science and International Affairs, July/October

Heymann P, Koutrika G & Garcia-Molina H (2007) Fighting spam on social web sites: A survey of approaches and future challenges. *IEEE Internet Computing* 11(6):36–45

Hickle K (2017) Victims of sex trafficking and online sexual exploitation. In Martellozzo E & Jane EA (eds.) *Cybercrime and its victims.* London: Routledge

Hier S (2008) Thinking beyond moral panic: risk, responsibility, and the politics of moralization. *Theoretical Criminology* 12(2):171–188

Higgins GE, Wilson AL & Fell BD (2005) An application of deterrence theory to software piracy. *Journal of Criminal Justice and Popular Culture* 12(3):166–184

Higgins GE, Fell BD & Wilson AL (2007) Low self-control and social learning in understanding student's intentions to pirate movies in the United States. *Social Science Computer Review* 3(25):339–357

Hillebrand C (2017) With or without you: the UK and information and intelligence sharing in the EU. *Journal of Intelligence History* 16(2):91–94

Hinduja S (2007) Neutralization theory and online software piracy: an empirical analysis. *Ethics and Information Technology* 9:187–204

Hirschi (1969) *Causes of delinquency.* Berkeley: University of California Press

Hoanca B (2006) How good are our weapons in the spam wars? *IEEE Technology and Society Magazine* 25(1):22–30

Holt JT (2007) Subcultural evolution? Examining the influence of on- and off-line experiences on deviant subcultures. *Deviant Behavior* 28(2):171–198

Holt TJ (2012) Examining the forces shaping cybercrime markets online. *Social Science Computer Review* 31(2):165–177

Holt TJ, Blevins KR & Burket N (2010) Considering the pedophile subculture online. *Sexual Abuse: A Journal of Research and Treatment* 22(1):3–24

Holt TJ & Lampke E (2010) Exploring stolen data markets online: products and market forces. *Criminal Justice Studies* 23(1):33–50

Holt TJ & Bossler AM (2013) Examining the relationship between routine activities and malware infection indications. *Journal of Contemporary Criminal Justice* 20(10):1–17

Holt TJ & Bossler AM (2015) *Cybercrime in progress. Theory and prevention of technology-enabled offences.* New York: Routledge

Holt TJ, Bossler AM & Seigfried-Spellar KC (2015) *Cybercrime and digital forensics. An introduction.* New York: Routledge

Holt TJ, Smirnova O & Chua YT (2016) *Data thieves in action. Examining the international market for stolen personal information.* New York: Palgrave

Holt TJ, Burruss GW & Bossler AM (2018) An examination of English and Welsh constables' perceptions of the seriousness and frequency of online incidents. *Policing and Society* (online first)

Holtfreter K, Reisig MD & Pratt TC (2008) Low self-control, routine activities, and fraud victimization. *Criminology* 46(1):189–220

Home Office (2010) *Cyber crime strategy.* London: Home Office.

Home Office (2016) *National cyber security strategy 2016 to 2021.* London: Home Office

Honan M (2012a) How Apple and Amazon security flaws led to my epic hacking. *Wired*, August. <https://www.wired.com/2012/08/apple-amazon-mat-honan-hacking/all/>

Honan M (2012b) How I resurrected my digital life after an epic hacking. *Wired*, August. <https://www.wired.com/2012/08/mat-honan-data-recovery/>

Huber M, Kowalski S, Nohlberg M & Tjoa S (2009) Towards automating social engineering using social networking sites. *CSE International al Conference on Computational Science and Engineering*

Hufnagel S (2017) Regulation of cross-border law enforcement: 'locks' and 'dams' to regional and international flows of policing. *Global Crime* 18(3):218–236

Hufnager S & McCartney C (eds.) (2017) *Trust in international police and justice cooperation.* Oxford: Hart Publishing

Hughes DM (2002) The use of new communication and information technologies for the sexual exploitation of women and children. *Hastings Women's Law Journal* 13(1):127–146

Hughes DM (2004) Prostitution online. *Journal of Trauma Practice* 2(3–4):115–131

Hunton P (2010) Cyber crime and security: a new model of law enforcement investigation. *Policing* 4(4):385–395

Hutchings A & Holt TJ (2015) A crime script analysis of the online stolen data market. *British Journal of Criminology* 55:596–614

Hutchings A & Ting Chua Y (2017) Gendering cybercrime. In Holt TJ (ed.) *Cybercrime through an interdisciplinary lens.* Abingdon: Routledge

IERC (2015) IoT Governance, Privacy and Security Issues. European Research Cluster on the Internet of Things. <http://www.internet-of-thingsresearch.eu/pdf/IERC_Position_Paper_IoT_Governance_Privacy_Security_Final.pdf>

Ikram M, Vallina-Rodriguez N, Seneviratne S, Kaafar MA & Paxon V (2016) An analysis of the privacy and security risks of android VPN permission-enabled apps. *Icm 2016 Proceedings of the 2016 Internet Measurement Conference*

Internet World Stat (2019) <https://www.internetworldstats.com/stats.htm>

Irani D, Balduzzi M, Balzarotti D, Kirda E & Pu C (2011) Reverse social engineering attacks in online social networks. In Holz T & Bos H (eds.) *Detection of intrusions* and malware, and vulnerability assessment. DIMVA 2011. Lecture Notes in Computer Science, 6739. Cham: Springer

Iqbal MS, Zulkernine M, Jaafar F & Gu Y (2018) Protecting Internet users from becoming victimized attackers of click-frauds. *Software: Evolution and Process* 30(3):e1871

Ismal RSM, Kwak D, Kabir H, Hossain M & Kwak KS (2015) The Internet of Things and healthcare: a comprehensive survey. *IEEE Access* 3:678–708

Irwin ASM & Milad G (2016) The use of crypto-currencies in funding violent jihad. *Journal of Money Laundering Control* 19(4):407–425

ITU (2016) *Child online protection (COP) guidelines*. International Telecommunication Union. <http://www.itu.int/en/cop/Pages/guidelines.aspx>

Jacques S, Garstka KK, Hviid M & Street J (2017) The impact on cultural diversity of automated anti-piracy systems as copyright enforcement mechanisms: an empirical study of YouTube's content ID digital fingerprinting technology <https://doi.org/10.2139/ssrn.2902714>

Jaishankar K (2007) Establishing a theory of cyber crimes. *International Journal of Cyber Criminology* 1(2):7–9

Jaishankar K (2009) Space transition theory of cyber crimes. In Schmallager F & Pittaro M (eds.) *Crimes of the Internet*. Upper Saddle River: Prentice Hall

Jaishankar K (2011) Victimization in the cyberspace: patterns and trends. In Manacorda S (ed.) *Cybercriminality: finding a balance between freedom and security*. Selected papers and contributions from the International Conference on 'Cybercrime: Global Phenomenon and its Challenges' Courmayeur Mont Blanc, Italy. International Scientific and Professional Advisory Council of the United Nations Crime Prevention and Criminal Justice Programme

James R (1996) Computer software and copyright law: the growth of intellectual property rights in Germany. *Dickinson Journal of International Law* 15(3):565–593

Jane EA (2014) 'Your a ugly, whorish, slut'. Understanding e-bile. *Feminist Media Studies* 14(4):531–546

Jane EA (2015) Flaming? What flaming? The pitfalls and potentials of researching online hostility. *Ethics and Information Technology* 17(1):65–87

Jane EA (2017a) Feminist flight and fight responses to gendered cyberhate. In Segrave M & Vitis L (eds.) *Gender, technology and violence*. London: Routledge

Jane EA (2017b) *Misogyny online. A short (and brutish) history*. London: Sage

Jansen J, Veenstra S, Zuurveen R & Stol W (2016) Guarding against online threats: why entrepreneurs take protective measures. *Behaviour & Information Technology* 35(5):368–379

Jenkins P (2001) *Beyond tolerance: child pornography on the Internet*. New York: New York University Press

Jewkes Y (2008) The role of the Internet in the twenty-first-century prison: insecure technologies in secure spaces. In Franko Aas K, Oppen Gundhus H & Mork Lommell H (eds.) *Technologies of insecurity: the surveillance of everyday life*. New York: Routledge-Cavendish

Jewkes Y & Yar M (2008) Policing cybercrime: emerging trends and future challenges. In Newburn T (ed.) *Handbook of policing*. London: Routledge

Jones R (2000) Digital rule. Punishment, control and technology. *Punishment & Society* 2(1):5–22

Jordan T & Taylor P (2004) *Hacktivism and cyber wars. Rebels without a cause*. London: Routledge

Junger M, Montoya L & Heydari M (2017) Towards the normalization of cybercrime victimization: a routine activities analysis of cybercrime in Europe. *International Conference on Cyber Situational Awareness, Data Analytics and Assessment (Cyber SA)*

Juels A, Jakobsson M & Jagatic TN (2006) Cache cookies for browser authentication. *IEEE Symposium on Security and Privacy*

Kaskaloglu K (2014) Near zero bitcoin transaction cannot last forever. *The International Conference on Digital Security and Forensics (DigitalSec2014)*

Kats J (1988) *Seductions of crime: moral and sensual attractions in doing evil.* New York: Basic Books

Kerstens J & Jurjen J (2016) The victim–perpetrator overlap in financial cybercrime: evidence and reflection on the overlap of youth's on-line victimization and perpetration. *Deviant Behavior* 37(5):585–600

Kethineni S, Cao Y & Dodge C (2018) Use of Bitcoin in Darknet markets: examining facilitative factors on Bitcoin-related crimes. *American Journal of Criminal Justice* 43(2):141–157

Khoo BH (2003) Police cooperation in fighting transnational organised crime: An Asian Perspective. In Broadhurst R (ed.) *Bridging the gap: a global alliance on transnational organised crime.* Hong Kong: Printing Department HKSAR

Khu-smith V & Mitchell C (2002) Enhancing the security of cookies. In Kim K (eds.) *Information security and cryptology – ICISC 2001. ICISC 2001.* Lecture Notes in Computer Science, vol 2288. Berlin: Springer

Kigerl A (2018) Profiling cybercriminals. Topic model clustering of carding forum member comment histories. *Social Science Computer Review* 36(5):591–609

Kim H, Yang S & Kang Kim H (2017) Crime scene re-investigation: a postmodern analysis of game account stealers' behaviours. <arXiv:1705.00242>

King A & Thomas J (2009) You can't cheat an honest man: making ($$$ and) sense of the Nigerian e-mail scams. In Schmallenger F & Pittaro M (eds.) *Crimes of the Internet.* Upper Saddle River: Pearson Prentice Hall

Klein JJ (2018) La rétribution et la dissuasion du cyber terrorisme. *ASPJ Afrique & Francophonie.* 1er trimestre, pp. 22–35

Kolaczek G (2009) An approach to identity theft detection using social network analysis. *First Asian Conference on Intelligent Information and Database Systems*

Koops BJ & Brenner SW (eds.) (2006) *Cybercrime and jurisdiction. A global survey.* The Hague: Asser Press

Koops B-J, Clayton Newell C, Timan T, Škorvánek I, Chokrevski T & Galič M (2016) A typology of privacy. *University of Pennsylvania Journal of International Law* 38(2):483–575

Kopecký K (2016) Online blackmail of Czech children focused in so-called 'sextortion' (analysis of culprit and victim behaviours). *Telematics and Informatics* 34(1):11–19

Korthagen I, van Keulen I, Hennen L, Aichholzer G, Rose G, Lindner R, Goos K & Nielsen RØ (2018) *Prospects for e-democracy in Europe.* European Parliamentary Research Service PE 603.213

Kortjan N & von Solms R (2013) Cyber security education in developing countries: a South African perspective. In Jonas K, Rai IA & Tchuente M (eds.) *e-Infrastructure and e-Services for developing countries. AFRICOMM 2012.* Lecture Notes of the Institute for Computer Sciences, Social Informatics and Telecommunications Engineering, vol 119. Berlin: Springer

Kranenbarg MW, Holt TJ & van Gelder JL (2019) Offending and victimisation in the digital age: comparing correlates of cybercrime and traditional offending-only, victim-ization-only and the victimization-offending overlap. *Deviant Behavior* 40(1):40–55

Kranzberg M (1986) Technology and history: 'Kranzberg's Laws'. *Technology and Culture* 27(3):544–560

Krone T (2004) A typology of online child pornography offending. *Trends and Issues in Crime and Criminal Justice* 279, Australian Institute of Criminology

Kruse CS, Benjamin F, Jacobson T & Monticone DK (2017) Cybersecurity in health-care: a systematic review of modern threats and trends. *Technology and Health Care* 25(1):1–10

Kumar KPK & Geethakumari G (2014) Analysis of semantic attacks in online social networks. In Martínez Pérez G, Thampi SM, Ko R & Shu L (eds.) *Recent trends in computer networks and distributed systems security. SNDS 2014.* Communications in Computer and Information Science, vol 420. Berlin: Springer

Lam WSE (2008) Language socialization in online communities. In Hornberger NH (eds.) *Encyclopedia of language and education.* Boston: Springer

Lambrecht M (2017) The time limit on copyright: an unlikely tragedy of the intellectual commons. *European Journal of Law and Economics* 43(3):475–494

Lamport L, Shostak R & Pease M (1982) The Byzantine generals' problem. *ACM Transactions on Programming Languages and Systems* 4(3):382–401

Landes W & Posner RA (2003) *The economic structure of intellectual property.* Cambridge: Harvard University Press

Larsson S, Svensson M & de Kaminski M (2012) Online piracy, anonymity and social change: innovation through deviance. *Convergence: The International Journal of Research into New Media Technologies* 19(1):95–114

Lavorgna A (2014a) Wildlife trafficking in the Internet age: the changing structure of criminal opportunities. *Crime Science* 3(5):1–12

Lavorgna A (2014b) Inhumane trade: human trafficking finds its way onto the Internet. *Jane's Intelligence Review*, December, pp. 50–53

Lavorgna A (2014c) Internet-mediated drug trafficking: towards a better understanding of new criminal dynamics. *Trends in Organized Crime* 17(4):250–227

Lavorgna A (2015a) Organised crime goes online: realities and challenges. *Journal of Money Laundering Control* 18(2):153–168

Lavorgna A (2015b) Dark coins. Digital currency opens loopholes for criminals. *Jane's Intelligence Review*, December, pp. 50–52

Lavorgna A (2015c) The online trade in counterfeit pharmaceuticals: new criminal opportunities, trends, and challenges. *European Journal of Criminology* 12(2):226–241

Lavorgna A (2016) Exploring the cyber-organised crime narrative: the hunt for a new bogeyman? In van Duyne PC, Scheinost M, Antonopoulos GA, Harvey J & von Lampe K (eds.), *Narratives on organised crime in Europe. Criminals, corrupters and policy.* Oisterwijk: Wolf Legal Publishers

Lavorgna A & Sergi A (2016) Serious, therefore organised? A critique of the emerging 'cyber-organised crime' rhetoric in the United Kingdom. *International Journal of Cyber Criminology* 10(2):170–187

Lavorgna A & Di Ronco A (2017) Fraud victims or unwary accomplices? An exploratory study of online communities supporting quack medicine. In van Duyne PC, Harvey J, Antonopoulos GA & von Lampe K (eds.) *The many faces of crime for profit and ways of tackling it.* Oisterwijk: Wolf Legal Publishers

Lavorgna A (2018a) Delitos informaticos. In Tenca M and Mendez Ortiz E (eds.) *Manual de prevención del delito y seguridad ciudadana* [Handbook of Crime Prevention and Citizes Security for Latin America]. Buenos Aires: Ediciones Didot

Lavorgna A (2018b) Brexit and cyberspace: implications for cybersecurity. In Carrapico-Farrand E, Niehuss A & Berthelemy C (eds.) *Brexit and internal security: political and legal concerns in the context of the future UK-EU Relationship*. London: Palgrave

Lavorgna (2019a) Cyber-organised crime. A case of moral panic? *Trends in Organized Crime* 22(4):357–374

Lavorgna A & Sugiura L (2019) Caught in a lie: the rise and fall of a respectable deviant. *Deviant Behavior* 40(9):1043–1056

Lavorgna A (2019) Organised cybercrime. In Holt TJ & Bossler A (eds.) *The Palgrave handbook of international cybercrime and cyberdeviance*. New York: Palgrave

Lazer DMJ, Baum MA, Benkler Y, Berinsky AJ, Greenhill KM, Menczer F, Metzger MJ, Nyhan B, Pennycook G, Rothschild D, Shudson M, Sloman SA, Sunstein CR, Thorson EA, Watts & Zittran JL (2018) The science of fake news. *Science* 359(6380):1094–1096

Lea J & Young J (1984) *What is to be done about law and order?* Harmondsworth: Penguin

Lee J (2017) *Sex robot. The future of desire*. London: Palgrave

Lemert E (1951) *Social pathology: a systematic approach to the theory of sociopathic behaviour*. New York: McGraw-Hill

Leppänen A & Kankaanranta T (2017) Cybercrime investigation in Finland. *Journal of Scandinavian Studies in Criminology and Crime Prevention* 18(2):157–175

Leukfeldt ER, Veenstra S & Stol W (2013) High volume cyber crime and organization of the police: the results of two empirical studies in the Netherlands. *International Journal of Cyber Criminology* 7(1):1–17

Leukfeldt ER & Yar M (2016) Applying routine activity theory to cybercrime: a theoretical and empirical analysis. *Deviant Behavior* 37(3):263–280

Leukfeldt R, Lavorgna A & Kleemans ER (2017a) Organised cybercrime or cybercrime that is organised? An assessment of the conceptualisation of financial cybercrime as organised crime. *European Journal of Criminal Policy and Research* 23(3):287–300

Leukfeldt R, Kleemans ER & Stol WP (2017b) A typology of cybercriminal networks: from low-tech all-rounders to high-tech specialists. *Crime, Law and Social Change* 67(1):21–37

Levi M, Doig A, Gundur R, Wall D & Williams M (2017) Cyberfraud and the implications for effective risk-based responses: themes from UK research. *Crime, Law & Social Change* 67(1):77–96

Levi M (2017) Assessing the trends, scale and nature of economic cybercrimes: overview and issues. *Crime, Law and Social Change* 67(1):3–20

Levy D (2012) The ethics of robot prostitutes. In Lin P, Abney K & Bekey GA (eds.) *Robot ethics. The ethical and social implications of robotics*. Cambridge: MIT Press

Levy S (1984) *Hackers: heroes of the computer revolution*. New York: Dell Publishing

Leiter B (2010) Cleaning cyber-cesspool. Google and free speech. In Levmore S & Nussbaum MC (eds.) *The offensive internet: speech, privacy, and reputation*. Cambridge: Harvard University Press

Lessig L (1999) *Code and the others laws of cyberspace*. New York: Basic Books

Lessig L (2004) *Free culture: how big media uses technology and the law to lock down culture and control creativity*. London: Penguin Press

Li H, Fei G, Wang S, Liu B, Shao W, Mukherjee A & Shao J (2017) Bimodal distribution and co-bursting in review spam detection. *Proceedings of International World Wide Web Conference (WWW-2017)*

Li Y, Chang MC & Lyu S (2018) In ictu oculi: exposing AI generated fake face videos by detecting eye blinking. <https://arxiv.org/pdf/1806.02877.pdf>

Liao K, Zhao Z, Doupe A & Ahn GJ (2016) Behind closed doors: measurement and analysis of CryptoLocker ransom in Bitcoin. *APWG Symposium on Electronic Crime Research (eCrime)*

Lin H & Bergmann N (2016) IoT privacy and security challenges for smart home environments. *Information* 7(3):44

Liong M & Cheng GHL (2017) Sext and gender: examining gender effects on sexting based on the theory of panned behaviour. *Behaviour & Information Technology* 36(7):726–736

Long J (2008) No tech hacking. A guide to social engineering, dumpster diving, and shoulder surfing. *Syngress*

Love C (2000) Courtney Love does the math <https://www.salon.com/2000/06/14/love_7/>

Lu Y, Luo X, Polgar M & Cao Y (2015) Social network analysis of a criminal hacker community. *Journal of Computer Information Systems* 51(2):31–41

Luca M & Zervas G (2016) Fake it till you make it: reputation, competition, and Yelp review fraud. *Management Science* 62(12):3412–3427

Lupton D (2014) *Digital sociology*. London: Routledge

Lusthaus J (2012) Trust in the world of cybercrime. *Global Crime* 13(2):71–94

Lusthaus J (2013) How organised is organised cybercrime? *Global Crime* 14(1):52–60

Lusthaus J & Varese F (2017) Offline and local: the hidden face of cybercrime. *Policing: A Journal of Policy and Practice* (online first)

Lyon D (1994) *Electronic eye: the rise of surveillance society*. Minneapolis: University of Minnesota Press

Lyon D (2007) *Surveillance studies: an overview*. Cambridge: Polity

Lyon D (2010) Liquid surveillance: the contribution of Zygmunt Bauman to Surveillance Studies. *International Political Sociology* 4:325–338

Lysonski S & Durvasula S (2008) Digital piracy of MP3s: consumer and ethical predispositions. *Journal of Consumer Marketing* 25(3):167–178

Mackey TK & Liang BA (2017) Health advertising in the digital age. Future trends and challenges. In Rodgers S & Thorson E (eds.) *Digital advertising. Theory and research*. London: Routledge

Majadi N, Trevathan J & Bergmann N (2016) Analysis on bidding behaviours for detecting shill bidders in online auctions. *IEEE International Conference on Computer and Information Technology*

Makin DA & Bye C (2018) Commodification of flesh: data visualization techniques and interest in the licit sex industry. *Deviant Behaviour* 39(1):46–63

Manion M & Goodrum A (2000) Terrorism or civil disobedience: towards a hacktivist ethics. *ACM Sigcas Computer and Society* 30(2):14–19

Mann D & Sutton M (1998) Netcrime. More change in the organization of thieving. *British Journal of Criminology* 38(2):201–229

Mann M & Warren I (2018) The digital and legal divide: *Silk Road*, transnational online policing and southern criminology. In Carrington K, Hogg R, Scott J & Sozzo M (eds.) *The Palgrave handbook of criminology and the global south*. Cham: Palgrave

Manning P (1991) Community policing as drama of control. In Greene J & Mastrofski S (eds.) *Community policing: rhetoric or reality*. New York: Praeger

Mantilla K (2015) *Gendertrolling: How misogyny went viral*. New York: Praeger

Marchetti M, Pierazzi P, Guido A & Colajanni M (2016) Countering advanced persistent threats through security intelligence and big data analytics. *8th International Conference on Cyber Conflict (CyCon)*

Marcum CD, Higgins GE & Ricketts ML (2014) Juveniles and cyber stalking in the United States: an analysis of theoretical predictors of patterns of online perpetration. *International Journal of Cyber Criminology* 8(1):47–56

Marcum CD, Higgins GE & Nicholson J (2017) I'm watching you: cyberstalking behaviours of University students in romantic relationships. *American Journal of Criminal Justice* 42:373–388

Marganski AJ (2017) Feminist theory and cybercrime. In Steinmetz KF & Nobles MR (ed.) *Technocrime and criminological theory*. Boca Raton (FL): CRC Press

Martellini M, Abaimov S, Gaycken S & Wilson C (2017) *Information security of highly critical wireless networks*. Cham: Springer

Martellozzo E (2012) *Online child sexual abuse: grooming, policing and child protection in a multi-media world*. London: Routledge

Martellozzo E (2017) Online sexual grooming. Children as victims of online abuse. In Martellozzo E & Jane EA (eds.) *Cybercrime and its victims*. London: Routledge

Martellozzo E & Jane EA (2017) Introduction: victims of cybercrime on the small 'I' internet. In Martellozzo E & Jane EA (eds.) *Cybercrime and its victims*. London: Routledge

Martin J (2014a) *Drugs on the dark net. How cryptomarkets are transforming the global trade in illicit drugs*. New York: Palgrave

Martin J (2014b) Lost on the Silk Road. Online drug distribution and the 'cryptomarket'. *Criminology and Criminal Justice* 14(3):351–367

Martin J (2016) Illuminating the dark net: methods and ethics in cryptomarket research. In Adorjan M & Ricciardelli Rose. *Engaging with ethics in international criminological research*. London: Routledge.

Mathiesen T (1997) The viewer society: Michel Foucault's 'Panopticon' revisited. *Theoretical Criminology* 1(2):215–234

Matzutt R, Hiller J, Henze M, Henrik Ziegeldorf J, Müllmann D, Hohlfeld O & Wehrle K (2018) A quantitative analysis of the impact of arbitrary blockchain content on Bitcoin. *Proceedings of the 22nd International Conference on Financial Cryptography and Data Security (FC)*

Maurer T (2016) 'Proxies' and cyberspace. *Conflict & Security Law* 21(3):383–403

McDonald K & Smith-Roswey D (2016) *The Netflix effect. Technology and entertainment in the 21ˢᵗ century*. London: Bloomsbury

McFarlane L & Bocij P (2005) An exploration of predatory behaviour in cyberspace: towards a typology of cyber stalkers. *First Monday*, 8(9)

McGlynn C, Rackley E & Houghton R (2017) Beyond 'revenge porn': the continuum of image-based sexual abuse. *Feminist Legal Studies* 25(1):25–46

McGough AS, Arief B, Gamble C, Wall D, Brennan J, Fitzgerald J, van Moorsel A, Alwis S, Theodoropoulos G & Ruck-Keene E (2015) Detecting insider threats using ben-ware: beneficial intelligent software for identifying anomalous human behaviour. *Journal of Wireless Mobile Networks, Ubiquitous Computing, and Dependable Applications* 6(4):3–46

McGuire M (2007) *Hypercrime. The new geometry of harm.* London: Routledge

McGuire M (2009) Online surveillance and personal liberty. In Jewkes Y & Yar M (eds.) *Handbook of Internet crime.* London: Routledge

McGuire M & Dowling S (2013) Cybercrime: a review of the evidence. *Home Office Research Report 75.* London: Home Office

McKenzie J (2017) Graduated response policies to digital piracy: do they increase box office revenues of movies? *Information Economics and Policy* 38(1):1–11

McLelland M (2019) Young people, online fandom and the perils of child pornography legislation in Australia. *International Journal of Cultural Studies* 22(1):102–118

McNally MM & Newman GR (ed.) (2008) *Perspectives on identity theft.* Crime Prevention Studies, vol. 23. Cullompton: Willan

Meland PH, Tøndel IA, Moe M & Seehusen F (2017) Facing uncertainty in cyber insurance policies. In Livraga G & Mitchell C (eds.) *Security and trust management. STM 2017.* Lecture Notes in Computer Science, vol 10547. Cham: Springer

Mennecke B, Terando WD, Janvrin DJ & Dilla WN (2007) It's just a game, or is it? Real money, real income, and real taxes in virtual worlds. *Communications of AIS,* Vol. 19

Merton RK (1938) Social structure and anomie. *American Sociological Review* 3:672–682

Middleton SE & Krivcovs V (2016) Geoparsing and geosemantics for social media: spatio-temporal grounding of content propagating rumours to support trust and veracity analysis during breaking news, *ACM Transactions on Information Systems (TOIS)* 34(3), article 16

Migicovsky A, Durumeric Z, Ringenberg J & Halderman JA (2014) Outsmarting proctors with smartwatches: a case study on wearable computing security. In Christin N & Safavi-Naini R (eds.) *Financial cryptography and data security. Lecture Notes in Computer Science,* vol 8437. Berlin: Springer

Miller V (2009) The Internet and everyday life. In Jewkes Y & Yar M (eds.) *Handbook of Internet crime.* London: Routledge

Miller C (2017) Australia's anti-Islam right in their own words. Text as data analysis of social media content. *Australian Journal of Political Science* 52(3):383–401

Milone M (2003) Hacktivism: securing the national infrastructure. *Knowledge, Technology and Policy* 16(1):75–103

Miró Llinares F (2011) La oportunidad criminal en el ciberespacio. Aplicación y desarrollo de la teoría de las actividades cotidianas para la prevención del cibercrimen. *Revista Electrónica de Ciencia Penal y Criminología,* num. 13-07

Mitnick KD & Simon WL (2001) *The art of deception: controlling the human element of security.* Hoboken: John Wiley & Sons

Moini R, Ismail B & Vialle E (2017) Censorship and surveillance of journalists: an unscrupulous business. *Reports Without Borders* <https://rsf.org/sites/default/files/rsf_report_censorship_and_surveillance_of_journalists_0.pdf>

Monahan T (2009) Identity theft vulnerability: neoliberal governance through crime construction. *Theoretical Criminology* 13(2):155–176

Morselli C, Décary-Hétu D, Paquet-Clouston M & Aldridge J (2017), Conflict management in illicit drug cryptomarkets. *International Criminal Justice Review* 27(4):237–254

Motoyama M, McCoy D, Levchenko K, Savage S & Voelker GM (2011) An analysis of underground forums. *ACM Internet Measurement Conference*

Moore T & Christin N (2013) Beware the middleman: empirical analysis of Bitcoin-exchange risk. In Sadeghi AR (eds.) *Financial cryptography and data security. Lecture notes in computer science,* vol 7859. Cham: Springer

Moskovitch R, Feher C, Messerman A, Kirschnick N, Mustafic T, Camtepe A, Lohlein B, Heister U, Moller S, Rokach L & Elovici Y (2009) Identity theft, computers and behavioural biometrics. *IEEE International Conference on Intelligence and Security Informatics*

MS-ISAC (2005) *Cyber security awareness.* New York: The Multi-State Information Sharing and Analysis Center. <http://mn.gov/mnit/images/cyber_security_awareness_handbook.pdf>

Mueller M (2017) *Will the Internet fragment? Sovereignty, globalization, and cyberspace.* Hoboken: Wiley

Müller P and Schulz A (2019) Alternative media for a populist audience? Exploring political and media use predictors of exposure to Breitbart, Sputnik, and Co., Information, Communication & Society (online first)

Munksgaard R & Demant J (2016) Mixing politics and crime – the prevalence and decline of political discourse on the cryptomarket. *International Journal of Drug* Policy 35:77–83

Nahar V, Li X, Zhang HL & Pang C (2014) Detecting cyberbullying in social networks using multi-agent system. *Web Intelligence and Agent System: An International Journal* 12(4):375–388

Nakamoto S (2008) Bitcoin: a peer-to-peer electronic cash system. <www.bitcoin.org/bitcoin.pdf>

Nathenson IS (1998) Internet infoglut and invisible ink: spamdexing search engines with meta tags. *Harvard Journal of Law and Technology* 12(1):44–146

Nazir M & Siu Man Lui C (2017) A survey of research in Real-Money Trading (RMT) in virtual world. *International Journal of Virtual Communities and Social Networking* 9(1)

Netanel NW (2003) Impose a non-commercial use levy to allow free peer-to-peer file sharing. *Harvard Journal of Law & Technology 17(1):2–44*

Ngo FT & Paternoster R (2011) Cybercrime victimization: an examination of individual and situational level factors. *International Journal of Cyber Criminology* 5(1):773–793

Nhan J, Huey L & Broll R (2017) Digilantism: an analysis of crowdsourcing and the Boston marathon bombings. *British Journal of Criminology* 57(2):341–361

NHS Digital (2019) Data Security Centre latest news. Available at: https://digital.nhs.uk/services/data-security-centre/data-security-centre-latest-news

Nieto A, Rios R & Lopez J (2018) IoT-forensics meets privacy: towards cooperative digital investigations. *Sensors* 18(2):492

Nussbaum MC (2010) Objectification and internet misogyny. In Levmore S & Nussbaum MC (eds.) *The offensive internet: Speech, privacy, and reputation.* Cambridge: Harvard University Press

O'Connell R (2003) *A typology of child cybersexploitation and online grooming practices.* Preston: Cyberspace Research Unit, University of Central Lancaster

O'Malley P (1996) Risk and responsibility. In Barry A, Osborne T & Rose N (eds.) *Foucault and political reason: liberalism, neo-liberalism and rationalities of government.* London: ULC Press

Odabaş M, Holt TJ & Breiger RL (2017) Markets as governance environments for organizations at the edge of illegality: insights from social network analysis. *American Behavioural Scientist* 61(11):1267–1288

Office for National Statistics (2018) *Crime in England and Wales: year ending June 2018.* London: Office for National Statistics

Ogilvie E (2000) Cyberstalking. *Trends & Issues in Crime and Criminal Justice* 166. Canberra: Australian Institute of Criminology

Okeke RI & Shah MH (2016) *Information theft prevention Theory and practice.* New York: Routledge

Olweus D & Limber SP (2018) Some problems with cyberbullying research. *Current Opinion in Psychology* 19(1):139–143

Orizio G & Gelatti U (2010) Public eHealth and new scenarios in terms of risks and opportunities: A specific focus on cyberpharmacies. *Social Semiotics* 20(1):29–41

Oude Breuil BC, Siegel D, van Reenen P, Beijer A & Roos L (2011) Human trafficking revised: legal, enforcement and ethnographic narratives on sex trafficking to Western Europe. *Trends in Organised Crime* 14(1):30–46

Ouimet M (2009) Internet and Crime Trends. In Schmallager F & Pittaro M (eds.) *Crimes of the Internet.* Upper Saddle River: Prentice Hall

Pajnik M, Kambouri N, Renault M & Šori I (2015) Digitalising sex commerce and sex work: a comparative analysis of French, Greek and Slovenian websites. *Gender, Place & Culture. A Journal of Feminist Geography* 23(3):345–364

Paoli L, Greenfield VA & Zoutendijk A (2013) The harm of cocaine trafficking. Applying a new framework for assessment. *Journal of Drug Issues* 43(4):407–436

Paquet-Clouston M, Décary-Hétu D & Bilodeau B (2018) Cybercrime is whose responsibility? A case study of an online behaviour system in crime. *Global Crime* 19(1):1–21

Patchin JW & Hinduja S (2016) Bullies move beyond the schoolyard. A preliminary look at cyberbullying. *Youth Violence and Juvenile Justice* 4(2):148–169

Pavan E (2017) Internet intermediaries and online gender-based violence. In Segrave M & Vitis L (eds.) *Gender, technology and violence.* London: Routledge

Pease K (2001) *Cracking crime through design.* London: Design Council

Peltier TR (2007) Social engineering: concepts and solutions. *Information Security and Risk Management* 15(5):13–21

Pereira F & Matos M (2015) Cyberstalking entre adolescentes: uma nova forma de assédio e perseguição? *Psicologia, Saúde & Doenças* 16(1):57–69

Peretti K (2009) Data breaches: what the underground world of carding reveals. *Santa Clara High Technology Law Journal* 25(2):375–413

Pérez-Marco R (2016) Bitcoin and decentralized trust protocols. *Newsletter of the EMS.*

Perry B & Olsson P (2009) Cyberhate: the globalisation of hate. *Information & Communicatios Technology Law* 18(2):185–199

Perry S & Roda C (2016) *Human rights and digital technology.* Cham: Springer

Peters MA (2018) The information wars, fake news and the end of globalisation. *Educational Philosophy and Theory* 50(13):1161–1164

Phillips W (2013) Don't feed the trolls? It's not that simple. *The Daily Dot*, June 10 <https://www.dailydot.com/via/phillips-dont-feed-trolls-antisocial-web/>

Phillips W (2015) *This is why we can't have nice things. Mapping the relationship between online trolling and mainstream culture.* Cambridge: The MIT Press

Philpot D (2017) Symbolic interactionism and technocrime. SWATing as episodic and agentic. In Steinmetz KF & Nobles MR (ed.) *Technocrime and criminological theory.* Boca Raton (FL): CRC Press

Phippen A (2017) *Children's online behaviour and safety. Policy and rights challenges.* London: Palgrave

Pittaro ML (2007) Cyber stalking: an analysis of online harassment and intimidation. *International Journal of Cyber Criminology* 1(2):180–197

Porcedda MG (2018) Regulation of data breaches in the European Union: private companies in the driver's seat of cybersecurity? In Bures O & Carrapico H (eds.) *Security privatization. How non-security-related private businesses shape security governance.* Cham: Springer

Poland GA & Jacobson RM (2011) The age-old struggle against the antivaccinationists. *The New England Journal of Medicine* 364:97–99

Popham J (2018) Microdeviation: observations on the significance of lesser harms in shaping the nature of cyberspace. *Deviant Behaviour* 39(2):159–169

Portnoff RS, Afroz S, Durrett G, Kummerfeld JK, Berg-Kirkpatrick T, McCoy D, Levchenko K & Paxson V (2017) Tools for automated analysis of cybercriminal markets. *International World Wide Web Conference Committee (IW3C2)*

Poster WR (2018) Cybersecurity needs women. *Nature*, 26 March

Powell B (2001) Is cybersecurity a public good? Evidence from the financial service industry. Independent Institute Working Paper Number 57, Sane Jose State University & The Independent Institute <http://www.independent.org/pdf/working_papers/57_cyber.pdf>

Powell A & Henry N (2017) *Sexual violence in digital age.* London: Palgrave

Pratt TC, Holtfreter K & Reisig MD (2010) Routine online activity and Internet fraud targeting: extending the generality of routine activity theory. *Journal of Research in Crime and Delinquency* 47(3):267–296

Pratt TC & Turanovic JJ (2017) Low hanging fruit. Rethinking technology, offending and victimisation. In Steinmetz KF & Nobles MR (ed.) *Technocrime and criminological theory.* Boca Raton (FL): CRC Press

Puddephatt A (2017) ICTs, privacy and the (criminal) misuse of data. In McGuire MR & Holt T (eds.) *The Routledge handbook of technology, crime and justice.* New York: Routledge

Puech M (2017) 'Black Mirror' ou l'ambiguïté du pire. *The Conversation*, June 26

Quayle E & Taylor M (2003) *Child pornography: an Internet crime.* New York: Routledge

Rao J & Reiley D (2012) The economics of spam. *Journal of Economic Perspectives* 26(3):87–110

Räsänen P, Hawdon J, Holkeri E, Näsi M, Keipi T & Oksanen A (2016) Targets of online hate: examining determinants of victimization among young Finnish Facebook users. *Violence and Victims* 31(4):708–726

Reep-van den Bergh CMM & Junger M (2018) Victims of cybercrime in Europe: a review of victim surveys. *Crime Science* 7(1)

Reese C (2013) Fantasy depictions of child sexual abuse: the problem of ageplay in Second Life. *Journal of Sexual Aggression* 19(2):236–246

Reese C (2018) The virtual simulation of child sexual abuse: online gameworld users' views, understanding and responses to sexual ageplay. *Ethics and Information Technology* 20(2):101–113

Rege A (2009) What's love got to do with it? Exploring online dating scams and identity fraud. *International Journal of Cyber Criminology* 3(2):494–512

Reitinger PR (2000) Encryption, anonymity and markets. Law enforcement and technology in a free market virtual world. In Thomas D & Loader BD (eds.) *Cybercrime: Law enforcement, security and surveillance in the information age.* London: Routledge

Reckless W (1967) *The crime problem.* New York: Appleton Century Crofts

Reeves C (2013) Fantasy depictions of child sexual abuse: the problem of ageplay in second life. *Journal of Sexual Aggression* 19(2):236–246

Reeves C (2018) The virtual simulation of child sexual abuse: online gameworld users' views, understanding and responses to sexual ageplay. *Ethics and Information Technology* 20(2):101–113

Reports Without Borders (2014) Enemies of the Internet. Available at: https://rsf.org/sites/default/files/2014-rsf-rapport-enemies-of-the-internet.pdf

Reynolds P & Irwin ASM (2017) Tracking digital footprints: anonymity within the bitcoin system. *Journal of Money Laundering Control* 20(2):172–189

Reyns BW (2010) A situational crime prevention approach to cyberstalking victimisation: preventive tactics for Internet users and online place managers. *Crime Prevention and Community Safety* 12(2):99–118

Reyns BW (2013) Online routines and identity theft victimization: further expanding routine activity theory beyond direct-contact offences. *Journal of Research in Crime and Delinquency* 50(2):216–238

Reyns BW (2015) A routine activity perspective on online victimisation: results from the Canadian General Social Survey. *Journal of Financial Crime* 22(4):296–411

Reyns BW, Henson B & Fisher BS (2011) Being pursued online. Applying cyberlifestyle-routine activities theory to cyberstalking victimisation. *Criminal Justice & Behaviour* 38(11):1149–1169

Reyns BW & Henson B (2016) The thief with a thousand faces and the victim with none: identifying determinants for online identity theft victimization with routine activity theory. *International Journal of Offender Therapy and Comparative Criminology* 60(10):1119–1139

Reyns BW (2017) Routine activity theort and cybercrime. A theoretical appraisal and literature review. In Steinmetz KF & Nobles MR (ed.) *Technocrime and criminological theory*. Boca Raton (FL): CRC Press

Rhumorbarbe D, Werner D, Gilliéron, Staehli L, Broséus J & Rossy Q (2018) Characterising the online weapon trafficking on cryptomarkets. *Forensic Science International* 283:16–20

Rice E, Rhoades H, Winetrobe H, Sanchez M, Montoya J, Plant A & Kordic T (2012) Sexually explicit cell phone messaging associated with sexual risk among adolescents. *Pediatrics* 130:667–673

Richardson J & Emerson J (2018) eDemocracy: an emerging force for change. *Stanford Social Innovation Review*. <https://ssir.org/articles/entry/edemocracy_an_emerging_force_for_change>

Rizi FS & Khayyambashi MR (2013) Profile cloning in online social networks. *International Journal of Social Networks* 11(8):82–86

Roberts L (2008) Jurisdictional and definitional concerns with computer-mediated interpersonal crimes: an analysis on cyber-stalking. *International Journal of Cyber Criminology* 2(1):271–285

Roberts LD, Indermaur D & Spiranovic C (2012) Fear of cyber-identity theft and related fraudulent activity. *Psychiatry, Psychology and Law* 20(3):315–328

Roberts K, Tolou-Shams M & Madera K (2016) Adolescent versus adult stalking: a brief review. *Journal of Forensic Psychology Practice* 16(4):236–252

Roesner F, Kohno T & Molnar D (2014) Security and privacy for augmented reality systems. *Communications of the ACM* 57(4):88–96

Rogers M (2019) Cyber terrorism. In Silke A (ed.) *Routledge handbook of terrorism and counterterrorism*. Abingdon: Routledge

Rowe NC (2017) Challenges of civilian distinction in cyberwarfare. In Taddeo M & Glorioso L (eds.) *Ethics and policies for cyber operations*. Cham: Springer

Salter M & Crofts T (2015) Responding to revenge porn: challenges to online legal impunity. In Comella L & Tarrant S (eds.) *New views on pornography: sexuality, politics, and the law*. New York: Praeger

Samanthula BK, Elmehdwi Y, Howser G & Madria S (2015) A secure data sharing and query processing framework via federation of cloud computing. *Information Systems* 48:196–212

Sanders T (2009) The sex industry, regulation and the Internet. In Jewkes Y & Yar M (eds.) *Handbook of Internet crime*. London: Routledge

Savchenko II & Gatsenko OY (2015) Analytical review of methods of providing internet anonymity. *Automatic Control and Computer Sciences* 49(8):696–700

Savona EU, Belli R, Curtol F, Decarli S & Di Nicola A (2009) *Trafficking in persons and smuggling of migrants into Italy. Analysing the phenomenon and suggesting remedies.* Transcrime

Scanlon JR & Gerber MS (2014) Automatic detection of cyber-recruitment by violent extremists. *Security Informatics* 3(5)

Schmitt M (ed.) (2013) *Tallin Manual on the international law applicable to cyber warfare*. Cambridge: Cambridge University Press

Schmidt A & Wiegand M (2017) A survey in hate speech detection using Natural Language Processing. *Proceedings of the Workshop AFNLP SIG SocialNLP*

Sela-Shayovitz R (2012) Gangs and the Web: gang members' online behavior. *Journal of Contemporary Criminal Justice* 28(4):389–405

Sellers BG & Arrigo BA (2017) Postmodern criminology and technocrime. In Steinmetz KF & Nobles MR (ed.) *Technocrime and criminological theory*. Boca Raton (FL): CRC Press

Shackelford SJ (2014) *Managing cyber attacks in international law, business, and relations: In search of cyber peace*. Cambridge: Cambridge University Press

Shalhoub-Kevorkian N (2012) In/security in everyday life: the Palestinian case. *The British Journal of Criminology* 52(1):55–72

Shamim I (2017) Child sexual abuse and exploitation online in Bangladesh: the challenges of the Internet and law and legal developments. In Shahidullah SM (ed.) *Crime, criminal justice, and the evolving science of criminology in South Asia*. London: Palgrave

Shannon D (2008) Online sexual grooming in Sweden – online and offline sex offences against children as described in Swedish police data. *Journal of Scandinavian Studies in Criminology and Crime Prevention* 9(2):160–180

Shapiro A (2017) Reform predictive policing. *Nature* 541(7638):458–460

Siadati H, Nguyen T, Gupta P, Jakobsson M & Memon N (2017) Mind your SMSes: Mitigating social engineering in second factor authentication. *Computers and Security* 65:14–28

Siegel D (2017) The criminalisation of legal prostitution. The Dutch Zandpad case. In van Duyne PC, Harvey J, Antonopoulos GA & von Lampe K (eds.) *The many faces of crime for profit and ways of tackling it*. Oisterwijk: Wolf Legal Publishers

Siegel D & van de Bunt H (eds) (2012) *Traditional organized crime in the modern world. Responses to socioeconomic change*. New York: Springer

Sikkenga J (2017) *Shitstorm-Prävention*. Wiesbaden: Springer Gabler

Simon J (2009) *Governing through crime. How the war on crime transformed American democracy and created a culture of fear.* Oxford: Oxford University Press

Simon J & Feeley M (2013) Folk devils and moral panics: an appreciation from North America. In Downes D, Rock P, Chinkin C & Gearty C (eds.) *Crime, social control and human rights. From moral panics to states of denial, essays in honour of Stanley Cohen.* Cullompton: Willan

Skidmore M, Garner S, Desroches C & Saggu Nikhita (2018) The threat of exploitation in the adult sex market: a pilot study of online sex worker advertisement. *Policing: A Journal of Police and Practice* 12(2):210–218

Sleat M (2018) Just cyber war? Casus belli, information ethics, and the human perspective. *Review of International Studies* 44(2):324–342

Smart C (1992) The woman of legal discourse. *Social and Legal Studies* 1(1):29–44

Smith RG (2009) Identity theft and fraud. In Jewkes Y & Yar M (eds.) *Handbook of Internet crime.* London: Routledge

Smith RG, Grabosky PN & Urbas G (2004) *Cyber criminals on trial.* Cambridge: Cambridge University Press

Smith Ekstrand V & Silver D (2014) Remixing, reposting, and reblogging: digital media, theories of the image, and copyright law. *Visual Communication Quarterly* 21(2):96–105

Smith GJD, Bennet Moses L & Chan J (2017) The challenges of ding criminology in the big data era: towards a digital and data-driven approach. *British Journal of Criminology* 57(2):259–274

Smith PK, Sundaram S, Spears BA, Blaya C, Schäfer M & Sanshu D (eds.) (2018) *Bullying, cyberbullying and student well-being in schools. Comparing European, Australian and Indian perspectives.* Cambridge: Cambridge University Press

Smithson J, Sharkey S, Hewis E, Jones R, Emmens T, Ford T & Owens C (2011) Problem presentation and responses on an online forum for young people who self-harm. *Discourse Studies* 13(4):487–501

Söderberg J (2010) Misuser inventions and the invention of the misuser: hackers, crackers and filesharers. *Science as Culture* 19(2):151–179

Soderlund G (2008) Journalist or panderer? Framing underage webcam sites. *Sexuality Research & Social Policy* 5(4):62–72

Solove DJ & Keats Citron D (2018) Risk and anxiety: a theory of data breach harms. *Texas Law Review* 96(737)

Sommer P (2004) The future for the policing of cybercrime. *Computer Fraud and Security* 1:8–12

Sorell T (2015) Human rights and hacktivism: the cases of Wikileaks and Anonymous. *Journal of Human Rights Practice* 7(3):391–410

Sparrow R (2017) Robots, rape, and representation. *International Journal of Social Robotics* 9(4):465–477

Spence-Diehl E (2003) Stalking and technology: the double-edged sword. *Journal of Technology in Human Services* 22(1):5–18

Spitzberg BH & Cupach WR (2007) The state of the art of stalking: taking stock of the emerging literature. *Aggression and Violent Behaviour* 12:64–86

Stallman RM (1984) The GNU Project. <https://www.gnu.org/gnu/thegnuproject.en.html>

Statista (2019) <https://www.statista.com/>

Steinmetz KF & Tunnell KF (2012) Under the pixelated Jolly Roger: a study of on-line piractes. *Deviant Behaviour* 34:53–67

Steinmetz KF (2016) *Hacked. A radical approach to hacker culture and crime.* New York: New York University Press

Steinmetz KF & Nobles MR (2017) Introduction. In Steinmetz KF & Nobles MR (ed.) *Technocrime and criminological theory.* Boca Raton (FL): CRC Press

Stohl M (2006) Cyber terrorism: a clear and present danger, the sum of all fears, breaking point or patriot games? *Crime, Law and Social Change* 46(4–5):223–238

Stone-Gross B, Abman R, Kennerer RA, Kruegel. C, Steigerwald DG & Vigna G (2013) The underground economy of fake antivirus software. In Schneier B (ed.) *Economics of information security and privacy III.* New York: Springer

Stottelaar, B., Senden, J. & Montoya (2014) Online social sports networks as crime facilitators. *Crime Science* 3(8)

Stratton G, Powell A & Cameron R (2017) Crime and justice in digital society: towards a 'digital criminology'? *International Journal for Crime, Justice and Social Democracy* 6(2):17–33

Suber P (2012) *Open access.* Cambridge: The MIT Press

Suler J (2004) The online disinhibition effect. *CyberPsychology & Behavior* 7(3):321–326

Sugiura L, Pope C, Weal MJ & Webber C (2012) Observing deviancy online. *Digital Research 2012*, Oxford

Sutherland EH (1939) *Principles of criminology* (3rd ed.) Philadelphia: Lippincott

Sutherland EH & Cressey DR (1978) *Criminology* (10th ed.) Philadelphia: Lippincott

Sutherland EH, Cressey DR & Luckenbill D (1995) Theory of differential association. In Herman NJ (ed.) *Deviance: a symbolic interactionist approach.* Lanham: General Hall

Swan M (2016) Blockchain temporality: smart contract time specifiability with blocktime. In Alferes J, Bertossi L, Governatori G, Fodor P & Roman D (eds.) *Rule technologies. Research, tools, and applications. Lecture Notes in Computer Science*, vol 9718. Cham: Springer

Switzer JS & Switzer RV (2016) United States taxation of virtual world economies: a review of current status. In Sivan Y (ed.) *Handbook of 3D3C platforms.* Cham: Springer

Sykes GM & Matza D (1957) Techniques of neutralization: a theory of delinquency. *American Sociological Review* 22(6):664–670

Szafranski R (1995) A theory of information warfare: preparing for 2020. *Airpower Journal*, Spring

Tade O (2016) Meet the 'Yahoo boys' – Nigeria's undergraduate conmen. *The Conversation*, 26 July

Taylor M, Quayle E & Holland G (2001) Child pornography, the Internet and offending. *The Canadian Journal of Policy Research* 2:94–100

Taylor PA (2005) From hackers to hacktivists: speed bumps on the global superhighway? *New Media & Society* 7(5):625–646

Taylor PA (2009) Hackers: cyberpunks or microserfs? *Information, Communication & Society* 1(4):401–419

Taylor M, Haggerty J, Gresty D & Hegary R (2010) Digital evidence in cloud computing systems. *Computer law & Security Review* 26(3):304–308

TechUK (2015) *Partners against crime. How can industry help the police to fight cyber-crime?* London: TechUK

Terralex (2017) *Cross-border guide to copyright 2017* <https://www.rpc.co.uk/perspectives/ip/terralex-cross-border-copyright-guide>

The Hollywood Reporter (2019) *Netflix, ABC Hacker promises more leaks:'Hollywood is under attack'*, June

The Mentor (1986) The conscience of a hacker. *Phrack* 1(7), phile 3 of 10 <http://www.phrack.org/archives/issues/7/3.txt>

Thomas J (2005) The moral ambiguity of social control in cyberspace: a retro-assessment of the 'golden age' of hacking. *New Media & Society* 7(5):599–624

Tokunaga RS (2010) Following you home from school: a critical review and synthesis of researc on cyberbullying victimisation. *Computers in Human Behavior* 26(3):277–287

Tosh DK, Shetty S, Sengupta S, Kesan JP & Kamhoua CA (2017) Risk management using cyber-threat information sharing and cyber-insurance. In Duan L, Sanjab A, Li H, Chen X, Materassi D & Elazouzi R (eds.) *Game theory for networks. GameNets 2017*. Cham: Springer

Treadwell J (2012) From the car boot to booting it up? eBay, online counterfeit crime and the transformation of the criminal marketplace. *Criminology and Criminal Justice* 12(2):175–191

Trevathan J & Read W (2006) Undesirable and fraudulent behaviour in online auctions. *Proceedings of International Conference on Security and Cryptography*

Tumblr (2017) *Everything ok?* <https://www.tumblr.com/psa/search/suicide>

Twitter (2017) Ad Policy: hate content, sensitive topics, and violence. <https://support.twitter.com/articles/20170425#>

UK Parliament (2018) Disinformation and 'fake news' – interim report <https://publications.parliament.uk/pa/cm201719/cmselect/cmcumeds/363/36303.htm>

Ungar S (2001) Moral panic versus the risk society: the implications of the changing sites of social anxiety. *British Journal of Sociology* 52(2):271–291

UNODC (2013) *Comprehensive study on cybercrime.* New York: United Nations

UNODC (2014) International Classification of Crime for Statistical Purposes. Principles, structure, application. <http://www.unodc.org/unodc/en/data-and-analysis/statistics/iccs.html>

UNODC (2016) Global report on trafficking in persons. United Nation Office on Drugs and Crime <http://www.unodc.org/documents/data-andanalysis/glotip/2016_Global_Report_on_Trafficking_in_Persons.pdf>

Vaciago G & Ramalho DS (2016) Online searches and online surveillance: the use of trojans and other types of malware as means of obtaining evidence in criminal proceedings. *Digital Evidence and Electronic Signature Law Review* 13:88–96

van de Weijer SGA, Leukfeldt R & Bernasco W (2018) Determinants of reporting cybercrime: a comparison between identity theft, consumer fraud, and hacking. *European Journal of Criminology* (online first)

Van Dijk J (2005) *The deepening divide: Inequality and the information society.* London: Sage

van Duyne PC & van Dijck M (2007) Assessing organised crime: the sad state of an impossible art. In Bovenkerk F & Levi M (eds.) *The organized crime community. Essays in honor of Alan A. Block.* New York: Springer

van Hardeveld GJ, Webber C & O'Hara K (2016) Discovering credit card fraud methods in online tutorials. *Proceedings of the 1st International Workshop on Online Safety, Trust and Fraud Prevention*

van Hout MC & Bingham T (2013) 'Silk Road', the virtual drug marketplace: a single case study of user experiences. *International Journal of Drug Policy* 24(5):385–391 van Wilsem JA (2013a). Hacking and harassment. Do they have something in common? Comparing risk factors for online victimization. *Journal of Contemporary Criminal Justice* 29(4):437–453

van Wilsem JA (2013b) 'Bought it, but never got it'. Assessing risk factors for online consumer fraud victimization. *European Sociological Review* 29(2):168–178

Vasek M & Moore T (2015) There's no free lunch, even using bitcoin: tracking the popularity and profits of virtual currency scams. In Böhme R & Okamoto T (eds.) *Financial cryptography and data security. FC 2015. Lecture Notes in Computer Science,* vol 8975. Cham: Springer

Vidal C & Choo KKR (2018) Situational crime prevention and the mitigation of cloud computing threats. In Lin X, Ghorbani A, Ren K, Zhu S & Zhang A (eds.) *Security and privacy in communication networks. SecureComm 2017.* Cham: Springer

Vigna P & Casey MJ (2015) *The age of cryptocurrency: How Bitcoin and blockchain are challenging the global economic order.* London: Picador

Vincent NA (2017) Victims of cybercrime. Definitions and challenges. In Martellozzo E & Jane EA (eds.) *Cybercrime and its victims.* London: Routledge

Virtanen SM (2017) Fear of cybercrime in Europe: examining the effects of victimization and vulnerabilities. *Psychiatry, Psychology and Law* 24(3):323–338

Vishwamitra N, Zhang X, Tong J, Hu H, Luo F, Kowalski R & Mazer J (2017) MCDefender: towards effective cyberbullying defence in mobile online social networks. *Proceedings of the 3rd ACM on International Workshop on Security and Privacy Analytics*

von Lampe K (2008) Organized crime in Europe: conceptions and realities. *Policing* (2)1:7–17

Waldron J (2010) Dignity and defamation: the visibility of hate. *Harvard Law Review* 123(7):1596–1657

Walker C, Wall D & Akdeniz Y (2000) The Internet, law and society. In Akdeniz Y, Walker C & Wall D (eds.) *The Internet, law and society.* Harlow: Pearson

Wall DS (2001) Maintaining order and law on the Internet. In Wall DS (ed.) *Crime and the Internet.* London: Routledge

Wall DS (2004) Digital realism and the governance of spam as cybercrime. *European Journal of Criminal Policy and Research* 10(4):309–335

Wall DS (2007) *Cybercrime: the transformation of crime in the information age.* Cambridge: Polity

Wall DS (2015) The Internet as a conduit for criminals. In Pattavina A (ed.) *Information technology and the criminal justice system.* Thousand Oaks: Sage

Wall DS & Williams M (2007) Policing diversity in the digital age. Maintaining order in virtual communities. *Criminology & Criminal Justice* 7(4):391–415

Wall DS (2008) Cybercrime and the culture of fear: social science fiction and the production of knowledge about cybercrime. *Information Communication & Society* 11(6):861–884

Wall DS (2009) Criminalising cyberspace. In Jewkes Y & Yar M (eds.) *Handbook of Internet crime.* London: Routledge

Wall DS (2012) The Devil drives a Lada: the social construction of hackers as cybercriminals. In Gregoriou C (eds.) *Constructing crime.* London: Palgrave

Wall DS & Yar M (2009) Intellectual property crime and the Internet: cyber-piracy and 'stealing' information intangibles. In Jewkes Y & Yar M (eds.) *Handbook of Internet crime.* Cullompton: Willan

Wall DS & Williams ML (2014) *Policing cybercrime: networked and social media technologies and the challenges for policing.* London: Routledge

Wardle C & Derakhshan H (2017) Information disorder: toward an interdisciplinary framework for research and policy making. Council of Europe report DGI(2017)09. <https://rm.coe.int/information-disorder-toward-an-interdisciplinary-framework-for-researc/168076277c>

Webber C & Yip M (2012) Drifting on and off-line: humanising the cyber criminal. In Winlow S & Atkinson R (eds.) *New directions in crime and deviancy.* London: Routledge

Weber RH (2015) Internet of things: privacy issues revisited. *Computer Law & Security Review* 31(5):618–627

Weimann G (2005). Cyber terrorism: the sum of all fears? *Studies in Conflict and Terrorism* 28:129–149

Weitzer R (2005) New directions in research on prostitution. *Crime, Law and Social Change* 43(4–5):211–235

Whine M (2003) Far Right extremists on the internet. In Thomas D & Loader B (eds.) *Cyber crime: law enforcement, security and surveillance in the information age.* New York: Routledge

Whittle H, Hamilton-Giachritsis C, Beech A & Collings G (2013) A review of online grooming: characteristics and concerns. *Aggression and Violent Behaviour* 18(1):62–70

Whitty M & Buchanan T (2016) The online dating romance scam: the psychological impact on victims–both financial and non-financial. *Criminology and Criminal Justice* 16(2):176–194

Whitty M (2018) Do you love me? Psychological characteristics of romance scam victims. *Cyberpsychology, Behaviour and Social Networking* 21(2):105–109

WHO (2010) Growing threat from counterfeit medicines. *Bulletin of the World Health Organization* 88(4):241–320

Williams F & MsChane M (2010) *Criminological theory* (5th ed.) Upper Saddle River: Pearson

Williams ML (2007) Policing and cybersociety: the maturation of regulation within an online community. *Policing and Society* 17(1):59–82

Williams ML, Edwards A, Housley W, Burnap P, Rana O, Avis N, Morgan J & Sloan L (2013) Policing cyber-neighbourhoods: tension monitoring and social media networks. *Policing and Society* 23(4):461–481

Williams ML & Levi M (2017) Cybercrime prevention. In Tilley N & Sidebottom A (eds.) *Handbook of crime prevention and community safety.* New York: Routledge

Williams M, Burnap P & Sloan L (2017). Crime sensing with big data: the affordances and limitations of using open-source communications to estimate crime patterns. *British Journal of Criminology* 57(2):320–340.

Willits D & Nowacki J (2016) The use of specialized cybercrime policing units: an organizational analysis. *Criminal Justice Studies* 29(2):105–124

Wilson D (2018) Algorithmic patrol: the future of predictive policing. In Završnik A (ed.) *Big data, crime and social control.* London: Routledge

Winters GM, Kaylor LE & Jeglic EL (2017) Sexual offenders contacting children online: an examination of transcripts of sexual grooming. *Journal of Sexual Aggression* 23(1):62–76.

WIPO (2017) What is intellectual property? <http://www.wipo.int/about-ip/en/>

Wolak JD, Finkelhor D & Mitchell K (2004) Internet-initiated sex crimes against minors: implications for prevention based on findings from a national study. *Journal of Adolescent Health* 35(1):183–191

Wood M, Wood G & Balaam M (2017) 'They're just tixel pits, man': disputing the 'reality' of virtual reality pornography through the story completion method. *Proceedings of the 2017 CHI Conference on Human Factors in Computing Systems*

Wortley R (1997) Reconsidering the role of opportunity in situational crime prevention. In Newman GR, Clarke RV & Shoham SG (eds.) *Rational choice and situational crime prevention.* Dartmouth: Ashgate

Wortley R & Smallbone S (2012) *Internet child pornography: causes, investigation, and prevention.* New York: Praeger

Wright A & De Filippi P (2015) Decentralized blockchain technology and the rise of Lex Cryptographia. <https://ssrn.com/abstract=2580664>

Wright S (2017) Mythology of cyber-crime—insecurity & governance in cyberspace: some critical perspectives. In Ramírez J & García-Segura L (eds.) *Cyberspace. Advanced sciences and technologies for security applications.* Cham: Springer

Wykes M (2009) Harm, suicide and homicide in cyberspace: assessing causality and control. In Jewkes Y & Yar M (eds.) *Handbook of Internet crime.* London: Routledge

Xu J & Chen H (2008) The topology of dark networks. *Communications of the ACM* 51(10): 58–65

Yar M (2005) Computer hacking: just another case of juvenile delinquency? *The Howard Journal* 44(4):387–399

Yar M (2008a) The rhetorics and myths of anti-piracy campaigns: criminalization, oral pedagogy and capitalist property relations in the classroom. *New Media & Society* 10(4):605–623

Yar M (2008b) Computer crime control as industry: virtual insecurity and the market for private policing. In Franko Aas K, Oppen Gundhus H & Mork Lommell H (eds.) *Technologies of insecurity: the surveillance of everyday life.* New York: Routledge-Cavendish

Yar M (2019) *Cybercrime and society* (2nd ed.). London: Sage

Yar M (2017) Toward a cultural criminology of the Internet. In Steinmetz KF & Nobles MR (ed.) *Technocrime and criminological theory.* Boca Raton (FL): CRC Press

Yip M, Webber C & Shadbolt N (2013) Trust among cybercriminals? Carding forums, uncertainty and implications for policing. *Policing and Society* 23(4):516–539

Young J & Matthews R (eds.) (1992) *Rethinking criminology: the realist debate.* London: Sage

Young KS (1998) Internet addiction: the emergence of a new clinical disorder. *CyberPsychology & Behaviour* 1(3):237–244

Zabyelina YG (2017) Can criminals create opportunities for crime? Malvertising and illegal online medicine trade. *Global Crime* 18(1):31–48

Zajko M (2018) Security against surveillance: IT security as resistance to pervasive surveillance. *Surveillance & Society* 16(1):39–52

Zavrsnik A (2008) Cybercrime. Definitional challenges and criminological particularities. *Masaryk University Journal of law and Technology* 2:1–29

Zhan Z, Xu M & Xu S (2013) Characterising honeypot-captured cyber attacks: statistical framework and case study. *IEEE Transactions on Information Forensics and Security* 8(11):1775–1789

Zhu X, Tao H, Wu Z, Cao J, Kalish K & Kayne J (2017) *Fraud prevention in online digital advertising*. Cham: Springer

Zhuge J, Holz T, Song C, Guo J, Han X & Zou W (2009) Studying malicious websites and the underground economy on the Chinese web. In Johnson ME (eds.) *Managing information risk and the economics of security*. Boston: Springer

Zimmer M & Kinder-Kurlanda K (eds.) (2017) *Research ethics for the social age. New challenges, cases, and contexts*. New York: Peter Lang

Zyskind G, Nathan O & Pentland A (2015) Decentralizing privacy: using blockchain to protect personal data. *Security and Privacy Workshops (SPW), 2015 IEEE*

INDEX

Page number in *italics* indicates when the term occurs in a table or figure.

4-1-9 scams, *see also* Advance-fee scams; Nigeria, 119

A

Access to data
legal, *see also* Data collection (legal); Methods of data collection in research, 27, 53–4, 65, 69, 123, 181, 189, 203–5, 213–16
illegal access, *see also* Hacking, 7, 14, 15, 17, 53, 54, 61, 63, 67, 73, 77, 119, 123, 147–9, 165, 170, 171, 176, 192, 203
ACABGang, 118
Accountability, 19, 61, 112, 119, 166, 185, 196, 218
Active monitoring, *see also* Methods of data collection in research, 214
Actus reus, 21
Administrators, 89–90, 118, 134, 136, 151–2, 154, 156, 159
Advance-fee scams, *see also* Frauds; Business opportunity scams; Romance scams; Sweetheart swindle scams; 4-1-9 scams, 116, 119–20, 126
Advance persistent threat, 73, 176
Advertisement frauds, *see also* Frauds, *116*, 124–5
Afghanistan, 61, 97
Africa, *see also* South Africa, 5, 15, 102, 119, 171, 184, 191, 204
Alibaba, 120
AlphaBay, 136, 155–6
Al-Qaeda, 178, 180
Amazon, 11, 69, 120, 125, 130, 204, 219
American, *see also* North America; United States
Android, 64, 134
Anglo-centrism, 30, 158
Anomie, *see also* Social structure approaches, 35–7, 51
Anonymity, 60, 69, 74–7, 82, 89, 90, 98, 104–5, 119, 123, 135, 154, 162, 179
Anonymous, 60, 135, 177

Antagonistic online behaviours, *see also* Hate speech; Harassment, 7, 81, 83, 90, 95, 111, 125
Anti-piracy campaigns, *see also* Copyright infringements, 162, 165
Anti-vax, *see also* Health frauds, 126
Apple, MacOS, 11, 65, 76, 130–1, 134–5
Arabic, 6, 93
Arab Spring, 184
Armchair jihadis, *see also* Cyber-jihad, 180
ARPANET, *10*, 11, 13
Artificial Intelligence, 5, *10*, 12–13, 68, 88, 104, 148, 174, 195, 218
Ashley Madison, 78, 135, 203
Ask.fm, 180
Australia, 72, 77, 85, 94, 96, 98, 101, 127, 177
Astroturfing, 171
Automatic data collection methods, *see also* Access to data, *19*, 24, 61, 155, 195, 214
Avatars, 101–2, 142
Awareness-raising, 69, 88, 105, 110–11, 139, 157, 172, 191, 198, 201, 205, 207, 219

B

Balkanisation of the internet, 183
Bangladesh, 96
Behavioural biometrics, *see also* Biometrics, 131
Belgium, 65, 192
Bidorbuy, 120
Bid shielding, *see also* Shill bidding; Frauds; Sale frauds, 121–1
Big data, *see* Data analytics
Biometrics, *see also* Behavioural biometrics, 131, 194, 195, 201, 218
Bitcoin, *see* Cryptocurrencies
BitTorrent, 134, 161
Blackmail, *see* Extortion
Blockchain, 144–147, 165, 167, 205, 218
Bolivia, 144

Botnets, bots, 61, *62*, 63, 68, 104, 118, 123–5, 150, 173, 175

Botswana, 97

Bugging, 192

Brazil, 110, 174

Brexit, 73, 174, 210

Brute-forcing, 64

Budapest Convention on Cybercrime, 12, 15–17, 20, 85, 191, 196

Bullying, *see also* Harassment, *83*, 90, 93–6, 109

Business opportunity scams, *see also* Advance-fee scams, 120

Byzantine generals, *see also* Blockchain; Proof-of-work, *144*, 145

C

Cambridge Analytica, 73, 203, 204

Cameroon, 184

Canada, 15, 72, 89, 127, 136, 199

Carding, carding forum 7, 25, 37, 121, 122, 129, 130, 141, 147–152

Card-non-present transactions, 147–8

Catfishing, 119

Censorship, 7, 14, 75, 76, 86, 177, 182–3, 206

Cerber, *see also* Ransomware, 134

Charity frauds, *see also* Frauds; Sale frauds, *116*, 120–2

Child pornography, *see also* Sex crimes, 12, 14–16, 21, 78, 83, 97–105, 114, 188, 193, 208

China, 6, 90, 127–8, 136, 144, 160, 174, 176, 182–3, 199–200

Class, 35–8, 40, 45, 46, 59

Classicism, classical school, neoclassicism 30–3, *31*, *32*, 50, 164

Clearnet, *see also* Dark web; Deep web, 141

Clickbait, 173

Clickjacking, 63, 118

Cloud computing, *10*, 12, 64–5, 67, 102, 130–4, 150, 164, 203–4

CloudFlare, 150

Codec, 103

Collective action problem, 209

Colombia, 133

Commercialisation of the internet, *10*, 11–13, 25, 34, 107, 161

Computer misuse, 16, 20, 22, 28

Computer science, 1, 6, 8, 13, 62, 88, 94, 125, 178, 186, 190, 213, 216–17, 220

Confidentiality, 7, 54, 70, 75–7, 112, 166, 170, 181, 191, 215

Conflict (in society) 30, *31*, 36, 38, 40, 45, 47, 100

Construction kits, *see also* Ransomware, 132

Convenience, *see also* Usability, 8, 64, 149, 213

Convictions, 21, 60

Cooperation, 7, 15, 72, 153, 176, 190–1, 196–200, 203, *209*, 210, 213, 220

Consensus (in society), 30, *31*

Control, *see also* Surveillance, 13, *18*, 25, 45, 47–8, *57*, 58, 72–3, 82, 90, 108, 110, 142, 153, 156, 169, 172, 182–5, 187–8, 194, 196, 206, 208, *209*, 217–18

Control theories, *see also* Self-control; Socialisation approaches, 24, 43–4, 137–8

Controlling cyberspace as political deviancy, *18*, 182–5

Cookies, 70, 72

Copyright (definition), *see also* Patent; Trademark, 160

Copyright infringement, *see also* Intellectual property infringement, 7, *10*, 11, 14–15, 37, 45, 60, 160–7

Cost, 26–7, 33, 50, 129, 139, 146, 154, 161–2, 165, 173–4, 201, 203

Council of Europe, 15, 93, 191

Counterfeits, counterfeit pharmaceuticals, 126, 153, 156–7

Cracking, 17, 54, 64

Crawling, 108, 179, 214, 216

Crime drop, 25, 28

Crime harvest, 211

Crime pattern theory, *see also* Opportunity theories, 34

Crime rates, 9, 19, 21, 25–6, 46

Crime statistics, *19*, 20, 24–8, 111, 119

Crimes against devices, 7, *18*, 20, *32*, 34, 53–79, 134, 171, 201, 203

Crimes against persons, 7, *18*, *32*, 34, 37, 46, 53, 81–114, *83*, 115

Crimes against property, 7, *18*, 25, *32*, 44, 60, 115–16, 141–67

Crimes of coercion, *see also* Extortion, 7, *18*, *32*, 34, 115, 131–9

Crimes of deception, *see also* Frauds, 7, *18*, *32*, 34, 106–7, 115–31

Crimeware, 141, 147, 149–52

Criminalisation, decriminalisation, 14, 15, 40, 50, 85, 102, 162

Criminal networks, *see also* Organised crime, 49, 60, 77, 100–1, 107, 108, 121, 142, 158–9

Criminology, 1–2, 6, 9, 16, 23, 29–50, 31, 55, 57, 59, 90, 91, 111, 126, 137, 143, 183, 186, 190, 216–17, 220

Criminological theory, *see* Theory

Crowdsourcing, *see also* Vigilantism, 136, 208

Cryptocurrencies, *see also* Digital currencies, 27, 64, 128, 143–7, 152, 154, 156, 171

Cryptography, 63, 75, 76, 142, 143, 146, 165

Cryptolocker, *see also* Ransomware, 132

Cryptoworms, 64

Critical criminology, *31*, *32*, 45–7

Critical infrastructures, 27, 73, 170–2, 177, 179, 198, 203

Crossdisciplinary, *see also* Multidisciplinary; Interdisciplinary, 1–2, 175, 186, 190, 213–17, 220

Culpability, 22

Cultural criminology, *see also* Critical criminology, 45–7

Cultures of invention, 13

CyberAngles, *see also* Vigilantism, 208

Cybercrime (definition), 3, 5–9, 12–18, 20

Cybercrime as a service, *see also* Ransomware as a service 150, 179

Cybercrime control industry, cybersecurity industry, 1, 25, 47, 51, 54, 57, 66, 73, 131–2, 137, 178–83, 186, 190, 202, 207, 209–10, 218

Cyber-facilitated hostile behaviours, *see also* Swatting, 94

Cyberespionage, 170, 175–7, 185

Cyber-jihad, *see also* Cyberterrorism, 179–81

Cyber-physical systems, 7, 12, 23, 217–18

Cyberpunk, 5, 28, 55, 143

Cyberspace (definition), 4–6

Cyberspace (genesis), 5

Cyberterrorism, *18*, 169, 177–82

Cybersecurity (definition), 181

Cyberwarfare, *see also under individual types*, 7, *18*, 169–77, 185–6

Cypherpunk, 143

Czech Republic, 85

D

Daesh, 60, 135, 178

Dark figure, *see also* Underreporting, 19, 22, 106, 133

Darknet, dark web, *see also* Clearnet; Deep web, 7, 136, 141, 154

Dark Overload, *see also* Ransomware, 136

Data analytics, 176, 195–6, 217

Data collection (legal), *see also* Hacking; Measuring cybercrime; Methods of data collection in research; Researching cybercrime, 9, *19*, 20–1, 24–7, 70–4, 104, 181–2, 193–6, 203, 213–17

Data science, 2

Data theft, *see also* Identity theft, *10*, 11, 53, 65, 117, 141, 145, 147–9, 162, 171

Dataveillance, *see* Surveillance

Datification, *see also* Data analytics, 195

De minimis trap, 188

DeepFake, 174

Deep web, *see also* Clearnet; Dark web, 15, 102, 134, 141, 157, 216

Democratisation of computing, 11, 13

Denial of service (DoS), *see also* Distributed denial of service, 17, 53, 61, 178

Determinism, *31*, 41

Deterrence, 26, 33, 50, 155, 164, 167, 186, 193, 202

Deviancy, deviant, *see also* Microdeviations; Controlling cyberspace as political deviancy, 3, *18*, 35–50, 53, 88, 91, 94, 97, 101, 111, 164, 169, 173, 182

Differential association theory, *see also* Psychosocial learning approaches, *31–2*, 40–2, 59, 152

Differential opportunity theory, 38

Digilantism, *see* Vigilantism

Digital currencies, *see also* Cryptocurrencies, 142–3, 152

Digital divide, *see also* Penetration rates, 5
geographical, 5, 200, 210
gender-based, 2, 5, 46, 51
age-based, 2, 5

Digital drift, 49, 50
Digital evidence, 189, 192–4
Digital immigrants, 2, 5
Digital natives, 2
Digital Single Market Strategy, 165
Digital society, 3, 183
Disruptive technology, 68
Distributed denial of service (DDoS), *see also* Denial of service, 60–1, *62*, 68, 150, 170
Domain name system, 117, 205
Dot-com economic bubble, 11
Double-role girls, *see also* Loverboys, 100
Doxing, 109, 134–6, 214
Doxware, *see also* Extortion; Leakware, 109, 131, 134–7
Dropbox, 134, 204
Drugs, drug markets, 7, 16–17, 20, 37–8, 59, 65, 141, 152–8, 167
Dystopia, 5, 28, 56, 72

E
eBay, 11, 120, 150
e-commerce, 23, 106, 120, 124, 137, 152, 156, 200, 205
e-companies, *see* Tech companies
Economics, 2, 143, 145, 213, 216
Ecuador, 144
eDemocracy, 184–5
Education, 1, 5, 28, 59, 68, 105, 110, 180, 206–8, 218, 220
Employability, 1
Encrypting ransomware, *see also* Ransomware, 132–4
Encryption, 68, 75–6, 103, 132–4, 143, 150, 154, 165, 179, 182, 203–5, 218
Engineering, 1, 58
English (language), 6, 124, 150, 180, 184, 210
e-patrol, *see* Vigilantism
Escrow, 121, 152, 156, 205
Espionage, *see also* Cyberespionage, 17, 63
Ethics
    behavioural implications 3, 27, 33, 55, 60, 101, 110–12, 167, 170, 193, 196
    in research 215–16
Europe, European Union *see also under individual countries*, 5, 13, 15, 20, 22, 25, 33, 72, 74, 84, 86, 87, 93, 102, 137, 145, 147, 158, 160, 165, 174, 176, 181, 187, 191, 198, 207, 210

Exploit kits, 66, 132, 150
Extortion, *see also* Crimes of coercion, *18*, 20, 46, 78, 99, 109, 115, 131–9, 159, 203
Eyepiramid, 63, 193
E-zubao, 127–8

F
Facebook, 12, 73, 79, 82, 85, 87–9, 95, 103, 118, 122, 125, 143, 175, 183, 203
Facial recognition, 195
Fair use, 160
Fake news, *see* Information pollution
Fake accounts, 124, 129, 173–5
Fancy Bear, 176
Fear, 14, 23, 27, 47, 57, 84–5, 91, 112, 116, 119, 130–1, 136, 174, 177–8, 181, 204
Feminism, *see also* Critical criminology; Gender; Gender-based theories, 46, 96
Filter bubbles, 82
Filtering, 88, 103, 105, 122–5, 166, 206
Financial data theft, *see* Data theft
Finland, 67, 155, 165, 170
Flaming, 95
FLocker, *see also* Ransomware, 134
Folk devils, 47, 57
Forbidden fruit effect, 14
Forced prostitution, *see also* Sex crimes, 83, 97–8, 100, 105–8
Forensics, 189, 190, 192, 194, 198
Fortnite, 3
France, 35, 86, 106, 117, 133, 173, 176, 182
Frauds, *see also under individual types*, 7, 14, 16–17, *18*, 20–3, 37, 47, 67, 71, 115–31, *116*, 138–9, 145–7, 156, 189, 198, 202–5
Freedom of expression, free speech, 48, 74, 76, 85, 90, 103
Free software, *see* Open source
Free will, 29, *31*, 33, 41
Friend verifier, 104

G
Gangs, 37–8, 45, 110, 118
Gatsby, 104
Gender, 45–6, 51, 59, 82, 84, 87, 92, 96–7, 110
Gender-based theories, *see also* Critical criminology, Feminist criminology, 45–6, 51
Gendered cyberhate, 97

Gendertrolling, 96
General theory of crime, *31*, 44
Generative adversarial networks, 174
Germany, 10, 61, 68, 85, 89, 96, 133, 157, 161, 165, 176, 182
GitHub, 61
GLACY, GLACY+, 191
Global, globalisation, 2, 5, 16, 20, 22, 25–6, 68, 72, 74, 87–9, 106, 112, 127, 134, 138, 143, 155, 159, 160, 167, 171–4, 179, 183, 192, 193, 196, 198, 208, 210, 219
Glocal, 7, 81, 112, 138, 210
GNU project, *see also* Open source, 163
Google, 12, 65, 69, 73, 82, 92, 123, 126, 134, 174, 177, 204, 207, 219
Governance, 7, 13, 27, 56, 68, 182, 183
Governing through crime, 48
Great Firewall of China, *see also* Balkanisation of the internet, 6, 183
Grooming, *see also* Sex crimes, 21, *83*, 92, 97–101, 103, 106, 108, 192
Grindr, 73
Guccifer 2.0, 176

H
Hacking
    definition, *18*, 54
    figures of, 22, 28, 172, 189
    hacktivism, *18*, 54, 55, 59–61, 66, 177, 183
    history of, *10*, 16, 20, 54–6
    identity construction of and subcultural elements, 54–9, 78, 135, 139
    cultural representation of, 12, 56, 77
Harassment, *see also* Bullying; Stalking; Trolling, 7, 14, 17, *18*, 20, 24, 42, 49, 81, *83*, 89–7, 109–13, 135, 207
Harms, 3, 7, 17, 23, 27, 57, 81–98, 101, 105, 112–13, 115, 120, 124, 126, 129, 130, 132, 138–9, 144, 147, 154, 156, 162, 169, 170, 173, 177–8, 181, 185, 187–8, 198, 204, 215
Hate
    hate crime, 17, 82, *83*, 84, 88, 97
    hate groups, 39, 88–90, 113, 125
    hate incident, *83*, 84
    hate sites, 88–90
    hate speech, 7, *18*, 81–8, *83*, 90, 96

Heath, healthcare, 66, 91, 109, *116*, 125–6, 133, 146, 149, 154, 156–7, 170, 218
Health frauds, *see also* Frauds, *116*, 125–6
Highly critical wireless networks, 171
History, 2, 6, 9–13, *10*, 29–30, 33, 62, 85, 96, 106, 127, 144, 158, 172, 178, 182, 218–19, 220
History of cybercrimes 9–13, *10*
Honeypots, 25, 104, 176, 192, 193
Human dimension of cybercrimes, 7, 167, 219
Human flesh searches, *see* Crowdsourcing
Human rights, 5, 85, 88, 129, 169, 177, 181–3, 193
Human trafficking, 106–8
Hyperspatialisation, 4, 208

I
ICQ, 150
Identity
    cloning, *see also* Profile cloning, 129
    collective, 6, 112
    concealment of, *see also* Anonymity, 154
    concepts of, 128
    construction of, see also Self-image, 47, 54–9, 94
    fraud, *see also* Frauds, 14, 115, *116*, 119, 128–31, 204
    theft, 12, 17, 22, 24, 53, 92, *116*, 128–31, 147, 149, 204
    revelation of, *see also* Doxing, 215
    sexual/gender, 84, 87
    verification of, 185, 201
Illegal markets (definition), 141
Illicit markets (definition), 141
Image-based sexual abuse, *see also* Sex crimes; Revenge porn, *83*, 97, 109–11
Inclusivity, 5, 81, 86, 95
India, 85, 86, 88, 96, 110, 112, 133
Indonesia, 145
Information and Communication Technologies (ICTs), 16, 94, 97, 104, 105, 108, 111, 122, 133, 169, 206, 208
Information pollution, *see also* Information warfare, 169, 172–5, 186
Information warfare, *see also* Cyberwarfare, 170, 172–5, 186

Inspire, 180
Instagram, 12, 175
Insurance, 146, 201–2
Intellectual property (definition), 160
Intellectual property infringement, *see also* Copyright infringement, 7, 12, *18*, 33, 40, 42, 156
Interdisciplinary, *see also* Crossdisciplinary; Multidisciplinary, 1–2, 175, 186, 190, 213–17, 220
International classification of crimes for statistical purposes (ICCS), 18
International Communication Union (ITU), 104
International cooperation (need of), *see also* Cooperation, 196–200
Internet Black Tigers, 178
Internet of Everything, *see also* Internet of Things; Ubiquitous computing, *10*, 67
Internet of Things, *see also* Internet of Everything; Ubiquitous computing, 12, 66–9, 77, 134, 149, 171, 194, 217
Internet Watch Foundation (IWF), 104
Intersectionality, 46
Investment frauds, *see also* Frauds; Ponzi schemes; Pyramid schemes, *116*, 126–8
Iran, 171, 177, 182
Ireland, 175
Italy, 2, 20, 21, 30, 63, 121, 125, 127, 135, 173, 182, 184, 192, 193

J
Japan, 15, 86, 145, 180–1
Just war theory, 170

K
KeRanger, *see also* Ransomware, 134
Keystroke dynamics, 131
KODAKOne, 165
Kosovo, 178
Kuwait, 97
Kwangmyong, 171
Kyrgyzstan, 144

L
Label, labelling, *see also* Social structure approaches, 3, 7, *31–2*, 36, 39–41, 45, 47, 148, 158, 178, 196
Language socialisation, 6
Late-modern criminology, *31–2*, 47–8

Latvia, 131
Lazarus group, 171
Leaking, *see also* Methods of data collection in research, 214
Leakware, *see* Doxware
Left-realism, *see also* Critical criminology, 45
Leeching, 53
Legal gaps, 16, 68, 85
Legal harmonisation, lack of, 14, 74, 85, 87, 93, 94
Legal highs, *see* New psychoactive substances
Legal sciences, 1–2, 6, 9, 186
Lemon markets, 151, 155
Lifestyle drugs, 157
Linguistic diversity, multilinguism, 6, 124
Local 2, 81, 88, 111–12, 138, 155, 159, 166, 167, 188–9, 219
Locker ransomware, *see also* Ransomware, 132, 134
Locky, *see also* Ransomware, 132
Loverboys, *see also* Double-role girls, 100
Loverspy, 63

M
Machine learning, 121, 155, 174, 195
MacRansom, *see also* Ransomware, 134
Macro theories, 30, *31*, 34, 37
Macros (virus), 132
Malaysia, 98, 119, 127
Malvertising, 63, 66, 122
Malware, *see also under individual types*, *10*, 11, 16, 17, 20, 22, 24, 61–4, 65, 114, 118, 122, 131, 132, 139, 150, 167, 170–2, 176, 177, 181, 203
Market-based crimes, 7, *18*, *32*, 46, 49, 116, 120, 141–60
Marxist criminology, *see also* Critical criminology, 45, 46
Masculinity, 38, 46, 59, 110
Mauritania, 97
Measuring cybercrimes, 6, 9, 18–28, 106, 123, 156, 202
Media, *see also* Social media; Moral panic, 12, 25, 27–8, 47, 54, 56–8, 77, 100, 136, 164, 178, 180, 184, 186, 219
Medical misinformation, *see also* Health frauds, 126
Megaupload, 165

Memes, 110, 161
Mens rea, 21
Methods of data collection in research,
     see also under individual types, 213–16
Micro theories, 30, *31*, 34, 37, 84
Microdeviations, 3
Military, 10, 11, 13, 57, 118, 169, 170,
     176, 178, 181, 219
Millennium bug, 178
Minecraft, 3
Mining
     data 73, 179, 195
     cryptocurrencies 64, 144
     opinion, *see* Sentiment analysis
Mirai, 68
Mirroring, *see also* Methods of data
     collection in research, 214
Money laundering, 145, 150, 155
Moral entrepreneurs, 57
Moral panic, 47, 56–8, 130, 178
Multi-agency, 199
Multidisciplinary, *see also* Crossdisciplinary;
     Interdisciplinary, 1–2, 175, 186, 190,
     213–17, 220
Mugging, 123
Mules, 61, 150, 154
Muslim 84–5, 89
Music industry, 132, 160–3
Myanmar, 88
Myspace, 12

N

Napster, 163
Natural language processing, 13, 88, 155,
     179, 195
Near field communication, 64
Neighbourhood informatics, 195
Netflix, 136, 165
Netherlands, 100–1, 104, 117, 137, 155–6,
     176, 189
Netiquette, 95, 207
Neuromancer, 5
Neutralisation techniques, neutralisation
     theory, *31–2*, 44–5, 55, 59, 152
New psychoactive substances (NPSs),
     153–4
New Zealand, 72, 165
Nigeria, 119, 207
No More Ransom, *see also* Ransomware, 137
North America, *see also* Canada; United
     States, 5

North Korea, 86, 171
Notice and take down, 161, 166

O

Official crime statistics, *10*
Online disinhibition effect, 24, 90
Online pharmacies, 156–7
Open access, 163
Open source, 61, 163
Open web, 12–13, 58, 60, 142, 163, 208,
     211
Operations, named
     Bayonet, 155
     Endeavour, 101
     Pacifier, 114
     PIN, 192
     Tovar, 132
Opinion spam, *see also* Frauds; Review
     frauds, 124
Opportunities
     criminal or criminogenic
         opportunities, opportunity
         structures *10*, 11, 17, 24, 26, 38–9,
         51, 54, 67, 89, 90, 105–8, 115, 120,
         125–6, 142, 153, 167, 180, 219
     opportunity theories, *see also* Rational
         choice theory; Crime pattern theory;
         Routine activity theory; Situational
         crime prevention, *31–2*, 33–5, 50,
         137, 210–11
Organised crime, 38, 107, 158–9, 162, 193
Out-of-band authentication methods, 118
Outsiders 39, 45, 79
Overpayment scams, *see also* Sale frauds;
     Frauds, 121

P

Paedophilia, 100–1, 192
Palestine, 184
Passwords, 23–4, 64–8, 76, 118, 130, 139,
     201, 205
Patent, *see also* Copyright; Trademark, 160
PayPal, 142, 150, 202
Peer-to-peer, 102–3, 126, 128, 143, 151,
     161
Pegida, 89
Penetration rates, *see also* Digital divide, 5
Perceptions, 3, 12, 21, 27, 33, 36, 48, 143,
     189, 219
Peru, 180
Petya, *see also* Ransomware, 133

Pharming, 205

Philippines, 101, 104–5, 127

Philosophy, 2, 30, 32, 47, 55, 86, 128, 220

Phishing, 20, 63, 118, 122, 133–4, 148, 156, 176–7, 199, 200

Phreaking, *10*, 11

Piracy, *see also* Anti-piracy campaigns; Copyright infringement, 39, 132, 162–4, 165

Pokémon Go, 175

Police recorded crime, *19*, 20

Policing, 7, 19, 27, 78, 103, 107, 110–11, 138, 155, 167, 187–200, 205, 207, 210

Policy-makers, 25, 28, 54, 56, 104

Political offences, *see also under individual types*, 7, *18, 32*, 169–185

Political mobilisation shutdowns, 183–4

Ponzi schemes, *see also* Investment frauds; Pyramid schemes, 127–8

Postal service, 119, 127, 155, 167, 175

Postmodernism, postmodern criminology, *31–2*, 46–8, 50

Post-truth, 173

Prevention, 7, 13, 19, 26, 27, 50, 51, 66, 90, 99, 113, 123, 137, 139, 142, 167, 187, 197–208, *209*, 210–11, 213, 217, 219

Privacy, 1, 7, 8, 48, 54, 56, 68, 69, 76–79, 92, 103–6, 112, 114, 135, 144, 154, 182–5, 193, 206, 208, 210, 213, 215

Process theories, *see also* Micro theories, 30, 40

Profile cloning, *see also* Identity cloning, 129

Proof-of-work, *see also* Blockchain; Byzantine generals, *142*, 146

Propaganda, *see also* Cyber-jihad, 78, 180–1

Proportionality (principle of), 170, 181

Proxies, 75, 93, 108, 170, 205

Psychology, 1–2, 30, 35, 36, 40, 41, 43, 59, 90, 100, 101, 128, 216

Psychonauts, 39, 154

Psychosocial learning approaches, *see also* Socialisation approaches; Differential association; Social learning, 40–3

Public goods, 1, 13, 203, 209, 215

Pyramid schemes, *see also* Investment frauds; Ponzi schemes, 127–8

Q

Qatar, 177, 207

QQ, 90

Quackeries, *see also* Frauds (health), 126

Quantum computing, 13, 218

R

Race, racism, 14, 48, 82, 86, 88, 179, 196

Radio-frequency identification (RFID), 218

Ransomware, *see also* Extortion; *see also under individual names and types*, 20, 27, 61, 62, 64–6, 131–4, 137–9, 145, 150, 171

Ransomware as a service (RaaS), *see also* Cybercrime as a service; Ransomware, 132, 134

Rape, 82, 96, 101, 110–11

Rational choice theory, *see also* Opportunity theories, 34, 50

Ratware, 63

Relative deprivation, 46

Researching cybercrime, *see also* Ethics (in research), 7, 213–17

Responsibility 21, 24, 44, 60, 66, 87, 90, 91, 103, 112, 139, 175, 182, 185, 192, 194, 200, 202, 204, 206, 208, *209*, 214, 218, 219

Responsibilisation thesis, 24

Reputation, *see also* Harms, 108, 124, 125, 129, 135, 151, 154, 159, 208

Revenge porn, *see also* Image-based sexual abuse, 21, 109, 110, 112, 135–6

Review frauds, *see also* Frauds; Opinion spam, *116*, 124–5

Rippers, 151, 159

Robbery, 17, 22

Robots, robotisation, 61, 111, 218

Romance scams, *see also* Advance-fee scams; Sweetheart swindle scams, 115, 119, 129

Romania, 159, 176, 191

Roomba, 68

Rousseau platform, *see also* eDemocracy; Voting systems, 184

Routine activity theory, *see also* Opportunity theories, 24, 34, 59, 82, 137, 139

Russia, 64, 144, 150, 169, 174–6

S

Sale frauds, *see also* Bid shielding; Charity frauds; Frauds; Overpayment scams; Triangulation frauds; Shill bidding, *116*, 120–4

Sarahah 93–4

Satana, *see also* Ransomware, 133

Saudi Arabia, 97, 172, 180, 189, 191

Scams, *see* Frauds

Scareware, *see also* Extortion, 131

Scurato (case), 193

Search engine optimisation (SEO), 123

Self-control, *see also* Control theories, 24, *31–2*, 44, 50, 59, 91, 113, 137–8, 164

Self-harm sites, 88–90

Self-help, 24, 206, 209

Self-image, 39, 45, 128

Self-reported crime surveys, *19*

Sentiment analysis, 195

Service providers, 27, 78, 86–7, 111, 118, 133, 150, 161, 194, 202, 204, 207

Sex, sexual 87, 89, 92, 96, 111–12

Sex crimes, *see also* Child pornography; Forced prostitution; Grooming; Image-based sexual abuse, 7, *18*, 21, 81, *83*, 97–111, 114, 121, 157, 167, 192, 198

Sex robots, *see also* Robotisation, 111

Sexism, 48, 59, 196

Shame, 33, 55, 96, 109, 113, 163–4, 208

Sharing of information, 11, 12, 118, 143, 161, 163, 167, 181, 197, 201, 204–5, 210

Shill bidding, *see also* Bid shielding; frauds; Sale frauds, 121–1

Shitstorm, 124

Silk Road, 155

Singapore, 133, 198

Situational crime prevention, *see also* Opportunities theories, 137, 139, 210

Skimmers, 148

Skype, 12, 103

Slander attacks, *see also* Sybils, 151

Sleuthing, 194

Smartphones, 5, 12, 63–4, 67, 91, 92, 94, 97, 124, 133, 134, 161, 216, 218

Smart contracts, 146–7

Smart devices, *see also* Cyber-physical systems; Wearable technology, 7, 12, 66–9, 77, 134

Smart homes, 67–8, 77

Snapchat, 94, 102

Social construction, 27, 39, 46, 47, 53, 56–8, 219

Social engineering, 7, 63, 117–19, 122, 129, 148, 157, 172, 176, 201

Social group, 3, 5, 34, 39, 47, *83*, 157

Social learning, *see also* Psychosocial learning approaches, *31–2*, 40, 42, 58, 59, 82, 91, 113, 152, 164

Social media, *see also under individual names*, 3, 5, 12, 58, 69, 72, 79, 85, 87–8, 96, 100, 103, 110, 113, 117, 122–6, 129, 141, 143, 157, 173–7, 180, 184, 194–6, 203, 218

Social structure approaches, *see also* Anomie; Strain; Subculture; Labelling, 30, 35–40, 45, 51

Socialisation approaches, *see also* Psychosocial learning approaches; Control theories; Neutralisation theory, 40–5

Sociology, social sciences 2, 7, 30, 35, 57, 59, 125, 128, 196, 213–17

Software as a service (SaaS), 64, 134

Sony, 171

SoundCloud, 164

South Africa, 15, 119, 204

South Korea, 86, 174

Space transition theory, *32*, 49–50

Spain, 60, 65, 118, 192, 199

Spam, 16–17, 63, 92, 122–4, 150, 156

Spoofing, 53, 118, 133, 205

Spyware, 63, 72, 150

SQL injections, 65

Sri Lanka, 178

Stalking, *see also* Harassment, 20, *83*, 90–3, 136, 207–8

Stalkers, typology of, 92

Stigma, stigmatisation, 3, 40, 74, 111, 119, 163

Strain, *see also* Social structure approaches, 36–37, 38, 43, 152, 164

Streaming, 94, 99, 101, 103, 161

Structural theories, *see also* Macro theories, 30

Stuxnet, 170–1

Subcultural theories, subculture, *see also* Social structure approaches, *31–2*, 36–9, 47, 50, 58, 59, 77, 84, 88–90, 95, 101, 135, 139, 143, 157

Sudan, 97

Supervisory control and data acquisition (SCADA), 170–1

Surveillance
by individuals, *71*, 72, 78–9
conventional, *71*, 72

corporate, 53, 70, *71*

dataveillance,7, 53, *71*, 72, 74

mass, *71*, 73, 182

personal, *71*, 72, 78–9

state, 53, 70, *71*, 182–5

technology of, 12, 62, 172, 192

use of, 13, 48, 68, 70–5, 158, 181–2, 187, 193, 208, 210

workplace, 72, 78

Swatting, *see also* Cyber-facilitated hostile behaviours, 94–5

Sweden, 99, 155, 157

Sweetie, Sweetie 2.0, 104

Sweetheart swindle scams, *see also* Advance-fee scams; Romance scams, 119

Sybils, *see also* Slander attacks, 151

Symbolic interactionism, 36, 39

Symphonic approach, 216–17

Syria, 176, 182

T

Taiwan, 174, 199

Tallin manual, 170

Tapping, 62, 192

Thailand, 136, 155

Tech companies, 11, 12, *19*, 27, 66, 68, 71, 72, 85, 87, 166, 173, 175, 182, 185–6, 196, 200–7, 218–9

Theories of crime, *see also under individual names*, 6, 24, 29–51, 59, 82, 91, 113, 137–9, 152, 164, 217, 219

Togo, 184

TOR, 75–6, 114, 141, 150, 155

Trademark, Patent, *see also* Copyright; Patent, 160

Trafficking, *see also* Market-based crimes; Crimes against persons; Sex crimes, 14–18, 20, 100–1, 103, 106–8, 111, 141, 153–9

Training, 27, 87, 120, 172, 188–92, 205, 207, 209

Transformation test, 16

Triangulation frauds, *see also* Sale frauds; Frauds, 121

TripAdvisor, 125

Trojans, 61–4, 132, 134, 193

Troll farms, 175

Trolling, *see also* Harassment, *83*, 90, 95–7, 125, 175

Trust, 27, 63, 84, 91, 98, 103, 109, 116, 118, 120–30, 150–1, 154, 155, 157, 174, 181, 189, 196–7, 199, 200, 202, 205

Tumblr, 90

Túpac Amaru Revolutionary Movement (MRTA), 181

Turkey, 61, 96, 183

Tutorials, 150–2

Twitter, 12, 87, 93, 96, 113, 129, 130, 174, 175, 180, 182, 183, 195

Typology, 3, *17*, 18

U

Uber, 203–4

Ubiquitous computing, *see also* Internet of Things; Internet of Everything, 4, 12, 91, 94, 149

Ukraine, 169–170

Undercover investigations, 103, 151, 192–3

Underreporting, *see also* Dark figure, 19–21, 26, 28, 99, 111, 125, 131

United Arab Emirates, 192

United Kingdom, 2, 10, 20–2, 24, 28, 30, 45, 47, 72–3, 77, 79, 84, 90, 96, 98, 99, 101, 105, 122, 133, 139, 157, 160, 173, 176, 182, 189–92, 207, 210

United Nations 5, 18, 102, 104, 106–7, 153

United States, *see also* North America, 10, 11, 15, 21–2, 25, 30, 35–7, 40, 57, 59, 71–3, 86, 96, 98, 101–2, 110, 127, 136, 147, 155, 160, 162, 165, 170, 172–6, 178, 182, 192, 199, 218

Upskirting, *see also* Image-based sexual abuse, 110

Usability, *see also* Convenience, 11, 112, 130, 149, 205–6

Utopianism, 58

Uzbekistan, 182

V

Vandalism, 38, 54

Venezuela, 129

Victimless crime, 26, 152, 162

Victims, victimisation 2, *17*, 20, 21, 23–4, 26–8, 34, 44–6, 51, 59, 61, *62*, 63–6, 76–8, 82, *83*, 84–8, 90–122, 126–39, 147–9, 152, 157, 166, 176, 188, 196, 198, 202, 204, 206, 209

Victim blame, 21, 24, 96, 111, 139
Victimisation surveys, *19*, 21, 22, 25
Vigilantism, 78, 105, 136, 206–8
Virtual ethnography, *see also* Methods of
    data collection in research, 214, 216
Viruses, 28, 62, 118, 132–3
Visual analyses, *see also* Methods of data
    collection in research, 214
Vodafone, 72
Voice-over-IP (VoIP), 72, 103, 179
Voting systems, *see also* eDemocracy, 184–5

W

WannaCry, *see also* Ransomware, 64, 133,
    171
Wearable technology, 149, 166
Web 2.0, *10*, 12, 47, 104
WhatsApp, 76, 88, 102

White collar crimes, 11, 27
White supremacists, 113
WikiLeaks, 60, 176
Wikipedia, 12
World Wide Web, *10*, 11
Worms, 62, 64, 170, 171

X

Xenophobia, 14, 15, 85

Y

Yahoo, 86
Yahoo boys, 119

Z

Zalora, 120
Zero-day attacks, 65, 176
Zombies, 61, *62*, 124

Lightning Source UK Ltd.
Milton Keynes UK
UKHW020812130821
388805UK00005B/525